The World of John Winthrop

Essays on England
and New England
1588-1649

MASSACHUSETTS HISTORICAL SOCIETY
STUDIES IN AMERICAN HISTORY
AND CULTURE

American Unitarianism, 1805-1865,
ed. Conrad Edick Wright (1989)

Massachusetts and the New Nation,
ed. Conrad Edick Wright (1992)

Puritanism: Transatlantic Perspectives on a Seventeenth-Century Anglo-American Faith, ed., Francis J. Bremer

Entrepreneurs: The Boston Business Community, 1700-1850,
ed. Conrad Edick Wright and Katheryn P. Viens (1997)

Transient and Permanent: The Transcendentalist Movement and Its Contexts, ed. Charles Capper
and Conrad Edick Wright

John Adams and the Founding of the Republic,
ed. Richard Alan Ryerson (2001)

Faces of Community: Immigrant Massachusetts, 1860-2000,
ed. Reed Ueda and Conrad Edick Wright

Henry Adams and the Need to Know,
ed. William Merrill Decker
and Earl N. Harbert (2005)

The World of John Winthrop: Essays on England and New England, 1588-1649,
ed. Francis J. Bremer and Lynn A. Botelho

The World of John Winthrop

Essays on England and New England

1588-1649

Francis J. Bremer and
Lynn A. Botelho
Editors

MASSACHUSETTS HISTORICAL SOCIETY
STUDIES IN AMERICAN HISTORY
AND CULTURE, No. 9

*Published by the
Massachusetts Historical Society
Boston, 2005*

*Distributed by the
University of Virginia Press, Charlottesville*

*Designed by Dede Cummings
and Carolyn Kasper / dcdesign*

Library of Congress Cataloging-in-Publication Data
The world of John Winthrop : essays on England and New England, 1588–1649 / Francis J. Bremer & Lynn A. Botelho, editors.
  p. cm. -- (Massachusetts Historical Society studies in American history and culture ; no. 9)
  Includes bibliographical references and index.
  ISBN-13: 978-0-934909-96-9 (paperback)
  ISBN-10: 0-934909-96-2 (paperback)
  ISBN-13: 978-0-934909-88-4 (hardcover)
  ISBN-10: 0-934909-88-1 (hardcover)
  1. New England–History–Colonial period, ca. 1600–1775. 2. Puritans–New England–History–17th century. 3. Massachusetts–History–Colonial period, ca. 1600–1775. 4. Great Britain–History–Early Stuarts, 1603–1649. 5. New England–Relations–England. 6. England–Relations–New England.
7. Transnationalism–History–17th century. 8. Winthrop, John, 1588–1649.
9. Governors–Massachusetts–Biography. 10. Puritans–Massachusetts–Biography.
I. Bremer, Francis J. II. Botelho, L. A. (Lynn A.) III. Series.
F7.W87 2005 974'.02–dc22
2005033980

To
Patrick Collinson
And
John Morrill

Contents

Introduction: Atlantic History and the
World of John Winthrop
Francis J. Bremer and Lynn Botelho 1

England's "Others" in the Old and New Worlds
Alden T. Vaughan and Virginia Mason Vaughan 22

The Practice of Piety in Puritan New England:
Contexts and Consequences
Mark A. Peterson 75

The Piety of Practice and the Practice of Piety
Tom Webster 111

Puritans in the Marketplace
Mark Valeri 147

The County of Massachusetts: The Governance
of John Winthrop's Suffolk and the Shaping
of the Massachusetts Bay Colony
Francis J. Bremer 187

The Ancient Constitution in the Old World
and the New
James S. Hart and Richard J. Ross 237

Performing Patriarchy: Gendered Roles and
Hierarchies in Early Modern England and
Seventeenth-Century New England
Richard Godbeer 290

"Justification by Print Alone?": Protestantism, Literacy,
and Communications in the Anglo-American
World of John Winthrop
David D. Hall and Alexandra Walsham 334

Notes on Contributors 387

Index 391

Introduction
Atlantic History and the World of John Winthrop

Francis J. Bremer and Lynn Botelho

"ATLANTIC HISTORY" HAS BECOME a popular approach for studying the Anglo-American past. Interested readers are swamped by articles and books that reflect this trend, and conferences and seminars invite discussions of the pre-industrial world from an Atlantic or shared perspective. Scholars from both sides of the watery divide have responded enthusiastically to this historical perspective, if not always effectively. This volume, and the conference from which it emerged, are themselves products of an Atlantic history approach. While we embrace the strategy of bringing together relevant aspects of the histories of England and her New England colonies, we also believe that such efforts require a broader contextual understanding.

In a recent attempt to bring this scholarly outpouring into a more meaningful framework, David Armitage has suggested dividing this emerging field into "three concepts of Atlantic History": "1. *Circum*-Atlantic history–the transnational history of the Atlantic world; 2. *Trans*-Atlantic history–the international history of the Atlantic world;

3. *Cis*-Atlantic history—national or regional history within an Atlantic context."[1] Armitage's last category has seen the most activity in recent years, and it is the one most relevant to this volume. Historians such as Roger Thompson, Michael Winship, and Carla G. Pestana have sought to explain the story of the English North American colonies by placing it within the broader context of British history.[2] Such historians, in part, have been reacting against the view of "American exceptionalism" that dominated historical thinking during the last half of the twentieth century. Promoters of exceptionalism sharply differentiated between the ways of the Old World and the New. They largely relegated England (and other European countries) to the background of the story, usually to some misty, physically distant past, and mostly insignificant to any meaningful explanation of how colonists settled a continent.[3] The broader Atlantic dimension was commonly ignored in attempts to tell what these authors viewed as the real story—that of America-in-the-making.

This trend in Atlantic history may appear new, a reaction to the narrow focus on exceptionalism. But if we step back a moment and look at the broader sweep of American historiography, we will recognize that claims for the uniqueness of the current Atlantic perspective are largely a trick of generational near-sightedness. Many new graduates of America's history doctoral programs fail to take seriously the historical literature written prior to the generation represented by their own advisors. Consequently, their claims of originality for the sub-field of Atlantic history do not stand the test of historiographic scrutiny. The fact is that the study of colonial-English political relationships has long and venerated traditions of working within an Atlantic perspective. Placing colonial institutional and political history within the context of England's greater imperial story dates at least as far back as the works of Herbert Osgood, Charles M. Andrews, and Lawrence Henry Gipson. More recently, such scholarship is

Introduction

carried forward by Richard Johnson, Stephen S. Webb, and Alison G. Olson.[4]

Similarly, colonial intellectual and religious history has long contextualized the American story within the broader English and European framework. One of the modern pioneering works in Atlantic intellectual history was Samuel Eliot Morison's two-volume *The Founding of Harvard College*.[5] Morison's perspective, broadened by his tenure as the first Harmsworth Professor of American History at Oxford University, anticipated the modern Atlanticist approach, placing the story of early Harvard firmly in the context of the history of European, and specifically English, higher education. Morison was not alone in this effort. Despite its title, *The New England Mind*, the first volume of Perry Miller's magisterial study, rested as much on a thorough reading of the writings of English puritan divines, such as William Ames and Richard Sibbes, as on colonial preachers in the vein of John Cotton and Samuel Willard.[6] Edmund S. Morgan's *Visible Saints* depicted New England religious practice as developments and variations on the theme of English Puritanism.[7] More recently, David D. Hall, Michael McGiffert, and other leading scholars of colonial New England intellectual history have approached their specific subjects with a deep awareness of the larger world of the Reformation and of sixteenth- and seventeenth-century English religious history.[8] The fact that some of the new Atlantic history fails to acknowledge these works of political, intellectual, and religious scholarship unfortunately speaks more to the authors' lack of interest in such aspects of the past—subjects increasingly considered traditional and old-fashioned—than to the originality of the new integrated Atlantic history itself.

On the other side of the Atlantic, historians focused upon England's own history have been reluctant to familiarize themselves with

American colonial history or to fully explore the connections between the mother country and her varied sixteenth- and seventeenth-century colonial ventures. Perhaps this reflects the view that parents can learn nothing from their children, representing a denial that the mother country could have been shaped in any way by its offspring! Yet here too the winds of change have stirred, initially through efforts to incorporate England's closest neighbors into her national history. In recent decades, the parochial preoccupations of England's Tudor and Stuart historians have been replaced by a growing awareness of the interrelationship between the histories of England, Scotland, and Ireland—though no one has yet to coin a universally acceptable term to refer to that larger sphere. Indeed, there is now a professorial chair at Cambridge University in "British and Irish history."

Aside from studies that focus on trade and immigration, new attention to the "Atlantic archipelago," as one scholar has termed it, has rarely extended to other members of England's budding imperial state.[9] Significant exceptions to this can be found in the controversial work of J. C. D. Clark on political discourse in the eighteenth century, in David Cressy's work on migration, and in Tom Webster's treatment of the effect of New England on the development of English puritanism in the years leading up to the Civil Wars.[10] But those are exceptions. It remains extremely rare to find any treatment of the colonies in studies of England's seventeenth-century political, legal, economic, or social history. Simply put, while Americanists are forced to acknowledge the presence of England—either for better or worse—in the development of these new communities, English historians have lost sight of the debt which English identity owes to the existence of the American colonies.

Despite some recent attempts (mostly by colonial scholars) to bring the subjects of Tudor-Stuart England and colonial New England together, much remains to be done. In most cases, trans-Atlantic stud-

Introduction

ies have only begun to achieve an integrated understanding of the shared history of England and New England. Indeed, the very use of the terms "New England" and "England" tend to encourage a focus on what made them distinct societies, rather than what united their peoples as members of a single society. For those working on English shores, the other side of the Atlantic mostly represents a place of import and export, or an annoying political nuisance drawing attention away from the more pressing business of real "Englishmen," those who lived and breathed island air. Few historians of England view American colonial history as relevant to their own interests. Historians of early New England have proven only marginally less myopic. In too many works, England is still depicted as a place that authored unnatural laws and taxes, based on questionable morals. Historians following this course betray their primary interest in American history. What is missing from our understanding of the Atlantic world is the organic nature of these two Englands, one new, one old.

To encourage greater communication between students of England and New England, Millersville University of Pennsylvania joined with the Massachusetts Historical Society and the Omohundro Institute of Early American History and Culture in 1991 to sponsor a conference on "Puritanism in Old & New England."[11] Leading historians and literary scholars came to the Millersville campus from all over the United States and the United Kingdom to spark a conversation on their shared history and to seek ways of incorporating the new insights into their own work. The stimulating conversations resulted in a selection of essays published as *Puritanism: Transatlantic Perspectives on an Anglo-American Faith* (Boston, 1994). Scholars have incorporated those essays into their own work, and contacts and friendships initiated at the conference have led to interesting new approaches. But the gathering at Millersville also reflected persistent professional shortcomings. English history specialists socialized mostly with their fellow historians of England, and the colonialists talked primarily with other colonialists. Similarly, scholars who have cited *Puritanism* in works dealing with Tudor-Stuart England have primarily referred to essays that focused on England, and early Americanists cite in their work the contributions that explored New England. Old paradigms die hard.

In 1999, Millersville University spearheaded another effort to provoke dialogue between the two groups of historians. The conference, "The Worlds of John Winthrop: England and New England, 1588-1649," marked the 350th anniversary of the death of John Winthrop, a man who symbolized the trans-Atlantic character of puritanism. Winthrop, born in the Armada year of 1588, grew up in the Stour Valley of East Anglia, where puritanism had achieved its greatest success in the Elizabethan Age. His uncle William had been a friend of the martyrologist John Foxe, and his father knew East Anglia's leading godly clergy. Winthrop rose to a position on the commission of the peace and aspired to join with like-minded magistrates in preserving the godly kingdom of the Stour Valley. He even hoped to achieve a seat in Parliament that might empower him to advance reform on a larger stage. But the policies of James I and Charles I thwarted these ambitions and threatened the viability of puritan reforms. Reluctantly, John Winthrop considered emigration, initially looking at Ireland before settling on New England. Chosen the governor of the Massachusetts Bay Company and its colony, he led the Great Migration to New England in 1630. Never abandoning hope for the reformation of his native land, he became the principal architect of the colonial puritans' "City on a Hill."[12]

The Massachusetts Historical Society and the Omohundro Institute of Early American History and Culture again joined with Millersville in sponsoring the new conference. Indiana University of Pennsylvania also provided substantial support. Clarion University of Pennsylvania and the Rothermere Institute for American Studies at

Introduction

Oxford University gave further assistance.[13] This time, organizers identified topics of relevance to English and American history and chose one scholar to address the topic from an English perspective and another to speak on the colonial dimension. This conference proved far more successful than its predecessor in stimulating dialogue about the trans-Atlantic dimension of seventeenth-century Anglo-American history.[14]

Looking to make these proceedings available to a broader audience, with the help of the Massachusetts Historical Society, we persuaded some of the conference participants to push the Atlantic approach and integrate English and American perspectives in their essays. We also commissioned a new essay exploring English views of "others" in the trans-Atlantic world to examine an important subject not directly addressed in the program. The result of our efforts is the volume before you.

For the seventeenth century, at least, both sides of the Atlantic arguably formed part of the same body politic, the same body spiritual, and the same body familial. What the authors of this collection of essays believe is that by viewing both shores simultaneously, as part of a collective whole, our understanding of the budding Anglo-American past will not only be much fuller, but, most importantly, more accurate. The following essays, each addressing one particularly key dimension of early modern life, aim to help in the rebalancing of the historiographical scale. At various points the authors shared their work with one another. Some chose to make reference to other essays, some did not.

Based on the research and interpretations presented here, the seventeenth-century relationship between old and New England fell into a number of overlapping categories. In some cases, old England served as a shibboleth by which the new societies compared themselves; the very fact that the colonists sought to create a *new* England suggests dissatisfaction with aspects of the world they left behind. On the other side of the Atlantic, for some Englishmen the colonies were the objects of negative comparison. Thus, during the 1640s, English Presbyterians crafted an image of the colonies as a breeding ground of heresy in order to warn their countrymen against adopting the New England Way.[15] A different form of relationship is found in the way New England colonists treated England as a rag bag from which they could pick at will, taking for their own use aspects of English culture they felt to be well regarded, useful, and good—while leaving others behind. The colonists were, after all, English men and women who sought to preserve and pass on to their posterity the best of the culture they knew. Finally, for much of their early history, England and New England moved more or less in tandem, borrowing, sharing, and growing as a people, separated, perhaps, only by a common language. In all cases, however, England was a factor in New England's self-construction. But with a few exceptions, such as the English Presbyterian effort to demonize colonial Congregationalism, the role New England played in the creation of English identity is—at present—less clear. Nevertheless, the engaging ideas that come into play and into practice on the western side of the Atlantic make it unlikely that New England will long remain that footling problem that has been traditionally portrayed by historians of England.

The issue of English identity formation in this period, and the extent to which that identity resulted from opposing peoples, things, and places, is the subject of Alden and Virginia Mason Vaughan's "England's 'Other's' in the Old and New Worlds." The Vaughans adopt a perspective far beyond the England/New England paradigm. In their view, the defining "other" was not the rustic New England colony or a misguided collection of Englishmen, but, rather, the wild Irish, the Scots, and the Welsh. Beyond the islands' coastlines, the English looked critically into Europe, then south past the Mediter-

Introduction

ranean into Africa, where the state of difference became magnified and further vilified. The English of New England shared the prejudices of their Atlantic brethren, with the added complexities generated by the close physical proximity of Native Americans. The stories are related, yet each has its own distinctive features, for while the Scot and the Wild Irish eventually assimilated into the ranks of the social order, beyond the Massachusetts pale remained the "Blacks" and the "Indians." As the Vaughans sum up their findings, "on both sides of the Atlantic, puritans shared most of England's perceptions and prejudices and, like other English men and women, largely defined and prided themselves by contrast to who they were *not*." In fundamental ways, the trans-Atlantic stance of defining and understanding the "other" firmly identified this aspect of early modern life as an ingrained characteristic of the inhabitants of both shores.

The identity of New England owed the most to the religious traditions of puritanism, ones that had been evolving in England since the earliest days of Henry VIII's Reformation. Thwarted in their efforts to transform England in accordance with their religious vision, many puritans left their homes in the 1630s to create a properly ordered society in America. Their desire to build a great and wonderful "city on a hill" formed the bedrock of their adventures as well as the foundation of many subsequent histories.

In his famous lay sermon on "Christian Charity," John Winthrop told his fellow colonists that "whatsoever we did or ought to have done when we lived in England, the same must we do and more where we go. That which the most in their Churches maintain as a truth in profession only, we must bring into familiar and constant practice." Not only *could* these fledgling architects of a godly polity in the wilderness be true to the teachings of Scripture in ways that their English brethren could not, they were *obliged* to do so for the sake of their souls and for the glory of God. They would be what their brethren back home could not be. And yet, though setting as their goal to craft a better order than England's, New Englanders soon discovered that among their colonial brethren, practice did not always follow profession of the truth.

Moreover, such truths appeared one way in the lived religion of the colonists and quite another back in England. One critical historiographical consequence of this difference is that puritan scholars facing each other across the Atlantic divide have largely failed to integrate the two sides of the story. The fact that English historians speak of "puritanism" while Americans study "Puritanism" symbolizes the differences that separate the two historical clans.[16] The questions, methods, and scholarly preoccupations of these two groups can be so different that two specialists here, Tom Webster and Mark Peterson, found it much more useful to write separate essays on puritan piety than to attempt to integrate their views into one. Webster's view of English puritanism is of a world of tension-laden dichotomies, where a dialectic of internal/external struggles became manifest in the external world. Puritans, according to Webster, survived in England because of overwhelming opposition to them as a variant form of antithetical self-identity. Peterson's understanding of colonial-based puritan piety turns Webster's Englishmen on their heads. In New England, he believes, "Puritanism" survived precisely because of the absence of opposition to it. The peace and freedom experienced in Massachusetts allowed church elders and elder statesmen alike to establish a material world of personal piety and an external structure that created, bolstered, and nourished one's internal piety and pursuit of grace. Clearly, Peterson's and Webster's essays illustrate the limitations of our trans-Atlantic model and the difficulty of integrating the histories of New England and England.

Nevertheless, the fact remains that the concerns of English historians have not been given comparable attention by American colonial historians; and the opposite is true as well. As each side listens to the other, both may gain new insight into what all puritans had in common and the ways in which historical and geographical contexts led to a unique flowering of piety.

The marketplace proved another setting in which New Englanders found themselves changed by the new circumstances of American life. Mark Valeri argues that puritans on both sides of the Atlantic strove to create and maintain a "moral economy of circulation," as opposed to a "market economy of exchange." Puritans, Valeri found, made a division between "good and bad commerce," with good commerce creating a "moral community" established and maintained by intellectual and theological ties, as well as by the bonds of kinship and social affiliation. Bad commerce, conversely, concentrated solely on profit and exchange, losing sight of and damaging frail humanity in the process. Valeri argues that the moral economy of English puritans stymied, but did not fully control, the unrestrained pursuit of profit, aided by the existing structures of church and state and the role they played in promoting and supporting this view of the marketplace. At the most fundamental level, English courts, civil and ecclesiastical, condoned the charging of interest, or "usury" in the language of the hotter Protestants, and settled grievances and suits in line with this philosophy. With the notable exceptions of puritan tradesmen such as Nehemiah Wallington, most were unable or unwilling to work and compete in the world of trade, credit, and finance as their consciences would have them do.

New England, with its external and structural manifestations of puritan piety and theology, initially succeeded in establishing a more godly marketplace. The "Puritan moral imagination" was so tightly held by most, and especially so by those in authority, that Winthrop and his associates successfully resisted England's legal culture of suit and countersuit, lawyers and agents, new tools of credit and exchange, in addition to usury and ungodly (as opposed to reasonable) profit. New England's marketplace would not be anything like England's.

Englishmen, regardless of religious identity, held orderly rule and governance dear. In areas such as the law, charter rights, and the structures of daily governance, English practice became the foundation for colonial use. But, as Francis Bremer reveals in "The County of Massachusetts: The Governance of John Winthrop's Suffolk and the Shaping of the Massachusetts Bay Colony," Winthrop and his fellow settlers drew selectively, albeit heavily, upon their English experiences in county government. More importantly, they drew upon their experiences in the godly country of the Stour Valley, adopting and modifying English courts and customs to suit colonial needs and religious aspirations. The influence can most readily be seen in the roles of magistrates, justices of the peace, and the amalgamated version of the assizes and quarter session courts. At the same time, colonial leaders rejected equally established aspects of English legal life, such as the offices of lord lieutenant and sheriff and the ecclesiastical courts and their canon law. Winthrop and his associates crafted a system of local government bent on maintaining the local peace and "calculated to create stability and order thousands of miles from home." At its most elemental level, the Massachusetts system would have been recognizable to any English man or woman, although without the familiar trappings of ancient practice and the state church. Rejection did not characterize the relationship between England and her New England colony. Rather, one finds selective borrowing and adaptation as a group of godly Englishmen strove to create a godly commonwealth in the wilderness.

In the opening phase of settlement, colonists did not explicitly lay claim to the idea of the "ancient constitution" and its attendant system of common law. As Richard Ross and James Hart explain in their

Introduction

essay, "The Ancient Constitution in the Old World and the New," even the second generation of colonists could not claim the ancient standing of their constitution, dating "time out of mind," when their own fathers had established it. Nevertheless, during these very years the English legal system became dedicated to this concept and lawyers of the common law attained particular regard. With the quickly shifting political circumstances generated by the English Civil Wars, and the subsequent political discourse of natural rights and social contracts, the ancient constitution fell in esteem as well as in usefulness. But as the sun set on the importance of the ancient constitution in England, it rose phoenix-like in the west. This once unjustifiable concept took on the mantle of godliness and sacredness. In order for this transformation to occur, colonial leaders needed to create an aura of godliness around the first charter as well as the common law which underpinned it. Prompted by events in England itself—not the least of them being the Crown's push in the 1680s to restrict colonial charters, as well as English municipal corporations—later generations of New Englanders turned selectively to the old country in an ironic bid to find the tools they needed to preserve and continue their distinctive standing as New England.

Our developing understanding of the seventeenth-century Atlantic world has shed new light on the relationship between New and old England, revealing a far more complex pattern of borrowing and adaptation than previously recognized. Additionally, the relationship proved not nearly as one-sided as we have assumed. In some areas, such as in the formation of identity, communication, and gender values, the relationship between the two sides of the ocean is better characterized as one of "cross fertilization," to borrow David Hall's and Alexandra Walsham's phrase, than of simple rejection. Richard Godbeer's "Performing Patriarchy: Gendered Roles and Hierarchies in Early Modern England and Seventeenth-Century New England" explores a shared paradigm of gender, hierarchy, and religion in a world without the modern rigidity of gender definitions. Male hierarchy governed the Atlantic world, but power favored role, class, or position more than simple gender. Thus, in certain circumstances men could find themselves as structural females, just as women could assume a structurally male persona. In the theological life of puritans, men assumed a bride-like position in relation to Jesus, whom ministers characterized as the bridegroom. In the complex manifestation of hierarchy in seventeenth-century England and New England, women crossed gender lines, becoming "male" in the market as they bought and sold, in the household as they supervised its running, and sometimes in the community in the absence of their husbands. The example of Queen Elizabeth, as Godbeer details, displayed the very real boundaries of gender identities but also surprising flexibility and ambiguity. Differences between England and Massachusetts certainly arose. Theaters with attendant cross-dressing and transgendered casts, for instance, did not exist in the colony. But, as Godbeer writes, at the convergence of religion, gender, and hierarchy, much more was the same.

David Hall and Alexandra Walsham explore an area of Atlantic history whose ties, bonds, and networks remained active and healthy. Their essay, "Justification by Print Alone? Protestantism, Literacy, and Communications in the Anglo-American World of John Winthrop," offers an intriguing and inspired look at the nexus of communication and religion, specifically "how particular groups or communities deployed the technologies of speech, writing, and printing in the maintaining of religion." In doing so, they call into question the long-held axiom that print and Protestantism were inextricably linked. Indeed, in light of Hall's and Walsham's work, historians must rethink the emphasis they have placed on print and publishing in the reforming process. The essay's suggestions about the importance and vibrant na-

Introduction

ture of spoken, oral, scribal modes of communication, and the fluidity of transmission between these methods of exchange, should alter the way we understand early seventeenth-century Atlantic culture.

In the world of John Winthrop, politics was not—nor could it be—separate from religion. Hall and Walsham unsettle another historical commonplace: that print and print culture marked the beginning of "rational public discourse." This long-held view, according to Hall and Walsham, erroneously overvalues the role of the printed word. Censorship and limited access to printing presses ensured that other methods of communication and dialogue not only continued from the medieval into the early modern world but actually flourished. As the authors demonstrate in the realm of religion, preaching and "gossip" acted as vital tools in undermining the status quo, voicing criticism, and fostering dissent. This too, they argue, held true for political discourse. One did not need the ability to read to participate in politics, nor did one have to write to engage in public dissent.

In areas such as communication, gender, and the construction of identities, both personal and national—aspects of early modern life embedded in the very hearts and minds of English men and women regardless of place—little differentiated the peoples of one shore from the other. Fundamental building blocks of the Anglo-American character or identity lay deeply ingrained, unquestioned, and unexplored by those in their grip. For more self-conscious acts, such as religion, governance, political theory, and economic exchanges, the relationships between old and New England underwent active and deliberate examination before colonists accepted or rejected them for use in the new land.

England clearly figured large in the world of New England. Yet, the role of New England in English thought, politics, government, and religion remains strikingly absent from most of the essays in this book. Historians still operate as if the existence of the Massachusetts colony altered not one wit of England, its identity, or the framework of its institutions. Could this be true? Contemporary Englishmen may not have noticed any change to their world as a result of their colonies or may have ascribed those changes to different causes. In any case, New England does not appear to have played the role logic suggests it should. What, therefore, does New England's absence from English historiography imply about the nature of John Winthrop's England? In the most critical light, it may suggest an inordinate degree of complacency or a staggering degree of hubris. At the very least, the failure to reckon seriously with the thoughts, ideas, and aims of New England possessed—and possesses—serious repercussions. It allowed a taproot of neglect to establish itself deep in the soil of colonial life and institutions. It fed the vine of rebellion and revolution and the eventual loss of much of England's North American colonies, the hallmark of the period that followed.

Did the tree not fall? Or have historians been deaf to the sound it made?

New England's absence from England's tale may not be the trick of some misshapen historiography, the product of scholars whose eyes and minds never extended to the lands across the Atlantic. Common sense suggests that the addition of the New World's resources and its markets, its challenges to English law, and its indigenous peoples, must have perforce shifted, if not even radically changed, the way England viewed itself and conducted its affairs. Is it possible that the emigration of over 20,000 Englishmen to New England in the 1630s caused no fundamental changes in the social and political order of the communities they left? Did the statements on religion and government from colonists that flowed from the London presses fall on deaf ears? Did the New England experience of Cromwell's major generals have no influence on their military careers? Could it have been mere coincidence that New England law codes were published in Eng-

Introduction

---

land as the Interregnum Parliaments took up the question of law reform? These are stories that historians of England have not investigated. Nor have they considered how the departure of Winthrop, John Cotton, John Davenport, and other lay and clerical leaders reconfigured the puritan movement that remained to challenge Charles I and his bishops in the 1640s.

Unfortunately, neither the "Worlds of John Winthrop" conference nor the essays in this volume have fully addressed these and other issues. What these essays do offer is a rethinking of the historical status quo and a further demonstration of the value of examining early American themes in the context of an expanded British history. The challenge still remains for historians of England to join in the task of telling the full story of the Anglo-American Atlantic.

Acknowledgments

Clearly this volume could not have happened without the conference that gave it birth. We would like to thank the administration of Millersville University of Pennsylvania for their support, and in particular President Joseph Caputo and Vice-President for University Advancement Jerry Eckert. President Larry Petit and Dean Brenda Carter at Indiana University of Pennsylvania offered their much-appreciated commitment to the project. The support of our colleagues in the history departments at Millersville and Indiana University of Pennsylvania also deserves thanks and acknowledgment. Dr. William M. Fowler, Jr., director of the Massachusetts Historical Society, and Dr. Ronald Hoffman, director of the Omohundro Institute of Early American History and Culture, generously supported the conference while giving us the freedom to shape it as we saw fit.

Dr. Fowler also provided us with an early commitment to publish this volume, a pledge without which it would have been difficult to persuade our authors to labor as hard as they have over these essays. More than any one person, Conrad E. Wright of the Massachusetts Historical Society is responsible for what is valuable in this collection. By insisting that we do more than merely revise and publish conference proceedings, Conrad made the meetings themselves a launching pad for a new round of rigorous research, collaboration, and writing. While Conrad set the goals, Donald Yacovone of the Massachusetts Historical Society was the editor who fought to make sure that we all remained true in the pursuit of those goals. Donald not only had the task of trying to insure that those essays authored by scholars thousands of miles removed spoke with a common voice, but also constantly reminded us that we needed to communicate not only to fellow scholars but to others without the specialized knowledge shared by the contributors. Daunting tasks indeed. As editors, we would like to thank him for his efforts while absolving him of responsibility for any infelicities of style and failures to be clear. We reserve special thanks for our contributors. Like the early colonists, they embarked on a journey with little idea of how long it would take to reach port. No one expected the complications caused by the dissolution of Northeastern University Press, the Massachusetts Historical Society's long-time distributor. And probably none of us understood the demands that such a complex collaboration placed on everyone. But all persevered, and for that we extend our thanks.

Notes

1. David Armitage, "Three Concepts of Atlantic History," in David Armitage and Michael J. Braddick, eds., *The British Atlantic World, 1500-1800* (New York, 2002), 15.
2. Roger Thompson, *Divided We Stand: Watertown, Massachusetts, 1630-1680* (Amherst, Mass., 2001); Michael Winship, *Making Heretics: Militant Protes-*

tantism and Free Grace in Massachusetts, 1636-1641 (Princeton, 2002); Carla G. Pestana, *The English Atlantic in an Age of Revolution, 1640-1661* (Cambridge, Mass., 2004).

3. For an excellent discussion of how Atlantic history relates to American exceptionalism, see Joyce Chaplin, "Expansion and Exceptionalism in Early American History," *Journal of American History* 89(2003):1431-1455.

4. See, for example, Herbert Osgood, *The American Colonies in the Seventeenth Century* (New York, 1904); Charles Maclean Andrews, *The Colonial Period of American History* (New Haven, 1934); Lawrence Henry Gipson, *The British Empire Before the American Revolution* (New York, 1936-1970). More recent works representative of this approach are Michael Kammen's *A Rope of Sand: The Colonial Agents, British Politics, and the American Revolution* (Ithaca, N.Y., 1968); Alison Olson's *Anglo-American Politics 1660-1775: The Relationship between Parties in England and America* (London, 1973); Philip Haffenden's *New England in the English Nation, 1689-1713* (Oxford, 1974); Richard R. Johnson's *Adjustment to Empire: The New England Colonies, 1675-1715* (New Brunswick, N.J., 1981); and Stephen S. Webb's *The Governors-General: The English Army and the Definition of Empire, 1569-1681* (Chapel Hill, 1979).

5. Samuel Eliot Morison, *The Founding of Harvard College* (Cambridge, Mass., 1935) and also his *Harvard College in the Seventeenth Century* (Cambridge, Mass., 1936). Morison was also noted for sailing upon and flying over the Atlantic as he researched his biography of Columbus and European explorations in North and South America; see his two volume *The European Discovery of America* (New York, 1971-1974).

6. Perry Miller, *The New England Mind: The Seventeenth Century* (New York, 1939) and *The New England Mind: From Colony to Province* (New York, 1953).

7. Edmund S. Morgan, *Visible Saints: The History of a Puritan Idea* (New York, 1963).

8. See, for example, David D. Hall, *The Faithful Shepherd: A History of the New England Ministry in the Seventeenth Century* (New York, 1972); Michael McGiffert, *God's Plot: Puritan Spirituality in Thomas Shepard's Cambridge* (Amherst, Mass., 1994); Michael Winship, *Seers of God: Puritan Providentialism in the Restoration and Early Enlightenment* (Baltimore, 1996); Stephen Foster, *The Long Argument: English Puritanism and the Shaping of New England Culture, 1570-1700* (Chapel Hill, 1991), and Francis J. Bremer, *Congregational Communion: Clerical Friendship in the Anglo-American Puritan Community, 1610-1692* (Boston, 1994).

9. This perspective is surprisingly absent in Steve Hindle's otherwise impressive book, *The State and Social Change in Early Modern England, c. 1550-1640* (New York, 2000). This is particularly relevant in that Hindle's volume and this one address virtually the same chronological span. An example of Atlantic-based studies of trade is David Harris Sacks, *Widening Gate: Bristol and the Atlantic Economy, 1450-1640* (Berkeley, 1991). For the later colonial period, Gretchen Holbrook Gerzina has impressively explored the effects of colonial migration into England of blacks, primarily West Indians, during the eighteenth century in her *Black London: Life before Emancipation* (New Brunswick, N.J., 1995).

10. J. C. D. Clark, *The Language of Liberty, 1660-1832: Political Discourse and Social Dynamics in the Anglo-American World* (New York, 1994); David Cressy, *Coming Over: Migration and Communication Between England and New England in the Seventeenth Century* (Cambridge, Eng., 1987); Tom Webster, *Godly Clergy in Early Stuart England: The Caroline Puritan Movement, c. 1620-1643* (Oxford, 1997). The study of witchcraft and its prosecution has also seen some use of a trans-Atlantic approach.

11. This was a follow up to an earlier 1975 conference on the same theme hosted by Thomas More College in Kentucky with funding from the National Endowment for the Humanities.

12. For Winthrop's background and life, see Francis J. Bremer, *John Winthrop: America's Forgotten Founding Father* (New York, 2003).

13. In initial discussions with Dr. Daniel W. Howe we hoped that the conference would be linked with an Oxford audience at the Institute's new home via teleconferencing, but construction delays made that impossible.

14. There were a number of interesting spinoffs from the conference. In conjunction with the conference, Dr. Lynn Botelho of Indiana University of Pennsylvania (an English historian) and Dr. Francis Bremer of Millersville University (a colonialist) each taught a semester-long class on the topic of seventeenth-century Anglo-America at their own campuses, with all sessions of each course telelinked to the other course. Thus, faculty and students on two sides of the Commonwealth of Pennsylvania discussed the English and American dimensions of the material. In the years leading up to the conference and afterwards, Dr. John Morrill of Cambridge University and Dr. Bremer collaborated on a number of projects in which they explored the English and American dimensions of common material through the juxtaposition of the careers and views of Oliver Cromwell and John Winthrop. These included an NEH Summer

Introduction

Seminar for Teachers on "Two Faces of Puritanism: Oliver Cromwell and John Winthrop," a team-taught summer graduate class, and a Liberty Fund Seminar in Lavenham, England, on the political ideas of Winthrop and Cromwell.

15. This is well explored in Ann Hughes's important new study, *Gangraena and the Struggle for the English Revolution* (Oxford, 2004).
16. Scholars have no settled opinion on whether or not they should capitalize the words "Puritan" and "Puritanism." For the most part, those writing on New England have seen Puritanism as a defined and fixed entity and have capitalized the terms, while those writing about Tudor-Stuart England have seen puritanism as a characteristic or orientation and declined to use capitals. We have chosen to allow the authors the freedom to exercise their own preference. The way they have used that discretion itself tells us something about the state of Atlantic studies.

England's "Others" in the Old and New Worlds

Alden T. Vaughan and Virginia Mason Vaughan

"[T]HE PEOPLE OF ENGLAND," boasted peripatetic physician Andrew Borde in the middle of the sixteenth century, "be as good as any people in any other lande, and nacion that ever I have travayled in, yea and much more better in many things, specially in maners & manhod."[1] A century later, Borde's assessment would have struck English readers as excessively modest about their virtues and insufficiently critical of other nationalities' vices. During those intervening years, England had taken giant strides toward self-definition and self-esteem. As Elizabethan and early Stuart writers compared their nation—its land, its inhabitants, its accomplishments—against a long list of external "others,"[2] the island kingdom gained a new confidence (rivals would say a new conceit) about its place among countries and among peoples. When in the early seventeenth century English emigrants expanded the "Circuit of Great Britaines Monarchie" into America, they carried with them England's ingrained notions about "others" for application and modification in the New World's quite different cultural context. In the "old" world and the "new," such precise description of "others" not only revealed English attitudes about the people they judged, but helped define English identity.³

Although England's confidence had been growing by fits and starts for several decades before 1588, the events of John Winthrop's natal year profoundly influenced England's perceptions of its own identity and its role in a changing world. The defeat of the Spanish Armada by a small but agile English navy and tempestuous weather—the latter frequently ascribed to God's intervention—settled England's future as a Protestant state and bolstered the English conviction that its "sceptred isle" had an exceptional, divinely-ordained destiny. Although England had been supporting Protestant forces in the Low Countries since 1585, the defeat of the Armada brought the struggle with Spain to the forefront of national consciousness, spurred virulent anti-Spanish propaganda, and inspired a euphoric wave of patriotism. Hack writer Robert Greene epitomized England's preening mood when he declared that Elizabeth thwarted the popish enemy "without aid of speare or horse, having the wind and sea Captains sent from above to quell the pride of such hereticall enemies of the Gospell."⁴ More than ever in English history, God seemed to be an Englishman and a Protestant to boot.⁵

Even before the Armada, English writers insisted on their countrymen's superiority. William Harrison's *Description of England* (1577) contended that the English are "merry without malice and plain without inward Italian or French craft and subtlety." Such patriotic preference grew exponentially in subsequent years. To the early seventeenth-century historian William Camden, Britain still seemed "the most flourishing and excellent, most renowmed [sic] and famous Isle of the whole world: So rich in commodities, so beautifull in situation, so resplendent in all glorie, that if the most Omnipotent had fashioned the world round like a ring, as hee did like a globe, it might have beene most worthily the onely gemme therein." England's island location on the western edge of Europe made it seem "*A world, divided from the world,*" protected from European vices and steadfast in virtue and plain-dealing. Early in the new century, John Davies of Hereford claimed that "wee open-harted are, / Scorning *Italian-hollow-heartednesse.*"[6] This sense of Englishness—admirable in all respects and superior to every other ethnic or national group—was lauded as the key to England's survival as a Protestant nation. By 1654, Oliver Cromwell was convinced that "the dispensations of the Lord have been as if he had said, *England* thou art my first-born, my delight amongst the Nations. . . . [T]he Lord hath not dealt so with any of the people round about us."[7]

Helping to construct a unique character for the English by differentiating themselves from the other peoples of the world was a flood of informative, though often inaccurate, books and other printed texts. Beginning in the mid sixteenth century and continuing well into the seventeenth, English readers consumed travel narratives (most notably the collections by Richard Hakluyt and Samuel Purchas), atlases (Abraham Ortelius and Gerard Mercator), chorographies (George Abbot and John Speed), dramas set in foreign lands (Christopher Marlowe and William Shakespeare), and hosts of poems and pamphlets that deplored—implicitly or explicitly—the vices of other nations and lauded English virtues. Sometimes these texts highlight physical differences between the English and other peoples, especially Moors, East and West Indians, Irish, Turks, Jews, and Spaniards, but English authors usually focused on differences in religion and customs, especially clothing, manners, and sexual habits.[8]

Few differences are discernible within that voluminous literature between Puritan writers—a meaningless term before the late sixteenth century and arguable for several decades thereafter—and authors who rejected that label. Yet by the second decade of the seventeenth century, writers in the coalescing Puritan movement were discernibly more critical than other English writers of Roman Catholic "others," especially Spanish and Irish, and less so than many other English writers of Jewish "others"; most authorial emphases were more individual than categorical.[9] And Puritans, like most Englishmen, couched much of their rhetoric about "others" in religious terms. The Anglican clergyman Samuel Purchas reflected a wide swath of English opinion in 1613 when he declared that "The tawney Moore, black Negro, duskie Libyan, Ash-coloured Indian, olive-coloured American, should with the whiter European become *one sheepe-fold*." Adherence to Christianity, Purchas seemed to say, was more significant than pigmentation or national affiliation, though he was clearly conscious of ethnographic categories.[10] Puritan writers would have agreed in principle, while insisting that the converts meet their definition of Christianity.

Face-to-face encounters with "others" may have been more formative for some English observers than literary encounters. Foreign traders and officials frequented England's commercial towns. Populous, polyglot London hosted every ethnicity, including scores of Africans, mostly in bondage to English masters, and a few dozen American Indians, mostly on visits to the English court or employed by promoters of England's American colonies.[11] But by and large, England viewed its "others" from afar, its perceptions shaped and its prejudices reinforced by English or foreign writers. By the time Winthrop reached adulthood, his countrymen harbored a broad array of ethnic stereotypes that would prove crucial in forging England's sense of itself and in shaping the assumptions of its overseas migrants.

The founders of English America—first around Chesapeake Bay, later in New England—encountered "others" close at hand: scatterings of continental Europeans, clusters of Scots and Irish, legions of American natives, and an initially small but growing number of free or enslaved Africans. While the relative paucity of non-English Europeans would encourage the colonists to co-opt them into the English mainstream, English America's perception of Indian and African cultural and physical otherness led increasingly to their separate and prejudicial treatment. In New England, as in old England, Puritans thought and acted much like their non-Puritan countrymen, but differences emerged, most notably in the Puritans' persistence (during Winthrop's lifetime and after) on the social and religious conversion of ethnic/racial others or their exclusion from Puritan-controlled society.

John Winthrop's English contemporaries often contrasted themselves with fellow inhabitants of the British archipelago.[12] While recognizing the ancient Britons as progenitors of the English as well as the Welsh and Scots, England's writers insisted that their own nation had progressed furthest from those barbaric origins. Although the Welsh had been incorporated politically into England as early as the twelfth century, they were still distinguishable by many non-English characteristics; by language, of course, but also by a persistent mysticism. "The Walsh men," Borde contended, ". . . do set much by their kynred & prophecyes."[13] Shakespeare's Owen Glendower (*1 Henry IV*), who professes to foretell the future, fits the stereotype. John Speed emphasized Welsh stubbornness, describing the ancient inhabitants of Wales as "a sturdy people against the *Romans*, but now most kinde and gentle towards the *English*, . . . except they be crossed and then they are the contrary."[14] Thus Shakespeare's Welsh Captain Fluellen in *Henry V* is stoutly loyal and courageous in battle but quarrelsome when the articles of war are improperly followed.

Scots, too, were simultaneously like and unlike the English. Borde's mid-sixteenth-century caricature reflected generations of bloody border wars and the Scots-French alliance that later spawned Mary Stuart, Elizabeth's Catholic rival for the English throne. Borde's Scot announces:

> I am a Scotyshe man and trew I am to fraunce
> In every cnuntrey, my selfe I do avaunce[;]
> . . . .
> An Englyshe man, I cannot naturally love
> Wherfore I offend them, and my lorde above[.]

After James's accession to the English throne, accounts of Scotland softened a bit. Camden admitted that "the Scottishmen subdued [the Picts], and established a kingdome in those parts, which with manlike courage and warlike prowesse, they have not onely maintained at home, but also purchased great honour abroad." Speed praised the Scots as a people "of good feature, strong of body, and of couragious minde" but considered those who lived closest to England to be "more beautified in manners, riches, and civilitie"; residents of the North are "more rude, retaining the customes of the *Wild-Irish*."[15]

Those "Wild-Irish" for several centuries had been England's most notorious insular "others." Central to its concern over Ireland were England's colonial settlements, where three major rebellions erupted during Elizabeth's reign: in 1566, spearheaded by Shane O'Neill; from 1579 to 1584, led by the Earl of Desmond; and, most deadly, from 1594 to 1603, the Earl of Tyrone's revolt. The Irish rebels (as England viewed them), supported by Philip II of Spain, posed a major threat to English security and heightened English excoriations of Irish character, culture, and religion.[16]

Colonial settlement clustered in the "pale" along the eastern coast, where English customs, language, and religion predominated. Outside the pale, the Irish "be slouthful, not regarding to sow & tille theyr landes, nor caring for riches[;] . . . they lak manners & honesti, & be untaught & rude, yet which rudenes with theyr meloncoli complexion causeth them to be angry and testy without a cause." The future Archbishop of Canterbury, George Abbot, contended that the Irish "naturally are rude and superstitious: the countrie good and fruitfull: but for want of tillage in divers places, they suffer it to growe into bogges, and desertes."[17] The Irish insistence on cattle herding rather than tillage struck Fynes Moryson, secretary to Lord Mountjoy at the end of Elizabeth's reign, as a basic defect in Irish character—a sign of sloth and indolence; he concluded that "They are by nature extremely given to idleness . . . [which] makes them also slovenly and sluttish in their houses and apparel."[18]

English writers often condemned Irish clothes and sartorial habits, especially the wearing of mantles. Moryson feared that mantles might serve "as [a] cabin for an outlaw in the woods, a bed for a rebel, and a cloak for a thief, and being worn over the head and ears, and hanging down to the heels, a notorious villain lapped in them may pass any town or company without being known." Hair style, as always, was contentious. Many Irish males wore long "glibs," which Edmund Spenser, secretary to Lord Grey in the 1580s, described as "a thicke curled bush of haire, hanging downe over their eyes, and monstrously disguising them, which are both very bad and hurtfull." Mantles and glibs symbolized for the English a hiding of the individual much as the Irish woods hid the rebels. Abiding in the forests and mountains, the wild Irish "lurkt, and lay in waite to doe mischiefe. These fast places they kept unknowne, by making the wayes and Entries thereunto impassable. . . . [T]here they made their Assemblies and Conspiracies without discovery."[19] By contrast, these writers imply, the Englishmen's shorter hair, relatively tight clothing, and plantations in open places reflected their forthright and upright character.

English Protestants lamented the persistence of Roman Catholicism among the Irish. Theological zeal to reform papist heretics combined with fear that Philip II's armies might use Ireland as a beachhead to attack England; Ireland could become a Spanish province. Already enmeshed in a surrogate war against Spain in the Low Countries, Protestant England could ill afford to lose Ireland to the Catholic king. Worse still, the English argued, Catholicism among the Irish had degenerated from its continental norms. Edmund Spenser charged that "not one amongst a hundred knoweth any ground of religion, or any article of his faith, but can perhaps say his Pater noster, or his Ave Maria, without any knowledge or understanding of what one word thereof meaneth." Moryson insisted that "they are by nature superstitious, and given to use witchcraft." Even while practicing rites of the Roman Church, "they intermix barbarous customs."[20] Compared to other European Catholics, whose faith was at least comprehensible (though reprehensible) to English—especially Puritan—observers, the Irish obscured their religion with crude, mystical elements.

English writers repeatedly distinguished between the "wild" or "mere" Irish—those who kept their native beliefs and lifestyles—and the "Old English" or Anglo-Irish, hybrid descendants of the native Irish and English colonists who settled in Ireland during the thirteenth century and after. Many descendants of English settlers had "gone native," intermarrying with the Irish, adopting their customs, speaking their language, and acquiring Irish names. Spenser complained that many "have degendred from their auncient dignities, and are now growne as Irish, as O'hanlans breech."[21] Sir John Davies, an important English official in Irish affairs, chided: "they did not only forget the English Language, & scorne the use thereof, but grew to bee ashamed of their very English Names, though they were Noble and of great Antiquitie; and tooke Irish *Surnames* and *Nicke-names*."[22] Such atavism subverted the colonial project to make

Ireland English and implicitly cast doubt on the inherent superiority of English values.

Davies's solution was to impose English law upon the entire country. "[H]eeretofore, the neglect of the Lawe, made the English degenerate, and become Irish," he charged, "and now, on the other side, the execution of the Law doth make the Irish grow civil, and become English."[23] The imposition of that law would require force. Through his spokesperson Ireneus, Spenser urged that England "send over into that realme, such a strong power of men, as should perforce bring in all that rebellious route and loose people, which either doe now stand out in open armes, or in wandring companies doe keepe the woods, spoyling the good subjects."[24] Only through the ruthless and consistent use of military force could the Irish be civilized into Englishness, which, of course, encouraged further rebellions and even more brutal tactics, as Cromwell's Irish campaign would later demonstrate.

Descriptions of the Irish circulating in Winthrop's England fueled the emerging sense of a unique, superior Englishness. "It was the Irish 'wilderness' that bounded the English garden," observed cultural critic Michael Neill; "Irish 'barbarity' that defined English civility; Irish papistry and 'superstition' that warranted English religion; it was Irish 'lawlessness' that demonstrated the superiority of English law and Irish wandering that defined the settled and centered nature of English society."[25] "Wild" Irishmen especially were a heaven-sent foil for England's self-fashioning.

The enemy most feared and hated by the Protestant English in the late sixteenth and early seventeenth centuries were the Spanish, especially while their nations were at war from the mid 1580s until James I's peace initiative in 1604. James sought to enhance the new alliance with Spain through dynastic marriages: first between Prince Henry and the Spanish Infanta and, after Henry's death in 1612, between Prince Charles and the Spanish princess. Militant Protestants loudly opposed these overtures. Puritans, argues Marvin Arthur Breslow, "saw Spain and the Roman Catholic Church as one inseparable danger[;] . . . they both appeared to the Puritan [and many Anglicans] to be seeking a Catholic Spanish universal monarchy."[26]

English contempt for Spain was fairly recent. Until the middle of the sixteenth century, Spain was barely distinguishable in English eyes from other European nations. Many English had disliked Philip II during his marriage to Mary Tudor, but once it was clear that Elizabeth would not follow her sister's path, his interest in England for a while seemed comparatively benign, and anti-Spanish sentiment abated. Then the papal bull of 1570 excommunicating Elizabeth and promising the remission of sins for her assassin refreshed English fears of Spain, as did Philip's assault on Protestantism in the Low Countries. Pamphlets from the Armada period, like most wartime propaganda, demonized the enemy, and the defeat of the Spanish fleet by Elizabeth's navy against overwhelming odds fed perceptions of Spanish arrogance. One wartime writer gloated: "[O]f the proude Spanish Fleete appointed for our overthrowe, containing so many ships in number, so well in all respects furnished . . . [there] returned very few, and those so sore afflicted, that the most of their men died either before or shortly after their return, utterly disappointed of their intent." Another pamphlet, excoriating the Spanish attack as a popish plot, gleefully proclaimed, "Great triumphes dost thou (Spaniard) tell, & thereby thy conquests boast / Yet doo both losse & shame thee haunt, & hunt thee home to Spanish coast." The same writer reported that documents on Armada ships disclosed Spanish plans "to roote out, and murther without any respect of religion, all the Inhabitants of England . . . even from the age of seven or tenne yeares upward."

Younger children would be branded on the forehead, "to the end they might know them hereafter, and to use them even as they doo use their *Indian* slaves: whose life is more wretched than a thousand deaths."[27] Thus English propagandists appropriated the "Black Legend" of Spain's cruel conquest of America as a warning that similar atrocities could be visited on the English.[28]

Shakespeare caricatured the arrogant but penurious Spaniard in the figure of Don Adriano de Armado, the lying braggart in *Love's Labour's Lost*—a "refined traveller of Spain, . . . That hath a mint of phrases in his brain" (1.1.161-175). Armado, named after the fleet of 1588, embodied the vices attributed by John Speed to Spaniards:

> They are extreamely proud, and the silliest of them pretend to a great portion of wisedome, which they would seeme to express in a kinde of reserved state, and silent gravitie, when perhaps their wit will scarce serve them to speak sense. But if once their mouthes be got too open, they esteeme their breath too precious to be spent upon any other subject than their owne glorious actions. . . . Superstitious beyond any other people: which indeede commonly attends those which affect to be accounted religious, rather than to be so. For how can heartie devotion stand with crueltie, lechery, pride, Idolatrie, and those other Gothish, Moorish, Jewish, Heathenish, conditions of which they still favour.

Speed's conclusion alluded, of course, to Spain's history before 1492 of occupation by Moors and the presence of many Jews. Spenser, for one, argued that the taint of Moorish blood was permanent: "after they were beaten out by Ferdinando of Arragon and Elizabeth his wife, yet they were not so cleansed, but that through the marriages which they had made, and mixture with the people of the land, during their long continuance there, they had left no pure drop of Spanish blood, no more than of Roman or Scythian."[29] The Spaniard thus made a most convenient enemy, chargeable not only with arrogance, cruelty, and heresy, but also with what would later be labeled "racial" impurity.[30]

Speed's condemnation of Spaniards for "Jewish . . . conditions" reflected a widespread English antipathy toward peoples identified culturally rather than geographically. The Rev. George Abbot attributed the Jews' lack of a homeland to "a curse upon them and their children, for putting Christ to death"; thus "they are scattered upon the face of the earth as runnagates: without certaine countrie, King, Priest, or Prophet." Abbot implicitly promoted the popular belief that all Jews had been expelled from England by King Edward I in 1290, although, as James Shapiro's meticulous study of Jews in Shakespeare's England reveals, some Jews lived in London in the early seventeenth century and long before. "[S]mall numbers of Jews began drifting back into England almost immediately after the Expulsion and began to arrive in large numbers during the Tudor period."[31]

Many Jewish refugees arrived from Iberia. Soon after Spain expelled the Jews from its boundaries in 1492, Portugal insisted on conversion or expulsion for its Jewish citizens. Some stayed in both countries and converted, at least outwardly, but a substantial number migrated to other parts of Europe. By Winthrop's day, a small community of Marrano Jews lived in London, working as merchants, physicans, and teachers of Hebrew. The English quietly tolerated them so long as they conformed outwardly to the rituals of the established church. Yet English opinion, like most of Europe's, remained profoundly anti-Semitic, associating Jews with heinous crimes against Christians and with usurious money-lending. Such sentiments were exacerbated by the trial and public execution in 1594 of the Portuguese Jew Roderigo Lopez, who had arrived in England in 1559, served for many years as physician to Queen Elizabeth, and stood accused of attempting to poison her.[32]

Barabas, the Machiavellian hero-villain of Christopher Marlowe's *The Jew of Malta*, exhibits the characteristics most frequently attributed to Jews in popular folklore. He boasts of his cruelty:

> I walk abroad a-nights
> And kill sick people groaning under walls:
> Sometimes I go about and poison wells.
>
> And Barabas is a miserly money-manager who exults
>   in the riches he extracts from Christian dupes.
> Thus trowls our fortune in by land and sea,
> And thus are we on every side enriched.
> These are the blessings promised the Jews,
> And herein was old Abram's happines.
> . . . .
> Rather had I, a Jew, be hated thus,
> Than pitied in a Christian poverty.
> . . . .
> I cannot tell but we have scrambled up
> More wealth by far than those that brag of faith.[33]

Tales also circulated in England—as elsewhere in Europe—of bizarre ritual murders in which Jews collected Christians' blood, which Shylock's lust for a pound of Antonio's flesh graphically reflects. In Shakespeare's *Merchant of Venice*, as in Marlowe's *Jew of*

Malta, Christian stereotypes and phobias about Jews reached a wide cross-section of England's populace.

Although John Winthrop may have shared to some extent the popular antipathy toward Jews, Puritan respect for the Old Testament, appreciation of ancient languages, and millennialist emphasis on the conversion of the Jews ameliorated such tendencies. At the turn of the century, Puritans were frequent clients of Marranos who taught and translated Hebrew. And if millennial hopes for the conversion of the Jews were to be realized, they had to be present on English shores. Thus in 1656 Oliver Cromwell officially reopened England to Jews. Although Puritan millennialism's focus on conversion of the Jews, in both England and America, would not occur until after Winthrop's death (few, if any, Jews inhabited English America before 1654), its early manifestations could be seen in Puritan views on the origins and conversion of American Indians.[34]

Aside from the Jews and the Spanish, early modern English men and women generally viewed continental Europeans through the prism of longstanding trading relationships, changing diplomatic priorities, and—especially important to the Puritan community—religion. Like John Speed, who described Europe as holding "the Sceptre of the Earth into her hand," an image that also graced the frontispiece of Abraham Ortelius's popular atlas, continental Europeans viewed their region of the world as the most advanced and civilized. Nations on the continent shared a common history and common values with Britain, dating back to the ancient Greeks and Romans. English stereotypes of continental nationalities, except for the Spaniards, were therefore largely benign: the Dutch were good traders and mechanics but bibulous; the French delighted in new fashions and gorgeous apparel; the Italians were lascivious and political; the Russians were rude and ignorant, but at least they were Christian, and so forth.[35] Not so in the farther corners of the continent, where peoples and cultures seemed vastly different from the English norm and where other religions competed with Christianity. During Winthrop's life, when the Ottoman Empire controlled most of the eastern Mediterranean rim and all of the Balkan peninsula, the Turks were for English commentators the most disturbing of the distant "others."

Unlike English disdain for the Irish and contempt for the Spanish, the Ottoman Empire inspired a mixture of respect and outrage. The empire's highly developed social structure and hierarchical government were comprehensible to the English. Citizens of the empire's major cities, moreover, shared a rich historical and cultural heritage with much of Europe, and a general prosperity, thanks to the extensive Ottoman commercial network. Most important, during its three-hundred-year expansionist history, the Ottoman Empire had shown remarkable military prowess. English writers frequently admired the discipline of the seasoned janizaries, who held their ranks when Christian armies fell apart. The Christian nations, by contrast, were too rent by religious divides and diplomatic rivalry to form a united opposition to the Turk—save for the alliance of Venetian, Spanish, and German forces which routed the Turkish galleys at Lepanto in 1571.[36] For many English writers, argues Daniel J. Vitkus, "the vast wealth, absolute hegemony, and steadfast discipline of the Islamic ruler and his loyal, united followers were cause for wonder and esteem."[37]

Although England remained comparatively isolated from Europe's ongoing warfare with the Ottoman Empire, its stock of information about the Turks was fuller than it was for many other groups. England's information came partly from regions that actively opposed the Empire's expansion—Germany, Hungary, Venice, and Spain—whose narratives circulated widely. And despite the prevailing distrust of Turks, English factors continued to deal with Turkish merchants at home and abroad. That did not prevent Turkish vessels in the Mediterranean, even in the English channel, from seizing English ships from time to time and enslaving the crews; English captivity narratives added to the fund of information and heightened English animosity. But information also came from first-hand encounters. "[R]eal meetings took place between Muslims and Britons: the latter ate at the same tables with visiting 'Turks' in London, encountered Barbary pirates in the jails of the southwestern sea towns or coastal villages of Ireland and the Channel Isles, and admired Ottoman *chiauses* [emissaries] in their processions to the Banqueting Hall. Britons. . . fought in Muslim armies, joined the Barbary Corsairs in piracy and pillaging, and entered as slaves into the intimacy of Muslim life, religion, and language."[38]

English writers emphasized the Turks' unalterable "otherness." John Speed was typical: "They are for the most part broad-faced, strong-boned, well proportioned, dull and heavie headed, of grosse understanding, idelely disposed, and yet greedie of wealth, luxurious in their diet, and beastly in their lustfull affections, without distinction of kindred or sexe, base minded, slaves to themselves, and their superiours in their owne Country: yet ignorantly proud, and contemptuous of other Nations."[39] Richard Knolles's lengthy *Historie of the Turkes* (1603) condemned Turkish polity: "*The Othoman* government in this his so great an empire is altogether like the government of the master over his slave, and indeed meere tyrannicall."[40]

English writers, like the rest of Christian Europe, decried the Turk's religion, describing Mohammed as a juggler, a renegade, a fraud. To Speed, for example, "Their Religion is a meere cousenage, thrust upon the silly people by the impious subtletie of one *Mahomet*." Another English tract described Islam as "a monstrous and most divelish religion favouring partly of Judaism, partly of Christianitie, and partly of Arrianism." The Turks proselytized this heretical religion wherever they could, desiring, one writer claimed, "nothing more then to drawe both christians and others to embrace their Religion and to turne Turke... bee it by any meanes good or badde, right or wrong."[41] As the Ottoman Empire advanced into Europe, Christians trembled at the conversion into mosques of cathedrals such as St. Matthias in Budapest.

Aside from his heretical religion, English writers most often castigated the Turk for cruelty.[42] After each major Ottoman campaign against Christian armies, vivid descriptions reached England of torture and merciless killings. Richard Knolles, for example, described Turkish behavior during the siege of Vienna in 1529: "the old men were slaine, the young men led away into captivitie, women ravished before their husbands faces, and afterwards slaine with their children, young infants were ript out of their mothers wombs, and others taken from their breasts were cut in pieces, or else thrust upon sharpe stakes, ... with many other incredible cruelties."[43]

Widely circulated accounts of fratricide committed by each emperor when he inherited the throne made the Turks seem peculiarly cruel in an uncommonly cruel era. Knolles began with Mahomet, who inherited the Turkish throne in 1450 and became the first emperor. He planned the murder of his youngest brother, "then but eighteene moneths old." Similarly, Selymus, who inherited the throne in 1512, eliminated his own kin and rivals, and Amurath, who succeeded to the throne in 1574, "caused his five brethren ... to be all strangled in his owne presence." Ismahel, a Turkish king in the same period, had his eight brothers beheaded.[44] This "Turkish pollicie" of eliminating rivals seems to have been common knowledge in Elizabeth's England. When Robert Greene presented the figure of Selimus (Selim I, 1512-1520) on the public stage, he included three stranglings and a scene in which the Emperor's advisor has his eyes gouged out and his arms cut off[45]; and when Henry V inherits the throne in Shakespeare's *2 Henry IV*, he reassures his brothers that "This is the English, not the Turkish court; / Not Amurath an Amurath succeeds, / But Harry Harry" (5.2.47-49).

Turkish sexual habits simultaneously fascinated and disgusted English writers. Speed contrasted the Emperor's palace, the Seraglio, which "surpasseth all other Courts under heaven for Majesty, and number of buildings, for pleasurable gardens, sweete-fountaines and rich furniture," with its fifteen hundred women "cloystered up for his pleasure and out of them one hundred and fiftie culled as choyce for his daily lust."[46] Far worse, another writer charged, Turkish men "are not contented with the abuse of women, for the satiating of their beastly humours, but they are so outragiously given over to the abominable sin of Sodomie, that it is impossible without horror to be uttered."[47] Nabil Matar notes that "Nearly every travel or captivity account includes references to Muslim sodomy and other sexual practices. . . . [S]odomy signified barbarity."[48]

English beliefs about Turkish hedonism contributed to anxieties—similar in some respects to fears of atavism in Ireland—about "turning Turk." Captured English seamen and pirates in the Mediterranean could choose a painful death or conversion; those who took the latter alternative often became "renagadoes," a word the *OED* attributes first to Richard Hakluyt's 1599 description of an English captive: "He was a Renegado, which is one that first was a Christian, and afterwards becommeth a Turke." Renegadoes adopted Turkish names, dress, and customs, and were circumcised. Like the Jews, some English writers argued, renegadoes were apostates who by their rejection of Christianity must wander the Mediterranean without a settled home, fitting precisely into neither Turkish nor Christian society. Unlike the few Christianized Portuguese Jews in London, the ethnically English renegadoes' conversion to Islam threatened England's sense of its own superiority.[49]

The Ottoman Empire during Winthrop's time controlled most of northern Africa and was linked to its Moorish inhabitants by ties of religion and commerce. Some travelers reported that the denizens of these regions varied in color and culture from Africans below the Sahara Desert, referring to the former as "tawny Moors" or "white Moors," to differentiate them from dark-skinned Moors to the south. "Moor" eventually referred—usually but not always—to a person with dark pigmentation, a verbal reminder of visual difference that, unlike the Irish "glib" or Turkish turban, was unalterable. English writers favored the proverb, "you can't wash the Ethiop white," to describe an impossible feat.[50] But just as the Ethiop could not turn white, the Englishman could not turn black. Thus, discussions of black Africans revealed less anxiety about transculturation than did descriptions of the Irish and the Turk, while the fear of hybridity through miscegenation lurked underneath quasi-scientific discussions of monstrous births and prodigies.[51]

The information about Africa available to English readers in the sixteenth century was largely fable, some of it dating back to Pliny and Herodotus. In the medieval travelogue of John Mandeville, they found images of monstrosity: "In Ethiopie are such men that have but one foote, and they go so fast it is a great mervaile, and that is a large foot that the shadow therof covereth the body from Sun or raine when they lye upon their backs, & when their children are first borne they looke like russet, and when they wax old then they bee all black." Such tales circulated well into the seventeenth century. Speed described the people of the Manicongo, for example, as anthropophagi who eat "shambles of mans flesh, as we have for meate. They kill their owne children in the birth, to avoide the trouble of breeding them, and preserve their Nation with stolen brats from their neighbouring Countries."⁵²

Perceptions of Africans had changed considerably when Dr. Borde's mid-sixteenth-century description noted that the Portuguese purchased black Moors for slavery, yet he wrote pejoratively about the Moors' religion and manners:

> I am a blake More borne in Barby
> Chrysten men for money oft doth me bye
> Yf I be unchristend, marchauntes do not care
> They by[e] me in markets be I never so bare
> Yet wyll I be a good dylygent slave
> Although I do stand in sted of a knave
> I do gather fygges and with some I whype my tayle
> To be angry wyth me what shal it a vayle[.]⁵³

English writers after Borde continued to condemn the apparent dearth of religion among sub-Saharan Africans. Abbot contended that the inhabitants of the torrid zone "have bin Gentiles: adoring Images, and foolish shapes for their gods: neither hearing of Christ, nor beleeving on Mahomet."⁵⁴ Other writers condemned their lack of civility. An English translation of Joannes Boemus's 1555 *Omnium gentium mores* claimed that most Africans "go naked: covering their privities with shiepes tayles."⁵⁵ Sixteenth-century accounts thus emphasized African monstrousness, heathenism, and barbarism.⁵⁶

Reports of sub-Saharan Africans by English eyewitnesses began to circulate in 1555, when Richard Eden tacked onto his edition of Peter Martyr Angleria's *Decades of the Newe Worlde of West India* a brief description of Africa. Eden claimed (though not by personal observation) that central Africa, the land of "the blacke Moores cauled Ethiopians or Negros" contained "no cities: but only certeyne lowe cotages made of bouwes of trees plastered with chauke and covered with strawe," most of the inhabitants were "pure Gentyles [pagans] and Idolatours." Eden also printed an eyewitness report by Robert Gainsh on the second English voyage to sub-Saharan Africa (1554), which described the people as "of beastly lyvynge, without a god, lawe, religion, or common welth, and so scorched and vexed with the heate of the soonne, that in many places they curse it when it ryseth."[57]

Gainsh seems here to attribute the Africans' color to the heat of the sun, a common belief among travel writers of the time. John Davies of Hereford, who posited the relationship between climate and body type in *Microcosmos* (1603), suggested that the sun also bore responsibility for the texture of the African's hair:

> And in the torrid *Zone* it is so hott
> That *flesh* and *Bloud* (like flaming *fire*) it fries,
> And with a *Cole*-blacke beautie it doth blot,
> Curling the *Haires* upon a wyry knott.[58]

In 1578, however, the seafarer George Best countered the climatological explanation of the African's darkness, arguing that people remained white in other parts of the Torrid Zone, such as New Spain. And "I my selfe," he testified, "have seene an Ethiopian as blacke as a cole brought into England, who taking a faire English woman to wife, begat a sonne in all respects as blacke as the father was, although England were his native countrey, and an English woman his mother." Best concluded that the black pigmentation "proceedeth rather of some natural infection of that man, which was so strong, that neither the nature of the Clime, neither the good complexion of the mother concurring, coulde any thing alter." Best's alternative explanation: blackness was a visible sign of the biblical curse laid upon Cham, the son of Noah, who disobeyed his father's command to abstain from "carnall copulation" with his wife on the Ark. All of Cham's posterity were accordingly accursed with a color "so blacke and lothsome, that it might remaine a spectacle of disobedience to all the worlde."[59]

Many English writers advocated an exegesis similar to Best's. The Rev. Thomas Cooper, for example, almost paraphrased it in a sermon of 1615 to the promoters of American colonization. That same year, George Sandys contended that Negroes "are descended of *Chus*, the Sonne of cursed *Cham*; as are all of that complexion. Not so by reason of their Seed, nor heat of the Climate: Nor of the Soyle, as some have supposed . . . but rather from the Curse of *Noe* upon *Cham* in the Posteritie of *Chus*." Sandys's narrative was published five times between 1615 and 1637. When Samuel Purchas included an extract in his *Pilgrimes* in 1625, he added in the margin: "*Chams* Curse continuing stil."[60]

Although as an avid Puritan Winthrop was unlikely to have attended theaters, stage representations of England's "others" were widely influential. Among the most pervasive was the association between blackness and damnation, dating back to the medieval mystery plays, wherein Lucifer's appearance in blackface signified his fall from grace, and the black faces of damned souls in the Doomsday pageant emblemized their fallen nature.[61] As early as 1584, Reginald Scot wrote in *The Discoverie of Witchcraft* that "A damned soule may and dooth take the shape of a blacke moore."[62] Not surprisingly, then, black Moors in George Peele's *Battle of Alcazar* (1587-1588), Shakespeare's *Titus Andronicus* (1592), and Thomas Dekker's *Lust's Dominion* (c. 1598) boast of their affinity with the devil and take pride in their evil deeds.

Besides the perverse and the demonic, English writers associated black skin with servitude. The first captive Africans reached England in the middle of the sixteenth century, and although their status is unclear, the enslavement of Africans throughout Iberia and its colonies was common knowledge and probably a formative precedent.[63] By the final quarter of the sixteenth century, black servants in England—most of them apparently in permanent bondage—were fairly common in London, as parish burial records suggest.[64] No later than 1617 the eminent Puritan preacher Paul Baynes distinguished between two fundamental categories of servants in England: they "are either more slavish, or else more free and liberall: the first are such whose bodies are perpetually put under the power of the Master, as Blackmores with us." Morover, Baynes added, "the children of [such] servants are borne the slaves of their Masters."[65] By the early seventeenth century, then, the three fundamental components of racial slavery—color, perpetuity, and inheritability—characterized England's treatment of its African "others." Not surprisingly, during this period the stage roles of black Moors (actually white actors in blackface) generally changed from the terrifying and exotic to the familiar and domestic, from African kings to lascivious serving maids.[66]

Before the end of the sixteenth century, the abundance of African servants prompted the government to order them out of England. Complaining that "blackamoores" were "so populous" that many able-bodied Christians were unemployed, the Privy Council in 1596 called on masters to relinquish their black servants so that "those kinde of people" could be "sent out of the lande." Five years later the problem persisted, causing Queen Elizabeth to demand that many of England's "Negroes and blackamoors" be expelled.[67] That effort also failed. The relatively few but influential owners of blackamores apparently relished the cheapness and social distinction of owning lifetime bondsmen, especially, perhaps, because they stood out as a different "kinde of people." In small numbers and under tight control, these "others" had an exotic appeal that reminded Englishmen of what they themselves most decidedly were not. While such "others" posed an economic threat to one segment of English society, they were useful for very different reasons to another, more powerful, social stratum.

American Indians presented a different sort of otherness. England had been aware of these overseas strangers since the late fifteenth century, of course, as reports circulated from Spain and Portugal of the peoples encountered by the early explorers, and by the second half of the sixteenth century, English writers were adding to a voluminous, if naive, ethnography. Much of it was nonsensical, exaggerated, and contradictory, but gradually the worst of the Indians' reputed features were proven false or grossly overstated. Indians were not ill-shaped monsters, as some early reports had contended; there were no man-hating Amazons; Americans were not, with a few exceptions and under certain circumstances, eaters of human flesh. Rather, America's natives were much like Europeans in their shape, their essential humanity, and the color of their skin. On the latter point, English readers had the testimony of numerous continental and English observers—including, after English colonies began, John Smith, William Strachey, John Rolfe, William Wood, Thomas Morton, and Roger Williams—that natives, at least along the eastern seaboard, were innately white and only superficially darkened by stains and the sun. Indians remained "other" to English eyes primarily because of their nurture, not their nature.[68]

By the time Winthrop reached Massachusetts Bay, a loose consensus had emerged about America's native "others."[69] The most universally acknowledged characteristic was their incivility—"beastly" behavior that reminded some observers of wolves or other free-ranging animals. In 1599, George Abbot had castigated America's inhabitants as "naked, uncivill, some of them devourers of mans flesh, ignorant of shipping, without all kinde of learning, having no rememberance of history or writing among them, . . . being utterly ignorant of scripture, or Christ, or Moyses, or any God."[70] Some English descriptions of the Indians, not surprisingly, noted minor parallels with the "wild Irish"—their animal-skin mantles, their insubstantial houses, their incomprehensible (to English ears) languages, their heathen rituals, which (to English eyes) smacked of devil-worship, superstition, and black magic.[71]

English writers agreed also that Indians, like the Irish, could be reformed. They too were sons of Noah—or, more precisely, descendants of his son Japhet, and thus from the same large branch of the human tree as the English. The Indians' pervasive barbarism was no more permanent than that of the ancient Britons. As the Puritan preacher William Crashaw reminded the Virginia Company of London in February 1610, "the time was when wee were as savage and uncivill, and worshipped the divell, as now they [the Indians] do, then God sent some to make us civill, others to make us christians. If such had not been sent us we had yet continued wild and uncivill, and worshippers of the divell." A decade later, Richard Whitbourne advocated charitable treatment of the natives because "we our selves were once as blinde as they in the knowledge and worship of our Creator, and as rude and savage in our lives and manners."[72] The message was clear and hopeful: just as Roman soldiers had thoroughly reformed the ancient English in the first three centuries of the Christian era, so would English settlers and preachers turn Indian "others" into civil Christians in the seventeenth century. The experience in Ireland, of course, suggested that it might not be easy. Nonetheless, the social and religious reformation of Irish and Indian "others" represented an important goal of Winthrop's contemporaries, especially of zealous Puritans.

Several encouraging scraps of evidence reinforced English expectations of rapid Indian conversion. Although, English writers insisted, the Spanish had created an animosity toward Christianity in their areas of exploration and colonization, England's gentler ways had already borne modest fruit. Thomas Hariot reported some success in spreading Anglicanism at Roanoke Island; at Jamestown, despite considerable Indian and colonial opposition, George Thorpe and others made promising headway before 1622; and, perhaps most telling, several Indians who had been in England between the 1580s and 1620s had embraced the Christian faith, the English tongue, and English "civility." The most publicized Indian converts were Hariot's friend Manteo and the Powhatan princess Pocahontas, alias Rebecca Rolfe, but several other instances of religious and social conversion presaged a successful missionary movement.[73] On the eve of Winthrop's departure for America, Puritan spokesmen generally proclaimed Indians to be temporary "others" whose current barbarism reminded the English of how necessary had been their own people's social and theological conversion and of how obligated true Christians were to effect a similar uplifting of America's natives.

In Winthrop's England, active discrimination against "others" was rare, except for the notable (and often neglected) case of African slaves, whose owners had almost unfettered control over their human property. Some Englishmen wielded swords against the Irish or pens against foreign and domestic strangers, but the vast majority had few occasions to act upon their prejudices. In England's American outposts, by contrast, colonists had a far freer hand to discriminate against aliens individually and collectively. Through their provincial and local governments and sometimes on their own, colonists imposed restrictions or even expelled aliens from the pale; in direst circumstances, they could be exterminated by war or execution. In England, otherness was objectified largely through words, in America, largely through actions.

Initially, Englishmen were eastern North America's conspicuous "others"—newcomers whose presence was often resented and sometimes vigorously resisted, and whose culture appeared grossly inferior in the eyes of the native majority.[74] By the time John Winthrop arrived in Massachusetts, nearly half a century after England's first footholds and nearly a quarter century after the first permanent colony, spheres of English hegemony were relentlessly expanding. The colonists' Indian neighbors, except for a few social and religious converts, were, like their Irish counterparts, outside the English pale.

Continental European settlers, as well as native "others," beleaguered Jamestown's early English colonists. Smatterings of Germans, Italians, Poles, and Frenchmen with minimal loyalty to King James lived within the pallisaded villages; several "damned Dutch-men," John Smith reported, almost destroyed the colony by conspiring with the Powhatans.[75] Fears persisted also of seaborne attacks by Spaniards, despite the nominal peace between Spain and England.[76] More serious was the colony's intermittent warfare with neighboring tribes from 1607 to 1614 that almost ended its existence (as Indian hostility had earlier obliterated the Roanoke outposts) and suggested from the outset that English and Indians would inhabit separate spheres.

For a few years after the Pocahontas-Rolfe marriage of 1614, the prospect of permanent separation disappeared, and colonial optimists predicted an eventual merger of peoples—on English terms, of course. After a treaty in which the Chickahominies agreed henceforth to be called "*Tassantasses*, or English men, and be King JAMES his subjects," members of that tribe "became as familiar amongst us, as if they had been English men indeede." Five years later, the first Virginia legislature ordered each community to "obtaine unto themselves by just meanes a certaine number of the natives Children to be educated ... in true Religion and civile course of life"; the most promising male students would be sent to a college for Indians being built in the town of Henrico. When most Indian parents declined to part with their children, the government welcomed whole families into English settlements and provided houses, clothes, cattle, and cornfields. In 1621 Virginia's governor boasted that Indians "were alwaies friendly entertained at the tables of the English, and commonly lodged in their bedchambers."[77] English America's most numerous and potent "others" seemed on the verge of assimilation.

Although the founders of Plymouth Colony arrived during Virginia's harmonious interlude, the *Mayflower*'s passengers harbored stereotypes of "cruell, barbarous, and most treacherous" Indians. According to William Bradford's hyperbolic recollection, the first wave of Plymouth pilgrims expected the natives to "tormente men in the most bloodie manner that may be; fleaing some alive with the shells of fishes, cutting of[f] the members, and joynts of others . . . [and] eate the collops of their flesh in their sight whilst they live."[78] But by the time Bradford recorded those early qualms, he had far more reason to prize Indians as friends and allies than to fear them as implacable "others." Plymouth Colony would probably not have survived its early years without the Patuxet Squanto's assistance as interpreter, guide, diplomat, and horticultural instructor, and the Wampanoag sachem Massasoit's material and military support.[79] For nearly half a century Massasoit and his heirs adhered to the agreement that "If any did unjustly war against him, we [the colony] would aid him; if any did war against us, he should aid us." Although the colony faced intermittent scares and occasional clashes with minor Algonquian tribes, for several decades the combination of Plymouth's firearms and Massasoit's warriors cautioned potential foes.[80] After Squanto's untimely death in 1622, Hobbamock, who lived at Plymouth during Squanto's residence and beyond, filled the colony's need for an effective culture broker. According to Bradford, Hobbamock "continued very faithfull and constant to the English till he dyed."[81] Thus on the eve of the Puritans' "great migration," Plymouth and its Indian "others" had already taken several small but important steps toward lessening their differences.

Virginia suddenly veered in the opposite direction. Whatever superficial harmony the colony enjoyed in 1620 evaporated with the Powhatan uprising in March 1622. Virginia's governor called for the "expulsion of the Salvages" from the English-dominated portion of Virginia, and the Virginia Company of London favored "rooting them out for being longer a people uppon the face of the Earth."[82] A relentless war from 1622 to 1632 created new areas of mutually exclusive English and Indian habitation, with Indians near the expanding settlements confined to proto-reservations, or, in a very few cases, accepted as liminal members of colonial society. The massacre also taught the Plymouth Colony, despite its good relations with the Wampanoags, to be wary of Indian friendship. "Hapie is he whom other mens harmes doth make to beware," cautioned Plymouth's first notice of the Powhatans' slaughter of some 350 Virginians. Plymouth quickly built a sturdy meetinghouse-fort, drilled its militia, slew several suspected Indian conspirators, and impaled their leader's head atop Fort Hill.[83]

By the time the *Arbella* and its sister ships set sail, Puritan spokesmen reported no fears of Indian opposition. Rather, Winthrop insisted the year before his migration, "We shall come in with the good leave of the natives who finde benifight allreaddy by our Neighbourhood, and learne from us to improve a parte [of the land] to more use then before they could doe the whole."[84] Part of Winthrop's confidence stemmed from the belief that industrious, sober settlers could do well what feckless Virginians had done poorly, but it stemmed also from a determination to make New England a mono-cultural utopia—almost wholly English, reformed Protestant, and pious. Potential immigrants to the New England colonies whose religious beliefs or customs clashed overtly with Puritan norms, as one Massachusetts leader pronounced, had "free Liberty to keepe away from us, and such as will come to be gone as fast as they can, the sooner the better." The staunch Puritans who controlled the provincial and town governments had no qualms about excluding or expelling anyone who violated community standards of belief and behavior. In 1637 Winthrop articulated the rationale: "If we here be a corporation established by free consent [of the members], if the place of our cohabitation be our owne, then no man hath right to come into us etc. without our consent."[85] During Winthrop's lifetime, the New England colonies, save Rhode Island, generally excluded—by law or custom—Catholics, Jews, Muslims, Baptists, Quakers, and other "heretics." Colonial leaders admitted non-English immigrants, such as "the Scottishe & Irishe gentlemen" who sought land in Massachusetts in 1634, and non-English servants, so long as they did not flaunt their otherness.[86] There were no "wild Irish," no Spaniards, no Turks, and initially no Moors.

The New Englanders could not, of course, deny regional cohabitation to American natives, but there seemed no need to try. The plague of 1616-1619 and a smallpox epidemic in 1633-1634 drastically reduced the Indian population along the Massachusetts coast; by the mid 1630s, most of the Bay Colony's native neighbors were nominally subject to England or cautiously friendly independent tribes. The Pequots' challenge to Puritan supremacy and expansion in 1636-1637 temporarily halted the trend, but within a few years, peaceful coexistence again seemed viable—a prospect not shared by the Indians in bondage for debt or for resisting Puritan forces in the recent conflict.

In a counterproductive attempt to maintain peace in English America, colonial authorities, wherever feasible, imposed English law on the Indians. Not only did they subject Indians who lived within an

English community to their rules, but colonial courts or officials judged Indians living in their own communities who were charged with wrongdoing against colonists—as were colonists who wronged Indians. Only Indian against Indian disputes within autonomous tribes could be adjudicated by Indians. Although many of Virginia's early regulations concerning Indians have not survived, there can be little doubt that the colony insisted from the outset on the supremacy of English jurisprudence in all cases to which an English person was a party.[87] Plymouth as early as the treaty of 1621 with Massasoit insisted that "If any of his did hurte to any of theirs [i.e., Plymouth's], he should send the offender that they might punish him." Other colonies imposed similar demands. In 1638, for example, the Quinnipiacs' treaty with the founders of New Haven Colony committed the tribe to submit its alleged offenders "to the consideration, censure & punishment of the English magestrate."[88] The imposition of Anglo-American jurisprudence partly sought to control the "others" in accordance with English notions of civility and partly to incorporate them, so far as possible, into the wider English society—to lessen, thereby, the characteristics that made them "other."

A similar dual purpose underlay colonial efforts to mold Indians into neo-Englishmen through religious and social conversion. Colonists sought to convert Indian women, too, though missionaries focused overwhelmingly on Indian men, assuming that women and children would follow their lead. As has often been argued by critics of the New England Puritans, the Massachusetts charter of incorporation's obligation to "wynn and incite the natives ... [to] the onlie true God and Savior of mankinde," and the governor's oath requiring his "best endeavour to draw on the natives of this country ... [to] the true God," resulted in only a handful of conversions before the 1640s. Then, after the Mayhews, father and son, converted a nucleus on Martha's Vineyard and John Eliot established the first "praying town" at Natick, Massachusetts, the Puritan missionary enterprise enjoyed appreciable success. Eliot's strategic innovation to isolate into special towns the Indians who agreed to be anglicized and Christianized shielded them from the most corrupting elements of colonial society and simultaneously from Indian traditionalists, especially sachems and shamans.[89]

The intertwined issues of sovereignty and ownership of land were additional obstacles to the assimilation of Indian "others." As in Ireland, Englishmen in America assumed the sovereignty of their government throughout its chartered boundaries, while tacitly admitting that English authority was unenforceable wherever natives were too strong to be coerced or too distant to be scrutinized. Only where tribes proved weak or where their land entered into the English sphere by purchase, confiscation, or conquest could sovereignty be effectively exercised. Virginia used all three tactics to acquire vast quantities of land by the early 1620s, including the foreclosure of Indian debts to the English that had tribal holdings as collateral.[90] New Englanders instituted similar practices, although the Puritans initially paid more attention than did their southern counterparts to biblical and theoretical justifications. In 1629, Winthrop asked rhetorically, "[W]hat warrant have we to take that lande which is and hathe been of longe tyme possessed by other sonnes of Adam?" Winthrop's answers (he offered several) drew heavily on England's erroneous assumption that "these salvadge peoples ramble over muche lands without title or propertye." As long as immigrants to America "leave them sufficient for their use," he concluded, "we may lawfully take the rest, there being more than enough for them and us."[91] Puritan writers thus conformed closely to the paradigm Anne Laurence observed among writers on Ireland: to justify territorial appropriation, "They needed to make the land seem desirable but its people reprehensible."[92]

By mid-century, New Englanders, much like English colonists elsewhere in mainland North America, seemed to have arrived at a modus vivendi. Except for the most populous and independent native nations, Indians lived either in small tributary tribes, on reservations, commingled with the colonial settlements, or, in New England, resided in closely-supervised praying towns. They appeared unlikely to threaten the colonies with attack or starvation, or to impoverish them by interrupting commerce. England's American extensions appeared (falsely) safe from the Indian "other."

Yet *individual* colonists remained vulnerable, not only to assault but to atavism. As in Ireland, Barbary, and the Turkish Empire, a captive or renegade might forsake English faith and customs. In Virginia, "runnagates" (some of them recently arrived from continental Europe) were numerous from the outset, despite the severe punishments that awaited those who fled to the Powhatans and were later captured. Some were shot, some hanged, some burned alive, some broken on the wheel. Other men permanently escaped from the Virginia Colony and merged with native society.[93] The evidence on renegades is necessarily sketchy; anonymity was their goal, and the colony was reluctant to advertize its cultural turncoats. The willingness of a colonist to shed the outward evidence of Englishness caused anxiety. After three years of captivity by Indians one settler had "growne so like, both in complexion and habit like a Salvage" that another Englishman took him for an Indian until he heard an unmistakable English accent.[94]

A few residents of the Puritan colonies also succumbed to cultural atavism. In the 1630s, a man from Plymouth's trading post on the Connecticut River "turned Indian in nakednes and cutting of haire" and married an Indian woman. The authorities eventually caught and whipped him for those and other transgressions. The Connecticut General Court in 1642 complained that "divers persons departe from amongst us, and take up their abode with the Indians in a prophane course of life," but the stipulated penalty (three years in the workhouse) seems never to have been imposed. Yet the problem remained. Five years later, Connecticut prohibited the leasing of land to Indians for fear that "many young [English] men are lyable to be corrupted" by working near them.[95] The message was unequivocal: Englishmen were to remain culturally English, while Indians, if possible, were to be transformed into neo-Englishmen. For an Englishman, especially a Puritan, to relinquish "civilitie" and Christianity for "savagery" was to recast himself as the Indian "other."

While English America largely excluded old world "others" and attempted to reform the new world's native "others," it soon forced African "others" into the colonies. Four years after settlement began in Bermuda and twelve years (perhaps fewer) in Virginia, "blackamores" arrived because—unlike in England—a shortage of labor overshadowed ethnocentric qualms. But colonials, even more than their cousins back home, showed little interest in transforming Africans into dark-hued Englishmen. There would be minimal anglicization: perhaps an English name, some colonial clothing (often specially made for bond-servants), and enough of the English language for owners and other Anglo-Americans to communicate with them. Africans in English America, and their immediate descendants, would remain the most clearly demarked "others" in Winthrop's time and beyond.

Given the customary status of Moors in England, the first Africans in Bermuda, not surprisingly, seem to have been held as long-term—though perhaps not permanent—workers. (The evidence for the earliest years is scanty.) By the mid 1630s, if not sooner, Bermuda contrived a unique form of enslavement for most of its black inhabitants: indentures for ninety-nine years.[96] In Virginia, most of the

Africans who arrived in 1619 remained in bondage far longer than European servants and, given the absence of recorded information about their ages or dates of arrival (the bases for terminating servitude), probably for life.[97] Although a few of Virginia's blacks eventually gained freedom, censuses from the 1620s suggest that most survivors of the colony's rampant warfare, disease, and malnutrition remained in menial positions.[98] By mid-century the colony's people of African origin or descent had increased to perhaps 300—not an appreciable number compared to later figures, nor a high percentage of Virginia's non-Indian population of about 15,000, but high enough to make Africans by far the largest non-English group in the English sphere.[99]

A variety of colonial documents reflect the Africans' continuing otherness. Individually and collectively, these coerced immigrants were rarely identified by their ethnicity or geographic origins but instead by "black" or its equivalent in Spanish and Portuguese ("negro") or Dutch ("negar," "neger"). Records designate many Africans only by such labels, sometimes with a first name but very often without names at all, in striking contrast to entries for English and continental Europeans in the same documents.[100] And although some Africans in Virginia became free and a few even owned black bondservants themselves, they continued to be identified in almost all surviving documents by color labels.[101] The Africans' otherness is also highlighted in several inventories of Virginia's early population, in which "Negroes" were not merely a separate category from Europeans or Indians but the *only* other category. In 1619, the enumeration contained three distinct categories: "En[g]lish and other Christians," "Indians in the service of sev[er]all planters," and "Negroes in the service of sev[er]all planters." The categories for a census of 1629, which was never taken or has disappeared, were "all the inhabitants . . . as well *Englishe* as Negroes," while a brief estimate of Virginia's population in the year of Winthrop's death similarly differentiated only between "*English*" and "*Negroes*."[102] Because "English" in all these censuses perforce included many non-English Europeans, Virginians appear to have discarded categorical distinctions among "others" that seemed important in England in favor of a bifurcated division of humankind into themselves and black Africans, with "English" always embracing other Europeans and sometimes, perhaps, partly anglicized Indians.

New Englanders were slower than Virginians to import workers they perceived as so physically and culturally different. Not that American Puritans harbored moral compunctions against owning Africans: in the 1630s, Puritans who created a plantation-based society on Providence Island in the western Caribbean (until Spain seized the island in 1641) imported and exploited sub-Saharan Africans as thoroughly as non-Puritan Englishmen and other Europeans did elsewhere.[103] And by 1638, if not earlier, Massachusetts had African slaves of its own. In 1637, Captain William Peirce exchanged fifteen captive Pequot boys and two women at Providence Island for "some cotton, and tobacco, and negroes, etc." How many Africans entered Massachusetts on Peirce's return is not recorded, nor is information about their names, sexes, or ages. The overwhelming likelihood is that they numbered a dozen or so (assuming a roughly equal exchange for the Pequots) and were enslaved as household servants or, in some cases, as farm or seaport workers.[104] Apparently they served well, for in 1645 Winthrop's brother-in-law Emmanuel Downing of Salem advocated further exchanges of New England Indians for Caribbean slaves. With "a Just warre" looming against the Narragansetts, Downing recommended that Indian captives be "exchange[d] for Moores, . . . for I do not see how wee can thrive untill wee gett into a stock of slaves suffitient to doe all our business." English servants, Downing complained, were determined to be free settlers themselves and hence of transient value to employers. "And I suppose you know verie well," he added, "how we shall maynteyne 20 Moores cheaper than one Englishe servant."[105]

New Englanders were far from unanimous in their approval of African slavery. The Rhode Island legislature in 1652 deplored the "common course practised amongst English men to buy negers, to that end they may have them for service or slaves forever" and prohibited any "blacke mankind or white being forced by covenent bond, or otherwise, to serve any man or his assighnes longer than ten yeares, or untill they come to bee twentie four yeares of age, if they be taken under fourteen . . . And at the end or [sic] terme of ten yeares to sett them free, as the manner is with the English servants." But Rhode Island was anomalous in early New England.[106] That Winthrop and most of his contemporaries chose not to favor the importation of numerous black laborers, contrary to the advice of Downing and the growing practice in Virginia, Maryland, and the island colonies, tells more about New England's continuing attraction for migrants from the British Isles and the nature of the New England economy than it does about Puritan sentiments on human equality.[107]

Yet the Puritans' indifference to the abuse of African "others" had limits. A Massachusetts law of 1641 forbid "any bond-slavery, villenage or captivitie amongst us; unlesse it be lawfull captives, taken in just warrs, and such strangers as willingly sell themselves, or are solde to us."[108] The final five words justified the acquisition of slaves in exchange for Pequot captives but did not apply to three or more Africans brought to Massachusetts in the spring of 1645. A Massachusetts ship had sailed to West Africa the previous autumn, where the crew seized several natives and eventually sold two in New England. Believing that the Africans had been "fraudulently & injuriously taken & brought from Ginny," the General Court condemned "the haynos & crying sinn of man stealing" and ordered that "the negers" be returned to Guinea.[109]

Benign as the General Court's action may have been in this case, its other actions at mid-century were ambivalent toward the Africans in their midst. The court decided in 1652 "that Scotsmen, Negeres, & Indians inhabiting with or servantes to the English" between the ages of sixteen and sixty were to "attend [military] trayninges as well as the English." Four years later, the court changed its mind on the last two categories: "henceforth no negroes or Indians, although servants to the English, shalbe armed or permitted to trayne."[110] And the few individuals of African heritage who lived for a significant time in early New England represented, not surprisingly, the lowest social class.[111] The first English settler of Shawmut Peninsula (later Boston), Samuel Maverick, had at least three black slaves by 1639 and would have had "a breed of Negroes" if the woman had not insisted that forced copulation was "beyond her slavery." Maverick's Africans may have arrived in 1638, as did, perhaps, "a Blackmore maid that hath long lived at *Dorchester*," according to a tract of 1643, who had "such a testimony given of her blamelesse and godly Conversion" that she was admitted to full church membership. This anonymous African-American woman subsequently proselytized among local Indians, a rare case of one colonial "other" attempting to entice members of another group of "others" into Anglo-American culture.[112]

According to "an eminent Person" quoted in 1652 by Roger Williams, "we have *Indians* at home, *Indians* in *Cornewall*, *Indians* in *Wales*, *Indians* in *Ireland*." Williams's readers would have readily understood: many British people, at home and abroad, lacked fundamental civility and godliness. As a Puritan clergyman, Williams cared more about the latter condition; his lay neighbors may have worried more about civil behavior. But both groups believed that the remedy was education. Savages in Ireland or Wales or America, several English spokesmen insisted, could be taught refined behavior, coherent English, and true religion. As the Puritan educator John Brinsley had argued twenty years earlier, God "ordained schooles of learning to be the principall meanes to reduce a barbarous people to civilitie, and thereby to prepare them the better to receive the glorious Gospel of Jesus Christ." Like Williams, Brinsley had in mind not only the Welsh, the Irish, and "the Virgineans," but "all other barbarous nations."[113] Thus ethnic "others" could become almost English. Their remaining traces of otherness would scarsely matter.

Although colonial efforts to transform Indians into neo-Englishmen failed dismally (with a few heralded exceptions), the prospect still burned bright when Winthrop died in 1649. In the long run, of course, most Indians in New England and elsewhere would oppose Christianity, or ignore it, or annex the most attractive parts to their traditional beliefs and rituals. English missionaries and magistrates would be frustrated but helpless. Because "we compell them not to the Christian faith, nor the profession of it, either by force of arms or by poenall laws," the Massachusetts legislature declared in 1646, native rituals and beliefs persisted, sporadic attempts to prohibit them notwithstanding.[114] Most Indians would also reject English definitions of civility and remain intentionally outside the English pale, where they continued to serve Anglo-Americans as the "savages" against whom to measure and praise themselves.

Neither Brinsley nor Williams breathed a word about Turks or Moors. They probably ignored the former because Turks were not only committed to their own faith, language, and customs (like the Indians) but because—except for transient visitors to England and encounters on the high seas—they were geographically beyond reach. But England's "blackamores," numbering at least in the hundreds by mid-century, and English America's "negroes," of far greater number and a much higher percentage of the whole population,[115] lay within easy reach but nonetheless outside most Englishmen's definitions of reformable humanity. In England, sub-Saharan Africans and their descendants would serve for many generations primarily as exotic servants, often in livery. Not long after Winthrop's death, if not before, silver collars engraved with the owner's name or crest would adorn many of England's black slaves.[116] In America, growing numbers of Africans would be subjected to ruthless systems of bondage and rigidifying categories of white and black.

Throughout Winthrop's life, in England and America, what most distinguished the Puritans' perspective on "others" from that of their countrymen was a greater concern for the social and religious reformation of individuals. Puritans deplored unreformed Englishmen almost as thoroughly they did unreformed Irishmen, Africans, Turks, and Indians (as Roger Williams had implied). One can argue endlessly over whether or not Puritans made genuine efforts to transform the "others" in their midst—or even if they *should* have tried—or only paid lip service to a reformist zeal. But in the New World at least, New England's greater harvest of Indian converts (largely post-Winthrop) and its occasional actions in defense of Africans' rights suggest that Puritans tried more intensely than their southern counterparts to inculcate their versions of civility and Christianity. Nevertheless, New England's exclusionist policies reveal severe limitations on such efforts. On both sides of the Atlantic, Puritans shared most of England's social perceptions and prejudices and largely defined themselves in contrast to whom they were *not*.

Endnotes

1. Andrew Borde, *The Fyrst Boke of the Introduction of Knowledge* (London, [c.1555]), sig. [A4v]. In all quotations (but not book titles), we have modernized the thorn and applied modern usage to "u" and "v," "i" and "j."

2. The historical/literary concept of "others" is explicated in Tzvetan Todorov, *The Conquest of America*, trans. Richard Howard (New York, 1984). In the eyes of mainstream commentators, England harbored several domestic categories of "others," including gypsies, vagabonds, and (in the words of Emily C. Bartels), the "'counterfeit' poor, the insane, religious and political heretics, witches, sodomites, and the like." *Spectacles of Strangeness: Imperialism, Alienation, and Marlowe* (Philadelphia, 1993), xiv. Limitations of space preclude consideration of such internal "others" in this essay.

3. John Speed, *The History of Great Britaine* . . . (London, 1627), 155.

4. Robert Greene, *The Spanish Masquerado* (London, 1589), sig. B3r.

5. Although "God is an Englishman" was George Bernard Shaw's derisive parody of English conceit, many English statements, beginning in the mid sixteenth century, expressed that notion. "God is English" appeared, for example, in [John Aylmer], *An Harborowe for Faithfull and Trewe Subiectes* . . . ([London], 1559), sig. [P4v].

6. Harrison, *The Description of England*, ed. George Edelen (Washington, D.C., 1968), 131, 447; Camden, *Remains Conerning Britain*, ed. R. D. Dunn (Toronto, 1984), 5; Ben Jonson, *The Masque of Blackness* (1616), in [*Works of*] *Ben Jonson*, ed. C. H. Herford, Percy and Evelyn Simpson (Oxford, 1925-1952), 8:177; John Davies, *Microcosmos: The Discovery of the Little World* (Oxford, 1603), 36.

7. "A Declaration . . . for a publique day of Thanksgiving," May 9, 1654, in Wilbur Cortez Abbott, ed., *The Writings and Speeches of Oliver Cromwell* (Cambridge, Mass., 1937-1947), 3:290-291.

8. For perceptive discussions of England's sense of difference from other nations, see John Gillies, *Shakespeare and the Geography of Difference* (Cambridge, 1994); and, with emphasis on language, Richard Helgerson, *Forms of Nationhood: The Elizabethan Writing of England* (Chicago, 1992). Important also is the sizeable and rapidly expanding literature on the formation of British identity and creation of the British empire, exemplified by David J. Baker and Willy Maley, eds., *British Identities and English Renaissance Literature* (Cambridge, 2002). Relevant also, from different perspectives, are Stephen Greenblatt, *Renaissance Self-Fashioning: From More to Shakespeare* (Chicago, 1980), and Bartels, *Spectacles of Strangeness*.

9. On perceptions of continental Europeans, see Marvin Arthur Breslow, *A Mirror of England: English Puritan Views of Foreign Nations, 1618-1640* (Cambridge, Mass., 1970).

10. Samuel Purchas, *Purchas His Pilgrimage, or, Relations of the World* . . . (London, 1613), 546. Although an Anglican, Purchas strongly influenced John Milton.

11. Peter Fryer, *Staying Power: The History of Black People in Britain* (London, 1984), 22-23; Alden T. Vaughan, "Trinculo's Indian: American Natives in Shakespeare's England," in Peter Hulme and William H. Sherman, eds., *"The Tempest" and Its Travels* (London, 2000), 48-59.

12. See especially Mark Netzloff, *England's Internal Colonies: Class, Capitalism, and the Literature of Early Modern England* (London, 2003).

13. Borde, *Fyrst Boke*, sigs. C1r-C1v.

14. Speed, *Theatre of Britaine*, 121.

15. Borde, *Fyrst Boke*, sig. [D1r]; Camden, *Remains*, 15; Speed, *Theatre of Great Britaine*, 131.

16. Among many important works on Renaissance England's perceptions of the Irish is the pioneer work by David Beers Quinn, *The Elizabethans and the Irish* (Ithaca, N.Y., 1966); and several works by Nicholas Canny, especially *Making Ireland British* (Oxford, 2001); Anne Laurence, "The Cradle to the Grave: English Observations of Irish Social Customs in the Seventeenth Century," *The Seventeenth Century* 3(1988):63-84; Patricia Coughlan, "'Cheap and Common Animals': The English Anatomy of Ireland in the Seventeenth Century," in Thomas Healy and Jonathan Sawday, eds., *Literature and the English Civil War* (Cambridge, 1990), 205-223; Sheila J. Cavanaugh, "'The fatal destiny of that land': Elizabethan Views of Ireland," in Brenda Bradshaw, Andrew Hadfield, and Willy Maley, eds., *Representing Ireland: Literature and the Origins of Conflict, 1534-1660* (Cambridge, 1993), 116-131; and Andrew Hadfield, "'The Naked and the Dead': Elizabethan Perceptions of Ireland," in Jean-Pierre Maquerlot and Michelle Willems, eds., *Travel and Drama in Shakespeare's Time* (Cambridge, 1996), 32-54.

17. Borde, *Fyrst Boke*, C3v; Abbot, *A Briefe Description of the Whole Worlde* (London, 1599), D1r-v. See also Fynes Moryson, "The Description of Ireland," in C. Litton Falkiner, ed., *Illustrations of Irish Topography, Mainly of the Seventeenth Century* (London, 1904), 231.

18. Moryson, "The Commonwealth of Ireland," in Falkiner, *Illustrations of Irish Topography*, 312. English writers were critical also of several Irish customs of landholding and distribution. See, for example, John Davies, *A Discovery of the True Causes Why Ireland Was Never Entirely Subdued* (1612; Shannon, Ireland, 1969), esp. 164, 167.

19. Moryson, "Commonwealth," 261; Edmund Spenser, *A View of the [Present] State of Ireland*, ed. Andrew Hadfield and Willy Maley (Oxford, 1997), 56; Davies, *Discovery*, 160-161.

20. Spenser, *Present View*, 85; Moryson, *Commonwealth of Ireland*, 314, 319.

21. Spenser, *Present State*, 70.

22. Spenser, *Present State*, 70; Davies, *Discovery*, 182.

23. Davies, *Discovery*, 217.

24. Davies, *Discovery*, 272; Spenser, *Present View*, 93.

25. Michael Neill, "Broken English and Broken Irish: Nation, Language and the Optic of Power in Shakespeare's Histories," *Putting History to the Question: Power, Politics, and Society in English Renaissance Drama* (New York, 2000), 338-372, 341.

26. Breslow, *Mirror of England*, 49-50.

27. *The Copie of a Letter Sent from Sea by a Gentleman, Who Was Employed in Discoverie on the Coast of Spaine by Appointment of the Generals of Our English Fleete* (London, 1589), Preface (italics removed); *The Holy Bull and Crusade of Rome* (London, 1588), 7, 8.

28. Among many condemnations of Spanish treatment of the American Indians are *The Holy Bull*, 9; Abbot, *Briefe Description*, sigs. D7r-v; and especially the English version of Bartolome de las Casas, *The Spanishe Colonie* (London, 1583).

29. Speed, *Prospect*, 23; Spenser, *Present View*, 50.

30. Breslow notes that by 1624, Puritan anti-Spanish sentiment was so heated that the Spanish were often declared to be non-Europeans of Moorish extraction. See *Mirror*, 72-73.

31. Abbot, *Briefe Description*, [B8v]; Shapiro, *Shakespeare and the Jews* (New York, 1996), 62. The analysis that follows depends heavily on Shapiro's work.

32. Shapiro, *Shakespeare and the Jews*, 68-72, 96.

33. Marlowe, *The Jew of Malta*, ed. James R. Siemon (London, 1994), 2.3.1768-78, 1.1.102-22; Shapiro, *Shakespeare and the Jews*, 96, 98, 103.

34. The role of Jews in Puritan millenialism is examined in many works, including David S. Katz, *Philo-Semitism and the Readmission of the Jews into England* (London, 1982); Theodore Dwight Bozeman, *To Live Ancient Lives: The Primitivist Dimension in Puritanism* (Chapel Hill, 1988); James F.

Maclear, "New England and the Fifth Monarchy Men: The Quest for the Millennium in Early American Puritanism," *William and Mary Quarterly*, 3d ser., 32(1975):223-260 (hereafter *WMQ*); and Richard W. Cogley, *John Eliot's Mission to the Indians before King Philip's War* (Cambridge, Mass., 1999), 10-18.

35. Speed, *Prospect*, 7, 8, 21, 25; ; Ortelius, *Theatrum Orbis Terrarum* (London, 1606); Borde, *Fyrst Boke*, sig. [K1r]. For an overview of the portrayal of European foreigners on the English stage, see A. J. Hoenselaars, *Images of Englishmen and Foreigners in the Drama of Shakespeare and His Contemporaries* (Cranbury, N. J., 1992).

36. The young King James VI of Scotland wrote a heroic poem celebrating the victory of the combined European forces at the Battle of Lepanto. See *The Poems of James VI of Scotland*, ed. James Craigie (Edinburgh, 1955).

37. Daniel J. Vitkus, ed. *Three Turkish Plays from Early Modern England* (New York, 2000), 11; Henry Blount, *A Voyage into the Levant* (London, 1636), 2-3.

38. Nabil Matar, *Islam in Britain, 1558-1685* (Cambridge, 1998), 6-11; and the same author's *Turks, Moors, and Englishmen in the Age of Discovery* (New York, 1999), 6; for English captives and their narratives, see chap. 2 and Appendix A, and Linda Colley, *Captives: Britain, Empire and the World, 1600-1850* (New York, 2002), 23-134. For English knowledge of Turks from a different vantage point, see Daniel Goffman, *Britons in the Ottoman Empire, 1642-1660* (Seattle, 1998).

39. Speed, *Prospect*, 35. See also George Sandys, *A Relation of a Journey . . . to the Turkish Empire* (London, 1615), preface; and the anonymous *The Policy of the Turkish Empire: The First Booke* (London, 1597), 7r.

40. Richard Knolles, *The Generall Historie of the Turkes* (London, 1603), 1154.

41. Vitkus, *Three Turkish Plays*, 9; Speed, *Prospect*, 35; Anon., *Policy of the Turkish Empire*, 2r-v, 19v. Samuel C. Chew notes that the "Renaissance inherited a confused and contradictory mass of grotesque notions concerning the Founder of Islam." See *The Crescent and the Rose: Islam and England during the Renaissance* (New York, 1965), 387.

42. C. A. Patrides shows how theological discourse in the period raised the spectre of Turkish cruelty as God's punishment for the sins of Christendom. See "'The Bloody and Cruell Turke': The Background of a Renaissance Commonplace," *Studies in the Renaissance* 10(1963):126-135.

43. Knolles, *General Historie*, 610.

44. Knolles, *General Historie*, 337-338, 501, 919, 922.

45. Robert Greene, *Selimus, Emperor of the Turks* (London, 1594), included in Vitkus, *Three Turkish Plays*.

46. Speed, *Prospect*, 35.

47. [Anon.,] *Policy of the Turkish Empire*, 46r.

48. Speed, *Prospect*, 35; [Anon.,] *Policy of the Turkish Empire*, 46r; Matar, *Turks, Moors, and Englishmen*, 112-113.

49. Abbot, *Description*, sig. C8v; Shapiro, *Shakespeare and the Jews*, 62-76.

50. See the illustration in Geoffrey Whitney's *A Choice of Emblemes* (Leiden, 1586) for an example. Karen Newman discusses the proverb in relation to Shakespeare's *Othello* in "'And wash the Ethiop white': Femininity and the Monstrous in *Othello*," in *Shakespeare Reproduced: The Text in History and Ideology*, ed. Jean E. Howard and Marion O'Connor (New York, 1987), 141-162.

51. See also James R. Aubrey, "Race and the Spectacle of the Monstrous in *Othello*," *Clio* 22(1993):221-238.

52. *The Voyages and Travailes of Sir John Maundevile* (London [1583]), sigs. Liiir-Liiiv; Speed, *Prospect*, 6.

53. Borde, *Fyrst Boke*, sig. [M3v].

54. Abbot, *Description*, sig. C7r.

55. *The Fardle of Facions, Conteining the Aunciente Maners, Customes, and Lawes, of the Peoples Enhabiting . . . Affrike and Asie*, trans., William Waterman (London, 1555), sigs. C2r-C3r.

56. For fuller discussion of the relevant sources, see our "Before *Othello*: Elizabethan Representations of Sub-Saharan Africans," *WMQ*, 3d ser., 54(1997):19-44.

57. Peter Martyr of Angleria, *The Decades of the Newe Worlde of West India*, trans. Richarde Eden (London, 1555), in Edward Arber, ed., *The First Three English Books on America* (Birmingham, Eng., 1885), 374, 384. Eden's and Gainsh's comments were reprinted in Richard Eden and Richard Willes, eds., *The History of Travayle in the West and East Indies, and Other Countreys Lying Either Way* (London, 1577), 337r-v, and later in Hakluyt, *Principal Navigations*, both the 1589 and 1598-1600 editions.

58. Davies, *Microcosmos*, 67. For an analysis of climate theory during this period, see Mary Floyd-Wilson, "Temperature, Temperance, and Racial

Difference in Ben Jonson's *The Masque of Blackness*," *English Literary Renaissance*, 28(1998):183-285.

59. George Best, *Discourse* (1578), reprinted in Hakluyt, *The Principal Navigations Voyages Traffiques & Discoveries of the English Nation*, 7 (Glasgow, 1904), 260-265.
60. Cooper, *The Blessing of Japheth* ... (London, 1615), 1-4; Sandys, *Relation of a Journey*, 136-137. Subsequent editions of Sandys book appeared in 1621, 1627, 1632, and 1637. Marginalia quotation from Samuel Purchas, *Hakluytus Posthumus, or Purchas His Pilgrimes* (London, 1625), 2:913. See also Speed, *Prospect*, 6.
61. See Annette Drew-Bear, *Painted Faces on the Renaissance Stage: The Moral Significance of Face-Painting Conventions* (Lewisburg, Penn., 1994), 38-41.
62. Reginald Scot, *The Discoverie of Witchcraft* (London, 1584), 456. For additonal evidence of England's pejorative attitudes toward blackness, see Winthrop D. Jordan, *White over Black: American Attitudes toward the Negro, 1550-1812* (Chapel Hill, 1968), 3-24.
63. John Hawkins, "the first voyage of *sir John Hawkins* ... " in Hakluyt, *Principal Navigations* (London, 1589), 521-522.
64. For example, W. Bruce Bannerman, ed., *The Registers of St. Olave, Hart Street, London, 1563-1700* (London, 1916), 121, 128, 131.
65. Paul Bayne[s], *An Entire Commentary upon the Whole Epistle of the Apostle Paul to the Ephesians* (London, 1643), 694-695. Baynes, successor to William Perkins at St. Andrews, Cambridge, died in 1617. Strong internal evidence indicates that whoever put his sermon into print in 1643 did not tamper with Baynes's text.
66. For example, Zanche in *The White Devil* (1612) and Zanthia in *The Knight of Malta* (1616).
67. "At the Court at Greenwich," July 18, 1596, John Roche Dasent, ed., *Acts of the Privy Council of England*, new ser., 26(1902):20-21; Paul L. Hughes and James F. Larkin, eds., *Tudor Royal Proclamations* (New Haven, 1969), 3:221-222.
68. Alden T. Vaughan, "Early English Paradigms for New World Natives," *American Antiquarian Society Proceedings* 102(1992):33-67; Vaughan, "From White Man to Redskin: Changing Anglo-American Perceptions of the American Indian," *American Historical Review* 86(1982):917-953. Revised versions of both essays appear in Vaughan, *Roots of American Racism: Essays on the Colonial Experience* (New York, 1995), 34-54 and 3-33 respectively.

See also Joyce E. Chaplin, *Subject Matter: Technology, the Body, and Science on the Anglo-American Frontier, 1500-1676* (Cambridge, Mass., 2001).

69. Among the many modern assessments of English colonial perceptions of the Indians, see especially Karen Ordahl Kupperman, *Indians and English: Facing Off in Early America* (Ithaca, N.Y., 2000); and several works by James Axtell, most recently *Natives and Newcomers: The Cultural Origins of North America* (New York, 2001), and Chaplin, *Subject Matter*.

70. Abbot, *Briefe Description*, sig. [E2]; Robert Cushman, "Reasons & considerations touching the lawfulnesse of removing . . . " in [William Bradford and Edward Winslow,] *A Relation or Journall of the . . . English Plantation Setled at Plimoth* . . . (London, 1622), 68.

71. Brief parallels between the Indians and Irish can be found, for example, in E. G. R. Taylor, ed., *The Original Writings and Correspondence of the Two Richard Hakluyts* (London, 1935), 1:71, 2:267, 328, 341, 377; William Wood, *New Englands Prospect* (London, 1634), 56, 79; Roger Williams, *A Key into the Language of America* (London, 1643), 72. See also Vaughan, "Early English Paradigms," in *Roots of American Racism*, 40-44.

72. William Crashaw, *A Sermon Preached in London before the Right Honourable the Lord La Warre . . .* (London, 1610), sig. [C4v]; Richard Whitbourne, *A Discourse and Discovery of New-Found Land* (London, 1622), reprinted in Gillian T. Cell, ed., *Newfoundland Discovered: English Attempts at Colonisation, 1610-1630*, Hakluyt Society Publications, 2d ser., 160 (London, 1982), 125. For elaboration on this line of English thought, see Vaughan, "Early English Paradigms," in Vaughan, *Roots of American Racism*, esp. 44-49.

73. Thomas Hariot, *A Briefe and True Report of the New Found Land of Virginia* (Frankfort, 1590), 27-28; Robert Hunt Land, "Henrico and Its College," *WMQ*, 2d ser., 18(1938):453-498; W. Stitt Robinson, "Indian Education and Missions in Colonial Virginia," *Journal of Southern History* 18(1952):152-168; Alden T. Vaughan, "Sir Walter Ralegh's Indian Interpreters, 1584-1618," *WMQ*, 3d ser., 59(2002):341-376.

74. For England's ability to create colonies amid much larger native populations, see Nicholas Canny, "Dominant Minorities: English Settlers in Ireland and Virginia, 1556-1650," in A. C. Hepburn, ed., *Minorities in History* (New York, 1979), 51-69.

75. For the Germans' treasonous actions, see John Smith, *The Proceedings of the English Colonie in Virginia* (London, 1612) in Philip L. Barbour, ed., *The Complete Works of Captain John Smith (1580-1631)* (Chapel Hill, 1986), 1:246, 250, 255, 256 (quotation), 266-267.

76. In 1614 the colony's treaty with the Chickahominies called for the tribe to "be ready and willing to furnish us with three or foure hundred bowmen to aide us *against the Spaniards.*" Ralph Hamor, *A True Discourse of the Present Estate of Virginia* . . . (London, 1615), 13.

77. Hamor, *True Discourse*, 13-16, 56-57; H. R. McIlwaine, ed., *Journals of the House of Burgesses of Virginia, 1619-1658/59* (Richmond, 1915), 1:10; Susan Myra Kingsbury, ed., *The Records of the Virginia Company of London* (Washington, D.C., 1906-1935), 1:588, 3:128-129; summary of Wyatt's letter in Kingsbury, *Virginia Company Records*, 3:550; Alden T. Vaughan, "'Expulsion of the Salvages': English Policy and the Virginia Massacre of 1622," in Vaughan, *Roots of American Racism*, 115-117.

78. William Bradford, *History of Plymouth Plantation*, ed. Worthington C. Ford (Boston, 1912), 1:57. Bradford may have reported accurately the pilgrims' initial fears, but he just as likely indulged in poetic license to magnify their accomplishments.

79. Bradford, *Plymouth Plantation* 1:199-203; [William Bradford and Edward Winslow,] *A Relation or Journall of . . . Plimoth . . .* (London, [1622]), 35-39. Squanto's career is traced in Neal Salisbury, "Squanto: Last of the Patuxets," in *Struggle and Survival in Colonial America*, ed. David G. Sweet and Gary B. Nash (Berkeley and Los Angeles, 1981), 228-246, and in the older but still useful article by L. N. Kinnicutt, "The Plymouth Settlement and Tisquantum," in *Proceedings of the Massachusetts Historical Society*, 48(1914-1915):103-118.

80. The intercultural events of Plymouth's first decade are documented in several sources, most notably Bradford, *Plymouth Plantation*, passim (the treaty is on 1:201-203); [Bradford and Winslow,] *Journall of Plimoth*, passim; and Phinehas Pratt, "A Declaration of the Affairs of the English People That First Inhabited New England," *Collections of the Massachusetts Historical Society*, 4 ser. (1858), 4:474-487. Modern discussions include Alden T. Vaughan, *New England Frontier: Puritans and Indians, 1620-1675*, 3rd ed. (Norman, Okla., 1995), 64-92; and Neal Salisbury, *Manitou and Providence: Indians, Europeans, and the Making of New England* (New York, 1982), 110-165.

81. Hobbamock's contributions are documented in Bradford, *Plymouth Plantation*, 1:225-26, 227n., 253, 346; [Bradford and Winslow,] *Journall of Plimoth*, 53-55; and Edward Winslow, *Good Newes from New England* (Lon-

don, 1624), reprinted in Alexander Young, *Chronicles of the Pilgrim Fathers* . . . (Boston, 1841), passim.

82. Francis Wyatt to ? (c. 1623-24), *WMQ*, 2d ser., 6(1926):118; Virginia Company to the Governor and Council in Virginia, Oct. 7, 1622, in Kingsbury, *Virginia Company Records*, 3:683.

83. Bradford, *Plymouth Plantation*, 1:273, 275-276; Pratt, "Declaration," 479-487; Winslow, *Good Newes*, 325-345.

84. Winthrop, "Reasons to Be Considered," in *Winthrop Papers* (Boston, 1929), 2:141. The improvements Winthrop believed the Indians had learned from the early settlers were, presumably, the use of domestic animals, fenced land, and animal dung manure. In fact, by 1629 Indians—for practical reasons as well as traditional habits—observed none of these European practices to an appreciable extent.

85. Nathaniel Ward, *The Simple Cobler of Aggawam in America*, ed. P. M. Zall (1647; Lincoln, Neb., 1969), 6; John Winthrop, "A Declaration in Defense of an Order of Court Made in May 1637," in *Winthrop Papers*, 3:423. See also Josiah Henry Benton, *Warning Out in New England* (Boston, 1911).

86. Nathaniel B. Shurtleff, ed., *Records of the Governor and Company of the Massachusetts Bay in New England* (Boston, 1853-1854), 1:129; *The Laws and Liberties of Massachusetts*, ed. Max Farrand (Cambridge, Mass., 1929), 24.

87. A treaty with the Chickahominies of 1614 allows the tribe to have its own laws but only after subjecting themselves to the English and agreeing to send any English offenders to the colony for punishment. Hamor, *True Discourse*, 12-14.

88. Bradford, *Plymouth Plantation*, 1:202; "Articles of Agreement" (Nov. 24, 1638), in Charles J. Hoadly, ed., *Records of New Haven Colony* (Hartford, Conn., 1857-1858), 1:1-5; *New Englands First Fruits: . . . With Divers Other Speciall Matters Concerning that Countrey* (London, 1643), 8.

89. Shurtleff, *Mass. Colony Records*, 1:17, 352. Recent studies of the controversial (then and now) Puritan missionary movement include, Charles L. Cohen, "Conversion among Puritans and Amerindians: A Theological and Cultural Perspective," in Francis J. Bremer, ed., *Puritanism: Transatlantic Perspectives on a Seventeenth-Century Anglo-American Faith* (Boston, 1993), 233-256; Cogley, *Eliot's Mission*; and the expanded version of William S. Simmons, "Conversion from Indian to Puritan" (orig., 1979) in, Alden T.

Vaughan, ed., *New England Encounters: Indians and Euroamericans, ca. 1600-1850* (Boston, 1999), esp.197-200.

90. John Rolfe, *A True Relation of the State of Virginia* (1616; New Haven, Conn., 1951), 6; Samuel Argall to Virginia Company, Mar. 10, 1618, in Kingsbury, *Virginia Company Records*, 3:92. Determining the legitimacy of the foreclosures—from an English legal standpoint, not to mention the broader context of Indian concepts and understandings—is impossible based on surviving records. The Indians surely resented the process and the outcome.

91. Winthrop, "General Observations, Autograph Draft," and "Reasons to Be Considered," in *Winthrop Papers*, 2:117, 140-141.

92. Laurence, "Cradle to Grave," 65.

93. George Percy, "A Trewe Relacyon of . . . Virginia," in *Tyler's Quarterly Historical and Genealogical Magazine* 3(1922):267, 280; Don Pedro de Zuñiga to Philip III, Aug. 1, 1612, in Alexander Brown, *Genesis of the United States* (Boston, 1890), 2:572.

94. John Smith, *Generall Historie*, in Barbour, ed., *Complete Works*, 2:250; Hamor, *True Discourse*, 27-28, 42-44; Nicholas Canny, "The Permissive Frontier: The Problem of Social Control in English Settlements in Ireland and Virginia," in K. R. Andrews, N. P. Canny, and P. E. H. Hair, eds., *The Westward Enterprise: English Activities in Ireland, the Atlantic, and America, 1480-1650* (Liverpool, Eng., 1978), 17-44, esp. 30-35.

95. *The Correspondence of Roger Williams*, ed. Glenn W. LaFantasie (Hanover, N. H., 1988), 1:126, 140, 145, 155, 158; J. Hammond Trumbull and Charles C. Hoadly, eds., *The Public Records of the Colony of Connecticut* (Hartford, Conn., 1850-1890), 1:78, 149-150.

96. J. H. Lefroy, ed., *Memorial of the . . . Bermudas or Somers Islands* (London, 1877-1879), 1:115, 127, 281, 308-309, 526; Helen Gosling, typescript of early Bermuda records, in Bermuda Archives, 2:6, 8, 12, 13, 18, and passim. The best comprehensive study of blacks in Bermuda is Virginia Bernhard, *Slaves and Slaveholders in Bermuda, 1616-1782* (Columbia, Mo., 1999), although we differ in some instances with its interpretation of the evidence.

97. Recent studies of the earliest Africans in Virginia include William Thorndale, "The Virginia Census of 1619," *Magazine of Virginia Genealogy* 33(1995):155-170; see also Michael Jarvis and Jeroen va Driel, "The

Vingboons Chart of the James River, Virginia, ca. 1617," *WMQ*, 3d. ser., 54(1997):392-393n.33); Engel Sluiter, "New Light on the '20 and Odd Negroes' Arriving in Virginia, August 1619," *WMQ*, 3rd ser., 54(1997):395-398; and John Thornton, "The African Experience of the 20. and Odd Negroes," *WMQ*, 3rd ser., 55(1998):421-434.

98. *Colonial Records of Virginia* (Richmond, 1874), 40-58; Annie Lash Jester and Martha Woodruff Hiden, eds., *Adventurers of Purse and Person: Virginia 1607-1625* (Princeton, 1956), 5-69; Alden T. Vaughan, "Blacks in Virginia: Evidence from the First Decade," in Vaughan, *Roots of American Racism*, 128-135. The extant lists of massacre victims do not appear to include any Africans, but the records are less precise for the heavy loss of life from the spring of 1622 until (and beyond) 1624.

99. [Anon.,] *A Perfect Description of Virginia* (London, 1649) in Peter Force, comp., *Tracts and Other Papers Relating Principally to . . . the Colonies in North America* (1837; New York, 1947), 2, no. 8:3.

100. See, for example, Jester and Hiden, *Adventurers of Purse and Person*, 22, 27; "Lists of the Livinge & Dead in Virginia," Feb. 16, 1623/24, in *Colonial Records of Virginia*, 40, 42, 45, 46, 49, 51; Nell Marion Nugent, ed., *Cavaliers and Pioneers: Abstracts of Virginia Land Patents and Grants, 1623-1800*, (Richmond, 1934), 1:28, 199, 258, 568.

101. On free blacks in early Virginia, see especially T. H. Breen and Stephen Innes, *"Myne Owne Ground": Race and Freedom on Virginia's Eastern Shore, 1640-1676* (New York, 1980), and the critique in Alden T. Vaughan, "The Origins Debate: Slavery and Racism in Seventeenth-Century Virginia," in Vaughan, *Roots of American Racism*, 150-152.

102. Thorndale, "Census of 1619," 168; H. R. McIlwaine, ed., *Minutes of the Council and General Court of Colonial Virginia, 1622-1632, 1670-1676* (Richmond, 1924), 196; *Description of Virginia*, 3.

103. For slavery on Providence Island, see Karen Ordahl Kupperman, *Providence Island, 1630-1641: The Other Puritan Colony* (Cambridge, 1993); and Newton, *Puritan Colonization*, 149-150, 258-261. For all areas of English settlement the classic work is Jordan, *White over Black*.

104. Winthrop to William Bradford, July 28, 1637, and Patrick Copeland to Winthrop, Dec. 4, 1639, in *Winthrop Papers*, 3:456-458, 157-159; *The Journal of John Winthrop*, ed. Richard S. Dunn, James Savage, and Laetitia Yeandle (Cambridge, Mass., 1996), 227, 246. Winthrop's journal entry

for July 13, 1637, specifies 15 boys and 2 women; Copeland's letter mentions 12 boys and no women.

105. Emmanuel Downing to John Winthrop, c. Aug. 1645, in *Winthrop Papers*, 5:38.

106. John Russell Bartlett, ed., *Records of the Colony of Rhode Island* (Providence, 1856), 1:243. Winthrop Jordan, following Charles M. Andrews, *The Colonial Period of American History* (New Haven, 1936), 30, notes that the colony was represented at that session of the legislature only by its two northern communities, Providence and Warwick, which probably held a quite different opinion on African slavery than did the seaport towns (Jordan, *White over Black*, 70n.58). By the eighteenth century, Rhode Island was the region's leading slave-holding colony.

107. By 1649, black servants in Virginia, Maryland, Bermuda, and Barbados, most of them enslaved by custom if not by statute, were numerous, though not yet predominant over white indentured servants. See especially Jordan, *White over Black*, 63-66, 71-82.

108. The law of 1641 was incorporated in 1648 into the *Laws and Liberties*, 4. Not shielded from slavery by the law were those "who shall be judged thereto by Authoritie"–i.e., persons sentenced to punishment for crimes. Massachusetts occasionally applied such penalties to colonists and Indians. See, for example, Shurtleff, *Mass. Colony Records*, 1:181, 246.

109. Shurtleff, *Mass. Colony Records*, 2:98, 129, 136, 168, 176; 3:49, 58; Dunn et al., *Winthrop's Journal*, 602-604; Petition of Richard Saltonstall in James Savage, ed., *Journal of John Winthrop* (Boston, 1826), 2:379-380.

110. Shurtleff, *Mass. Colony Records*, 3:268, 397.

111. An analysis of Massachusetts court cases involving blacks is Robert C. Twombly and Robert H. Moore, "Black Puritan: The Negro in Seventeenth-Century Massachusetts," *WMQ*, 3rd ser., 24(1967):224-242. Using evidence from the second half of the seventeenth century and the early eighteenth, the authors conclude that "Massachusetts never forced Negroes into this status [slavery]" and that "Negroes and whites received essentially equal treatment before the law." We are not persuaded that either conclusion is correct. As Downing's letter and the Rhode Island statute suggest, most of New England's black servants were almost certainly held for life (Rhode Island's, for a time, excepted), with their issue. Under such circumstances, some blacks, probably most, would have

been punished summarily by their owners and thus would not appear in court records.

112. John Josselyn, *An Account of Two Voyages to New-England* (London, 1674), in Paul J. Lindholdt, ed., *John Josselyn, Colonial Traveler* (Hanover, N.H., 1988), 24; *New Englands First Fruits*, 5. See also Lorenzo Johnston Greene, *The Negro in Colonial New England, 1620-1776* (New York, 1942), 15-22.

113. Roger Williams, *The Hireling Ministry None of Christs, or A Discourse Touching the Propagating the Gospel of Christ Jesus* (London, 1652), 13; [John Brinsley,] *A Consolation for Our Grammar Schooles* (London, 1622), dedication, 3.

114. "Against Blasphemy of the Name of God," in Shurtleff, *Mass. Colony Records*, 2:176-177.

115. No accurate count is possible of the number of English America's people of African origin or descent in the 1650s, but the combined figure for Virginia, Maryland, New England, Bermuda, Barbados, and the lesser islands must have been many thousands. Barbados alone had an estimated 20,000 by 1655. Hilary McD. Beckles, "The 'Hub of Empire': the Caribbean and Britain in the Seventeenth Century," *The Origins of Empire: British Overseas Enterprise to the Close of the Seventeenth Century*, ed. Nicholas Canny (New York, 1998), 224.

116. For the debate in England and the colonies over conversion of Africans, see Alden T. Vaughan, "Slaveholders' 'Hellish Principles': A Seventeenth-Century Critique," in Vaughan, *Roots of American Racism*, 55-81; for collared slaves in England, see Fryer, *Staying Power*, 22-23.

The Practice of Piety in Puritan New England: Contexts and Consequences

Mark A. Peterson

AN UNUSUAL FEATURE OF Charles Hambrick-Stowe's masterful 1982 study, *The Practice of Piety*, is that its title page displays a reproduction of the title page of another book bearing virtually the same title, a 1620 edition of Lewis Bayly's *The Practise of Pietie*. This is clearly more than a failure in what marketing executives call "product differentiation." What are we to make of this telescoping collapse of history and historiography, of distant past and nowadays, as we think about the meaning of the practice of piety in Puritan New England?

Perhaps one explanation for this curious conflation lies in the common belief that the inner feelings expressed in acts of piety transcend the petty realities of particular places and times. The pious strive for access to the infinite and the eternal; that, and not the ephemera of the moment, is what matters to them. For that reason, historians have often found it tempting to describe the pious practices of particular groups as a kind of living anatomy lesson, in which the thoughts and feelings of a particular individual can be taken to stand for those of the group. In his magisterial study *The New England Mind* (1939), Perry Miller treated the piety of New England Puritans as a defining characteristic of a uniform species and felt at liberty to draw his examples from "whichever authors happen to express a point most conveniently," citing dozens of different Puritan writers, in widely varied circumstances, over the course of a century.[1] This method allowed Miller to probe deeply into the subtle and complex workings of a system of belief and practice without requiring that any single example, any given member of the species, demonstrate each and every one of its distinctive features. But at the same time, this ethnographic approach can make it difficult to explore the subject of Puritan piety historically, to follow important variations across space and changes over time. Miller himself acknowledged this problem in his opening chapter, "The Augustinian Strain of Piety," in which he described the practice of piety as the animating spirit of the Puritan movement. As Miller put it:

> when the wave of religious assertion which we call Puritanism is considered in the broad perspective of Christian history, it appears no longer as a unique phenomenon, peculiar to England of the seventeenth century, but as one more instance of a recurrent spiritual answer to interrogations eternally posed by human existence. The peculiar accidents of time and place did indeed entice Puritanism into entertaining a variety of ideas which were the features of its epoch, yet it was animated by a spirit that was not peculiar to the seventeenth century or to East Anglia and New England.[2]

The Practice of Piety in Puritan New England

Following Miller, we might agree that certain practices of piety identified English Puritans during the lifetime of John Winthrop, and that this form of piety was a central motivating force in the transplantation of thousands of English Puritans overseas. We might also say that the ostensible purpose of Puritan devotion, the inner experience of the individual believer engaged in the practice of piety, may have been extraordinarily similar across the generations, and may have depended very little on geography as well. A godly woman reading devotional manuals in a quiet moment, a godly man reviewing sermon notes during weekday family devotions, a child learning her catechism at her mother's feet—these practices could have been experienced in much the same way in Boston, Lincolnshire, as in Boston, Massachusetts, or in Dublin, Leiden, Bermuda, Barbados, Providence Island, or any other place that the Puritan movement reached during the diaspora of the early Stuart period. A century after John Winthrop's death, the same devotional practices and the same supporting texts still circulated in New England and throughout the Anglophone Protestant world, even as descendants of New England's first Puritan migrants spread farther into the American "wilderness."[3]

But the fact that there were common, perhaps universal, qualities present in this "animating spirit" does not therefore mean that Puritan piety was always and everywhere the same. For example, although historian Tom Webster argues that antagonism between the godly and the profane lay at the heart of English Puritan piety, Francis Bremer has suggested that in the local world of the Stour Valley in Suffolk, where the young John Winthrop was nourished in his Puritan faith, the external antagonism Webster describes was largely absent until the 1620s. When it did arise, Winthrop and others like him were forced to consider migration in order to reconstitute the godly community they had known and feared they might be losing.[4] In other words, if we are to understand the significance of the practice of piety for the worlds of John Winthrop—the world that nurtured him in England, the world that forced him to leave, and the world he helped to create in America—we need to attend not only to the ethnography of piety, but also to its history and to the "peculiar accidents of time and place" that shaped Puritan piety's evolution as it expanded into the Atlantic world of English colonization.

In this essay, I intend to sketch out the general dimensions of this evolutionary process. It will not be a comprehensive survey of the practice of piety in Puritan New England, in part because that subject has already been thoroughly anatomized by several generations of scholars.[5] Instead, I wish to investigate the political, social, and cultural dimensions of the practice of piety in New England, focusing on three main areas.

First, I want to consider how devotional practice as a form of identity formation and cultural boundary demarcation can be useful in understanding the ways that migration to New England reshaped the Puritan tradition. When Winthrop and his fellow migrants left behind "the luxury of persecution," the practice of piety as a form of habitual opposition to a dominant culture, how did the practice of piety reshape itself as a tool for constructing and identifying allegiances in a world without profane masses and overweening bishops?[6] To answer this question, it will be particularly important to pay attention to the differences between New England and the other colonial ventures in which settlers of Puritan inclinations attempted to establish their pious habits in less favorable conditions than the New England settlers enjoyed. In this way, the value and influence of the Puritan hegemony over religious culture in New England can best be measured.[7]

Second, the practice of piety in John Winthrop's England, in whatever form it assumed, was built upon and sustained by a broad and deep religious infrastructure. Leaders of the established church and dissenters alike were devoted to devotion. England's churches, clergy, educational system, publishing trade, even the built environment and the material world of everyday life were well organized to provide the foundation and means for the practice of piety. It is plausible to say that in England the supply of the means of grace exceeded demand. In colonial New England and throughout the scattered reaches of England's new world plantations, conditions were initially reversed. In many instances, the migrant population, defined by its common demand for devotional machinery, moved to places where the material resources for practical divinity were scarce and expensive. To understand the distinctive development and maintenance of devotional traditions in colonial New England, it is critical to understand how society produced and distributed the resources essential to Puritan devotion and how the variable production and distribution of these resources shaped the further development of Puritan piety.

Finally, if early New England's peculiar conditions reshaped the practice of piety, or at least its context and meaning, setting it on a path distinct from its European origins and from other colonial ventures, did the region's continuing growth and evolution lead to further divergence or to convergence? In other words, how did New Englanders' awareness of the strength and distinctive qualities of their devotional traditions shape their relationship to the larger Christian world? A tentative answer to this question will be suggested by a brief examination of the encounter between New England Puritans and continental pietists as the seventeenth century gave way to the eighteenth.

During John Winthrop's lifetime, the practice of piety in England was by no means restricted to Puritans. Believers across the spiritual and ecclesiastical spectrum of English worship shared devotional traditions with roots in medieval Catholicism. But the style in which Puritans practiced their devotion and the opposition it engendered distinguished them. By forming conventicles within the parish church for private worship and communion, by leaving their parish churches to go gadding after sermons, by calling for special fast days, by strictly observing the sabbath in opposition to James's *Book of Sports*, English Puritans practiced their piety ostentatiously. Their exclusivist spiritual vigor drew the ire of a broad range of opponents. Ecclesiastical authorities, worldly cynics, and common folk still devoted to pre-Reformation customs and rhythms of life could all find common ground in mutual Puritan-loathing. Unless Puritans gained the favor of a protective patron or a sympathetic bishop, their precisianist devotional style often put them on the short end of temporal power relationships, a position they eagerly accepted in return for their presumably higher status and influence in the kingdom to come.[8]

The series of decisions by communities of the godly to migrate to New England, beginning with the Plymouth colonists in 1620, made the kingdom, or rather commonwealth, arrive sooner than anticipated, at least insofar as power relationships are concerned. The ease with which the puny and legally flimsy Plymouth colony, led by its diminutive general Miles Standish, suppressed the carousing of Thomas Morton's Merrymount revelers in a kind of *opera buffa* conflict between the godly and the profane, foreshadowed the shape of things to come once the more powerful and legally chartered Massachusetts Bay colony emerged.[9] The "Great Migration" of tens of thousands of Puritans to New England from the late 1620s through the early 1640s meant that they not only left behind their numerically dominant enemies in England, but also gained the power in their new home to suppress the profane and build their vision of the proper practice of piety into the very foundations of church, society, and state.

This radical move may not have been John Winthrop's intention in 1631 when he and the colony's General Court linked political freemanship to membership in its churches. But the heightened fervor of the migrants who followed the Winthrop fleet's wake in the mid 1630s pushed the churches to define themselves by standards derived from the vigorous practice of piety.[10] Narratives of individual conversion became the norm for Massachusetts church gathering and admissions by the late 1630s. These conversion narratives were, in effect, formalized public expressions of the inward experiences engendered by the devotional techniques of practical piety. The godly in England had identified one another and segregated themselves from the ungodly by their common affinity for these very practices and techniques. Thus, in the "free aire of a new world" there seemed little reason not to use these standards to define the boundaries of their new churches.

Little reason, that is, when considered from the point of view of the nonconforming clergy, minor gentry, middling merchants, prosperous yeomen, and comfortable artisans who provided leadership and material resources for the Massachusetts Bay colony. But a brief comparison with the politics of piety in other English colonies where Puritans of various sorts played significant roles reveals the distinctiveness of the Massachusetts settlement. In Bermuda, the interest of the godly in the colonizing venture emerged slowly, as a series of ostensibly conforming clergymen sent over by the company's directors in London revealed their dissenting sympathies. Without the unanimous support and virtual independence that the Massachusetts clergy would later enjoy, Bermuda's Puritans had to promote their version of true piety in conditions that replicated, on a small scale, those they had left behind in England. As early as 1617, clergymen such as Lewis Hughes gathered what were essentially conventicles of pious and devoted colonists from among the profane mass of settlers. By the

1630s, this nonconformist faction had gained considerable strength on the island. They formed what their enemies called a "government of ministers," holding private weekly devotional meetings, pressing for universal catechism, and in 1644 pushing for the creation of an independent covenanted church, with a self-selected pastor and elders, free of company control. For this presumptuous act, their fellow Bermudans indicted the self-appointed leaders of the independent church for high treason. Although the company directors acquitted them of this charge, the dissenters never gained the corporate support necessary to remake Bermuda's society on the model of Massachusetts. Throughout the period of Bermuda's corporate existence, which ended, like that of Massachusetts, in the mid 1680s, the godly remained a dissenting faction, and the practice of piety there played a divisive role in the politics and social development of the island.[11]

A similar story could be told about the fate of Puritan piety in the Chesapeake colonies. Unlike Bermuda, the Puritan colonists who migrated to Virginia never came close to forming a "government of ministers" over this sprawling colony. Nevertheless, in counties south of the James River, particularly Isle of Wight, Nansemond, and Lower Norfolk, several hundred Puritan migrants attempted to create godly communities, and in the 1630s they appealed to John Winthrop, John Davenport, and other New England leaders for support in their venture. Three New England ministers were sent to Virginia in the early 1640s and had considerable success in cultivating recruits, but the arrival of Gov. William Berkeley in 1642 brought an end to the relative freedom of these communities, and their ministers were banished. The Royalist Berkeley fiercely opposed nonconformity, and his opposition emboldened local vestrymen, in Virginia's highly decentralized system of religious authority, to persecute Puritans even in counties where they made up a substantial portion of the population. The new governor outlawed attempts to practice godly piety through informal or unsanctioned worship services. William Durand, a lay preacher who led one such meeting, was arrested and his conventicle dispersed. By 1649, most of Virginia's Puritans had fled to neighboring Maryland, where Gov. William Stone had recently adopted a policy of religious toleration. In the Chesapeake, as in Bermuda, Puritan piety was a divisive force, and the godly in Virginia, with even less institutional support than Bermuda's Puritans, quickly faded from view.[12]

On Providence Island, the colony in the western Caribbean founded at roughly the same time as the Massachusetts Bay experiment, and with an even more powerful array of Puritan supporters, the relationship between the practice of piety and the formation of society also differed markedly from the Massachusetts model. The Puritan grandees who kept firm control of the island's government—the Earl of Warwick, Lord Saye and Sele, and Lord Brooke—rejected the innovations of the Bay Colony, especially the linkage of government participation with church membership and the construction of churches around a single narrowly defined form of piety. Unwilling to relinquish their customary political and social authority to an unpredictable set of middling settlers, and accustomed to treating Puritan clergymen as dependent clients rather than as equals, the Providence Island grandees attempted to create a godly colony by the force of their own wills and the wisdom of their governance from afar. In their eyes, Providence Island would be a place where the godly could escape England's ecclesiastical tyranny and use their freedom to discover new light on the nature of true piety, rather than be forced into another form of devotional tyranny as in Massachusetts Bay. But the need to develop an exportable staple crop and maintain a strong military force on this island in the heart of the Spanish Caribbean represented huge obstacles to growth. Additionally, the unwillingness of Puritan clergy and laity alike to migrate to a colony where they could not be equal participants in the venture discouraged many of the godly from settling on Providence Island. Those who did (many of them refugees from Bermuda) remained an insecure minority during the colony's brief existence. When Puritan ministers such as Hope Sherrard tried to maintain a community of godly worship amid the island's motley assortment of colonists, conflict resulted, ending in the suspension of the sacrament and the collapse of religious observance altogether. Despite the overwhelming support of Warwick, Brooke, and other powerful Puritans, their hoped-for tolerant and godly utopia failed to emerge. The Providence Island colonists found the practice of piety there to be just as divisive and unsettling as it had been at home.[13]

These brief comparisons with Bermuda, Virginia, and Providence Island are meant to highlight the distinctiveness and peculiarity of the Massachusetts model. The relationship in Massachusetts between Puritan devotional techniques and the construction of churches and governments was not simply the practical expression of an abstract Puritan ideal, but the product of two unique circumstances. By leaving behind their profane enemies in England and placing control of government and churches in the hands of those most devoted to one rather precise form of godliness, the Massachusetts system evolved in conditions unknown in the rest of the Puritan world. And yet, even among the relatively homogeneous population of immigrants to New England, the creators of Massachusetts orthodoxy discovered new enemies, internal ones, to replace the external opponents they left behind in the process of consolidating their power.

One dissenting group appeared among those who saw the elaborate machinery of practical piety as so much legalism and hypocrisy, a glorification of the means of grace and the signs of sanctification at the expense of true grace and real saintliness. Anne Hutchinson and her fellow "antinomians," the most outspoken critics of the dominant brand of practical piety, represented what scholars over the past

The Practice of Piety in Puritan New England

decade have identified as a deep and potentially subversive strain of opposition to an excessively formalized definition of right religious experience and its privileged place at the heart of Massachusetts's church polity.[14] Michael Winship's recent revisionist account of the Hutchinson affair, which he persuasively renames the "free grace" controversy, emphasizes the idea that Puritan practical piety was itself generally a unifying factor among the godly—how the godly knew and identified one another. But the attempt to codify piety in doctrinal terms could be wildly divisive, especially in the hands of vengeful or hot-headed zealots.[15]

Another form of opposition appeared among those who rejected not a precise definition of the practice of piety itself but its association with the state. Here, Roger Williams's sharp critique of the persecuting tendencies within the Massachusetts churches has gained the most attention. Other free thinkers, however, such as Samuel Gorton, Robert Child, and William Pynchon, similarly opposed the state power that one particular version of godliness had appropriated. Even orthodox clerics such as Thomas Hooker preferred to keep the practice of piety at a greater distance from the functions of the state, as the formation of Connecticut's alternative to Massachusetts's polity would suggest. Despite the horrified response of much of the rest of the Puritan world, the ability of Massachusetts Bay to enforce its radical coupling of devotional piety and state formation by expelling powerful dissenters created a strong and durable system—the so-called "New England Way." The remarkable continuity and staying power of the Massachusetts variant of the practice of piety came at the high price of ruthlessly eradicating alternative forms of religious devotion and alternative ways of linking piety to social and political organization.[16]

In addition to these internal enemies, the godly migrants of Massachusetts discovered in the native population of the region another challenge to their vision of piety and its place at the center of church and state. The obligation to bring the means of grace to Indians suffering from its absence had been high on various lists of reasons that English Puritans had used to justify migration.[17] If the profane majority in England's rapidly degenerating society had scorned godly nourishment, surely some population in New England starved for this spiritual food. In the words that the Massachusetts Bay Company's official seal so wishfully and plaintively put in the mouth of an Indian, "come over and help us!" The fantasy of Indian desire for Christian instruction was based on the notion that native Americans were naturally given to piety but unschooled in right doctrine and practice.[18] This belief justified the heroic efforts made, after a late start, by John Eliot, whose work sought to inculcate among Indian converts the regular habits, the ways of life, necessary to sustain this practice. It is no coincidence, then, that the name applied to Christianized Indians under Eliot's model referred to the habitual practice of piety rather than to the content of their faith—they were not called "Protestant Indians" or "Reformed Indians" but "praying Indians." Nor is it surprising that the first non-scriptural work Eliot translated into the local Indian language was *Manitowompae Pomantanoonk*, Lewis Bayly's *The Practice of Piety*.[19] Eliot's work among the Indians of Massachusetts continued to be extremely appealing to practical pietists throughout the Atlantic world through the end of the century and beyond. Richard Baxter read Cotton Mather's *Life of the Renowned John Eliot*, also known as *Triumphs of the Reformed Religion in America*, on his deathbed in 1691, and it revived him long enough for Baxter to send Mather a complimentary note.[20] August Hermann Francke, the director of the Halle Institute in Saxony, was profoundly impressed by Increase Mather's description of Eliot's missions, which he translated into German and published at Halle in 1696.[21]

Of course, another view of native Americans existed from the beginnings of colonization as well, a view that depicted Indians as pagan devils, with no natural inclination to piety, whose practice thereof would necessarily be the most extreme form of hypocrisy. The ugliest consequences of this vision emerged during King Philip's War when, after thirty years of Eliot's missionary work, praying Indians who favored their Indian allegiances over their devotional ones received the most extreme brutality from their English counterparts.[22] The creation of unusual forms of Indian missions under Eliot's guidance *and* the dreadful treatment of lapsed praying Indians during wartime were consistent with the distinctive importance that the practice of piety held within New England society. Clearly, the stakes involved in the acceptance or rejection of Puritan piety were extraordinarily high.

Yet another, and still more complex consequence of the enshrinement of practical divinity at the center of the church/state complex was its effect on the lives of women. In many cases, women seemed to be—and were portrayed as—the best practitioners of Puritan devotion. Their conversion relations and accounts of their inner experiences became models of true faith. Several recent scholars have made provocative arguments that explore how early modern notions of feminine nature encouraged the belief that women were more given to piety than men.[23] Over the course of the century, women came to dominate Massachusetts church membership and played a profound role in the inculcation of family devotional practice.[24] Yet by assigning piety as the central qualification for participation and leadership in the government, Puritans blurred and confused traditional lines of gender distinction. Unintentionally, the colony forced women into an unusually prominent place in society and the state, pushing them forward in ways that male leaders then found hard to accept. From Anne Hutchinson, an early and formidable voice of this newly unleashed power, to Anne Bradstreet, astute commentator on the ironies of her situation, to the previously obscure voices of the victims of witchcraft persecution, historians have listened with greater attention in recent decades to women's expression of their peculiar position as exemplars of the primary qualification for participation in a system that excluded them.[25]

Finally, when considering how the practice of piety in early Massachusetts excluded rival varieties, it may be worth looking more closely at alchemical, hermetic, or other forms of "occult" practice. Historians have suggested that the orthodox leaders of Massachusetts rejected these alternative forms of practical divinity that integrated a particular understanding of the nature of matter and the structure of the cosmos with the work of Christian redemption and refinement. But these beliefs and practices were popular among some godly and learned reformers of early seventeenth-century Britain and continental Europe. Recent work on the range and depth of alchemical practice in New England, especially its connection to the treatment of sickness, raises questions about the extent to which alchemy may have been an acceptable part of the forms of ritual and communal behavior that constituted the practice of piety.[26] Alchemical practice shared certain sociological features with the Puritan practice of piety. Both manifested a tension between the need to separate themselves from the vulgar or the profane and the obligation to use their rarefied knowledge or abilities to improve society as a whole. There were, of course, indications of possible conflict between those possessing alchemical or hermetic beliefs and the orthodox powers in Massachusetts. The expulsion of Robert Child in 1646 and the unwillingness of John Winthrop, Jr., to settle in the Bay Colony are two important instances. Nonetheless, recent scholarship has demonstrated a fairly broad current of alchemical and hermetic practice in early New England. When the Harvard College-trained alchemical adept George Starkey left New England in 1650 to work with Samuel Hartlib and Robert Boyle in London, he did so not because he lacked fellowship, interest, or support among other New Englanders, but because he needed better equipment to conduct his chemical and spiritual experiments. His was a rarefied form of quasi-religious devotion that New England could not yet supply the material resources to practice.[27]

The reasons behind Starkey's departure turn us to a second and somewhat overlooked aspect of the development of devotional culture in early New England. All the various means of grace that sustained the intense form of piety enshrined in the New England Way required the extensive outlay of material resources.[28] In England, the important elements of the infrastructure that produced these resources had long been in place: an active printing and publishing trade, an elaborate educational system, and above all, a wealthy and powerful established church, intricately woven into the fabric of social life, whose buildings and institutions created a sacralized landscape and culture. In New England, these institutions had to be created *de novo* and the enabling materials imported from overseas.[29] In either case, the task of producing the material resources needed to sustain the practice of piety was bound to be complicated, risky, and expensive.

A second feature distinguished the development of devotional piety in New England from other godly colonizing ventures: the colony's extraordinary success in accumulating resources and directing them in a sustained way toward the cultivation of godliness. Perhaps the most obvious example of this point can be seen by conceptualizing preaching as a commodity or scarce resource. The godly sermon, "a central element to Puritan piety," was not always easy to come by, even in England.[30] There, pious lay people faced the difficult challenge of identifying the truly orthodox, learned, and charismatic preachers from among a crowd of indifferent, "dumb," or "dead" hirelings, and protecting their favorites from hostile authorities. But the Puritan hot-house colleges at Cambridge and, to a lesser extent, Oxford, regularly produced gifted clergymen, and the godly laity tracked them down.[31] In the early colonial ventures, settlers usually could find no preacher at all. Few clergymen of reputation and standing in Britain would risk the hazards and isolation of trans-Atlantic life, which meant that even the most devout lay colonists, like the pilgrim brethren at Plymouth, suffered through decades of instruction at the hands of incompetents, imposters, and charlatans.[32] The absence of orthodox clergymen could turn even a colony of the godly into a breeding ground for heresy, schism, or religious indifference.[33]

Fully aware of these dismal examples, the founders of Massachusetts determined to improve upon them. During the 1630s, their task eased as many Puritan clergymen proved increasingly ready to flee Britain and lead migratory ventures. Additionally, after the doctrinal crises of the mid 1630s when antinomian heresies and other politically radical challenges to orthodoxy came in the baggage of newly arrived clergy, colonial leaders saw wisdom in the idea of training clergymen in New England. In 1636, the general court directed that £400 be used to found a college at Newtown. Once operations began in earnest following the antinomian crisis, these initial funds were supplemented in future years by the proceeds of the Charlestown ferry, by rents from farm lands reserved for the college's benefit, and by occasional taxes levied on the population of all the United Colonies (Massachusetts, Plymouth, Connecticut, and New Haven).[34] Under the immediate supervision of a president and tutors, and guided by overseers representing the government and the leading clergymen of the Bay colony, a successful college could be counted on as a training ground for orthodox preachers. Harvard's founders believed they had guaranteed a continuing supply of the chief commodity necessary for the practice of piety, "when our present ministers shall lie in the dust."[35]

The Practice of Piety in Puritan New England

The forms of clerical and lay leadership necessary to uphold the standards for practical piety placed considerable demands on the colony's resources. Ideally, each church should have had two university-educated clergymen, a pastor and a teacher, as well as an ordained lay ruling elder and two deacons to oversee the disciplinary and pragmatic needs of the church and congregation. In principle, this system produced specialists in the cultivation of piety, an efficient division of religious labor among expensively trained professionals. In reality, this ideal was not always achieved, especially among poorer rural churches that could barely afford a single minister's salary.[36] But the ideal remained powerful, and in more urban and populous communities like Boston or New Haven, where sufficient resources existed, churches often did sustain more than one clergyman. Over the course of the seventeenth century, more than 60 percent of the college's graduates did become orthodox ministers. The vast majority of these highly trained intellectuals, the "thinking class" as one historian calls them, remained in the colonies, in stark contrast to the "brain drain" so characteristic of colonial societies throughout the world.[37]

With respect to the demands of practical piety, the colony's decision to found a college before it established a printing press made a good deal of sense. In addition to the vaunted primacy of the preached word over the written text in Puritan circles, it was also the case that books proved more stable and reliable commodities than clergymen, and easier to predict and control. A man who seemed perfectly orthodox in one context might become a dangerous radical in another, but books, once printed, remained fairly fixed commodities, and their importation and distribution could be controlled and censored more easily than the shifting opinions of radical clergymen. In the long run, colonial leaders preferred to keep the entire process of education, training, and ordination of ministers under local control, while the literary foundations for the practice of piety favored in New England could be safely (if expensively) sustained through the importation of standard devotional works from overseas.[38] With the establishment of a colonial press, its initial religious output, not surprisingly, favored meeting those particular and distinctive demands of Massachusetts piety not satisfied through imports. The *Bay Psalm Book* supplied a guide to the form of psalm-singing that the godly in New England wanted but that official use of the Common Prayer book had prevented in England.[39] The *New England Primer* forged a vital link between literacy and catechetical training in the colony's innovative educational system, a connection that Puritans in other plantations had hoped for but failed to sustain. In Bermuda, the Puritan clergyman John Oxenbridge met considerable resistance when he attempted to introduce "Universal Catechising [of] all men and women weekly ... and pressed upon us with great vehemency and that all shall be tied to answer according to that Catechism of Mr. Oxenbridge's called Baby Milk or some other."[40] It is significant in this light that John Cotton, Jr., the first Harvard-trained minister to gain a pulpit in the Plymouth colony, began his ministry by introducing universal religious education to make sure that folks in Plymouth, like those in Massachusetts, could answer according to an orthodox catechism.[41]

By the 1660s, the press in Massachusetts began to produce locally the devotional tracts that it had previously imported, and these works would increase in numbers and volume through the end of the century. This new indigenous output symbolized the region's economic and cultural maturation—it now made financial sense to produce these popular works locally. But it also reflected New England's vigorous material response to what Charles Hambrick-Stowe has called "the devotional crisis of the second generation." The piety of the founders had been forged in their conflict with profane opposition in England. Absent that confrontation, the second and subsequent generations needed other means to sustain the intense devotional culture around which they had built their social and political lives. The outpouring of devotional titles from regional authors and the Boston press, and their enduring popularity among the colonial population, strongly indicated how material resources would direct—and be directed by—the practice of piety in New England.[42]

Work on the history of books as commodities and as material objects has broadened and deepened our understanding of their role in the culture of Puritan piety. If the intellectual content of a devotional manual was an essential element of spiritual practice, so too were the kinds of interpersonal relationships—communities of devotion—that could be solidified or cemented by the exchange of books as gifts, tokens of friendships, and fellow-feeling.[43] But the power of printed matter to shape the inner lives of readers was not fixed at the point of production or in the act of exchange or acquisition. In the library amassed by the Mather family, a substantial part of which is now held by the American Antiquarian Society, there are dozens of what I would call, for want of a better word, "composite" books. These are collections of pamphlets published (usually in Britain) over a span of decades, which Increase or Cotton Mather collected and bound together between two covers so that the assembled pamphlets construct an overarching political, ecclesiastical, or theological argument. These arguments, often stating or defending implicitly the position of the Massachusetts government and churches, were contained in no single title but emerged from the whole. Such composite books represent a form of intellectual labor, of value added to the original works. In this case, English pamphlets became a distinctly American book, an English production retooled for New England consumption.[44] Similarly, other books bear the signs of use by several generations of the Mather family, containing the signatures of Richard, Increase, Cotton, and Samuel Mather, and laden with palimpsests of marginal notes. Subject indexes appear on the flyleafs, suggesting the way certain critical texts were read and re-read and amended by generation after generation of users, cultural artisans revising and reforming the tools of their trade.[45]

Elsewhere, I have discussed in detail the proliferation of Boston's silver trade. The remarkable skill and refinement of these products, and the extraordinary demand for them on communion tables throughout New England, even in poor and remote frontier settlements, is yet another indication of how the cultivation of an intense and rarefied form of Puritan piety shaped the material life of the colony.[46] Silver was not strictly necessary for the Lord's Supper in any theological sense; in a pinch, the sacramental bread and wine could have been served in wooden tankards and trenchers. But the near-ubiquitous presence of silver communion vessels throughout New England by century's end resulted from the intense and widespread cultivation of a form of piety that demanded communion silver; that is, it gained strength from the rich array of symbolic reinforcements that silver lent to the meaning of the sacrament. Silver symbolized the expense of Christ's sacrifice for the souls of worthless sinners. It stood for the purity, refinement, and endurance of the bodies of the saints in heaven, once the earthly dross was no more. Each engraved silver communion cup offered New England's saints an additional set of visible and tangible metaphors for grasping the elusive process of salvation, and provides us with another way to observe the central drama of Puritan piety.

Although the intense logocentrism of Puritan culture has long been remarked upon, the importance of material objects and physical rituals, like silver and its use in the sacrament as an aspect of Puritan piety, is a subject deserving further investigation. Great headway already has been made in scholarship on another of the tangible and enduring objects of this culture of piety, namely gravestones. Nevertheless, more work could be done on the material culture of funerary practices: burial rituals, funeral processions, the uses of portraiture, and the iconography of mourning, as well as tokens of remembrance such as gloves and rings.[47] In addition, the built environment, particularly houses and churches, including their design, construction, and furnishing, has received considerable attention, most recently in the provocative work of Robert St. George. Still, the intersection between buildings, both public and domestic, and the practice of piety deserves further elaboration.[48] Samuel Sewall's diary reveals the way in which artifacts of the built environment served as a constant reminder of the acts of the saints. From his annual visits to the Plymouth meetinghouse and burying ground at the time of his birthday, to his attention to the houses that had once been home to a John Cotton or a John Harvard, Sewall lived in a landscape that gradually became invested with sacred meanings.[49] But further systematic efforts to bring the techniques of material culture studies to bear upon the relationship between the practice of piety and the built environment might yield rich rewards.

Yet another aspect of the material, physical, and ritualistic versions of piety deserving examination is the strong tradition of military training that evolved in the New England colonies. From the militia training days observed by every village and town in the New England Confederacy, to Boston's elite Ancient and Honorable Artillery Company, military service always presented an occasion for communal worship. The military sermons of the clergy invited to preside at these meetings have received scholarly analysis, as have the social and political importance of these organizations.[50] Overlooked, however, has been the effect of military drill itself on the inner lives and communal cohesiveness of New England's adult male citizenry. Because Puritans frowned on traditional forms of communal dancing, military drill and psalm-singing were, in all likelihood, the only two legitimate forms in early New England culture of what the historian William McNeill has called "keeping together in time." The power that McNeill ascribes to this "muscular bonding" as a force for creating a kind of religious ecstasy, became "a strange sense of personal enlargement; a sort of swelling out, becoming bigger than life." It also maintained strong feelings of communal solidarity, all suggesting the importance of examining this version of physical or ritualistic piety as a way further to comprehend the strength and longevity of Puritanism in New England.[51] In sum, strong scholarship exists on most, if not all, of the elements that constituted the material world of Puritan piety in New England, but it still remains for these pieces to be assembled into a unified whole and aligned with the scholarship on material Christianity in Europe and America.[52]

George Starkey may have been wise to leave New England in 1650 for want of the equipment necessary to practice his version of alchemical piety. But in the half century following his departure, virtually every other form of devotional equipment, every other means of grace or tool for the practice of piety, was imported or produced in New England, turning a landscape of cultural scarcity into a world of plenty.[53] Many authors have suggested that the establishment of European immigrant colonies in the new world resulted in the thinning out, stripping down, or simplification of European culture.[54] As Dr. Johnson put it in describing the depopulation of western Scotland, "a nation scattered in the boundless regions of America resembles rays diverging from a focus. All the rays remain but the heat is gone."[55] But with respect to the distinctive culture of godliness built around the practice of piety, New England proves the exception to this rule. By focusing their material resources on the replication of an extremely narrow band within the spectrum of English culture, singling out a kind of laser beam of Puritan piety, New England's colonists managed to retain, at times perhaps increase, the heat, the intensity, and the longevity of a subculture that dissipated in England and in all other English plantations. The use of material and cultural resources to cultivate Puritan piety helps to explain its remarkable concentrated persistence in New England, an increasingly anachronistic quality in Britain's realm as the seventeenth century closed. Just imagine the shocked incomprehension of British soldiers stationed in Boston in 1768, whose customary recreations on Sunday—their one day of leisure each week—tended toward loud music, dancing, gambling, horse racing, and general carousing—when confronted with the restrictions of the Puritan sabbath still devoutly maintained in New England's metropolis.[56] It must have been like entering a time warp, like a trip to Plimoth Plantation for the modern tourist, but without the refuge of the visitor center or the comforting knowledge that you can leave at the end of the day.

The persistence with which New England clung to the practice of piety, and the intensity with which it devoted its resources to sustaining this cultural system, must have looked odd, even hypocritical, to outside observers, as numerous travelers' accounts in the later seventeenth and eighteenth centuries suggest.[57] The Puritan colonies' later clerical leadership was deeply concerned with continuity and comprehension, to make sure that the widespread piety of the first generation would be sustained broadly throughout the colony's growing population. This ambition underlay the outpouring of new forms and means of devotion in the later seventeenth century, as well as innovations in church polity such as the so-called Halfway Covenant of 1662.[58] Of course, some of these innovations met fierce opposition from those who retained an older English Puritan view that true piety necessitated a division between the godly and the profane, even in New England. But the larger effect of all this pious cultivation, especially when viewed by outsiders, seemed like an effort to convert and keep converted a population that by European or colonial standards was already notable for its godliness.

For those New Englanders who concerned themselves with how their own society appeared from abroad, the late seventeenth century was an important time to assess the place of New England in the larger Protestant tradition. The loss of the Massachusetts charter, the surprising upheavals Protestants faced under Charles II and James II and during the Glorious Revolution, the increasing belligerence of Louis XIV on the European continent, together with the revocation of the Edict of Nantes and the flight of the Huguenots, prompted New Englanders' anxious attention to the larger Protestant world and their role within it.[59] On some level, English nonconformity, the remnants of a once powerful tradition, must have looked enfeebled to New England observers. The failure of the Heads of Agreement to bring lasting union among English Presbyterians and Independents, and the continuing marginal status of dissenters in Britain even after a Dutch Calvinist was placed on the throne, diminished any hope that the Glorious Revolution would be glorious for English nonconformists.[60] The more vigorous and evangelical elements of the Church of England sometimes would seem equally appealing to anglophilic New Englanders of a dissenting sensibility. Henry Newman, for instance, the son and grandson of prominent Puritan ministers in New England, chose to leave his homeland, settle in London, conform to the Anglican church, and take up a position as secretary in the newly formed Society for the Promotion of Christian Knowledge. He served the SPCK for thirty years, fostering cooperation among international Protestant missionary and refugee societies, all the while maintaining strong ties with New England's clerical elites, including Cotton Mather, Benjamin Colman, and Thomas Prince. Similarly, the societies for the reformation of manners encouraged by Anglicans and dissenters alike at the end of the seventeenth century had a strong appeal among New England's clerical elites.[61]

But if English nonconformity was less than wholly inspiring to turn-of-the-century New Englanders, and if none of the other English plantations remotely approached the New England model, the (re)discovery of continental pietism appeared as something of a revelation, or at least a mirror, in which a new reflection of New England's image in the wider world became visible.[62] Although his father had had literary contact and correspondence with some of the forerunners of continental pietism during his two extended European sojourns, Cotton Mather's active encounter with this tradition began in the first decade of the eighteenth century. Versions of the works of August Hermann Francke, director of the pietist institute at Halle, in Saxony, found their way into Mather's hands via correspondents in London (among them Henry Newman). Soon, Mather resolved to send Francke some of his own publications, which he called "the true American pietism."[63]

What impressed Mather so greatly about Halle pietism, and what he hoped to convey to Francke by describing some of his accounts of New England's culture of pious devotion, was the extraordinary vigor that pious discipline gave to evangelical and reforming works. Mather translated and redacted for publication in Boston a seventy-page letter in which Francke had described the achievements of the Halle institute, a success nothing short of astonishing. "Dr. Franckius is a Person truly Wonderful for his vast Erudition; but much more so for his most shining Piety; and yet more so for his most peerless Industry; and most of all so, for the Astonishing Blessings of God upon his Undertakings to advance His Kingdom in the World."[64] These many undertakings included the creation of an enormous orphanage, a home for widows, and the development of a school for the training of missionaries who were sent by the Danish government to serve on the

Malabar coast of India. Other schools formed at Halle educated children of the godly nobility, women, and the poor. Additional impressive accomplishments included the establishment of an infirmary and a pharmaceuticals business—combining piety with healing—and above all, in Mather's eyes, the operation of a printing press that turned out Bibles and devotional tracts in many languages and at a prodigious rate. As Mather put it: "Within a few Years, and since the light of Evangelical Piety thus breaking forth in the Heart of Germany, there have been more Volumes of the Scriptures vended than in the whole Period of the Time, from the Reformation until Now; and never were they so cheap since the World began."[65]

The relationship between "the light of evangelical piety" and the peerless industry of Francke's institute inspired Mather and like-minded New England clergymen to expand their own efforts to apply the practice of piety to the cause of worldly reformation. Mather could honestly describe New England's long tradition of such work in his letter to Francke as the "true American pietism" because Francke's vigorous evangelical pietism bore the closest resemblance to the New England Way among all the various forms of Protestant religious culture rimming the greater north Atlantic world. Although these pietistic reform movements would eventually diverge in the eighteenth century, it is instructive to consider how Mather and Francke arrived at such similar positions. Both men emerged from (and aimed to complete) what they viewed as partial reformations—one English Calvinist, one German Lutheran—movements that considered the cultivation of piety to be the most practical alternative to the overt institutional reforms of the powerful established churches that seemed doomed to failure. In the case of New England and Halle, the vigor and persistence of these efforts were possible because of unusual circumstances and rare forms of protection. In New England, a lenient charter and a formidable ocean separating believers from the pressures that nonconformists faced in England, made it possible to keep Puritan piety at the center of church and state. In Halle, the almost as formidable and often fickle protection of the Prussian monarchy shielded advocates from their orthodox Lutheran and Reformed antagonists.[66]

This last section, tentative and highly speculative as it is, has moved us far afield from John Winthrop's experience. But these later developments in Puritan piety experienced by his children and grandchildren, and by their contemporaries who scattered across the English Atlantic, nonetheless formed important parts of the world John Winthrop helped create. In the far-flung realms of the Puritan diaspora, the necessity for a context of external antagonism for Puritan piety to develop seems more problematic than it may have been to English Puritans. Or more precisely, it might better be said that the longevity and vitality of Puritan piety in the colonies were best sustained in places with a minimum of external antagonism. Of internal antagonism, there was no end. New England Puritans, like their English counterparts, were driven by the need to find and denounce an alien "other" within their own psyches, to create internal enemies among themselves, or single out deviants from the true path. External antagonism, however, does not appear to have been necessary to sustain piety in the colonies. Indeed, the "light of evangelical piety" burned brightest and longest in those places most protected from hostile winds, but was snuffed out where external antagonists proved strongest. On this issue, then, the obscure gentleman from Suffolk had very good instincts. The Stour Valley of John Winthrop's youth had been a protective enclave that nurtured Puritan piety and formed Winthrop's sense of self and security. In the 1620s, when external threats to this world loomed large, Winthrop gambled on moving to a distant refuge where these dangers might be banished, where church and state alike could be created by and for those devoted to the practice of piety. In hindsight, he did the right thing.

Endnotes

1. Perry Miller, *The New England Mind: The Seventeenth Century* (Cambridge, Mass., 1939), vii. Tom Webster's essay in this volume on the practice of piety among English Puritans follows a remarkably similar strategy.
2. Miller, *New England Mind: The Seventeenth Century*, 4. Charles Hambrick-Stowe echoes and expands upon these observations, see *The Practice of Piety: Puritan Devotional Disciplines in Seventeenth-Century New England* (Chapel Hill, 1982), 25-39.
3. See Charles Hambrick-Stowe, "The Spirit of the Old Writers: The Great Awakening and the Persistence of Puritan Piety," in Francis J. Bremer, ed., *Puritanism: Transatlantic Perspectives on a Seventeenth-Century Anglo-American Faith* (Boston, 1993), 277-291.
4. Francis J. Bremer, "The Heritage of John Winthrop: Religion along the Stour Valley, 1548-1630," *New England Quarterly* 70(1997):515-547.
5. Many titles might be included on a list of significant works that bear on this field; some of the more influential, arranged chronologically, are Miller, *The New England Mind: The Seventeenth Century*; Norman Pettit, *The Heart Prepared: Grace and Conversion in Puritan Spiritual Life* (New Haven, 1966); David D. Hall, *The Faithful Shepherd: A History of the New England Ministry in the Seventeenth Century* (Chapel Hill, 1972); Michael McGiffert, *God's Plot: The Paradoxes of Puritan Piety, Being the Autobiography & Journal of Thomas Shepard* (Amherst, Mass., 1972); E. Brooks Holifield, *The Covenant Sealed: The Development of Puritan Sacramental Theology in Old and New England, 1570-1720* (New Haven, 1974); Hambrick-Stowe, *The Practice of Piety*; Charles L. Cohen, *God's Caress: The Psychology of Puritan Religious Experience* (New York, 1986); Harry Stout, *The New England Soul: Preaching and Religious Culture in Colonial New England* (New York, 1986); David D. Hall, *Worlds of Wonder, Days of Judgment: Popular Religious Belief in Early New England* (New York, 1989); Horton Davies, *The Worship of the American Puritans, 1629-1730* (New York, 1990); Amanda Porterfield, *Female Piety in Puritan New England: The Emergence of Religious Humanism* (New York, 1992); Michael P. Winship, *Making Heretics: Militant Protestantism and Free Grace in Massachusetts, 1636-1641* (Princeton, 2002).
6. Tom Webster, "The Piety of Practice and the Practice of Piety," 111-146.
7. A cautionary note: this portion of the essay is structured in a way that often suggests "New England" was more or less synonymous with Mass-

achusetts Bay. The disproportionate power and wealth of the Bay Colony, and the focus of this volume on its leading citizen, will stand as my excuse for perpetuating this misleading synecdoche. Important differences between the practice of piety in Massachusetts and in the other New England colonies will be acknowledged.

8. For the most recent, thorough, and insightful study of the rise of the puritan or "precisionist" impulse within English reformed piety, see Theodore Dwight Bozeman, *The Precisianist Strain: Disciplinary Religion and Antinomian Backlash in Puritanism to 1638* (Chapel Hill, 2004).

9. See William Bradford, *Of Plymouth Plantation, 1620-1647* (New York, 1981), 226-232, and Thomas Morton, *New English Canaan* (1643; New York, 1972), for the two opposing sides of this conflict.

10. Edmund S. Morgan, *Visible Saints, The History of a Puritan Idea* (Ithaca, N.Y., 1963), is the most economical of the many accounts of this development in Massachusetts's polity. Philip Gura, *A Glimpse of Sion's Glory: Puritan Radicalism in New England, 1620-1660* (Middletown, Conn., 1984), is particularly useful in describing how this seemingly radical swing in Massachusetts polity may actually have been a way to fend off even more radical alternatives.

11. See Charles M. Andrews, *The Colonial Period of American History*, vol. 1, *The Settlements* (New Haven, 1934), 214-235; also Alison Games, *Migration and the Origins of the English Atlantic World* (Cambridge, Mass., 1999), 132-138, 156-160.

12. See Kevin Butterfield, "Puritans and Religious Strife in the Early Chesapeake," *Virginia Magazine of History and Biography* 109(2001):5-37; also Perry Miller, "Religion and Society in the Early Literature of Virginia," in Miller, ed., *Errand into the Wilderness* (Cambridge, Mass., 1956), 99-140.

13. On religious life on Providence Island, see Karen Ordahl Kupperman, *Providence Island, 1630-1641: The Other Puritan Colony* (Cambridge, 1993), 221-266; Games, *Migration*, 153-156.

14. Two notable studies in this vein are Andrew Delbanco, *The Puritan Ordeal* (Cambridge, Mass., 1989), and Janice Knight, *Orthodoxies in Massachusetts: Rereading American Puritanism* (Cambridge, Mass., 1994). For earlier discussions that bear on the issue of practical piety in the antinomian controversy, see also Pettit, *The Heart Prepared*, and William K. B. Stoever, *"A Faire and Easie Way to Heaven": Covenant Theology and Antinomianism in Early New England* (Middletown, Conn., 1978).

15. Winship, *Making Heretics*.

16. Gura, *A Glimpse of Sion's Glory*, makes the strongest case for the significance of Puritan radicalism in the shaping of Massachusetts orthodoxy. But see also David S. Lovejoy, *Religious Enthusiasm in the New World*, (Cambridge, Mass., 1985); Timothy Hall, *Separating Church and State: Roger Williams and Religious Liberty* (Chicago, 1998); Michael P. Winship, "Contesting Control of Orthodoxy among the Godly: William Pynchon Reconsidered," *William and Mary Quarterly*, 3d ser., 54(1997):795-822.

17. For a general discussion, see Neal Salisbury, *Manitou and Providence: Indians, Europeans, and the Making of New England, 1500-1643* (New York, 1982), 141-181; specific primary texts include John White, *The Planters Plea* (London, 1630); Robert Cushman, "Reasons and Considerations Touching the Lawfulness of Removing out of England into the Parts of America" (1621), in Alexander Young, ed., *Chronicles of the Pilgrim Fathers* (Boston, 1841), 239-249.

18. Although critical of the approach of Massachusetts Bay colonists toward Indian relations, Roger Williams's *A Key into the Language of America* (London, 1643) was one of the most significant texts in advancing this vision of the natural piety of native Americans.

19. In fact, among the comprehensive collections of the American Antiquarian Society, Eliot's 1665 translation of Bayly is the earliest devotional title published in North America in *any* language, English included.

20. Cotton Mather, *Triumphs of the Reformed Religion in America: The Life of the Renowned John Eliot* (London, 1691); for the reference to Baxter's response, see Thomas J. Holmes, *Cotton Mather: A Bibliography of His Works* (Cambridge, Mass., 1940), 3:1129.

21. Increase Mather, *Ein Breiff von dem glucklichen Fortgang des Evangelii bey den West-Indianern in Neu=Engeland an den beruhmten Herrn Johann Leusden* (Halle, 1696)–copy in Houghton Library, Harvard University, Cambridge, Massachusetts.

22. Jill Lepore, *The Name of War: King Philip's War and the Origins of American Identity* (New York, 1997).

23. See Porterfield, *Female Piety*; Margaret W. Masson, "The Typology of the Female as a Model for the Regenerate: Puritan Preaching, 1690-1730," *Signs* 2 (1976): 304-315; Richard Godbeer, "'Love Raptures': Marital, Romantic, and Erotic Images of Jesus Christ in Puritan New England, 1670-1730," *New England Quarterly* 68 (1995): 355-384; for an alternative

analysis, see Elizabeth Reis, *Damned Women: Sinners and Witches in Puritan New England* (Ithaca, N.Y., 1997).

24. Porterfield, *Female Piety*; Laurel Thacher Ulrich, *Good Wives: Image and Reality in the Lives of Women in Northern New England, 1650-1750* (New York, 1980); Hall, *Worlds of Wonder*; Gerald Moran and Maris Vinovskis, *Religion, Family, and the Life Course: Explorations in the Early Social History of America* (Ann Arbor, Mich., 1992).

25. Jane Kamensky, *Governing the Tongue: The Politics of Speech in Early New England* (New York, 1997), offers a fascinating approach to these issues, not directly through the examination of the practice of piety, but through the related subject of the politics of speech. See also Carol Karlsen, *The Devil in the Shape of a Woman: Witchcraft in Colonial New England* (New York, 1987); Reis, *Damned Women*; Lyle Koehler, *A Search for Power: The 'Weaker Sex' in Seventeenth-Century New England* (Urbana, Ill., 1980); Marilyn J. Westerkamp, "Anne Hutchinson, Sectarian Mysticism, and the Puritan Order," *Church History* 59(1990):482-498; James F. Cooper, "Anne Hutchinson and the 'Lay Rebellion' against the Clergy," *New England Quarterly* 61 (1988): 381-397.

26. John Brooke, *The Refiner's Fire: The Making of Mormon Cosmology, 1644-1844* (Cambridge, Mass., 1994), 3-29, dismisses the possibility that members of the "magisterial reformation" in Massachusetts could have introduced hermetic or alchemical traditions into colonial America, and looks to radical spiritists—Baptists, Quakers, and other seekers—as the source for early American hermeticism. Jon Butler, *Awash in a Sea of Faith: Christianizing the American People* (Cambridge, Mass., 1990), 67-97, also draws a sharp distinction between orthodox Christianity and magical or occult beliefs, while Richard Godbeer, *The Devil's Dominion: Magic and Religion in Early New England* (Cambridge, Mass., 1992), and David Hall, *Worlds of Wonder*, 71-116, both see more room for ambiguity and syncretism, though they address popular or folk magic more extensively than elite or learned alchemical practice.

27. On Starkey's career, and on the depth and range of alchemical practice in early New England, see William R. Newman, *Gehennical Fire: The Lives of George Starkey, an American Alchemist in the Scientific Revolution* (Cambridge, Mass., 1994); see also Walter W. Woodward, "Prospero's America: John Winthrop Jr., Alchemy, and the Creation of New England Culture" (Ph.D. diss., University of Connecticut, 2001). The role of alchemical practice in the religious, scientific, and reforming dreams of seventeenth-century Euro-

pean intellectuals has received extensive attention; see for example Charles Webster, *The Great Instauration: Science, Medicine, and Reform, 1626-1660* (London, 1975); Frances Yates, *The Rosicrucian Enlightenment* (London, 1972); Mark Greengrass et. al., eds., *Samuel Hartlib and Universal Reformation* (Cambridge, Eng., 1992); Betty Jo Dobbs, *The Janus Face of Genius: The Role of Alchemy in Newton's Thought* (Cambridge, Eng., 1991).

28. I treat this subject at greater length in *The Price of Redemption: The Spiritual Economy of Puritan New England* (Stanford, 1997). The text that follows summarizes this argument in part, while attempting to turn attention to other related aspects of the material basis for the practice of piety.

29. Butler, *Awash in a Sea of Faith*, 37-66, has a useful discussion of the colonists' need to recreate the kind of sacralized landscape they had known in Europe, and singles out New England for its speed in doing so, compared with the other English colonies.

30. For a more extended discussion, see John Morgan, *Godly Learning: Puritan Attitudes towards Reason, Learning, and Education, 1560-1640* (Cambridge, 1986), 95-141; Tom Webster, "The Piety of Practice and the Practice of Piety," 134.

31. See Bremer, *Congregational Communion*, 17-63; Stephen Foster, *The Long Argument: English Puritanism and the Shaping of New England Culture, 1570-1700* (Chapel Hill, 1992), 20-24.

32. See Mark A. Peterson, "The Plymouth Church and the Evolution of Puritan Religious Culture," *New England Quarterly* 66(1993):570-593; George F. Willison, *Saints and Strangers* (New York, 1945), 343-372; Bradford, *Plymouth Plantation*, 163-181. The difficulty of attaining reliable, vital, and orthodox clergy was a problem in every Calvinist colony, even those like New Netherlands with some support from an established church; see Randall Balmer, *A Perfect Babel of Confusion: Dutch Religion and English Culture in the Middle Colonies* (New York, 1989).

33. John Winthrop's son Samuel settled in Antigua, where he suffered from the absence of godly community among the "vices" and "madness" of the other colonists, and pleaded with his brother John to help the colony acquire a "godly, able, grave minister." The island's failure to acquire such a minister may have contributed to Samuel Winthrop's eventual conversion to Quakerism; see Larry D. Gragg, "A Puritan in the West Indies: The Career of Samuel Winthrop," *William and Mary Quarterly* 3d ser., 50(1993):778-781.

34. Samuel Eliot Morison, *The Founding of Harvard College* (Cambridge, Mass., 1935), 169, 292.
35. The phrase in quotation marks is from *New England's First Fruits*, (London, 1643), the early promotional pamphlet for Massachusetts Bay's educational and missionary efforts. For an insightful discussion of the importance of the founding of Harvard College in solidifying orthodoxy, and the very high price the colony paid for this, see Darren Staloff, *The Making of an American Thinking Class: Intellectuals and Intelligentsia in Puritan Massachusetts* (New York, 1998), 91-100.
36. Nonetheless, by the end of the first decade of Massachusetts's settlement, the twenty churches in the colony were served by thirty-four ministers; in other words, fourteen of the twenty churches were served by two ministers: see Staloff, *Thinking Class*, 92.
37. See Samuel Eliot Morison, *Harvard College in the Seventeenth Century* (Cambridge, Mass., 1936).
38. On the early importation, distribution, and control of books, see Hall, *Worlds of Wonder*, 43ff.
39. See George Parker Winship, *The Cambridge Press, 1638-1692* (Philadelphia, 1945).
40. See Andrews, *Colonial Period*, 1:231.
41. Peterson, "Plymouth Church," 585-588; *Plymouth Church Records, 1620-1859, Publications of the Colonial Society of Massachusetts* 22:142-144.
42. Hambrick-Stowe, *Practice of Piety*, 242-277.
43. See Hall, *Worlds of Wonder*, 18-31, 236-237.
44. See, for example, Mather Library, American Antiquarian Society, Worcester, Massachusetts, Shelf 3, Volume 22, which is a compilation of six titles: [Z. Cawdrey], *A Preparation for Martyrdom* (London, 1681); *The Common Prayer Book Unmasked* (n.p., 1660); John Geree, *The Character of an Old English Puritan, or Non-Conformist* (London, 1649); John Corbet, *An Account . . . of the Practices and Principles of Several Nonconformists* (London, 1682); *A Few Sober Queries Upon the Late Proclamation, for enforcing the Laws against Conventicles . . .* (London, 1668); and Phillip Nye, *The Lawfulness of an Oath of Supremacy* (London, 1683).
45. See, for examples, the Mather Library copy of Christopher Ockland, *Anglorum Praelia* (London, 1582), Shelf 7, vol. 39, or J. H. Alsted, *Theologia Polemica* (Hanover, 1627), Shelf 17, vol. 9.

46. Mark A. Peterson, "Puritanism and Refinement in Early New England: Reflections on Communion Silver," *William and Mary Quarterly* 3d ser., 58 (2001): 307-346; Peterson, *Price of Redemption*, 82-84, 113-114.

47. See Allan Ludwig, *Graven Images: New England Stone-Carving and Its Symbols* (Middletown, Conn., 1966); *Puritan Gravestone Art*, Dublin Seminar for New England Folklife (Boston, 1977); David Stannard, *The Puritan Way of Death* (New York, 1977); and Steven C. Bullock and Sheila McIntyre's forthcoming work on funeral gloves.

48. Robert Blair St. George, *Conversing by Signs: Poetics of Implication in Colonial New England Culture* (Chapel Hill, 1998).

49. M. Halsey Thomas, ed., *The Diary of Samuel Sewall* (New York, 1973), 1:162, 1:367; St. George, *Conversing by Signs*, 169; see also Robert J. Dinkin, "Seating the Meetinghouse in Early Massachusetts," in St. George, ed., *Material Life in America* (Boston, 1988), 407-418; Joseph Wood, *The New England Village* (Baltimore, 1997).

50. For studies of the role of the militia in Massachusetts society and politics, see T. H. Breen, "The Covenanted Militia of Massachusetts Bay: English Background and New World Development," in *Puritans and Adventurers* (New York, 1980), 25-45; Louise A. Breen, "Religious Radicalism in the Puritan Officer Corps: Heterodoxy, the Artillery Company, and Cultural Integration in Seventeenth-Century Boston," *New England Quarterly* 68(1995):3-43.

51. William H. McNeill, *Keeping Together in Time: Dance and Drill in Human History* (Cambridge, Mass., 1995), 2.

52. See Colleen McDannell, *Material Christianity: Religion and Popular Culture in America* (New Haven, Conn., 1995); David Morgan, *Visual Piety: A History and Theory of Popular Religious Images* (Berkeley, 1998).

53. Indeed, in the 1670s, Leonard Hoar, a distinguished Puritan clergymen and medical practitioner, arrived to assume the Harvard presidency, with plans for building the first chemical laboratories in the new world, plans that went unfulfilled when his presidency was riven by controversy and ended abruptly with his sudden death. Had Hoar's dreams become reality, even this esoteric form of practical piety might have flourished in New England as well. (As it is, the still mysterious causes for the controversy that undermined Hoar's tenure in office may yet yield further knowledge of the standing of alchemical or hermetic experiments within New Eng-

land orthodoxy). See Morison, *Harvard College in the Seventeenth Century*, 2:390-414; John Langdon Sibley, *Biographical Sketches of the Graduates of Harvard University* (Cambridge, Mass., 1873), 1:228-252.

54. See, for example, Jack P. Greene, "Interpretive Frameworks: The Quest for Intellectual Order in Early American History," *William and Mary Quarterly*, 3d ser., 48(1991):515-530; Cole Harris, "The Simplification of Europe Overseas," *Annals of the Association of American Geographers* 67 (1977): 469-483; Harris, "European Beginnings in the Northwest Atlantic," in David D. Hall and David Grayson Allen, eds., *Seventeenth-Century New England, Publications of the Colonial Society of Massachusetts*, 63:119-152.

55. Samuel Johnson, *Journey to the Western Islands of Scotland*, cited in Bernard Bailyn, "New England and the Wider World," in Hall and Allen, *Seventeenth-Century New England*, 326.

56. For an immediate view of this cultural conflict, see Oliver Morton Dickerson, ed., *Boston Under Military Rule, 1768-69, as revealed in A Journal of the Times* (Boston, 1936).

57. Ned Ward, *A Trip to New England, with a Character of the Country and People*, George Parker Winship, ed. (1699; New York, 1970); *John Dunton's Letters from New England* (1867; New York, 1966); *John Josselyn, Colonial Traveler*, ed. Paul J. Lindholdt (Hanover, N. H., 1988).

58. See David D. Hall, "Declension Politics," in *The Faithful Shepherd*; Foster, *The Long Argument*, 175-230; Hambrick-Stowe, *Practice of Piety*, 242-277; and Robert Pope, *The Halfway Covenant: Church Membership in Puritan New England* (Princeton, 1969).

59. Cotton Mather's *Magnalia Christi Americana* is the most weighty literary example of this more general trend.

60. On the divergence of interests and loss of close connections between New England Puritans and English Dissenters, see Francis Bremer, *Congregational Communion*, 253-256.

61. On Henry Newman and the SPCK, see Leonard W. Cowie, *Henry Newman: An American in London, 1708-1743* (London, 1956). Samuel Newman, first generation Puritan migrant, was the author of the largest and most comprehensive Biblical concordance written in any modern European language until the nineteenth century; see Cotton Mather, "Bibliander Nov-Anglicus, The Life of Samuel Newman," in *Magnalia Christi Americana* (1702; New York, 1972), Book III, 113-116. On the popularity of reforming societies, see Richard P. Gildrie, *The Profane, the Civil, and the Godly: The*

Reformation of Manners in Orthodox New England, 1679-1749 (University Park, Penn., 1994), 202-207.

62. The best account of this relationship is that of Richard F. Lovelace, *The American Pietism of Cotton Mather: Origins of American Evangelicalism* (Grand Rapids, Mich., 1979), but see also Ernst Benz, "The Pietist and Puritan Sources of Early Protestant World Missions (Cotton Mather and A. H. Francke)," *Church History* 20(1951):28-55; Benz, "Ecumenical Relations between Boston Puritanism and German Pietism: Cotton Mather and August Hermann Francke," *Harvard Theological Review* 54(1961):159-193.

63. *Diary of Cotton Mather, Collections of the Massachusetts Historical Society*, 7th ser. 8:23.

64. Cotton Mather, *Nuncia Bona e Terra Longinqua: A Brief Account of Some Good & Great Things a Doing for the Kingdom of God in the Midst of Europe* (Boston, 1715), an edition of which is reprinted along with an edited version of Francke's Latin original, in Kuno Francke, "Further Documents Concerning Cotton Mather and August Hermann Francke," *Americana Germanica*, vol. 1, no. 4(1897):32-66.

65. Cotton Mather, *Nuncia Bona e Terra Longinqua*, in Kuno Francke, "Further Documents," 61-62.

66. On the rise of Halle pietism, its associations with English Puritanism, and its relationship to the Prussian state, see F. Ernest Stoeffler, *The Rise of Evangelical Pietism* (Leiden, 1965); Stoeffler, *German Pietism during the Eighteenth Century* (Leiden, 1973),1-87; Richard L. Gawthorp, *Pietism and the Making of Eighteenth-Century Prussia* (Cambridge, 1993).

The Piety of Practice and the Practice of Piety

Tom Webster

THE INITIAL RESPONSE TO yet another study of piety among English puritans might well be the same sense of satiety verging on revulsion that one feels when the cheeseboard arrives at the end of a prodigious feast. Surely, a sufficient number of eminent writers have dealt with this topic crisply and efficiently long before any of us were born. David Hume covered the field when he described "the most obstinate reformers," having "had leisure to imbibe a stronger tincture of the enthusiastic genius," upon Elizabeth's accession, when "they imported it, in its full force and virulence" into England. The next generation, according to Hume, formed "certain assemblies" where, "as moved by the spirit, they displayed their pious zeal in prayers and exhortations, and raised their own enthusiasm, as well as that of their audience, to the highest pitch, from that social contagion, which has so mighty an influence on holy fervors, and from the mutual emulation which arose in those trials of religious eloquence."[1] In this essay, I will try to work beyond Hume's characterization, partly to show that religious historians have produced new angles of vision in the past 250 years.

In order to open up the puritan piety of John Winthrop's England, I want to explore three general themes. The first may be placed under the banner of "necessary context," which means far more than the laudable desire to trace the socio-economic, cultural, and political environments of puritan piety. The second could be more or less held together under the label of "the importance of language," providing that this is taken in its broadest sense. The third, rather less Delphic, is "how did this happen?"—an effort to return to the godly in their fasts and conferences to ensure that this thesis is strongly "applied." I share Patrick Collinson's concern about the counter-productivity of studies that are solely the "minute examination of inert specimens, pinned out on boards." If any group should be observed "alive and kicking," it is the godly.[2]

I will begin by making it clear what I mean by "necessary context." Puritan piety was structured by a "compare and contrast" approach, drawing both within the individual believer—the internal life—and in terms of the believer's relationship with "external" conditions. Three of the primary "internal" dichotomies were weakness/strength, activity/passivity, and success/suffering. As will appear shortly, these seemingly opposing characteristics have penetrable boundaries, with each side containing the potential of its opposite. The struggles of impotence, inadequacy, and weakness appear in the clergyman John Brinsley's advice for devout Protestants failing to find assurance:

> This therefore is the wisdom and goodnesse of our God, to leave such wants and weaknes in his dearest servants, to beate downe the pride of our hearts . . . and to teach us to give all the glory and promise, both of our justification, and salvation, to him alone in Jesus Christ . . . and that we have

enough, if we be found cloathed in the glorious Robes of his righteousnesse.[3]

To suggest that a recognition of weakness was to lead inexorably to a gift of strength from an external, divine source is not quite the whole story, however. This route was fraught with danger. To leap from such insecurity to confidence was to risk "security," the *image* of strength which all too likely would be revealed as nothing more than a veneer, the mask of a hypocrite. The diarist Ralph Josselin illuminated this path when he noted that "I desire to loath myself, but yet I attain not to an inward spiritual frame."[4] To reach the strength, one embraced the weakness to make space for the strength of the "new man" of Colossians 3.10, often through a reading (and application) of Matthew 16.24.[5] This easily could be achieved through the failure to live up to the Law. As the acclaimed theologian William Perkins saw it, "You are as Gods corne, you must therefore goe under the flaile, the fanne, the milstone, and the oven, before you can be Gods bread."[6] This is more than mere hyperbole. When the preacher John Rogers writes of "the mightie worke of the holy Ghost, whereby a sinner humbled by the Law," is "quite driven out of himselfe," he reiterated the sentiments of another godly minister, Robert Bolton, who stated plainly that "those who would come to Christ . . . must be utterly unbottomed of themselves." As Bolton explained elsewhere, the means of such self-destruction was not internal, but dependent upon "a *mercifull violence*" with which "thou bee pulled out of the world, by the power of the Word, and happily weaned from the sensuall, insensible poison of all bitter-sweete pleasures, and fellowship with the unfruitfull workes of darknesse."[7]

One of the consequences of this "hollowing-out" of the self was a belated recognition of human impotence, of human indebtedness, and, most importantly, of complete dependence upon God. Richard

Sibbes, a renowned writer of practical divinity, made this clear: "We are beholding to God for all the ill that we do not; either it is his not offering occasions, or else his giving us strength in the occasions."[8] This subjection seems, initially, to lay all the emphasis on the passivity of the activity/passivity dichotomy. However, there is also a divinely empowered activity contained within this passivity. As Geoffrey Nuttall noted, "the Puritan movement, in its various phrases, has evinced itself to be a movement towards immediacy in relation to God."[9] One symptom of this immediacy could be found in an active piety with a newly solid foundation. John Preston, Sibbes's friend and colleague, felt confident about the obligation of activity: "If you have faith, use it: many have it, that doe not use it. This is a thing that you are able to do: For though *God* work in you all the worke of faith, as it is received; yet know, he doth not worke in you only but by you; he makes you instruments: . . . to move of your selves."[10] The comfort brought with it a responsibility.

This prescription was so ingrained in the godly *mentalité* that the first element of Sir Robert Harley's "Character" was the desire "to practice what others profess. Is one that dares do nothinge in the wor[ship] of god or course of his life but whatt gods word warra[n]ts hym & dares not leave undone anythinge that that worde co[mman]ds hym."[11] Samuel Clarke's encomium for the ministerial career of Robert Harris rested on proof of his godliness in life rather than in his writing:

> these evidences were best read by others in the course of his life, by his exact walking with God in piety, charity, humility, patience, and dependence upon him. . . . His life was a Commentary upon his Doctrine, and his practice the Counterpane of his Sermons.[12]

The activity consequent upon the formation of the "new man" (if we can forgive the gender specificity of the Holy Ghost) is, so far, rather vague. The more practical consequences, and their concomitant pietistic elements, will emerge when we move to the more "external" dimension. At this point, it remains to integrate the third dichotomy for the "internal" sphere, success/suffering. In this area, the cross-fertilization is particularly important, especially the success to be found within suffering. Various categories of affliction existed, or at least there were various sources of affliction: failure to attain assurance, suffering of abuse, or perceived persecution by external authorities, for instance. On the level of piety, however, without the familiar forms for the pursuit of success within affliction, puritanism would not be the faith that we know. As the preacher Samuel Ward noted, "Zeale comes of a word framed of the very sound and hissing noise, which hot coales or burning iron make when they meet with their contrary." Zeal was two-sided: it produced love, joy, and hope but also used "the contrary of hatred, anger, griefe, &c. As so many mastives [mastiffs] to fly upon the throat of Gods enemies, the Devill, his Angels, Sinne, the world with the lusts thereof."[13] If zeal produced suffering, so much the better, in a sense. Sibbes was convinced that "[t]he more afflictions here, the more comfort here, but especially hereafter."[14] He had a clear confidence both that adversity was inevitable and that it could be successfully, and profitably, weathered. His opening doctrine in a sermon on the acquisition of assurance was that "*God's children are exercised with sharp conflicts in the faith of principles, yea, of God's providence.*" His immediate conclusion, however, was that this "should comfort such as God suffers to cast forth mire and dirt of incredulity. It is the common case of God's children . . . and therefore we ought not to be dejected too much; and the rather because . . . *God's children, though they be thus low, yet shall they recover,* and after recovery comes a triumph."[15] A period of suffering could, indeed, *should* be a period of spiritual growth and strengthening.

The opportunity to grow is at the heart of a way in which puritans found a confidence in adversity, indeed, found a confidence *from* adversity. The confidence was rooted, once again, not in human resolution or strength, but in divine omnipotence. Jeremiah Burroughes, the moderate Congregationalist, was sure that preachers telling their flock that God would provide support would only produce conviction tempered with incredulity. After such experiences, however, "we can say to you that you yourselves have found it so by experience, that God hath made former afflictions to be great benefits to you, . . . such experiences will exceedingly quiet the heart and work it to contentment." Afflictions operated as clear evidence that dependence upon God was reliable. Sibbes captured the spirit in a phrase that was rather more adversarial, a critical element to which I will return, when he stressed that "He suffers his children to meet with oppositions, that they may see they can stand by an almighty power above their own, and above the power of their enemies."[16]

We must move from the "internal" tensions to the "external" ones. I have placed quotation marks around these terms throughout for two reasons. First, the "internal" dichotomies were not, of course, autochthonous to each individual believer. Even the most solitary parts of piety were acquired by a process that was at least partly public, whether through sermons, printed works, or family disciplines (themselves with a public dimension to their dissemination). Second, such "internal" perceptions and activities impinged on public spaces, through the shaping of perceptions of that "external" world (to which we will turn below) and through the matters of activity and parts of the sufferings touched upon above. Similarly permeable boundaries will appear in the treatment of "external" elements, which is the next area to be explored. This is not to downgrade the division to merely a questionable heuristic device. Rather, this interaction existed within a period of the emergent and fragile status of the public/private distinction and represented a necessary condition for puritan piety.[17] The same will be true through explorations of the dichotomies of carnal/pious, pride/humility, and unworthy/(un)worthy.

When we look at the distinction between carnal and pious individuals, drawing attention to the fact that the relationship between the representation and the reality is "not quite fair" is to miss the point. When Robert Bolton categorized the profane, those who could be seen as pious constituted a tiny and almost negligible minority. He rounded up "the usual suspects," but the profane also included "all formall Hypocrites" (compared to "the foolish Virgins, and that proud Pharisee"), "all final back-sliders" prone to become either "sensuall Epicures" or "scurrilous deriders of the holy way," and, most strikingly, "all unsound Professors for the present, of which you would little thinke what a number there is." As he concluded, "let these and all other strangers to the puritie and power of godlinesse be set apart, and tell mee how many true-hearted *Nathaniels* wee are like to find."[18] Bolton's account makes vividly clear the scale of the challenge set out by John Sprint: "Though a corporal separation cannot be had, yet in spirit thou must separate thyself." "We suffer for separating within the Church."[19] The circumstances of spiritual separation within institutional inclusion brought both tests and opportunities.

The matter of representations and perceptions will be explored in a later section, but here it is more pertinent to touch upon the dichotomy of pride/humility. The search for humility is *de rigueur* for the most facile account of puritan piety. Humility's obverse has been comparatively neglected, however, which is surprising since Perkins had declared that "there is no greater enemie to faith than pride."[20] It might cause raised eyebrows to find this dichotomy in the "external" category. Surely the search for humility is an "internal" element. On the contrary, it operated on a comparative level. This is implicit in Robert Bolton's characterization of the properly pious Christian:

> No walking with God, no sweete communion and sound peace at his Mercy-seate, except for his sake, and keeping a good conscience, thou be content to denie thyself, thy worldly wisdome, naturall wit, carnal reason, acceptation with the world, excellencie of learning, favour of great Ones, credit and applause with the most; thy passions, profit, pleasures, preferment, neerest friends, ease, libertie, life, every thing, any thing. And feare no losse; for all things else are nothing to the least comfortable glimpse of God's pleased face.[21]

We might note a hint of selfishness in the conclusion, that one gains more than one loses, or one wins in the long run. The significant point here is the implied, and failing, "other"—the proud worldling, misdirected and failing, more to be pitied than envied. This can be seen in one way in John Bunyan's famous sighting of the godly women of Bedford, his envy producing his humility.[22] In the other direction, it verges on becoming pride for Nathaniel Sparrowhawk, a laymen of Dedham in Essex. His search for humility took him to solitary fasting. He mentioned that "I could walk up and down the room rejoicing in Him and hitting those out of the window that were otherwise engaged."[23]

This dangerous tension between pride and humility is related to the third dichotomy noted above, the system of unworthy/(un)worthy, which draws out the tension more fully. The tension, the public/private element, the superficial problem and its solution are all to be found in a brief prescription of Richard Sibbes: "*Labour to maintain humility, enjoy a sense of thy unworthiness, and wants, and continual dependence on God, and thus humble thyself to walk with him.*"[24] To place unworthy against (un)worthy may appear to be a paradox and certainly requires a little explanation. The first part is plain, expressing the unworthiness of the worldlings, formalists, and hypocrites. The second does not contrast any *inherent* worthiness. One should gain a sense of one's own unworthiness. In doing so, one could conclude that one has worthiness in this recognition, not, however, through something one has *within* one's self, but by a space opened by that evacuation of misconceived worth, space to be occupied by divine empowerment. The public/private factor is a consequence of the recommendation to "*humble thyself to walk with him.*" This was a crucial element in the zeal for the reformation of manners. This is not to suggest that the desire to reform was a puritan monopoly, but that "it was the godly who felt most keenly the need to express their religious calling, to validate their individual spiritual condition in a stream of other-directed works of charity and reform." These sentiments "prompted Puritans. . . to take the lead in the pursuit of the reformation of manners."[25]

Preston traced the route from private to public and back again to private. Good faith leads to love, which sets one on work, concluding that "*we are to be judged not onely by our faith and love, but also by our workes, that no man hath faith and love, that none are new creatures, that none hath sincerity, but workes will follow.*"[26] Thus, public works, as a fruit of faith and love, could act as a reassurance for the troubled saint. "If a man have a treasure within, there will be silver in his speeches and actions; but if his heart be nothing worth, his speeches and actions will be but meere drosse. . . . Therefore let no man say he hath faith and love, and as good a heart as the best, though his actions be not so good, though hee be not so strict in his carriage; for it cannot be my brethren."[27]

Such actions might tend to be divisive (with, of course, the best of intentions). Bolton called upon the saint "to addresse himselfe with resolution, and conscience to discharge this Christian duty of reproving, when a just occasion and a calling thereunto doe require and exact it at his hands." He set forth four reasons and in this context the fourth was the most important. Admonition should be declared "in respect of God Himselfe." In these days, even when "the world is pestered with all the pollutions and abominations," in which "iniquity mightily abound with much tyranny and triumph," in which "Satan, more is the pitty, hath innumerable swarmes of knights of the Post, as they say, at a becke to do him any desperate service," such a reproof would show that "here and there God hath a Champion, who fearlesse in the face of man, dare with an undaunted and holy resolution, defend His wayes, and stand on his side."[28] By implication then, one stood on God's side in matters of social mores, aligning oneself against the profane—likely to be reprobate—and alongside the pious—likely to be the elect.

A theme that has emerged at many points in the preceding analysis, implicitly or explicitly, is of linguistic practice. To put it more broadly, this is a collection of tropes joined under the banner of language, abuses, internalizations, inversions, and perceptions. What I wish to explore further is linguistic positioning, the relationship between perception and reality, the sense of inclusion and exclusion and the place of the "other" and, most importantly, the structuring effects of these tropes upon godly piety.

Initially, this may seem to be old hat. We have all learned to see puritans through their own eyes as "the godly," and to see that when one is accused of being a puritan it "tells us about both halves of a stressful relationship."[29] But I would like to take this insight a little further. In an otherwise splendid and persuasive article on Robert Harley's "Character" of a puritan, Jacqueline Eales concluded that it "strongly suggests that behind the rhetoric and the satire on both sides, there existed a particular strain of godly piety, practice and action which contemporaries would have recognized, and which can usefully be labeled by historians as puritan."[30] I take issue with the phrase "behind the rhetoric and satire," which misses the point. Looking for an "essence" of a puritan that exists outside of language ignores the importance of the relationship between language and the structuring of reality. This is not to suggest, I hasten to add, that "reality" does not exist, merely that the language that is available lays down the parameters of experience. One works within these limits. One can test their boundaries and they may, and do, change; but this merely changes the limits. One cannot operate beyond the limits of language. The available language structures perceptions and thereby reality; there is no perception of reality that is "free" from language, that is "culture-free."[31]

That this quasi-philosophical stance has utilitarian value will become more evident if we return to the issue of suffering. The various categories of affliction touched upon above, need a closer examination. On the wider scale, there were enemies to godliness on the international level, be they Spanish, Papist, Turkish, or Islamic; or, more specifically, the forces drawn up against Frederick, James VI & I's son-in-law, in the Thirty Years War despite the difficulty of establishing a clear "Catholic versus Protestant" line between those conflicting forces.[32] On an ostensibly individual level, a discontented member of their community or of the ecclesiastical courts often hurled abuse at puritan men and women. The description of such as "ostensibly individual" is crucial. If such people were labeled "puritan" or any equivalent term and one saw oneself as sharing substantial amounts of common ground with such "persecuted" people, one would feel part of a persecuted community. When Samuel Rogers, an insignificant young chaplain in Bishops Stortford, heard of Matthew Wren's rigorous visitation of the diocese of Norwich in 1636, he made the following note in his diary:

A deep sadnes hath taken hold on mee [from] many motives; 1. the church of god held under hatches, the walls of Jerusalem beaten downe; pore suffolke and northfolke lying desolate by that cursed wretch wren; the plauge abroad; 2. this wofull place; in whose companyes I am afraid to be for feare of some evell speech.[33]

This fear, anxiety, and sadness was no less because Rogers had not been touched by the visitation. "His" company had been, as he saw it, ravished, and remained under threat. Through his vicarious suffering, Rogers felt himself to be under threat.

Such a position becomes more readily comprehensible if we turn to the means of comfort broadcast from godly pulpits. Verbal abuse could be turned into a positive experience, almost to a sign of regeneracy, either through acceptance or inversion. When the MP Bulstrode Whitelock wrote of his mother, who was criticized "for being too much of the persuasion of the Puritane," he concluded positively: "Certainly she feared God truely, and if that be to be a Puritan, she was so."[34] According to his contemporary minister John Brinsley, "Wee shall stop the mouthes of all the wicked, when we may beare the reproach as a crown, and so have much boldnesse in the day of triall, to stand forth for any good cause."[35] Bolton emphasized the point explicitly by describing those delivering the abuse as "the children of darknesse," the recipients as the "children of light," and comforted the recipients by showing them how to turn such abuse to their own advantage. "Let every one, who in sinceritie of heart seekes to bee saved, ever hold it a speciall happinesse and his hi[gh]est honor to be singled out from the universall pestilent contagion of common prophaneness, and the sinful courses of the greatest part; and to be censured as singular in that respect." If, by "all sorts of unregenerate men, thou art hunted for thy holiness as a Partridge on the mountains, at least by the poison and persecution of the tongue; I say, then thou are certainely in the hie way to Heaven."[36]

This brings us to the necessity of a perceived "other," the desire to have one to hate or pity, perhaps to be threatened by; and a sense of "us" and "them," a source of comparison that works to the benefit of "us." Bolton reassured his readers that to persecute believers "is a certain mark [that] thou are a limb of Satan."[37] The apologetic testimony of John Johnson in the Star Chamber, where he claimed that the name of brother was limited to those who were of "their own faction and opinion," affirms the practice and promotion of this trait.[38] It could only be exacerbated by advice warning against worldly friends and commending godly supporters: one should depend upon "godly men, for they will proove our surest friends. Vicinitie and neighbourhood will faile, and alliance and kindred will faile, but grace and religion will never faile."[39] Sibbes made some of the advantages fairly clear: "Oh, it is a notable signe of a spiritual heart to seek spiritual company; for when their hearts join together, they warm one another, and are hereby guarded from temptations."[40] Comfort from like-minded friends could intensify the sense of "us" and "them."

We will move on to the "application" of such calls below, but the primary point to be noted here is the way in which the addressees are referred to as "us," particularly when this "us" is set against "carnal" men and "the wicked." The experience of such a division by the church within a church required very sharply drawn lines. Sibbes characterized the profane with very little charity:

> There is a mixture in the Church (as in a house) of good and bad vessels, but the godly are especially God's house. As for hypocrites and false professors, they are no more in the house, than the excrements are in the body; they are in the body, but

not *of* the body, and therefore as Ishmael they must be cast out at length.[41]

The greatest extent to which this inversion can be seen is in the willingness of believers to adopt the label "puritan." Thomas Scott, the MP for Canterbury, was prepared to accept the term in the 1620s, which was, according to Richard Cust, a view of contemporary politics characterized by "division and polarization."[42] In Harley's "Character" he not only accepted the nomenclature of "puritan" but used it to invert the accusation of unlawfulness and a tendency to promote disorder: "To thinges Indifferent he thinkes hym self not borne a bondeman & wonders why He is stilled [styled] a man of disorder when he is so wiling to obey all law com[m]ands."[43] When Samuel Ward embraced the word, he moved on to describe such puritans in Petrine terms with quite a congratulatory tone:

> But with that which most call Puritanisme, I desire to worship God. For singularity, Christ calls for it, and presseth and urgeth it; What singular thing doe you; or what odd thing doe you; shall God's peculiar people doe nothing peculiar? . . . Judge you which of these men shall please: I beleeve none shall ever please Christ, till they appear odde, strange, and precise men to the common sort.[44]

This rhetoric might be described as the "Queer Nation" strategy, where one takes a pejorative term and adopts it, thus disempowering the abuse, indeed, turning the insult into an unintended compliment. It is a possibility worth investigating that the strategy is most frequently employed during periods of persecution or marginalization, be they Whitgiftian, Bancroftian, or Laudian.[45] In any case, "Puritan" was not the most extreme way of striking back. Without any note to suggest that the word was meant in the broad, inclusive sense, Ward adopted "Christian" to describe the godly. Similarly, Bolton could shift quietly from "the saints" to "understanding men" coming to a climax with "christians."[46]

The extremes of devotional treatises should not be taken to denote linguistic practice wholly separated from "reality." Alongside such rhetoric lay a "genuine" ability, or a confidence in such an ability, to differentiate between the godly and the profane. In response to those who poured scorn on such a capacity, the famous Congregationalist Thomas Goodwin responded with conviction, claiming that "there are many rules in the Word it is meet to judge who are saints. . . . It is not a profession of faith joined with morality, and no great scandal, but a profession of faith of such a strictness that will rise to holiness, that you are to judge men saints by."[47] As Peter Lake has stated, what "marked out puritans was the seriousness with which they took entirely orthodox notions of election and reprobation and applied them to their own lives and experience. In their drive to externalize, express and validate their status as elect vessels of God they were led into certain devotional activities and exercises and into a distinctive preciseness or scrupulosity about their own and other peoples' moral conduct."[48]

This is not to say, however, that the two are separate, that there is an "untampered-with reality" underneath the linguistic practice. Perception/reality is never an either/or option; the two are always interrelated and necessarily so. It is only helpful on one level to seek to remove the "crust" of perceived experience to grasp at the "reality." Once one has been armed with ways of looking at the world, one is more likely to find things; this is a reciprocal relationship with the one reinforcing the other.[49] To exclude the perceptions and self-perceptions from an account of puritan piety would stop us from understanding the sense of urgency, the passion, and the requirements of responsibility on the part of the godly. Without this system, the harshness of puritan defense mechanisms would be less comprehensible. Bearing in mind the tendency for inversion, this makes more sense: puritans were castigated for popularism, disorder, disloyalty, and so forth–they became scapegoats for so much–but such castigations failed by feeding into inversion. As the contemporary songwriter Elvis Costello observed, "even a scapegoat must have someone to hate."[50] Feeling a part of a tiny minority standing "on God's side," one assumes a huge responsibility to reform "the other" and to maintain one's suitability as an elect vessel of God.

We are coming to appreciate some crucial elements that fed into puritan piety, to different degrees at different times and different places. We must first understand that a siege mentality dominated the puritan world-view, with dangers and threats on every side, on various scales and experienced on communal and individual levels. This element existed in a reciprocal relationship with puritan piety. As stability and success were much sought-after, they also could be unattainable in terms of piety. While John Brinsley offered the saints comfort in times of anxiety by drawing attention to the ways in which God's love exceeded that of human parents, he also promised the favor of the Lord "so long onely as thou makest conscience, thus to walke with thy God in all his Commandements, as his obedient child, and doest steadfastly purpose so to continue all thy dayes, thou mayest be assured of his love, as of thy tender Father."[51] As Richard Greenham, an Elizabethan minister renowned for his pastoral care, demanded, "every day must have a dayes increase in godlinesse."[52]

Secondly, puritans lived in a world of "compare and contrast." When considering the heterogeneous field of the unregenerate, particularly the hypocrites among the godly, one could never, should never, escape the literal sense of "there but for the grace of God go I." The tension, and anxious sense of good fortune, served as a constant reminder of one's dependence upon God—and therefore of humility—and also a sign that one was among the godly. At different times and places, puritans might have a growing prevalence, but it must be asked whether dominance, or undisputed dominance, was ever possible, indeed desirable.[53] If in any community such success should come to pass, we might conclude that "it *is* puritanism, Jim, but not as we know it." Even with such dominance, puritanism would still need constant maintenance. The puritan, and puritanism in the broader sense, remained context-dependent, fluid, contingent, and inherently unstable. The question of spiritual and social success—who holds which place in a community, who lives with and through which labels, who has the power—always awaited return of the jury. Puritanism *had to be* contingent, or put in more positive terms, puritan piety depended upon a series of dynamic relationships, between the saint and God, between the saint and the formalists *et al*, between the saint and the saints, and between the saint and her/his self.

Building upon questions of identity, the godly faced two conflicting models of self. The first, acquired directly or mediated through sermons and so on, threatened the impossibility of keeping a stable self through time.[54] The second, admirable but intimidatingly difficult to attain, was the stable self, drawing upon endless Foxeian examples with which the godly would be all too familiar. A narrative represented the means for maintaining this "discordant concordance." One would have to write a story about oneself, sometimes literally so, crafted without complete control and necessarily constructed in conjunction with other people's stories, both *about* the individual saint and others.[55] Such stories floated in constant negotiation, always in danger of taking a wrong turn and linked to the notion of "tradition" on both an individual and communal level. By tradition I mean the pre-structured version of the past into which one is received by the community of saints and which limits one's horizons of expectation in the present. Thus, no present selves can be completely innovative, one is merely an heir to an established tradition, an heir to presumed truths. A tradition, however, is a combination of sedimentation and innovation. The tradition received is the product of generations of presumed truths (taken-for-granted statements) which limit horizons of expectation, but do not determine their focal point. Each generation has an opportunity of innovation, albeit limited. Traditions need not be received passively; indeed, passivity represents an action, a choice.[56] The idea of a puritan "resting easy" is a contradiction in terms. Puritan piety, by definition, always existed in these fragile, changeable, and changing relationships.

This dynamism became both sharper and more manageable with the rise of covenant theology at the end of the sixteenth and the start of the seventeenth centuries.[57] The ambiguities of covenant in scripture helped to promote ambiguities within the divinity, which, in turn, enhanced the tensions within puritan piety. The theology drew out two forms of covenant. The first viewed the covenant as a contract, a bargain, in which God and the saved had reciprocal duties. The duties of the saved included self-denial and a life devoted to worship, be it individual, communal, or reformatory in the sense of improving society. The demands of the reciprocal covenant were balanced by a purely theocentric covenant. God might expect the best efforts of covenanted humans, while recognizing that perfection lay beyond the means of humans. Ultimately, the second covenant stressed the impotence of creatures and their dependence upon God. The covenant of grace was, as John von Rohr has shown, conditional and absolute *at the same time*.[58] After inevitable human failure, the godly could turn to John Preston's reassurance of theonomy: "If thou art in covenant with God . . . then thy election is sure; and be sure that God will never alter it, for his is unchangeable."[59] Thus we have, at a theological level, the combination of activity and passivity, confidence

The Piety of Practice and the Practice of Piety

and (profitable) anxiety, that has recurred at various points in this account of puritan piety.

Moving from the individual to the intra-social dimension of saintly communities, we find the enactment of social covenanting parallel to, and probably imitative of, the individual covenant between God and the saint. Their semi-formal and voluntary nature possibly allows us only to view the tip of the puritan iceberg. Some can be found in London, Worksop, Dorchester, and Boston for instance. Perhaps the most substantial is the 13,000 word covenant subscribed by around twenty parishioners in Wethersfield, intended as an aid "for the continuance of love, and for the edifying of one another," and as a means "to turn to the Lord in all sincerity." Richard Rogers left an account, presumably for evangelical purposes, in his devotional treatise,[60] and it certainly proved successful in encouraging an obscure Suffolk gentleman by the name of John Winthrop to renew his personal and social covenants.[61] As John Cotton told his fellow minister Samuel Skelton, "in some congregations in England the ministers and all the professors among the people have entered into such a covenant to yield professed subjection to the gospel of Christ, so far as they conceive Christ requireth of them in their places in these times."[62]

It is not, however, wholly accurate to refer to such undertakings as purely intra-social. The Wethersfield covenant made it plain that its subscribers were no Brownists—that they were merely devout members of the Church of England. The necessity of "the other" appears more clearly in Samuel Ward's call for a similarly intense commitment. He opened by saying that "I hope the Lord hath his fifties amongst us, though but thin sowne in comparison of the swarmes of professed Recusants, and Church-Papists, of prophane Atheists, key-cold Worldlings, and luke-warme Professors." Then he turned to abuse from the other side, as it were, the Brownists, who accused puritans of resembling "the prophet Hosea his Cake [Hosea 7.8], halfebaked upon the hearth, having one side, that is the outside to the world-ward, in publicke service, scorched a little and browned over; but the inside to God-ward, in private and family duties, no better than dough." The first thing to stress, therefore, is the necessity of the "external," be it critic or ne'er-do-well. The second dimension, touched upon above, is whether such intensifications of "us" and "them" were more common at times of crisis or extraordinary pressure. The Wethersfield covenant was drawn up in 1588 and when Ward came to the conclusion of his Jeremiad he asked "how then should we please the stomache of God? Who hath indeed brooked and borne us a long time, I doubt but wamblingly. How near were wee going in 88, and in the Powder treason?"[63]

More positively, we should see the practices of puritan piety caught in a web of perceptions and tensions, with the strains and emphases differing according to time, place, and socio-political conditions. Puritanism represented a form of habitual contingency, if you will forgive the paradox, operating at the individual and intra-social level. The godly always kept an eye on the chaotic, disorderly, profane world, a world which they sought to differentiate themselves from and extend their influence over. It was, in the broadest terms, what Jerald Brauer has called "a profound existential affirmation of a special way in which human beings are oriented in their cosmos."[64]

There has been, so far, a great deal of reflection that could be described as detached from "real experience," a supreme irony given that I have insisted upon the impossibility of a context-free account of puritan piety. It is necessary, and I hope profitable, to give some space to bringing this analysis down to earth—to give some account of how one came to be positioned in such piety. I will move from the isolated, solitary practices of piety through those of the "community of saints,"

and on to the public dimension, both in terms of worship and in terms of the reformation of manners. However, one must keep in mind that the public/private distinction is somewhat artificial, more a boundary to be transgressed than to be observed.[65]

Solitary piety was, for the godly, the most dangerous circumstance. As Sibbes warned, "the strongest enemy is in our own bosom." Therefore, "we should be watchful over ourselves when we are alone, for every man cannot use privacy well. . . . Oh, when we are sequestered from others, our thoughts are a fit shop for the devil. Take heed, therefore, of privacy and idleness."[66] Self-examination lay at the heart of solitary piety: by "a serious examination of a man's own estate, he may know whether he hath faith or not, whether there be a work of grace upon his head or not."[67] Such introspection, rigorously practiced, could lead to assurance but only via humility. According to John Preston, "the more empty the soule is, the more a man is humbled, the more he sees into himselfe (as faith come with an empty hand) the faster hold is taken on CHRIST." "And take this withall, Humiliation doth not weaken assurance, but workes the contrary: Indeed, the less sincerity, and the less mourning for sin, and the less Humiliation, the less assurance. . . . Therefore a man should make a daily practice of Humiliation, for it is to a man's great advantage, it is a thing too much omitted, we should take time for it."[68] This could lead to a total renunciation of the self. The preacher Thomas Taylor demanded that "all selfe-respects, selfe-seeking, selfe-aymes, must be renounced and the Christian wholly vanish into nothing," leaving the saint, as his friend and colleague Arthur Hildersham hoped, "resting onely upon the free grace of God in Christ."[69]

The means for reaching such a haven (and limitations of literacy have to be borne in mind) were fourfold. Prayer assumed the primary position, partly to lead one toward humility, but also as a form of daily preparation, to help one to "put on the armour of light" (Rom. 13.12), often before one rose in the morning.[70] Lady Brilliana Harley told her son that "Experimentally, I might say that privet prayer is one of the beest means to keepe the harts of our God, as to a frinde."[71] There was also the broader sense of meditation, often appraising one's conduct through each day in the evening, "shutting up the Day in *Examination*, and viewing it over," "to peruse and *examine* the several parts of my *Life every Evening*, how this course hath been kept of me, where it hath to keep it still, where it hath not, to seek pardon and recovery."[72] In addition, one might spend time reading, either Scripture itself, Foxe's *Book of Martyrs*, or works of practical divinity. (The Geneva Bible, of course, protected the reader from misunderstanding or misapplication with its prodigious marginal notes.) The scale of this reading could be considerable. Ignatius Jordan, the magistrate of Exeter, read the whole Bible twenty times over, marking the "highlights" with asterisks, completed Foxe seven times, and relished Richard Rogers' *Seven Treatises* "and other practical books," making voluminous notes upon them.[73] Finally, one could bring these disciplines together by keeping a diary. A written record established distance between oneself and one's critical acumen by creating a material site for one's present experience and one's past and a vital aid to one's self-assessment. These various disciplines could all come together in the diary. Isaac Ambrose set his personal experiences in one column of his diary, Biblical texts that placed him in a teleology of grace in the next, and textual uses in a third, thus integrating his self wholly in Scripture.[74]

A multitude of fruits could be found at the intra-social level. The company of the godly could provide comfort to embattled saints: "though thou shouldst come amongst the Saints with a sad heart . . . yet the presence and faces of those, whom hereafter thou shalt meete in Heaven . . . should disperse and dispell them all, and infuse comfortable beames of heavenly lightsomenesse and spiritual mirth."[75] How one was regarded in such circles could, in itself, prove to be reas-

The Piety of Practice and the Practice of Piety

suring. To return to the obscure Suffolk gentleman, when Winthrop sought the approval of his worldly contemporaries he felt a disregard for the "society of the saints." When he fought against excessive concern for having "an ill name with the most where I live," he concluded that "I will say with Paul, I pass not for man's judgement. . . . Walk with God, and never fear but thou shalt be honoured by the godly."[76] Samuel Rogers noted that he was "sweetly touched by Mr Marshalls sermon but readye to drop againe, I have need of continuall underpropings to hold up my tottering soule."[77]

A godly company meant far more than mere personal utility. The preacher Robert Some outlined a Christian's duties, concluding that one must "walk in newness of life" and always recall that "a principal branch whereof is to be unity with the godly."[78] Sibbes pointed out the reciprocal benefits: "so for company, by which we may either do good or receive good; for that is a great help to our watch—company—for one strengthens another, as stones in an arch."[79] One's success in this field could be used as evidence, almost as a requisite, of loving God. "It is a hundred times more easie to love godlinesse in the Saints, than in *God* himselfe, because he is remote farre from us, and they are amongst us, and are visibly seene."[80]

The piety of the godly working together was more than the sum of the parts. Nicholas Bownd saw it as "a great many of firebrands layde together, in which though there be some heate when they are apart by themselves, yet being layd together, it is doubled, and otherwise everyone would dye of itselfe."[81] William Gouge imagined the union of saints in the most divine terms:

> And because worship is done to God, not onely in materiall Temples, but also in the communion of Saints, yea and in the bodies and soules of particular Christians, they are also called *Gods Houses*.[82]

This perceived power of saintly union is pertinent to the public/private distinction. We are familiar with this tension through the meanings of the conventicle,[83] but the distinction is transgressed from another angle, too. Puritans who came together for private rituals of piety could turn such acts to public ends. For instance, Sir Robert Harley's fasts intended to seek God's help for: ministers harassed by the ecclesiastical courts, the Feoffees for Impropriation, the state of Protestantism in Europe, the prospect of a parliament, and the suppression of Popery and Arminianism at home.[84] Similarly, Robert Bolton attributed the failure of the Spanish Match to the fervent fasting and prayer of the godly.[85] At its most extreme, godly fasting received credit for the death of Samuel Harsnet as he traveled north to become Archbishop of York.[86] Private pieties could have very public consequences.

When we turn to the category of "public piety" one might assume that many of the ambiguities and linkages that have been a recurrent theme might, at least, diminish if not disappear. To an extent, they do. At the same time, it should come as no surprise that this is not the whole story. To begin with, it must be made clear that I define "public piety" in its broadest sense. This includes, of course, public worship and devotional duties enacted within the parish church, but it also includes the pieties contained within the idea of "the reformation of manners." I will start with the tight definition of public worship and move outwards, drawing attention to connecting themes and relationships which act as a matrix within which to locate puritan piety.

To open with an assertion that sermons were a central element to puritan public piety is platitudinous, but also true. Thomas Taylor stated that the "preaching of the word is the greatest blessing that the Lord bestoweth upon any people." John Rogers called upon ministers to "Preach Christ Crucified in a Crucified Phrase." There "is no more weighty part of any Minister's duty," Rogers proclaimed, "no none more like unto it, than to Preach the word of God." Through the sermon, they won the approval of the godly.[87]

The sermon was not, of course, the be-all and end-all of godly worship. We should not ignore the Eucharist, and here again we can allow John Rogers to speak for many. For him, "The Word and Sacraments be the two breasts of the Church."[88] The sacrament of the Lord's Supper could be "a gracious and speciall meanes for the increase of our assurance."[89] John Preston emphasized the empowering effects of the rite, promising that if one was a good communicant, "thou wouldst be strengthened to do all things, thou wouldst find thy heart able to doe this, thou shouldst find a change in thy heart, that thou wouldst doe it without difficulty, thou wouldst finde thy selfe turned and changed, thou wouldst have new affections, and a new life."[90] A principle gain of the godly piety regarding communion was exactly that, the *koinōnia*, the spirit of unity and the bond of love among the communicants, the universal communion of Christians with Christ, and with one another in Christ. Thomas Goodwin looked for "a communion, the highest outward pledge, ratification and testimony of love and amity among his members themselves . . . a love-feast, in that they eat and drink together at one and the same table."[91] After one particularly fruitful Eucharist, Samuel Rogers found his greatest help in a renewed sense of godly society:

> Saboth; and sacrament at [St Stephen's] Coleman [Street]: broken to peices with joy; drunk with comfort; this is a day of rejoicing, and strength; for the joy of the L[or]d, hath bin my strength; A sweet communion of Saints, at mr Roules his house at dinner; a sweet refreshing at mr Simonds; one of a most sweet, godly spirit; and now I lye downe with praises.[92]

Such joy was hard-earned. A rigorous preparation by self-examination was required to find if one had "a competent measure of Repentance, Knowledge, faith and Love."[93] Humility lay at the heart of the experience. "The sense of unworthinesse is our worthinesse; A little vessell that is empty, will receive more than a great one that is full; A broken Christ requires a broken heart."[94] It is worth noting the appearance of the adoption of Canticles as a source of humility regardless of gender. Thomas Brooks made the point with clarity:

> In this sacrament Christ comes forth and shews his love, his heart, his bowels, his blood, that his children may no longer say, Doth the Lord Jesus love me? Doth he delight in us? &c.; but that they may say with the spouse, "I am my beloved's, and his desire is towards me." Solomon's Song 7.10.[95]

We should, however, avoid getting swept away in too great a sense of a "group hug." The sense of worthy communicants could only be acquired through a rigorous exclusion of the "unworthy" that extended well beyond the beginning and end of the service. One set of parishioners was called before the ecclesiastical courts for refusing to take communion with their own minister, wanting to receive "with Mr Gifford, vicar of Maldon," a neighboring parish.[96] Perhaps the crucial word in this testimony is "with," that is, searching for a proper sense of exclusive unity with the godly. Additionally, we should not underestimate the consequences of dispensing communion to the unworthy. Preston warned his auditors that "if you be unworthy receivers, you cannot do your selves a worse turne, than to offer to come to the sacrament without faith, to provoke *God* more, *to eate and drinke your owne damnation*. . . . Know that thou hast had warning given thee, that thou receivest unworthily and art *guilty of the body and blood of Christ*; that is, thou commitest such a sin as those did that killed

Christ."⁹⁷ Two Northamptonshire ministers, John Barry and Anthony Stackhouse, wanted to exclude one parishioner with a reported "appetite for incontinence." In another case, Barry so doggedly refused to admit a communicant with an inadequate understanding of the ritual that he canceled one communion altogether.⁹⁸

Mentioning the extension of (self-)examination before the communion (which could extend to over a week before the service) draws attention to the permeability of the line between the divine service and the wider world. Such permeability also applies to other areas. For the godly, traveling to the service of a neighboring godly minister could, in itself, constitute an act of piety. The journey, spent singing psalms or simply talking, reinforced the sense of kinship among the puritans. Samuel Rogers often found himself "refreshed with the societye of the faithfull," "delivered in journye," or he would note that "our good discourse in the journye was that which most refreshed mee."⁹⁹ The same could be said for the journey home, or for the examinations, discussions, even repetitions of the sermons in conventicles in the afternoon. This "boundary stretching" also extends to the "reformation of manners." In addition to the predictable sermons invoking a sense of godly charity and personal reformation, the godly in a parish (where they held the reins of governance) might decide that "warning shall be give in the church the next Sabbath to the parish" concerning unwanted immigrants, or to ask the minister to make declarations concerning poor relief or moral disciplinary matters.¹⁰⁰

To move on to the reformation of manners in an account of puritan piety might, initially, seem strange, but we need to touch upon the ambiguities within the term. "Reformation" could mean improvement (at least from a godly perspective), as in providing funds for the establishment of lectures in a parish or for godly education. It could also mean the establishment of programs to assist the disadvantaged. A minister "with two or three of the auncients of the towne . . . do visitt the poore and chiefly the suspected places, theat understandinge the miserable estate of those yt wante and the naughtie disposition of disordered persons, they may provide for them accordinglie."[101] The term "manners" possesses a similar ambiguity when it applies to changing the ways things are done, whether they be the recreational activities of others (the profane) on the Sabbath, the "merry English" repertoire, or the practice of divine worship and the habits of the godly. There is a constant tension here between the voluntary and the involuntary, the embraced and the imposed. Understood in this way, the reformation of manners further contributes to the fragmentation of the public/private division.[102]

Where has this peregrination through the nodes of English puritan piety taken us? It has taken us across the period between 1590 and 1640, which Henry Parker described as dominated by "the ethical puritans." During this era, according to Patrick Collinson, "puritan piety became progressively an interior matter," and Parker claimed that "the most ordinary badge of puritans is their more religious and conscionable conversation than that which is seen in other men."[103] Parker could be accused of being disingenuous and Collinson, in this particular phrase, of not telling the whole story. Puritan piety could rarely, if ever, exist as a quiet, introverted faith, or at least not safely so. It existed through and depended upon a series of tensions and practices, negotiated through an experience of "us" and "them," good and bad relations, public and private, inside and outside, self and other, with each component feeding into and off of its partner.

The ultimate dichotomy of the elect and reprobate and the tendency to dichotomize within seventeenth-century English discourse underpinned puritanism. These variably elastic tensions contributed to the inherent difficulties of constantly maintaining a church within a Church and heightening our awareness of the pros and cons of the "spectrum" model for English Protestantism. There was much common ground within the broad spectrum of Protestantism that the godly could locate themselves, but such a place was negotiated within an omniscient sense of "us" and "them." Moreover, this negotiation never could be wholly quiescent. A constant sense of threat, both internal and external, coursed through the community of saints. As Nathaniel Ward observed, "The Kingdome of Satan finds instruments inough in such as crowd fast inough for advantages ag[ain]st Xt [Christ] and the truth."[104] The words laid before the Long Parliament by Stephen Marshall might also apply to historians of this field: "Many *great things* are yet to be done; much rubbish to be removed; many obstacles to be cleared."[105]

Endnotes

1. David Hume, *The History of Great Britain: The Reign of James I and Charles I*, ed. Duncan Forbes (1754; Harmondsworth, Eng., 1970), 73, 76.
2. Patrick Collinson, *The Puritan Character: Polemics and Polarities in Early Seventeenth-Century Culture* (Los Angeles, 1987), 16.
3. John Brinsley, *The True Watch and Rule of Life* (London, 1637), 180-181.
4. Alan Macfarlane, ed., *The Diary of Ralph Josselin, 1616-1683* (London, 1976), 348; see also, Collinson, *Puritan Character*, 11.
5. Matt. 16.24: "Then said Jesus unto his disciples, If any man will come after me, let him deny himself, and take up his cross, and follow me."
6. William Perkins, "A Treatise of Tending unto a Declaration, Whether a Man be in the Estate of Damnation or in the Estate of Grace," *Workes* (London, 1631), 2: 410, 419.
7. John Rogers, *Doctrine of Faith* (London, 1627), "Epistle to the Reader"; Robert Bolton, *Instructions for a Right Comforting Afflicted Consciences with Antidotes Against Some Grievous Temptations* (London, 1631), 210; Bolton, *Some*

Generall Directions for a Comfortable Walking with God (London, 1630), 6, emphasis added.

8. Richard Sibbes, "The Beast's Domination over Earthly Kings," *Works*, ed. A. B. Grosart (Edinburgh, 1826-1864), 7:526.

9. Geoffrey F. Nuttall, *The Holy Spirit in Puritan Faith and Experience* (Chicago, 1992), 134.

10. John Preston, *The Breast Plate of Faith and Love*, 5th ed. (London, 1634), 1st pagination, 239.

11. Jacqueline Eales, "Sir Robert Harley, K.B., (1579-1656) and the 'Character' of a Puritan," *British Library Journal* 15(1989):150. I have omitted the erasures that Dr. Eales noted in her transcription.

12. Samuel Clarke, *A Collection of the Lives of Ten Eminent Divines* (London, 1662), 303.

13. Samuel Ward, "A Coale from the Altar to Kindle the Holy Fire of Zeal," in Ward, *A Collection of Sermons and Treatises as Have Beene Written* (London, 1636), 236, 238; see also, Patrick Collinson, "Towards a Broader Understanding of the Early Dissenting Tradition," in Collinson, *Godly People* (London, 1983), 547.

14. Sibbes, "The Glorious Feast of the Gospel," *Works*, 2:484.

15. Sibbes, "The Saints Happiness," *Works*, 7:67.

16. Jeremiah Burroughes, *The Rare Jewel of Christian Contentment* (1655; London, 1840), 79; Sibbes, "The Saints Happiness," 67.

17. An interesting engagement from an unfamiliar angle can be found in Matthew Johnson, *An Archaeology of Capitalism* (Oxford, 1996), 160-166. See also J. Brewer, "'This, That and the Other': Public, Social and Private in the Seventeenth and Eighteenth Centuries," esp., 8-9, where he shows a good deal of interpenetration and an unstable, shifting boundary between the two "as if public and private are shifting territories on a map," and J. Barry, "A Historical Postscript," both in Dario Castiglione and Lesley Sharpe, eds., *Shifting the Boundaries: Transformation of the Languages of Public and Private in the Eighteenth Century* (Exeter, Eng., 1995); A. Vickery, "Golden Age to Separate Spheres? A review of the Categories and Chronologies of English Women's History," *Historical Journal* 36(1993):383-414; Robert B. Shoemaker, *Gender in English Society 1650-1850: The Emergence of Separate Spheres* (London, 1998).

18. Bolton, *General Directions*, 4-5. The reality of these tensions is one of the main lessons gained from Peter Lake, *The Boxmaker's Revenge: "Orthodoxy,"*

"Heterodoxy," and the Politics of the Parish in Early Stuart London (Manchester, Eng., 2000).

19. John Sprint, as quoted in Henry Ainsworth, *Counterpoyson* (Amsterdam, 1608), Sig. A, cited in Patrick Collinson, "Sects and the Evolution of Puritanism," in Francis J. Bremer, ed., *Puritanism: Transatlantic Perspectives on a Seventeenth-Century Anglo-American Faith* (Boston, 1993), 158; see also, Collinson, "The Cohabitation of the Faithful and the Unfaithful," in O. P. Grell, J. I. Israel, and N. Tyacke, eds., *From Persecution to Toleration: The Glorious Revolution and Religion* (Oxford, 1991), 51-76.

20. Perkins, "Estate of Damnation," 419.

21. Bolton, *General Directions*, 52.

22. John Bunyan, *Grace Abounding to the Chief of Sinners*, ed. W. R. Owen (Harmondsworth, Eng., 1987), 14.

23. G. Selement and B. Wooley, eds., *Thomas Shepard's Confessions, Publications of the Colonial Society of Massachusetts* 58(1981):63.

24. Sibbes, "The Saints Happiness," 75.

25. Peter Lake, "Defining Puritanism—Again?" in Bremer, ed., *Puritanism*, 11-12.

26. Preston, *Breast Plate*, 2nd pagination, 212.

27. Preston, *Breast Plate*, 2nd pagination, 213.

28. Bolton, *General Directions*, 120-125.

29. Collinson, *Puritan Character*, 19; see also Peter Lake, "Matthew Hutton: A Puritan Bishop?" *History* 44(1979):182-204.

30. Eales, "Sir Robert Harley," 149.

31. See Collinson, *Puritan Character*, 21-22, 23, 25-26, and also Collinson, "Ben Johnson's *Bartholomew Fair*: The Theatre Constructs Puritanism," in David L. Smith, Richard Strier, and David Bevingtron, eds., *The Theatrical City: Culture, Theatre and Politics in London, 1579-1649* (Cambridge, 1995), 157-169; Collinson, "Ecclesiastical Vitriol: Religious Satire in the 1590s and the Invention of Puritanism," in J. Guy, ed., *The Reign of Elizabeth I: Court and Culture in the Last Decade* (Cambridge, 1995). This is not to suggest that these pieces endorse my view, but rather move in this direction.

32. See Thomas Cogswell, *The Blessed Revolution: English Politics and the Coming of War, 1621-1624* (Cambridge, 1989) and Peter Lake, "Constitutional Consensus and Puritan Opposition in the 1620s: Thomas Scott and the Spanish Match," *Historical Journal* 25(1982).

33. Tom Webster and Kenneth Shipps, eds, *The Diary of Samuel Rogers, 1634-38*, Church of England Record Society 10 (Woodbridge, Eng., 2003), 84.
34. B[ritish] L[ibrary], Additional Manuscripts 53726, f 59r.
35. John Brinsley, *The True Watch*, 1st pagination, 28.
36. Bolton, *General Directions*, 6, 7, 8.
37. Bolton, *A Cordiall for a Fainting Christian* (London, 1644), 10.
38. P[ublic] R[ecord] O[ffice], Star Chamber 5 A 49/34, depositions of John Johnson and Thomas Edmunds, quoted in Collinson, *English Puritanism* (London, 1983), 19.
39. John Dod and Robert Cleaver, *A Plain and Familiar Exposition of the Thirteenth and Fourteenth Chapters of the Proverbs of Salomon* (London, 1609), 199.
40. Sibbes, "The Saints Happiness," 73.
41. Richard Sibbes, *The Saints Cordialls* (London, 1637), 215; for a broader treatment, see Collinson, "The Cohabitation of the Faithful."
42. Richard Cust, *The Forced Loan and English Politics, 1626-1628* (Oxford, 1987), 177.
43. Eales, "Sir Robert Harley," 150.
44. Ward, "A Coal from the Altar," 269-270; a "peculiar people" is from 1 Peter 2.9. It might prove worthwhile to trace the uses and frequency of Petrine influence in godly portrayals of the world and the saints' relation to it, not least to balance the emphasis on Pauline influence.
45. See also Collinson, "Comment: Concerning the Name Puritan," *Journal of Ecclesiastical History* 31(1980), passim, esp. 487-488.
46. For instance, Ward, "A Coale," 72-73; Bolton, *General Directions*, 95-97, 137-139.
47. Thomas Goodwin, *The Works of Thomas Goodwin* (Edinburgh, 1861-1865), 1:11-12.
48. Peter Lake, "Puritan Identities," *Journal of Ecclesiastical History* 35 (1984):116.
49. Collinson, *Puritan Character*, 19-27.
50. Elvis Costello, "Miss Macbeth."
51. Brinsley, *True Watch*, 1st pagination, 173.
52. Richard Greenham, *Workes* (London, 1612), 689.
53. Collinson, "A Comment," 487.

54. This sections draws fully upon Paul Ricoeur, "Life in quest of narrative," and Ricoeur, "Narrative identity," both in David Wood, ed., *On Paul Ricoeur: Narrative and Identity* (London, 1991), 20-33 and 188-199, particularly for the phrase "discordant concordance."
55. Tom Webster, "Writing to Redundancy: Approaches to Spiritual Journals and Early Modern Spirituality," *Historical Journal* 39(1996):33-56.
56. Ricoeur, *Time and Narrative*, trans. Kathleen Blamey and David Pellauer (Chicago, 1984-1988), 2:7-29; 3:216-229; Ricoeur, "Myth as the Bearer of Possible Meanings," in M. J. Valdes, ed., *A Ricoeur Reader: Reflection and Imagination* (London, 1991), 483-484.
57. Michael McGiffert, "Grace and Works: The Rise and Division of Covenant Divinity in English Puritanism," *Harvard Theological Review* 75(1982):463-502.
58. John von Rohr, *The Covenant of Grace in Puritan Thought* (Atlanta, Ga., 1974), 53-85.
59. Preston, *Life Eternall or a Treatise of the Knowledge of the Divine Essence and Attributes* (London, 1631), 2nd pagination, 84-85.
60. Collinson, "Towards a Broader Understanding of the Early Dissenting Tradition," in Collinson, *Godly People*, 544-546; David Underdown, *Fire from Heaven: Life in an English Town in the Seventeenth Century* (London, 1992), 91-92; Richard Rogers, *Seven Treatises* (London, 1603), 477-495.
61. *Winthrop Papers* (Boston, 1929-), 1:197, 209-210.
62. David D. Hall, "John Cotton's Letter to Samuel Skelton," *William and Mary Quarterly*, 3rd ser. 22(1965):484.
63. Ward, "A Coal," *Sermons*, 302, 303. To "wamble" is to move unsteadily or to have a sense of nausea. This possibility is supported by Stephen Foster's observation of covenant renewal in New England post-1677 in his "Not What, But How–Thomas Minor and the Ligaments of Puritanism," in Bremer, *Puritanism*, 50.
64. Jerald C. Brauer, "Types of Puritan Piety," *Church History*, 56(1987):39-58, quoted, 43.
65. An omission should be noted. There is not space in a work of this length to deal with "recruitment" and conversion. Perhaps there is little to be said about this field, since by the end of the sixteenth century a sufficient number of godly households existed to sustain the community. However, there was considerable regional variation in puritan presences, some places with disproportionate numbers, others with relatively few. How does one come

to godliness in such isolated circumstances? To put it synechdochically, we know the details of Richard Baxter's conversion in a godly household, but less about how his father became the solitary puritan in Eaton Constantine. Many of the cases dealt with in Patricia Caldwell, *The Puritan Conversion Narrative: The Beginnings of American Expression* (Cambridge, 1993) and Charles Cohen, *God's Caress: The Psychology of Puritan Religious Experience* (Oxford, 1986) pre-date the emigration of their subjects.

66. Sibbes, "The Christian's Watch," *Works*, 7:300, 304.

67. Thomas Brooks, *Heaven on Earth* (1654; Edinburgh, 1982), 26.

68. Preston, *The Saint's Qualification* (London, 1637), 28-29.

69. Thomas Taylor, "The Principles of Christian Practice," in *Works* (London, 1653), 5; Arthur Hildersham, *CLII Lectures on Psalm LI* (London, 1635), 638.

70. Cf. Sibbes, "Christian's Watch," 303.

71. Thomas Taylor Lewis, ed., *Letters of Lady Brilliana Harley*, Camden Society, 1st series, 58 (London, 1854), 15.

72. John Rogers, "Sixty Memorials for a Godly Life," in Cotton Mather, *Magnalia Christi Americana* (London, 1704), 3:112, 110.

73. Clarke, *A Collection*, 453.

74. Isaac Ambrose, *Prima, Media, and Ultima* (London, 1674), 163-168.

75. Bolton, *General Directions*, 86-87.

76. *Winthrop Papers*, 1:197, 209-210.

77. Webster and Shipps, *Diary of Samuel Rogers*, 15.

78. Robert Some, *A Godly Treatise of the Church* (Cambridge, 1592), Sig. E8v, quoted in Peter Lake, "Robert Some and the Ambiguities of Moderation," *Archiv für Reformationsgeschichte*, 71(1980):256.

79. Sibbes, "Christian's Watch," 303.

80. Preston, *Breast Plate*, 1st pagination, 228-229.

81. Nicholas Bownd, *The Doctrine of the Sabbath* (London, 1595), 212.

82. William Gouge, *The Saints Sacrifice: Or, a Commentarie on the CXVI Psalme* (London, 1632), 259; this is developed further in Tom Webster, *Godly Clergy in Early Stuart England: the Caroline Puritan Movement, c.1620-1643* (Cambridge, 1997), 136-140.

83. Patrick Collinson, "The English Conventicle," *Voluntary Religion, Studies in Church History* 23(1986):223-261.

84. BL, Add Ms 70062, unfoliated heads of prayer.
85. Robert Bolton, *A Threefold Treatise* (London, 1634), 16-17.
86. Mather, *Magnalia*, 3:44.
87. Thomas Taylor, *A Commentarie upon the Epistle of S. Paul Written to Titus* (Cambridge, 1612), 49; John Rogers, *A Godly and Fruitful Exposition upon the First Epistle of Peter* (London, 1650), 236, 632. The theater and broader "popularity" of the sermon is dealt with in Collinson, "Elizabethan and Jacobean Puritanism as Forms of Popular Culture," in Christopher Durston and Jacqueline Eales, eds., *The Culture of English Puritanism, 1560-1700* (London, 1996), 47-48.
88. Rogers, *Doctrine of Faith*, 215.
89. Brinsley, *True Watch*, 1st pagination, 185.
90. Preston, *Breast Plate*, 1st pagination, 208.
91. Goodwin, *Works*, 2:292; see also, John Dod and Robert Cleaver, *Ten Sermons Tending Chiefly to the Fitting of Men for the Worthy Receiving of the Lords Supper* (London, 1632), 13.
92. Webster and Shipps, *Diary of Samuel Rogers*, 154-155.
93. Dod and Cleaver, *Ten Sermons*, 2.
94. Richard Vines, *A Treatise of the Institution, Right Administration, and Receiving of the Sacrament of the Lords Supper* (London, 1657), 280-281.
95. Brooks, *Heaven on Earth*, 27, and see also, 81-82, 141, 195; Preston, *Breast Plate*, 1st pagination, 53; Perkins, "Oeconomie: Or, Household-Government," *Workes*, 3:690; Dod and Cleaver, *A Godly Form of Household Government* (London, 1630), Sig. Gr. The place of Canticles in the masculine search for humility is dealt with in Tom Webster, "'Kiss me with the kisses of his mouth': Gender Inversion and Canticles in Godly Spirituality," in Tom Betteridge, ed., *Sodomy in Early Modern Europe* (Manchester, Eng., 2002).
96. E[ssex] R[ecord] O[ffice], AEA 12, f 89r, cited in Collinson, "The Godly: Aspects of Popular Protestantism," in Collinson, *Godly People*, 9.
97. Preston, *Breast Plate*, 1st pagination, 207-208.
98. N[orthamptonshire] R[ecord] O[ffice], CB A43 ff 30-31; A30 f 8; 52 f 36.
99. Collinson, "Elizabethan and Jacobean Puritanism," 48-50; Webster and Shipps, *Diary of Samuel Rogers*, 98, 87, 24.
100. ERO, D/P 14/8/7; D/P 14/18/1A f 37.

101. R. G. Usher, ed., *The Presbyterian Movement in the Reign of Queen Elizabeth as Illustrated by the Minute Book of the Dedham Classis, 1582-89* Camden Society, 3rd ser., 8(1905):100.
102. Collinson, "Sects and the Evolution of Puritanism," in Bremer, *Puritanism*, 163.
103. Henry Parker, *A Discourse Concerning Puritans* (London, 1641), 8-9, 53; Collinson, "Towards a Broader Understanding," 539.
104. BL, Harl Ms 3783 f 11.
105. Stephen Marshall, *Meroz Cursed, or, a Sermon* (London, 1641), 46.

Puritans in the Marketplace

Mark Valeri

IN HIS 1654 *Wonder-Working Providence*, Edward Johnson celebrated the remarkable transformation of the New England wilderness.[1] Johnson, a founder of Woburn, Massachusetts, representative to the General Court, militia captain, and erstwhile surveyor and mapmaker, recalled that New England once consisted of a few isolated villages, beset by hunger and poverty, but by 1652 it had developed into a prosperous society of well-settled towns with thriving commercial traffic and human concourse. Boston epitomized this change. Once a "poor country village," situated among "hideous Thickets" with wolves and bears, it now boasted nascent manufactures, unbounded opportunities for "trade by Sea," and every imaginable craft or artisanship, from shoemaking to house-building.

Foreseeing what appeared to him to be "some sumptuous City," Johnson discerned God's hand in the circulation of goods in and around Boston Bay. The town had become an entrepôt for goods flowing from New England to Virginia and the West Indies; even "that Grandmother of us all," Great Britain, looked to Boston for essential commodities. It was "the very Mart of the Land," where "French, Portgualls and Dutch" came "for Traffique." Its houses and public buildings, its "good shopps well furnished with all kind of Merchandize," its "crowded" wharves, and its streets filled with people "inriching themselves by their trades" evidenced "a well-ordered Commonwealth."²

Johnson envisioned a society in which material commodities and divine truths circulated to the benefit of all members. He believed that God had ordained the expansion of New England as an instrument of divine rule in the world, and that trade would be a means of such expansion. It was an ominous sign, then, that "of late the Lord hath given a check to our traffique." Merchants had fallen on hard times after the economic boom of the late 1630s. Decreased immigration, scarcity of money, depressed prices, shipwrecks, piracy, and Indian wars had made "Merchants and traders themselves sensible of the hand of the Lord against them." These scourges could mean only that New Englanders perverted the true meaning of commerce, provoking divine punishment. Johnson recounted how avarice, greed, and self-serving ambition had led many to profane the sabbath or to treat their neighbors in a mercenary fashion. Boston's more aggressive entrepreneurs also had invited antinomians, Anglicans, and other enemies of the Puritan way to reside in New England in order to increase opportunities for trade and profit. Ill-motivated traders "would willingly have had the Commonwealth tolerate divers kinds of sinful opinions to intice men to come and sit down with us that their purses might be filled with coyn, the civil Government with contention, and the Churches of our Lord Christ with errors." No wonder, he concluded, that "the Lord was pleased" to "let in the King of Terrors among his newplanted Churches."³

Johnson's narrative reflected a persistent tension in Puritan economic sensibilities between aspirations for commercial expansion (New Englanders' "enriching themselves by their trades") and fears of free economic exchange (the link between "sinful opinions" and "purses . . . filled with coyn"). Many historians have contended that proto-capitalistic impulses shaped the Puritans' understanding of the economy (Johnson's reverence for commerce).[4] By contrast, the following essay emphasizes Puritan ambivalence toward, even resistance against, the new economy or what may be termed in shorthand as "the market."[5] To be sure, reformed Protestants praised economic productivity, championed new industries, and admired diligent merchants whose profits furnished comfortable homes and funded religious activities. Yet when the faithful conducted their business according to impersonal social laws and secular legal precedents (as the market often required) rather than to the need of the local community, their leaders protested. Puritans such as Edward Johnson never reconciled a godly economy to a market economy of exchange.

To recover Puritan economic sensibilities in New England, we must read the leaders of the first generation in Massachusetts Bay in the context of a long history of godly teaching about England. Elizabethan reformers critiqued new commercial measures—especially usury—and disparaged the established Church for its lack of supervision over economic life. John Calvin's Geneva inspired these reformers to envision congregational discipline over commercial exchange. Episcopal policy prevented them from establishing disciplinary institutions in England; but Puritans nonetheless promulgated a moral discourse against many market-driven behaviors. These Puritan economic ideals informed a full system of moral discipline that flourished in the churches and political institutions of early New England.

Economic changes during the last four decades of the sixteenth century provoked a great moral debate among English Protestants. The most salient of these developments are quite familiar: rising population; a relatively mobile labor force, a turn to the production of market goods (e.g. wool, linen, iron); specialization in production, an increase in the distance between sites of production and exchange (i.e. the rise of middle-distance merchants who transported goods throughout the kingdom and overseas merchants); an intensified reliance on bonds, bills, or other forms of paper credit; and a sharp rise in commercial litigation. English social commentary from the 1560s through the 1620s by humanist writers, religious leaders, and civil servants focused on the moral implications of new exchange practices that fell outside the bounds of customary, local prohibitions. Merchants who bought grain where plentiful, transported it to locations suffering from a dearth, and sold it at high prices did not necessarily violate local prohibitions against engrossing, regrating, or forestalling (i.e. hoarding grain from one area until a shortage, then selling it at high prices in the same area). Were they guilty of engrossing by other standards? Did enclosure in the 1600s still fall under the category of oppression of the poor, given that new patterns of husbandry often employed the indigent? What were the best means to care for the poor, whose numbers rose at alarming rates? Was increasing social stratification inherently fractious and vicious, or was it an acceptable cost of the nation's prosperity? What *was* the commonweal, after all?[6]

Usury in particular signified new and troublesome modes of exchange. Before the English Civil War, few economic issues roused such heated and extended debate, and few appeared as symptomatic of the market. Many religious commentators, dissenting and Anglican, noted usury as the bane of England in general, London in particular. As the Canon of Windsor, William Harrison, observed in 1587, usury was "now perfectly practiced almost by every Christian and so commonly that he is accounted but for a fool that doth lend his money for nothing." Bare mention of the city evoked complaints that usury had fouled the metropolis with avarice, fraud, and sheer mammonism. Such charges did not fall far from the truth. London loan-brokers routinely charged as much as 30 to 50 percent on loans during the early seventeenth century. According to humanist Thomas Decker, "Upon *Usury* hast thou," London, "begotten *Extortion* . . . *Hardness of heart*, a very murderer, and *Bad Conscience*," along with "*Scriveners*," who have begotten "common *Brokers*," who produce "common Theeves." From the open pulpit outside of St. Paul's Cathedral in 1627, preacher John Grent summarized half a century of apprehension about usury in London: "amids your great dealing, and traffique," there are "Merchants, most odious among you," i.e. "merchants" of "*Time*, Usurers," who personified the "deceit and misrepresentation" that threatened to undo the commonwealth. Such was "the chiefe *Symptome* of a Cities sicknesse."[7]

Grent and other preachers employed usury as a synecdoche for the abuse of nearly any form of credit. Usury became synonymous with oppression when merchants sold goods on credit at unfair prices; with "rent racking"—lodging provided on credit at inflated rates; with unfair labor practices, such as when debtors worked off their loans at low wages; and with engrossing when creditors waited until a grain shortage to demand payment in kind from farmer-debtors. Charging any loan fees, using loan brokers, or profiting from rates of exchange in foreign goods or currency were all considered usurious. Usury stood for a form of exchange that disregarded the moral dynamics of neighbor-to-neighbor relations and looked instead to rational laws of supply and demand.[8]

Growth of usury and other new exchange patterns outside of London also troubled Protestant moralists. When Thomas Carew, a fevent preacher in the cloth-producing town of Bildeston in Suffolk, learned that local clothiers paid low wages to spinners and weavers while earning substantial profits, he condemned them for practicing what he characterized as a form of usury. Likewise, his colleague from nearby Cavenham, Bezaleel Carter, denounced well-to-do parishioners who were "gripers, grinders of the poor, extortioners, usurers" and in many other ways "merciless."[9]

By associating usury with falsehood, lying, and deceit, Puritan preachers made the practice appear as a complete reversal of true commerce: communication and union within society. Premised on dissimulation, usury broke social bonds. Miles Mosse claimed in 1595 that "to cover their sinne, and to upholde their credite," usurers "have devised faire cloakes to shroude their ragged garments, and have begotten a more cunning, and subtile kinde of traffique in the world," so that there were "thirteine thousand devises, which men of evil conscience have invented" to practice their wicked art. It was "now one thing now another," inflated prices or unfairly low wages, high rents, or the taking of pawns, "alwaies being *usurie*, and yet never plainely appearing to be *usurie*." Usury so appalled Wiltshire preacher George Webb in 1609 that he declaimed from the Paul's Cross pulpit that "truth has been set to sale" in the market.[10]

For many Puritans, the spread of usury revealed the socially ruinous implications of market exchange in general; and the failure of religious and political institutions to limit usury signified a disastrous lack of moral resolve.[11] Puritans who condemned usury judged quite correctly that neither the crown, Parliament, and the secular courts, nor the church, its bishops, and local ecclesiastical tribunals did much, despite all the protests, to prohibit usurious practices or other commercial vices. Advisors to the Court such as Francis Bacon defended usury as politically and economically expedient, and the House of Commons raised legal limits on interest. More troubling to Puritans, civil courts refused to prosecute violations of statutes against usury. The case of one John Hemlyn of Exwicke, who appeared before a lower court in 1601 on charges of "very hard dealing by usery and other extreame courses," was typical. The Privy Council advised the lower court to issue only a modest verbal admonition: Hemlyn needed "a more Christian and charytable consideracion of thes his neighbours." Relatively few usury, engrossing, and price-gouging cases came to trial. Many Puritans concluded that the government was irremediably prone to such laxity.[12]

The Church of England fared no better. Anglican moral discipline depended on ecclesiastical courts organized on several levels. At the top, Tudor-Stuart bishops held consistory courts and courts of appeal, organized into different branches, to hear cases of great importance. Archbishops and bishops also promulgated occasional injunctions that specified liturgical and moral regulations and informed visitations by episcopal officials who set up temporary courts to examine priests and churchwardens within their parishes. Archdiaconate and diocesan courts met more regularly to hear cases as presented by churchwardens of local parishes.

Although Elizabethan ecclesiastical courts exercised a nearly omnipresent moral supervision, their effectiveness depended greatly on the energy and personal predilections of religious officials. While often zealous in enforcing regulations requiring conformity of their clergy, bishops notoriously failed to supervise the laity, and the number of presentments for usury remained minuscule. Archdeacon courts tended to commute penances for small fines rather than enforce official injunctions against usury and the like.[13]

Church courts performed even worse under James I and Charles I. Episcopal administrations, pressed for money, increasingly turned to monetary fines as a means of discipline. The resulting ease of commutation of penance, the inability of courts to compel defendants to appear, and the desire to keep citizens within the Church rather than push them toward dissent, led to leniency, especially an unwillingness to use excommunication. Episcopal injunctions and court records from 1603 to 1630 show that the chief disciplinary concerns of the church remained enforcement of conformity and upkeep of the established ministry, rather than protection of just exchange. From the perspective of the godly sort, episcopal discipline was far too unwieldly, distant, and preoccupied with administrative orthodoxy to attend to the moral dilemmas of commercial transactions at the local level.[14]

Puritans made it known that the established church had become a conduit for unjust modes of commerce. As a group of Puritan nobility complained to the council of the Archbishop of Canterbury in 1569, "the care and diligence, that properly belongeth to the office of bishops" was "of late years so diminished and decayed" that many people" engaged without penalty in "a manner of life of contempt or libertie." In a 1578 sermon, Thomas White maintained that behind London's usury and oppression lay a blend of religious and moral infidelity. Episcopal discipline, with its crypto-Catholic sacerdotalism, was grounded in lies. It was no mere coincidence, White believed, that in London "decyte," "Idolatrie," "Lying," and "covetousness" combined to dim all conscience and promote "usury, which for mischiefe . . . surpasse them all." John Udall's *The State of the Church of England*, a satiric dialogue against prelates, included a usurer who loved bishops for their moral indifference and hated Puritans for their obnoxious interference.[15]

In a great flood of pamphlets beginning with Thomas Wilcox and John Field's *Admonition to Parliament* in 1571, Puritans demanded reformation of discipline within the Church. They asserted that England needed local, corporate, and visible institutions to combat usury and other inhumane forces in the economy. William Fulke's *A Briefe and Plaine Declaration* typified such tracts. Despite some "presentments" to ecclesiastical tribunals for serious vices, Fulke claimed, "little or none amendmente" in behavior "at all doth followe." Using John Calvin's terminology, Fulke contended that "there ought to be in every Church" a "Consistory or segnorye of Elders or governors, which ought to have the hearinge, examination and determining of all matters, pertaining to Discipline and Governement of the Congregation." Clearly, Fulke argued, a bishop was incapable of administering "exhortation" to "every particular person within his charge."[16]

Fulke's language alerts us to one of the more important models for English Puritans, in contrast to which they judged established discipline so feeble. Influenced by their contacts in Geneva and by French Reformed congregations in London, many of the godly idealized the regime of John Calvin, who promoted rigorous religious supervision over merchants in his city. Dozens of Marian exiles had resided in Geneva when Calvin had produced his most extensive commentary on prices, wages, rents, usury, and other matters of exchange. Calvin prodded the Genevan Consistory (clerical and lay leaders of the church) to initiate a sweeping campaign to restrict usury, forestalling, and profiteering. The Consistory obliged, spending no small amount of time chastising, rebuking, and excommunicating offenders. On their return to England, these exiles agitated for moral reform with this Genevan model in mind. Here, they found, was personal, localized, and immediate application of church discipline: the Genevan saints censured usury and other controversial exchange practices as moral offenses.[17]

The publication of Calvin's writings on moral discipline also influenced the godly in England, who made quick work of reproducing his writings on society and ethics. From 1548 to 1630, 136 separate editions of his works appeared, most between 1570 and 1590. In 1562, Robert Fills translated *The Laws and Statutes of Geneva* (London, 1562), so that English Christians "may behold as in a glass, a Christian Reformation, and empty themselves [in] imitation" of it. Shorter selections of Calvin, especially his many condemnations of usury, appeared in the numerous English tracts on that subject throughout the late sixteenth and early seventeenth centuries. Calvin's understanding of social obligation in general found its way, through his successor Theodore Beza and the Frenchman Philip Duplessis Mornay, into Puritan treatises on federal, or covenant, theology.[18]

It is difficult to identify the precise social effects of these Calvinist ideals, but they did encourage real restrictions against novel exchange practices among the godly as they conducted business. Local courts and church tribunals in areas of strong Puritan influence heard far more cases against usury, engrossing, and oppression than in other regions. From Dedham, in the Stour Valley where Winthrop was raised, we have one of the few surviving manuscripts of an Elizabethan Presbytery. The records of the Dedham classis show how Puritans established an organ of communal moral discipline, directed it to local economic matters, and in doing so made explicit reference to Geneva. Wherever possible, late Elizabethan and early Stuart reformers created underground conventicles and disciplinary bodies that circumvented the established courts. In Norwich and Northampton, for example, Puritans organized classes, heard sermons that highlighted the sins of commerce, and punished usurers. Recent studies of Dorchester, and of the Suffolk towns of Bildeston and Bury St. Edmonds during the early seventeenth century, demonstrate that when radical Protestants gained control over local politics, they enacted severe statutes and used them against reputed usurers, engrossers, and profiteers.[19]

After 1580, however, the royal court brooked little campaigning for elders, consistories, or presbyteries. To some extent the pronouncements of Puritans on discipline represented only so much wishful thinking, and their legislative efforts proved futile. Yet Puritans did not abandon their positions on usury, exchange practices, and church polity. William Perkins and William Ames, to illustrate, could not legally denounce bishops, advocate the overthrow of episcopacy, or institute consistories, but they still maintained that godly churches ought to institute local moral discipline. Furthermore, they held that the powers of censure and excommunication ought to compel individuals to submit their private consciences to the community, particularly in important matters such as credit and prices. Perkins in fact fastened on economic sins as key subjects for discipline. "Usurers and oppressours," as well as "ingrossers," he insisted, should not be admitted to the Lord's Table.[20]

Since they could not establish Genevan-style courts and tribunals, the Puritan divines who taught the generation of John Winthrop and John Cotton relied chiefly on preaching, teaching, and devotional writing to promote social and economic reformation. Puritans claimed to derive their program for reformation from the Word of God. They drew from scriptural exegesis rather than, say, from abstract and universal moral concepts or purely pragmatic analyses of the needs of state. So they wrote and preached about the meaning of biblical rules for the immediate relationship between people in the same community: specific moral dilemmas in particular societies.[21]

William Perkins and William Ames, widely read in old and New England, argued to this effect: proper preaching and teaching amounted to the application of the Word to specific social dilemmas. Illustrating their method in the cases-of-conscience genre of moral writing, they turned the Bible toward contemporary economic issues. Perkins suggested that merchants or financiers who had the least qualm about their credit relations confer with good Christian neighbors about the meaning of biblical prohibitions against usury. Should such consultation burden their consciences, they should refrain from the Lord's Table until they amended their ways. Ames took an even more stringent position. Quoting from several scriptural texts about usury, he argued that moneylenders could invest in commercial ventures and reap the rewards of shared profits as long as they also shared the risks of such ventures. Lenders should know their borrowers, however, and speak honestly with them about the moral worthiness of their intentions. Creditors should find out how their debtors used the money before they collected anything above the principal, lest the creditor commit the sin of usurious lending to the needy. He even went so far as to support the controversial decree of the Dutch Reformed Church, which barred bankers from communion on the grounds that they made impersonal, fixed contracts on loans and thereby neglected the moral dynamics of creditor-debtor relationships.[22]

So Puritans began to form a moral community—a community of discipline—through networks of ideas as well as of kinship and social affiliation. They attempted to convince their readers, students, and local parishioners of the necessity of a virtuous vocation. They explained the importance of charity and justice in business practices. They condemned raising prices or lowering wages under market pressures in order to increase profits. They even attempted to define the limited conditions under which interest might be charged on a loan. Puritan preachers and divines in England embedded their discipline—their restraints on commerce—in tomes of Calvinist divinity and the practical recommendations of sermons.[23]

In Nehemiah Wallington, a London artisan, we can see how Puritan words shaped the mental worlds of ordinary practitioners. Wallington realized that his business, making wooden utensils, would succeed in secular terms only if he capitulated to the vicious rules of the market: the "lying, deceit, oppression, bribery," and "usury" that filled the stalls of London. Other woodworkers raised their prices when strangers appeared. They also charged more for goods bought on credit, or unloaded bad coins on unsuspecting customers. Not Wallington. Having sat through numerous Puritan sermons—nineteen in one week—and having dedicated hours to reading Perkins and Ames, Wallington could not in good conscience adopt the venal measures of his colleagues. He had learned to apply the Ten Commandments to his business in a straightforward way—one that prohibited the self-serving rationalizations of more modern-minded Londoners. He contented himself with a modest income, and, perhaps, some measure of moral satisfaction.[24]

We have other instances of how Puritan teaching retarded, rather than energized, godly enthusiasm for new modes of exchange in the market. Richard Napier, a physician influenced by reading Calvin, Bucer, and other reformers, and the brother of a highly successful London merchant, accepted Calvinist teaching that condemned as usurious profit-taking from a disadvantaged neighbor. Concluding that it was well nigh impossible to avoid usury in the economic climate of the 1620s, he charged no interest on hundreds of loans—to the dismay, we might imagine, of his brother. Joyce Jeffries, a godly widow of some means, made some five hundred loans during a ten-year period starting in 1638. Unlike other creditors who played the market and charged up to 30 percent on loans, Jeffries never charged more than 10 percent, lent chiefly to neighbors and kin at lower rates, abated the accounts of those who died in debt, frequently forgave the debts of widows, and only once pursued a debtor in court.[25]

Many Puritans nonetheless longed to expand the scope and power of religious discipline over the economy. During the 1620s, they increasingly looked to the settlement of New England as an opportunity to institute, in churches and civil government, their ideals of reform. Winthrop placed generous and merciful exchange of wealth at the center of his manifesto, "A Modell of Christian Charity." John White, Puritan pastor in Dorchester, England, promoted American colonization as the latest and best opportunity for English Calvinists to fulfill the divine mandate for the economy. In England, "idlenesse, riot, wantonnesse, fraud, and violence" ruled, the result of overpopulation and corrupt morals. In New England, people would be compelled to "labour, frugality, simplicity, and justice." Farmers, fishermen, merchants, and artisans could find in Massachusetts a good living and could produce, sell, trade, and make a profit and harm no one in the process. Such would be the case, White argued, if moral leaders—"good Governours, able Ministers"—defined and enforced the moral obligations of exchange. "When the frame of the body is thus formed and furnished with vitall parts, and knit together with firme bands and sinews" of discipline, then common folk and even poor people would benefit from the prosperity of the whole.[26]

Winthrop justified immigration to New England in similar terms. In England, he argued in his "General Observations" of 1630, monopolies and corruption in the courts constricted economic circulation, so that "yt is almost impossible for a good upright man to maynteyne his charge and to live comfortably in this profession." New England afforded the opportunity for a more "Christian" exchange; its fertile land could be turned to a virtuous and profitable trade. This was possible, Winthrop wrote in 1645, if New Englanders rejected a market economy based on "naturall corrupt libertyes." New England's mandate derived, not from a license for self-interested pursuit of gain, but from the freedom to exchange in "subiection to Authoritye," and to enjoy the "ordinances" of preaching and church discipline. This, according to Winthrop, was "the main end (professed) of our coming hither." True "liberty," he warned settlers in 1642 who wished to return to England, did not allow them to desert "the commonwealth" because of their individual needs. They ought to maintain solidarity with their neighbors in New England, even if this meant "to suffer affliction with thy brethren."[27]

Winthrop and fellow magistrates held fast to this challenging discipline and wished to make it a prerequisite for all new immigrants.

Prospective settlers, Winthrop asserted, must pursue their economic callings with diligence and be devoted to "unitie bond, and waie of pietie." This excluded anabaptists, antimomians, libertines, and other enemies of the Puritan way, who cared little for either a proper calling or true piety. Winthrop and his Assistants forbade merchants from dealing with rogue English traders and their French and Indian partners in northern New England, who might corrupt commercial ethics in Massachusetts. "Let not any Merchants, Inkeepers, Taverners, and men of Trade in hope of gain," Edward Johnson warned, "fling open the gates so wide, as that by letting in all sorts you mar the worke of Christ intended."[28]

Massachusetts's Puritans did not believe that their strict standards for admission to the colony would eliminate the need for moral supervision over all settlers. Behind the corruption of exchange lay sin; and sin abounded everywhere. Religious and political leaders accordingly promoted disciplinary measures to enforce the desired boundaries of economic activity. Ministers preached with remarkable consistency against self-serving business practices. Pastors and lay elders formed eccelsiastical tribunals to censure avaricious merchants and idle workers. Church members elected civic officials who repeatedly intervened in economic affairs. Judges were appointed to bring the guilty to justice. These disciplinary institutions—the church, the civil magistracy, and the courts—gave institutional expression to Puritan ethics. When members of these bodies attempted to control the terms of economic exchange, they upheld a moral agenda that characterized Calvinism.

New England divines identified moral discipline as one of the distinctive feature of their churches. Cotton's *Keys of the Kingdom of Heaven* (London, 1644), Hooker's *Survey of the Summe of Church-Discipline* (London, 1648), and Richard Mather's *Church-Government and Church-Covenant Discussed* (London, 1643) all focused on this corporate control over individuals' public behavior. Thomas Shepard reminded his congregation that the "end of coming hither" to New England was "the ordinances of God." Some commoners, such as John Dane and James Cudworth, claimed that they had come to New England for the very purpose of finding a godly community that would protect them from the temptations of a dishonest life. Dennis Geere, an otherwise unknown immigrant, in 1635 testified that the religious community in New England had convinced him to repent of usury, which he had practiced in London. He had learned by the discipline of the church to devote his estate to the common good of church and plantation.[29]

In practical terms, Calvinist discipline also consisted of lay officers (elders and deacons) exercising the power of censure and, in the words of John Cotton, "sitting in the presence of the Congregation, and hearing and judging cases before them." Anglican bishops, he reminded critics of the New English diaspora, were "removed from the people," both incapable and unwilling to "attend to every offence of every private brother." The Church of England turned a blind eye to the "oppression" of the marketplace, the various ways in which profit-mongering and "lying" pitted neighbor against neighbor in the new economy. New England, he believed, would follow a different path. He and other preachers such as Thomas Hooker insisted that New England's churches wield censures such as excommunication to fight against the temptation to reduce social relationships to impersonal transactions for the sake of profits.[30]

In New England Congregationalism, members, who chose their pastors, also elected lay leaders. Along with pastors, these officers confronted parishioners whom they suspected of sins such as lying, heresy, outbursts against public authorities, Sabbath-breaking, absence from public worship, drunkenness, fornication, and economic vices such as oppression. Elders and ministers attempted to expose unwanted behavior in public interviews. They admonished the guilty. If the sinner remained unrepentant, the case came before the whole congregation for disclosure and comment. Ministers and officers censured, administered public rebuke, temporarily suspended from communion, or, as a last resort, excommunicated the obdurate sinner. During the first few years in Massachusetts, Winthrop confidently believed that these measures would preserve the moral economy of the colony. He noted that many "profane and notorious evill persons" experienced conversion through the preaching, godly counsel, and "practice of Discipline" of his church in Boston.[31]

The actions of the officers and pastors of Boston's First Church revealed the extent to which they attempted to promote godly exchange. They confronted merchants and entrepreneurs suspected of oppression or other sins, as well as the idle unemployed, in interviews and examinations. As John Cotton instructed church members in 1638 who voted to readmit Richard Wayte, a tailor who had confessed to cheating his customers and lying about it, the people together "rightly binde[,] and upon good growndes any man under wroth[,] god bindes that person." After officers admonished one woman, ironically named Temperance Sweete, for selling wine with "some iniquity" in "the pryce thereof," she "penetentially made open acknowledgment" before the congregation, after which she "reconciled to the Church." Such a disciplinary procedure did not promote a modern, which is to say individuated, economic conscience.[32]

From 1630 to 1654, Boston's First Church passed some forty sentences of excommunication. About one-third of them dealt with sabbath breaking or heresy. Another third involved drinking and fornication. Eight cases dealt directly with economic vice, six with libel and violence. The number of cases devoted to commerce is significant in itself. More importantly, ministers and church officers treated the sins of the market as of a piece with other forms of social disintegration: as deviant as heresy, disorderly as drunkenness, violent as fisticuffs, and factious as adultery. Unjust prices, deceit, lying, and even harm to others all threatened to break social solidarity and, in this sense, reflected what Puritans judged as the dangers of impersonal economic exchange. Tailor Thomas Marshall found the church so ready to question or censure "his Dealing," on accusations of unfair prices, that he left the Bay Colony in 1644.[33]

Puritans frequently linked the corruption of the circulation of goods to the corruption of verbal exchange, e.g. slander and lying. When the church excommunicated William Franklin in 1646 for overcharging a Dutch resident for some industrial equipment, the elders noted the interconnections between his "extortion, deceipt, and lying." Tanner William Harvey fell "into Scandall" by ignoring his business (sloth too was a sin) and by compounding his "negligence in his Calling" with "lyes and forgeryes."[34]

The case of Anne Hibbens is particularly revealing. She ran afoul of the First Church after a dispute with local carpenters. She accused them of charging unjust fees and doing shoddy work on her house. Church elders heard her charges, called in another carpenter to review the work, and judged her complaint invalid. Hibbens nonetheless persisted with accusations and sought a second opinion on the work from other carpenters. All of this, the church officers concluded in 1640, warranted her excommunication because she presumed to "bring out the Trueth" in accordance with her private opinion rather than subject herself to the religious community. Her "Judgeing and Condemning" of the worth of the carpenters' labor led to other vices—"uncharitable Jealousies and Suspicion," "Irregular dealing," "obstinate Judgeing," "sundry Untruethes," and general disobedience to church and husband.[35]

Much has been written about the case of Robert Keayne, the Boston merchant whom pastors and elders admonished in 1639 "for selling his wares at excessive Rates." He underwent examination and censure by the church. Keayne contested the facts of the accusation but never doubted the use of ecclesiastical discipline in economic matters. He did not question the church's duty to censure usury or inflated prices. He recognized such activities as shamefully antisocial and charged his accuser with the equally antisocial sins of covetousness and bearing false witness.[36]

Keayne's account of the affair, and Winthrop's commentary on it, demonstrate that the issue at stake was not the right of a merchant to make a good profit. It was the manner in which he determined his prices and how he conducted commercial exchange with his neighbors. Even though a faithful church member, Keayne operated his business according to pure commercial acumen. As Bernard Bailyn has described Keayne's business accounts, we can see "Keayne's mind working in abstractions . . . and slipping unconsciously into quantitative measurements"; he displayed a "calculating trait" and could be "unforgiving" of debtors and less fortunate people around him. The market, Winthrop wrote, taught men such as Keayne to behave in a rational, calculating way: "there was no law in force to limit or direct men in point of profit in their trade," and "it is the common practice, in all countries, for men to make use of advantages for raising the prices of their commodities." Keayne—whom Winthrop admired in other respects—had become, in Winthrop's phrase, "a hard dealer in his course of trading." By Winthrop's judgment, Keayne should have known better. He was "an ancient professor of the gospel." His neighbors and friends previously had warned him against "false principles" of the market, and urged him to consider the needs of the local community in his dealing. If the church in Boston was to live up to its disciplinary mandate, it had to censure someone who neglected such advice.[37]

Churches outside of Boston pursued similar measures, although not in as spectacular a way as in the case of Robert Keayne. We can turn, for example, to John Fiske and his small congregation at

Wenham, Massachusetts. Trained under Cambridge Puritans, Fiske immigrated in 1637, was an assistant to pastor Hugh Peter in Salem, and became the minister in Wenham soon thereafter. He kept detailed notes of church meetings, and his notebooks show how Fiske and church officers applied biblical rules and Calvinist theology to a wide range of social behaviors. Members cited scripture in debating standards for membership, the acceptability of the Cambridge Platform, relief for the debts of failed farmers, and moral complaints against individuals. When deliberating the affairs of the town and church, members made no appeal to general social or economic principles other than what was "profitable" to the community at that time. Fiske and the officers focused on the needs of the poor in town, the command to maintain a "particular calling" for the sake of order, the urgency to "avoid all appearances" of capitulation to the worldly culture of the market, and the mandate to speak plainly, truthfully, and directly to local circumstances.[38]

Many disciplinary cases in Wenham involved members of the community who laced their economic violations with slander. Church members, for example, admonished the wife of one Phineas Fiske for loudly demanding on the Sabbath that another church member repay a loan. According to "the church's mind," this implicated Mrs. Fiske in Sabbath-breaking, slander, and covetousness. Robert Gowing, another member of the church, committed "lying" and the "public scandal (of covetousness or oppression)." Goodman Badger came under censure for claiming that he could not contribute money to the church because he had given alms to poor strangers.[39]

The Wenham congregation, like other first-generation Puritan churches, considered business transactions matters of religious concern and subject to its review. From 1644 through 1671, the church initiated action against thirty-seven instances of censurable behavior. Twenty of them involved slander, lying, and public arguments; eleven concerned economic vices, from idleness to oppression; and five revolved around absence from church or Sabbath violations. Only one case involved drunkenness. When two members fell into a disagreement over the worth of a cow that one Mr. Read gave as room rent, the church intervened, examining accounts of the cow's value. The elders also adjudicated disputes over the division of estates, the price of corn in the town, and business contracts.[40]

In addition to spiritual censures such as excommunication, New England's Puritan leaders employed a second means of moral discipline: temporal punishments at the disposal the General Court (the legislative body of the colony) and the law courts it established. In his *Discourse on Government,* John Davenport provided a standard reformed rationale for cooperation between the church and civil institutions in the New World. God created the church to care for the souls; God ordained the state to guard the temporal interests and the peace of society.[41]

Many of the economic statutes enacted in Massachusetts revised the English common law along Mosaic lines. Unlike English precedent, they included provisions for debt relief, the annulment of contracts or deeds signed under economic duress, a limitation on servitude to seven years, the requirement that eldest sons receive twice the inheritance of other heirs, and severe restrictions on usury. The regulations set a relatively low ceiling on interest rates and prohibitions against interest on loans outside of those intended for commercial investment. The colony also enacted prohibitions against idleness and libel. Thomas Lechford, a critic of the Bay Colony's establishment, was not far from the mark when he complained that New Englanders jettisoned English common law, and natural law, "upon pretense that the Word of God is sufficient to rule us."[42]

Legislators also denied merchants and laborers the right to set their prices or wages according to the law of supply and demand.

During the early 1630s, the General Court periodically limited prices on essential goods such as bread and on wages for artisans. Thereafter, the Court ceded the authority to regulate prices and wages to the colony's townships, a decision in accord with the Puritan conviction that local communities should control the dynamics of exchange. Puritans did not gainsay the general notion of selling goods for a profit, but they distrusted merchants who set their prices without regard to the needs of their immediate neighbors. Such was the case with merchant Keayne. Found to have sold nails at three pence a pound above the going rate, he provoked a hefty fine and a censorious discourse by John Cotton. The minister considered the market vicious when "a man might sell as dear as he can, and buy as cheap as he can." Good Christians could not "take the advantage" of a scarcity of goods, "another's ignorance" of customary prices, someone's urgent need for particular commodities, or even business losses, and raise prices accordingly. Again, the circumstances of particular communities overrode impersonal economic laws. "A man may not sell above the current price," by which Cotton meant the level as determined by local conditions: "a price as is usual in the time and place." If neighbors could not form a consensus on prices, Cotton averred, then the magistrates ought to set them in behalf of the commonweal.[43]

In England, Puritans often had campaigned in behalf of underpaid laborers; in New England, they saw invidious forces moving wages unduly upward. During the 1630s, when Massachusetts suffered a shortage of artisans, many newcomers demanded uncustomarily high wages. The General Court intervened, setting strict limits to the amount of pay given to tradesmen and craftsmen. Winthrop defended salary caps on the ground that they protected the production and flow of goods within the commonwealth. "A general Complaint" against carpenters, masons, and other artisans, he wrote, elicited the Court's response. The Governor and his Assistants noted that highly paid laborers, content with their incomes, sometimes worked only half as much as needed. They also used their ill-gotten money on useless consumer items from other colonies. Worse, some workers, such as one otherwise unnamed "Richard," a servant in Dorchester, accumulated their excessive pay with unjust intentions. Instead of putting his nestegg back into circulation or land, Richard took off for England. This betrayal, according to Winthrop, occassioned a providential judgment. "Cavaliers" robbed Richard of his money in England and obliged him "to return to New England again," much humbled and more obedient.[44]

The General Court issued dozens of other economic regulations, including ceilings on the production and sale of alcohol, limits on trade with Indians, and restrictions on traffic in timber products and beaver pelts.[45] Even during the 1640s and 1650s, when periods of depression, increasingly localized variations in the economy, and rapid economic change made regulation by the Court in Boston impractical, magistrates often continued to restrict commercial freedoms. Massachusetts legislators rescinded regulatory statutes but still empowered local magistrates to fine and imprison "ill disposed persons" who took advantage of such "liberty to oppresse and wronge their neighbours" by demanding "excessive wages" or asking "unreasonable prizes" for goods. Although the Court allowed interest rates of up to 8 percent on commercial loans, and eventually permitted an even higher rate on bills of exchange, it did not intend thereby to "be a colour or countenance to allow any usurie amongst us contrary to the Law of God." This provision gave rulers the right to judge whether loan contracts were usurious by virtue of their effect on debtors. When the General Court handed over an ironworks at Saugus to private investors in 1650, it strictly limited prices and proscribed business with foreign customers, disappointing the new owners.[46]

At each turn in the legislative history, Winthrop justified the General Court's rulings with reference to the needs of particular groups at the time: farmers or merchants, creditors or debtors, producers or consumers. The leaders of the colony did not doubt their right to control exchange for the sake of their society. The promotion of manufactures, building of wharves, and various attempts to provide a stable source of credit all spoke of the value Puritans placed on production and trade. They did not, however, disclose an acceptance of market principles concerning exchange.[47]

On the local level, farmers and merchants faced the effects of the General Court's legislation in the judiciary system. Initially the only court was the Court of Assistants, the upper body of the General Court, which had administrative, legislative, and judicial authority. During the 1640s, the General Court established quarterly or inferior courts, along the English model, for the counties of Essex, Middlesex, and Suffolk. In 1651, the General Court also established an inferior court in Boston to deal with commercial litigation.[48]

All of these courts meted out punishments for violation of economic statutes, adjudicated business disputes between colonists, and in a rather *ad hoc* fashion issued warnings against unseemly behavior such as speculation in land, trading with the French, and unfair loan practices. From 1628, when it met prior to Winthrop's departure for New England, through 1643, a period when the records are fairly complete, the Court of Assistants alone handled over 400 judicial cases. Except for alcohol consumption, no matter occupied the Assistants as much as economic exchange. Even other issues, such as libel, improper treatment of servants, or sumptuary violations, often involved commercial practices. The most frequent problem was drinking (some 90 cases), followed by fraud or violations of wage and price statutes (50); fornication (45); seditious speech and contempt of authority (44); libel, swearing, and other speech crimes (37); theft

(35); neglect of civic duty—e.g. causing fires, cultivating lands outside of proper boundaries, neglecting the watch (32); master-servant relations (29); battery or murder (21); scandalous comportment and sumptuary violations—e.g. improper clothing, gaming, tobacco use (19); and illegal trading with Indians (12). Comparative figures emerge from the records of county courts, locations of first hearing for minor cases. In one year alone, for example (starting with March 1658), the Essex County court fined one Mr. Wade "for excessive prices," Robert Payne and William Bartholomew "for selling dear," and dealt with one complicated case of usury (involving the worth of a cow paid for land).[49]

In many respects, the courts emulated the model of discipline set by the church: the application of biblical rules to local social relations. The collective judgment of neighbors—common opinion, personal testimonies, informal presentations—took precedence over impersonal legal procedures. In 1640, for example, the magistrates declared that the worth of property seized for nonpayment of certain debts be evaluated by a committee consisting of three judicious and impartial men to be chosen by the creditor, the debtor, and the town marshal. In 1644, the General Court ruled that all debt cases be tried first in the court closest to where the creditor or debtor lived, in order to facilitate the judgment of neighbors in the community where disputes arose.[50]

During the early 1640s, Governor Winthrop contended that he and other members of the Court of Assistants should have personal, discretionary powers to apply scripture to legal cases as they saw fit. His critics complained of arbitrary government and despotism. They campaigned for a full set of laws that would define moral offenses and their attendant punishments. Some urged, for example, that all public lying be punished by a fine of forty shillings—a law that would leave the Assistants little room for leniency or harshness based on their personal judgments. Winthrop maintained that strict legalism along these lines depersonalized the concept of justice. "The qualitye of the person and other circumstances" ought to be considered. Such a law could not account for differences between an otherwise honest youth caught in a harmless lie and a crafty old businessman who slandered his competitors. Furthermore, he continued, powers of discretion allowed mature Christians to administer "Admonition" and "Reproofe," which was to say to treat wayward members of the community as fellow Christians, subject to discipline and reform as well as punishment.[51]

Winthrop, to be sure, had personal motives for defending the discretionary powers of the Court of Assistants; he was its most prominent member. Yet his moral reasoning followed the paradigm inherited from Calvin and accepted by his godly mentors in England. Puritans strove to protect the community by the flexible and pragmatic application of the Bible to problems of exchange. The leaders of New Haven took these Puritan moral ideals to an extreme. There, legal proceedings took place in simplified lay language. Magistrates and people appealed to a literal reading of the Bible, addressing themselves to *ad hoc* remedies for local problems. Most New Haveners took their leaders' advice to settle disputes over debt and property ownership by informal conciliation and arbitration by neighbors; judges acted as spiritual advisors and counselors, rather than as mediators between plaintiffs and abstract legal precedents.[52]

The leaders of the Bay Colony so embraced the particular discourse of Calvinist ethics that they could not be reconciled fully to a secular court system. The idea of a civil judiciary chafed against their moral values. Intending the courts to be agents of corporate harmony and communal negotiation, Puritans resisted barratry and litigiousness. A 1635 Boston town meeting prohibited anyone from initiating lawsuits without permission from church elders. The Puritan agenda for communal harmony led the inhabitants of towns such as Lancaster, in Middlesex County, to covenant with each other "to end all differenc[es] by arbitration" rather than "goe to lawe with another in actions of debts or damages." So too the First Church in Boston. In a 1649 meeting, the members voted to censure any of their number who "should goe to law one with another without the Consent of our brethern." As usual, the ministers and magistrates in New Haven would not be bested in moral zeal; they banned lawyers from the colony altogether.[53]

Puritans feared the incursion of secular jurisprudence into their moral world because the language of law, predicated on natural principles, threatened to unravel the bonds created by deference to godly discourse and communal discipline. Winthrop repeatedly set biblical rules above what he deemed to be mere law. He organized his "Modell of Christian Charity," largely an address about the social agenda of the settlement of New England, according to a series of scriptural passages. Some thirteen years later, the Governor faced a vexing decision regarding Massachusetts's relations with two French grandees in Canada; and he again turned to the Bible. Charles de la Tour asked Winthrop for permission to supply himself with goods and munitions from Boston merchants in his fight against his rival Charles D'Aulnay. Winthrop agreed. This provoked protests from members of the Massachusetts government who thought that New Englanders had no business providing arms or any other form of assistance to French Catholics. In a lengthy address to his critics, Winthrop laid out his defense in terms of scriptural logic: New Testament texts that commanded charity to strangers and Old Testament passages that commended commercial transactions with pagans.[54]

New Englanders such as Winthrop and John Davenport often contrasted this biblical-Calvinist model of social negotiation to English precedents for civil adjudication by common and natural law. Davenport insisted that the distinguishing mark of Puritans was their reliance on the Bible for every sort of practical direction, from "ethicks, economicks," and "politicks" to "church-government." He portrayed Massachusetts Bay as a community ruled by this conviction. A unique utterance defined New England's "theocratie," a social order under "the Laws of God." Only church members—believers who understood the grammar of the text—were allowed to vote, because they were "fitter" than unbelievers "to judge and determine according to God," the moral dynamics of social relations. In economic terms, the saints were best qualified to judge between proper and improper modes of exchange, because they were "civilly honest, and morally just" and "have judgement" in matters of "Humane Contracts, mens Goods and Lives, and outward Liberties."[55]

Thomas Shepard provided a full discussion of the relationship between civil law and the Bible in his treatise on Christian liberty. "Laws and orders enacted in any place" by civil magistrates, he contended, were "good" only if they followed the rules "expressly mentioned in the word" of God or directly derived from the Word. The usefulness of such laws, furthermore, depended on how magistrates made a "prudent collection and special application" of the "rules, recorded in Scripture, to such special and particular circumstances which may promote the public weal and good of persons" in particular "towns" or other social groups. By Shepard's reading, this conviction superseded any appeal to moral rights or legal prerogatives putatively derived from natural law. Secular ethics or civil jurisprudence, from his perspective, tended to abstraction and obfuscation. Winthrop reflected the Puritan view in 1641 when he criticized a preacher for a political discourse filled with principles from "the old Roman and Grecian governments." New England, Winthrop opined, had different rules for moral thinking; and "if religion and the word of God makes men wiser than their neighbors," then "we may better frame rules of government for ourselves than to receive" the opinions of others, based "upon the bare authority of the wisdom, justice" of "heathen commonwealths."⁵⁶

New England Puritans instituted the moral teaching of their Calvinist predecessors by making a local, flexible, and circumstantial application of scriptural rules to the market. Such was the thrust of Winthrop's exhortation, once again, in the *Arbella* speech. Take, for instance, his discussion of private property. Universal laws or regulations—what he described as "the Lawe of nature"—implied an inflexible and impersonal defense of the right to private property. Without denying that right in all respects, Winthrop urged variation in its application. The "Lawe of the Gospell," he asserted, taught people to relate to each other not merely as "one man to another," with absolute rights, but "as a brother in Christ," united "in the Communion of the same spirit." The need of neighbors thus overrode natural principles of individual rights to ownership. The Bible called Christians to set aside the primacy of their property when certain "seasons and occasions," such as the "perills" of the settlement of New England, demanded "extraordinary liberallity." Service to "the community" of "the church" in exile implied, in this instance, that Christians "must sell all and give to the poor as they did in the Apostles times."⁵⁷

Winthrop had been trained as a lawyer, but he, like other Puritans, criticized his profession. John Cotton spoke for most Puritan leaders when he described "Advocates" as motivated by a drive for success rather than a love of truth. Lawyers, he claimed, "bolster out a bad case by quirks of wit, and tricks and quillets of Law," using "their tongues as weapons of unrighteousness" for "corrupt Causes." Following a line of teaching from I Corinthians 6–and influenced by Calvin and the English Puritans–Davenport argued that Christians should not sue other Christians in unchristian judicatories. Unbelievers' "unacquaintance with the Law of God," Davenport reasoned, blinded them from seeing the fundamental rules for proper moral judgments. The principles of common law, natural law, or, worse, mere reason of state, were unreliable and unsuited to true justice. To Davenport, this explained the "preverting of *Justice* by Magistrates of worldly spirits" in England. "All true Moral Justice," he concluded, rested on the election of godly rulers by godly citizens. The Puritan moral imagination resisted creation of legal culture that became the chief means of arbitration in a market society.[58]

To explore this arena differently, we should consider an observation made by Max Weber in an essay rarely cited by historians of Puritanism and the market. Weber opined that the market represented an "absolute depersonalization" of social exchange, and therefore challenged organic ethical systems. He claimed that "the more the world [of the market] follows its own immanent laws, the less accessible it is to any imaginable relationship with a religious ethic of brotherliness. The more rational, and thus impersonal, capitalism becomes, the more this is the case." In pre-market societies, ethical norms "regulated" "personal relations"; "but it is not possible to regulate," Weber explained, the complicated and impersonal relations between holders of bonds, notes of exchange, or mortgages, and their distant debtors. So, "where the market is allowed to follow its own autonomous tendencies, its participants do not look toward the persons of each other but toward the commodity; there are no obligations of brotherliness or reverence, and none of those spontaneous human relations that are sustained by personal unions."[59]

What Weber portrays as an archaic notion of fraternal and interpersonal ethics challenged by the market system perfectly describes Puritan attitudes toward market-induced exchange. New England merchants, to be sure, eventually found it impossible to pursue profits without deploying lawyers, agents, and new instruments of credit. Despite their reverence for prosperity, many Puritans protested. Men such as Edward Johnson, to return to our opening example, predicted savage judgments from God. Puritan jeremiads, like their disciplinary institutions, expressed the central convictions of their economic ethics.[60] They drew from a long history of Calvinist moral discourse, which stretched back through their Elizabethan forebears to Geneva. Those jeremiads ceased only when New Englanders experienced a fundamental transformation of their moral imagination.

Notes

1. Johnson had come to Massachusetts in 1630 aboard the *Arbella*, a companion of Gov. John Winthrop and other notables of the Bay Colony. The full title of Johnson's work was *A History of New England from the English Planting in the Yeere 1628, until the Yeere 1652: Wonder-working Providence of Sion's Saviour in New England* (London, 1654). See Sacvan Bercovitch, "The Historiography of Johnson's Wonder-Working Providence," *Essex Institute Historical Collections* 104(1968):139-161; and Ormond Seavey, "Edward Johnson and the American Puritan Sense of History," *Prospects* 14(1989):1-29.
2. Johnson, *Wonder-working Providence*, ed. J. Franklin Jameson (New York, 1937), 70-71, 247-248. All following citations to this text will be from the 1937 edition.
3. Johnson, *Wonder-working Providence*, 247, 254.
4. Perry Miller set the standard interpretation with his subtle and dynamic application of the Weber thesis to early New England: Miller, *The New England Mind: From Colony to Province* (Cambridge, Mass., 1953), 19-57; and Miller, *Nature's Nation* (Cambridge, Mass., 1967), 14-49. See, for permutations on Miller, Stephen Foster, *Their Solitary Way: The Puritan Social Ethic in the First Century of Settlement in New England* (New Haven, 1971); and *The Long Argument: English Puritanism and the Shaping of New England Culture, 1570-1700* (Chapel Hill, 1991). In his *The New England Merchants in the Seventeenth Century* (Cambridge, Mass., 1955), Bernard Bailyn argued that merchants, operating out of a pragmatic and modern business ethic, contested ministers and their retrograde ethics. Three more recent studies stress the proto-capitalistic mindset of Puritan New England: John Frederick Martin, *Profits in the Wilderness: Entrepreneurship and the*

Founding of New England Towns in the Seventeenth Century (Chapel Hill, 1991); Stephen Innes, *Creating the Commonwealth: The Economic Culture of Puritan New England* (New York, 1995); and Mark A. Peterson, *The Price of Redemption: The Spiritual Economy of Puritan New England* (Stanford, 1997). Less driven by debates about the Weber thesis, historians of English Puritanism have located the godly among middling merchants and their neighbors who supported entrepreneurial ventures yet stood apart from the great traders and counselors of state who drove England into the market system. Among many important studies on Puritan merchants, see David Harris Sacks, *The Widening Gate: Bristol and the Atlantic Economy, 1450-1700* (Berkeley, 1991); and Robert Brenner, *Merchants and Revolution: Commercial Change, Political Conflict, and London's Overseas Traders, 1550-1653* (Princeton, 1993). For older studies, which are more heavily indebted to Marxist or Weberian theories, see Christopher Hill, *Society and Puritanism in Pre-Revolutionary England* (1958; New York, 1997); and David Little, *Religion, Order, and Law: A Study in Pre-Revolutionary England* (New York, 1969). The best studies of English Puritans and the market in local contexts are William Hunt, *The Puritan Moment: The Coming of Revolution in an English County* (Cambridge, Mass., 1983); David Underdown, *Fire from Heaven: Life in an English Town in the Seventeenth Century* (New Haven, 1992); and Paul S. Seaver, *Wallington's World: A Puritan Artisan in Seventeenth-Century London* (Stanford, 1985). The two most recent, synthetic works, which suggest Puritan reticence to embrace new economic exchange practices, are Craig Muldrew, *The Economy of Obligation: The Culture of Credit and Social Relations in Early Modern England* (New York, 1998); and Keith Wrightson, *Earthly Necessities: Economic Lives in Early Modern Britain* (New Haven, 2000).

5. We can usefully define the early modern market, or what we mean by a market economy, with reference to Fernand Braudel's work. In Braudel's terms, the market took shape as sites for exchange moved beyond city stalls to regional fairs, then to international ports and distant cities, where extended networks of supply and demand determined prices more than did local custom, civic code, and religious doctrine. There was more to this development, however, than prices and wages. Once dependent on commodities and coins, seventeenth-century merchants utilized a plethora of negotiable papers: bonds, bills, and increasingly complicated contracts. They developed public institutions for investment, speculation, and credit, such as banks, brokerages, and stock exchanges. The use of third parties—lawyers, agents, and law courts—to adjudicate disputes

gradually displaced local negotiation over simple account books. Accounting measures in themselves became more complicated in order to rationalize rising interest rates, shifting supply and demand, and fluctuations in the values of different currencies. Fernand Braudel, *Civilization and Capitalism, 15th-18th Century*, vol. II: *The Wheels of Commerce*, trans. Sian Reynolds (1982; Berkeley, 1992).

6. Wrightson, *Earthly Necessities*, 150-213.
7. William Harrison, *The Description of England* (1587), ed. George Edelen (Washington, D. C. and New York, 1994), 203; Thomas Decker, *The Seven Deadly Sins of London* [1606], ed. Edward Arber (London, 1879), 22; John Grent, *The Burthen of Tyre* (London 1627), 7, 10. For lending rates in London, see Peter Earle, *The Making of the English Middle Class: Business, Society and Family Life in London, 1660-1730* (London, 1989), 50, 118.
8. For usury's association with nearly all forms of commercial transactions and credit, see [Anon.], *The Death of Usury* (Cambridge, 1594); for the general inhumanity of exchange practices, see Nathanael Homes, *Usury is Injury, in an Examination of its Best Apologie, Alleaged by a Countrey Minister, Out of Doctor Ames* (London, 1640).
9. Thomas Carew, "Caveat for craftsmen and clothiers," in *Certaine Godly and Necessarie Sermons* (London, 1603); and Bezaleel Carter, *Christ his Last Will, and John his Legacy* (London, 1621), 56-86. Both texts are discussed and cited in Patrick Collinson, "Christian Socialism in Elizabethan Suffolk: Thomas Carew and his *Caveat for Clothiers*," in Carole Rawcliffe, Roger Virgoe, and Richard Wilson, eds., *Counties and Communities: Essays on East Anglian History* (Norwich, Eng., 1996), 161-178.
10. Miles Mosse, *The Arraignment and Conviction of Usurie* (London, 1595), 65-60; George Webbe, *Gods Controversie with England* (London 1609), 58.
11. In his *Worlds Apart: The Market and the Theater in Anglo-American Thought, 1550-1750* (New York, 1986), Jean-Christophe Agnew shows how Puritans rhetorically linked usury, verbal misrepresentation, social fraction, and the emergent market.
12. The case of Hemlyn is recounted in Acts of Privy Council, 31:79, quoted in R. H. Tawney, ed., *Tudor Economic Documents: Being Select Documents Illustrating the Economic and Social History of Tudor England* (London, 1924), 2:175. For Bacon, see Francis Bacon, *The Essayes or Counsels, Civill and Morall* [written 1597-1625, first pub. 1625], ed. Michael Kiernan (Cambridge, Mass., 1985), 126-128. See also Norman Jones, *God and the Moneylenders: Usury and Law in Early Modern England* (Oxford, 1989). Under the

Stuarts and with the advice of mercantilist advisors such as Thomas Mun and Edward Misseldon, even the bare remnants of Elizabethan usury law were rescinded.

13. Martin Ingram, *Church Courts, Sex and Marriage in England, 1570-1640* (New York, 1987); Ronald A. Marchant, *The Church Under the Law: Justice, Administration and Discipline in the Diocese of York, 1560-1740* (Cambridge, 1969), 174-177, 214-221. See W. P. M. Kennedy, ed., *Elizabethan Episcopal Administration: An Essay in Society and Politics* (London, 1924), 1:iii-ccxix for general statistics.

14. See Ingram, *Church Courts*; and John Addy, *Sin and Society in the Seventeenth Century* (New York, 1989). Churchwarden, archdeacon, and episcopal court records show that the only cases involving economic vices were a few sabbath violations and faulty record-keeping of parish finances. Ecclesiatical court records from the period, parish records, and episcopal visitation records show only a handful of presentments or charges for usury, engrossing, extortion, etc.

15. The Earl of Leicester to Matthew Parker, 1569, in Edward Cardwell, ed. *Documentary Annals of the Reformed Church of England* (Oxford, 1844), 1:351; [Thomas] W[hite], *A Sermo[n] Preached at Pawles Crosse . . . November 1577* (1578), 45, 51; [John Udall], *The State of the Church in England* (n.p., 1588?). See also Walter Travers, *A Defence of the Ecclesiastical Discipline Ordayned of God To Be Used in His Church* (London, 1588), 136. Puritan charges of usury among priests were not completely inaccurate: see B. A. Holderners, "The clergy as money-lenders in England, 1550-1700," in Rosemary O'Day and Felicity Heal, eds., *Princes & Paupers in the English Church, 1500-1800* (Totowa, N. J., 1981), 195-209. In his "Puritans and the Church Courts, 1560-1640," in Christopher Durston and Jacqueline Eales, eds., *The Culture of English Puritanism, 1560-1700* (London, 1996), 58-91, Martin Ingram suggests that Puritan complaints after 1580 were overstated; but he also shows that Puritan insistence on local, visible, zealous, and regular discipline differed greatly from Anglican campaigns to reform the courts from the top down.

16. [William Fulke,] *A Briefe and Plaine Declaration, Concerning . . . the Discipline and Reformation of the Church of Englande* (London, 1584), 51, 84, 134.

17. Patrick Collinson, *The Elizabethan Puritan Movement* (Berkeley, 1967), 114-141. For Calvin, the Consistory, and usury, see Mark Valeri, "Religion, Economy, and Discipline in Calvin's Geneva," *Sixteenth Century Journal* 28(1997):123-142.

18. P. G. Lake, "Calvinism and the English Church, 1570-1635," *Past & Present* 114 (1987):32-76. For Fills's edition of Genevan statutes, see *The Laws and Statutes of Geneva*, trans. Robert Fills (London, 1562), n. p. For a typical edition of Calvin, see James Spottswood, *The Execution of Neschech . . . or A Short Discourse Shewing the Difference Betwixt Damned Usurie and that which is Lawfull, Whereunto there is Subjoyned an Epistle of . . . John Calvin* (Edinburgh, 1616). For the influence of Calvin on English reformers, see [Thomas Cartwright,] *A Full and Plaine Declaration of Ecclesiastical Discipline* (n.p. 1574); Walter Travers, *A Defence of The Ecclesiastical Discipline Ordayned of God To Be Used in His Church* (London, 1588), 124; and a typical complaint from an Anglican about the pernicious influence of Calvin: Matthew Sutcliffe, *A Treatise of Ecclesiastical Discipline* (London, 1590), sig. B2r, 1-10, 86, 94, 135, 158. For use of Calvin as an authority against usury, see, for one of many examples, Miles Mosse, *The Arraignment and Conviction of Usurie* (London, 1595).

19. Dedham Classis, "Minute Book, 1582-1589," in Roland G. Usher, ed., *The Presbyterian Movement in the Reign of Queen Elizabeth as Illustrated by the Minute Book of the Dedham Classis, 1582-1589* (London, 1905), 59, 71, 97-100. Marshall M. Knappen, *Tudor Puritanism: A Chapter in the History of Idealism* (Chicago, 1939), 409-411; Collinson, *The Elizabethan Puritan Movement*, 323-329. For an example of Puritan anti-usury preaching, see Robert Bolton, *Two Sermons Preached at Northampton at Two Severall Assises There* (London, 1639). For Dorchester, see Underdown, *Fire from Heaven*. John Craig, "Puritans and the Marketplace: England" (paper presented at Millersville University conference, John Winthrop's Worlds: England and New England, 1588-1649, September 1999) shows how in the village of Bury St. Edmonds, as in Puritan Dorchester, the godly gained control and promoted local trades yet also enacted strict economic regulation. The theme of Puritan control over the local economy is stressed also in Diarmaid McCulloch, *Suffolk and the Tudors: Politics and Religion in an English County, 1500-1600* (Oxford, 1986); and, in a much more focused study, Collinson, "Christian Socialism in Elizabethan Suffolk."

20. For the powers of censure in a corporate communal setting, see Henry Ainsworth, *The Communion of Saintes* (Amsterdam, 1607), 355-378; and William Perkins, *The Workes of that Famous and Worthy Minister of Christ, in the University of Cambridge* (Cambridge, 1608), 1:316-395. The Perkins quote is from *Workes*, 1:734. See below for Ames.

21. Hunt, *The Puritan Moment*, 113-129; Theodore Dwight Bozeman, *To Live Ancient Lives: The Primitivist Dimension in Puritanism* (Chapel Hill, 1988). For

a clear statement on the relation between the Bible and preaching as vehicles for practical ethics, see William Perkins, *The Art of Prophesying*, in Ian Breward, ed., *The Works of William Perkins*, Courtenay Library of Reformation Classics, vol. 3 (Abington, G. B., 1970), 333-334. For the localism and realism of Calvinist ethics, see William J. Bouwsma, *John Calvin: A Sixteenth Century Portrait* (New York, 1988); for an analysis of distinctions between the sort of ethical reasoning discussed here and more analytical, abstract, and universal moral reasoning, see Stephen Toulmin, *Cosmopolis: The Hidden Agenda of Modernity* (Chicago, 1990).

22. Perkins dealt with the issues mentioned here in the second half of *The Whole Treatise of the Cases of Conscience* (London, 1628). For Perkins's fullest discussion of usury, see his *Workes* (1608), 1:63-64, 734-735. William Ames, *Conscience with the Power and Cases Thereof* (n.p., 1639), sig. A2, 236-244. Ames's discussion of "Contracts" on 227-235 shows his familiarity with market transactions. For the currency of Perkins and Ames, see "Charles F. Robinson and Robin Robinson, "Three Early Massachusetts Libraries," in *Publications of the Colonial Society of Massachusetts*, 28:107-186.

23. On the links between kinship networks, Puritan divinity, and Calvinist self-understanding, especially as it related to Winthrop, see Francis J. Bremer, "The Heritage of John Winthrop: Religion along the Stour Valley, 1548-1630," *New England Quarterly* 70(1997):515-547.

24. Seaver, *Wallington's World*, 129-130 (Seaver quoting from Wallington's manuscripts); see also 14-66, 127-138. According to Seaver's reading, viii, "Wallington's mental world is not separated by a gulf of incomprehension from the mental world of the Protestant intelligentsia; on the contrary, his categories of thought and angle of vision were profoundly shaped by their preached and written words."

25. Michael McDonald, "An Early Seventeenth-Century Defence of Usury," *Historical Research* 60(1987):353-360; Robert Tittler, "Money-lending in the West Midlands: The Activities of Joyce Jeffries, 1638-1649," *Historical Research* 67(1994):249-263. Tittler argues that religious conscience could spur some forms of money-lending, yet act as a brake against newer credit practices.

26. John Winthrop, "A Modell of Christian Charity," in *Winthrop Papers* (Boston, 1929-), 2:282-295; John White, *The Planter's Plea: or the Grounds of Plantations Examined* (1630; Rockport, Mass., 1930), 34; for White on production, see esp. 2-5. For White's economic preaching, see Underdown, *Fire from Heaven*. In his *New England Merchants*, 23, Bernard Bailyn maintained that Puritan "ideals were put into use in the very first years

of the Puritan settlements and helped to shape the development of institutions and traditions from the start. Nowhere else did Calvinist doctrines of social ethics find such full application." For arguments about motives for settlement, see Virginia DeJohn Anderson, "Migrants and Motives: Religion and the Settlement of New England, 1630-1640," *New England Quarterly* 58(1985):339-383; and David Cressy, *Coming Over: Migration and Communication Between England and New England in the Seventeenth Century* (New York, 1987).

27. Winthrop, "General Observations on the Plantation of New England," in *Winthrop Papers*, 2:112; see esp. 114-116; and *The Journal of John Winthrop, 1630-1649*, ed. Richard S. Dunn, James Savage, and Laetitia Yeandle (Cambridge, Mass., 1996), 588, 317, 416 (in order of quotations here).

28. Arthur Tyndal to Winthrop, Nov. 10, 1629, cited in Rutman, *Winthrop's Boston*, 136; Johnson, *Wonder-Working Providence*, cited in Bailyn, *New England Merchants*, 105. See Bailyn, *New England Merchants*, 13-14, 105-106, for requirements for policies on trade with non-Puritans and toleration of strangers in Boston. Winthrop discusses profane merchants in his *Journal*, 331-334.

29. Shepard, "The Parable of the Ten Virgins," in *The Works of Thomas Shepard*, ed. John A. Albro (Boston, 1852-1853), 2:376. For John Dane, see "John Dane's Narrative, 1682," in *New England Historical and Genealogical Register* 8(1854):154, cited in Virginia DeJohn Anderson, *New England's Generation: The Great Migration and the Formation of Society and Culture in the Seventeenth Century* (New York, 1991), 41-42. For Cudworth, see Johnson, *Wonder-Working Providence*, cited in Bozeman, *To Live Ancient Lives*, 113. For Geere, see his will, reprinted in *New England Historical and Genealogical Register* 37(1883):229.

30. John Cotton, *The Keyes Of the Kingdom of Heaven* (London, 1644), 41-42; Cotton, *On the Holinesse of Church-Members*, 20. For Cotton's general reflections on discipline, see *The True Constitution of a Particular Visible Church* (London, 1642), 2-3. See also Thomas Hooker, *A Survey of the Summe of Church-Discipline* (London, 1648), esp. 36-40.

31. Winthrop, *Journal*, 106, see also 111-112. For elders and the system of censures, see John Cotton, *The True Constitution of a Particular Visible Church*, 2-3.

32. The first excommunication listed in the records, in fact, was "for scandalous oppression" by one Robert Parker. First Church, Boston, *Records of the First Church in Boston, 1630-1868*, ed. Richard D. Pierce, *Publications of*

the Colonial Society of Massachusetts, 39:20. For Cotton and Wayte, see James F. Cooper, Jr., "The Confession and Trial of Richard Wayte, Boston, 1640," *William and Mary Quarterly,* 3rd. ser. 44(1987):310-332, quote from 326. For Temperance Sweete, First Church, *Records,* 39:28.

33. First Church, *Records,* 39:42-45; see 12-160 for the statistical profile.

34. First Church, *Records,* 39:45-46, 49. Likewise the Roxbury church excommunicated Hannah Webb in 1642 for the "grosse sins" not merely of selling her bread at too high a price but also for "lying and shifting" in the public market, Roxbury Church Records, published in *A Report of the Record Commissioners Containing the Roxbury Land and Church Records* (Boston, 1881), 83.

35. First Church, *Records,* 39:31-33. For further reflection on Hibbens, see Richard Godbeer's essay in this volume: "Performing Patriarchy: Gendered Roles and Hierarchies in Early Modern England and Seventeenth-Century New England."

36. First Church, *Records,* 39: 25. Bernard Bailyn, "Introduction" to Robert Keayne, *The Apologia of Robert Keayne* (1964; Gloucester, Mass., 1970), x; see Keayne's text, 48-60. Innes, *Creating the Commonwealth,* 184-185.

37. Bernard Bailyn, "The 'Apologia' of Robert Keayne," *William and Mary Quarterly,* 3d ser., 7(1950):568-587; Winthrop, *Journal,* 307, 397.

38. John Fiske, *The Notebook of the Reverend John Fiske,* 1644-1676, ed. Robert G. Pope, *Publications of the Colonial Society of Massachusetts,* 47:133, 226; see also 61-66.

39. Fiske, *Notebook,* 22, 26-27, 34-35, 47-48, 56, 61, 72-73, 92, 130, 201-202.

40. Fiske, *Notebook,* passim.

41. For Davenport's *Discourse about Civil Government in a New Plantation...* (1637), I have used a later edition that was misattributed to John Cotton (Boston, 1663), 7, 11; Bozeman, *To Live Ancient Lives,* 160-192. For a study of the general theory of church and state, see T. H. Breen, *The Good Ruler: A Study of Puritan Political Ideas in New England, 1630-1730* (New Haven, 1970).

42. Thomas Lechford, *Plain Dealing,* cited in Bozeman, *To Live Ancient Lives,* 188. For revisions of English law, see Bozeman, *To Live Ancient Lives,* 177; for a survey of statutes, see Bailyn, *New England Merchants,* 33-34, 104; and Rutman, *Winthrop's Boston,* 181, 207, 222-223.

43. Cotton's remarks were recorded by Winthrop in his *Journal,* 308.

44. Winthrop, *Journal*, 102, 430.
45. Much of the literature downplays these early regulatory statutes as temporary expedients that fell by the way during the 1640s and 1650s, see Darrett Rutman "Governor Winthrop's Garden Crop: The Significance of Agriculture in the Early Commerce of Massachusetts Bay," *William and Mary Quarterly*, 3d ser., 20(1963):396-415; Margret E. Newell, *From Dependency to Independence: Economic Revolution in Colonial New England* (Ithaca, N.Y., 1998), esp. 56-57; Innes, *Creating the Commonwealth*, 160-191; and Peterson, *The Price of Redemption*, 7-12. There is little evidence, however, that John Winthrop, John Cotton, John Davenport, and other Puritan leaders ever abandoned their central conviction that the church and government ought to control prices, wages, and credit rates.
46. Massachusetts Bay Colony, *The Book of the General Lawes and Libertyes* (Cambridge, Mass., 1648), 43, 51; Nathaniel B. Shurtleff, ed., *Records of the Company of the Massachusetts Bay* (Boston, 1853), 1:160, 5:62-63; Rutman, *Winthrop's Boston*, 239. For the Saugus ironworks, see Shurtleff, *Records*, 3:31, 59-61, 92-93, 142; and Innes, *Creating the Commonwealth*, 237-270.
47. For Winthrop's comments, see his *Journal*, 342, 345, 353-354, 414.
48. The nomenclature for these courts eventually changed, especially after 1692. The Court of Assistants became the Superior Court of Judicature (the court of appeal). The county or Quarterly Courts became Courts of Common Pleas, and dealt with civil matters; General Sessions of the Peace, somewhat like criminal courts, were then added at a county level. For a brief narrative, see Rutman, *Winthrop's Boston*, 234-235; and the relevant essays in Daniel R. Coquillette, ed., *Law in Colonial Massachusetts, 1630-1800, Publications of the Colonial Society of Massachusetts*, vol. 62.
49. Massachusetts Bay, Court of Assistants, *Records of the Court of Assistants of Colony of the Massachusetts Bay, 1630-1692*, ed. John Noble and John Fr. Cronin (Boston, 1901-1928), 2:passim; Essex County, Quarterly Courts, *Records and Files of the Quarterly Courts of Essex County Massachusetts*, ed. George Francis Dow (Salem, Mass., 1911-1975), 2:118-119, 146.
50. See Bailyn, *New England Merchants*, 48-49.
51. John Winthrop, "John Winthrop's Discourse on Arbitrary Government," in *Winthrop Papers*, 4:468-482 (quotations from 475-476; the illustration on lying from 474).
52. Cornelia Hughes Dayton, *Women before the Bar: Gender, Law, and Society in Connecticut, 1639-1789* (Chapel Hill, 1995), 29-30.

53. Rutman, *Winthrop's Boston*, 154-155; Roger Thompson, *Sex in Middlesex: Popular Mores in a Massachusetts County, 1649-1699* (Amherst, Mass., 1986), 169; First Church, Boston, *Records*, 39: 52. For a study of how Puritans attempted to shape the courts around the concept of negotiation and harmony, see also David Thomas Konig, *Law and Society in Puritan Massachusetts: Essex County, 1629-1692* (Chapel Hill, 1979).

54. For Winthrop's "Modell of Christian Charity," see "Notes 1A, 1B, 1C" in , Winthrop, *Journal*, 726; for the French affair, see "John Winthrop to Richard Saltonstall and Others," 1643, in *Winthrop Papers*, 4:402-410; and Winthrop, *Journal*, 444-449.

55. [Davenport, attributed to] Cotton, *A Discourse about Civil Government*, 12, 14-15, 19-20.

56. Thomas Shepard, "For a Time of Liberty," in *Works*, 3:346-347; Winthrop, *Journal*, June 1641, 359-360. Shepard argued that "it is not now *lex nata*" (natural law) "but *lex data*" (revealed law) "which is the rule of moral duties." Only "the whole Scriptures contain the perfect rule of all moral actions." Shepard, "The Morality of the Sabbath," in *Works*, 3:44.

57. Winthrop, "Modell of Christian Charity," 284.

58. John Cotton, *An Exposition upon the Thirteenth Chapter of the Revelation* (London, 1655), 163, cited in Rutman, *Winthrop's Boston*, 233-234; and [Davenport, attributed to] Cotton, *Discourse about Civil Government*, 20, 23; see also 19-20. For Winthrop's opinion of lawyers, see his *Journal*, 345, 360. For legal culture and the market, see Bruce H. Mann, *Neighbors and Strangers: Law and Community in Early Connecticut* (Chapel Hill, 1987).

59. Max Weber, *From Max Weber: Essays in Sociology*, trans. H. H. Gerth and C. Wright Mills (New York, 1946), 331; and *Economy and Society*, ed. Gunter Roth and Claus Wittich (Berkeley, 1978), 636-637. Quoted in Robert N. Bellah, "Max Weber and World-Denying Love: A Look at the Historical Sociology of Religion," *Journal of the American Academy of Religion* 67(1999):277-304 (quotations from 297 and 297 n.26).

60. For the jeremiad, see Harry S. Stout, *The New England Soul: Preaching and Religious Culture in Colonial New England* (New York, 1986), esp. 67-123.

The County of Massachusetts: The Governance of John Winthrop's Suffolk and the Shaping of the Massachusetts Bay Colony

Francis J. Bremer

THE SUCCESSFUL ADAPTATION OF English institutions to New England by John Winthrop and his fellow magistrates may have been the puritans' "greatest achievement" and insured the Bay Colony's success.[1] Massachusetts leaders wielded authority and interpreted their charter powers in light of administrative experiences in old England, particularly in Suffolk and Essex, fashioning a simplified version of English local government for New England. Surprisingly, most historians of the colonial era have missed this insight and by ignoring the forms and functions of English local government they have misapprehended key aspects of colonial American history. This essay seeks to explore the parallels between English and colonial civil order and focuses historical attention on the institutions and practices of East

Anglia, in the eastern region of England, the home of most first-generation New England settlers.

At the heart of this argument is the participatory character of English local government. In regulating the counties of England, the Crown in the late sixteenth and early seventeenth centuries depended upon local elites to perform the various executive, judicial, and regulatory tasks essential to maintaining the peace and order of the realm. The men tapped to perform these tasks saw themselves not only as Englishmen, but also as representatives of their "country," as many referred to their own counties. They embraced the chance to advance local interests (and their own) while serving the monarch. They freely adapted the formal legal powers invested in them to local conditions and found ways to mitigate or evade unpleasant measures mandated by the central government. Local English political culture at that time possessed a surprising amount of flexibility, allowing county leaders the scope to exercise much discretion in the exercise of their offices. In doing so, they often helped to shape innovations in policy and institutional structures.

The Commission of the Peace, whose members were justices of the peace, was the key agency of government at the county level, with responsibility for a wide range of administrative and judicial tasks. It represented the principal stage upon which local elites exercised power and preserved social order. During the late Elizabethan period, Commission duties and its membership—Crown appointed—expanded. In the county of Suffolk, where John Winthrop and many of the future Massachusetts colonists lived, the Commission increased from forty-five at the accession of Queen Elizabeth in 1558 to nearly seventy during the 1590s. Despite the increasing numbers and a high turnover rate, the Commission represented a relatively small number of men from a large county, giving the office a mark of status. Such recognition became the prime incentive for men to assume the responsibilities of a justice of the peace.[2] Distinctions of rank within the Commission generally followed social standing, with those justices of the "quorum"—members of which had to be present for some of the court's functions—possessing more authority and rank than their fellow justices. Traditionally, the quorum had been composed of Commission members learned in the law, but the position increasingly fell to those with higher social positions regardless of legal background.[3]

The Commission met four times a year as a court of criminal jurisdiction, commonly known as "Quarter Sessions." Twice a year, the Commission joined with two justices of the nation's central courts to hold assize sessions for the adjudication of capital offenses.[4] The central courts at Westminster, including Chancery, King's Bench, and Common Pleas, dispersed pairs of judges on different circuits to the various counties to administer justice. Those judges brought a national perspective to the assizes, making the sessions something of a legal compromise between centralization and decentralization. As the legal historian J. S. Cockburn commented, "assizes provided relief locally without endangering the essential uniformity and impartiality of the common law."[5]

At both Quarter Sessions and the assizes, county sheriffs and their bailiffs, high constables and petty constables, and local coroners reported offenses and presented to the justices those bound over for criminal activities. Local people formed juries of inquiry, grand juries brought indictments, and the court empanelled trial juries to assist the bench in dealing with criminal trials. While Quarter Sessions could sentence offenders to death, this became less common over time, with the assize court eventually trying most felons. For lesser offenses, in addition to imposing fines and other penalties such as whipping and requiring offenders to stand in the stocks, the justices might demand financial sureties to guarantee that offenders would maintain the peace in the future, an increasingly common measure.[6] In addition to its judicial duties, Quarter Sessions also convened to conduct administrative business and issue orders to repair roads and bridges, maintain jails, supervise parish poor relief, license alehouse keepers and other traders, and review judicial orders.

Commission members also acted in other settings. Single justices of the quorum, or a pair of local justices, served as arbitrators and sought to settle local disputes before they required the attention of the courts. They admonished and corrected minor offenders, imposed bonds for good behavior, and when necessary bound individuals over for appearance at Quarter Sessions. At one point, Queen Elizabeth's government planned to have enough justices of the peace to insure that no Englishman would be farther than six or seven miles from one.[7] The expansion of the commission never quite achieved that goal, but by the 1620s a magisterial presence existed in most towns and parishes of Suffolk. As the weight of the full commission's business increased, small groups of justices in each locality began to meet in special sessions to deal with the legal matters of their designated division of the county. These smaller meetings, which occurred as often as once a month, became known as petty sessions. There, lesser offenses could be handled quickly and thus removed from the Quarter Sessions workload.[8] This institutional innovation developed as a local, rather than national, initiative, and showed how local leaders adapted their legal powers to better serve the needs of their county.[9]

The range and importance of the duties of the Justice of the Peace made the position important, one that ambitious men could use to build considerable local influence. Large numbers of inactive members of the Commission testified to the honorific quality of the appointment. An untimely dismissal represented a loss of face that the victim felt keenly. Minor gentlemen also concerned about their local status, occasionally served as justices and held positions in local governmental below the Commission of the Peace. In most English counties, including Suffolk, a separate administrative layer existed below the Commission consisting of the head constables. Men of some local status occupied this position, but we know relatively little about them. They oversaw the administrative and judicial activity within divisions of the county–called variously hundreds, lathes, or wapentakes, depending on the region.[10] Gentlemen aspiring for the higher levels of office could also serve an apprenticeship as subsidy (tax) collectors (as distinct from commissioners)[11] or on ad hoc commissions established by the Crown.

Other governmental institutions, some wielding authority that paralleled that of the Commission of the Peace, also represented local interests. Each county contained numerous towns, and while many came under the jurisdiction of county offices, others had a more complex relationship with the county officials. Boroughs were towns or cities with municipal corporations established by royal charter and possessing independent powers of self-government. In general, a correlation existed between the size and importance of a town and its status, but new towns might lack charters, while older ones with declining populations generally held on to their legal advantages. The organization of incorporated boroughs varied greatly, from the complexity of London's government to that of small towns. In London, perhaps one in ten of the adult male population held some office, creating a tradition of self-government and independence remarked upon by contemporaries. Elsewhere, such as Sudbury, in Suffolk, a smaller elite controlled affairs. Thus, towns originated many administrative initiatives: the first compulsory poor rate appeared in Norwich and efforts in the late sixteenth century to cope with rising poverty appeared earliest in London.

Boroughs claimed a certain independence from the county commission. Although most Englishmen lived under town or county, not borough, government, nearly all understood the chartered rights and privileges held by borough residents. Boroughs held their own courts, administered their own affairs, and raised their own militia forces. Because each had its own governing responsibilities, the relationship between boroughs jealous of their privileges and county officials often led to intense friction. Such difficult relationships shed light on a generally underappreciated feature of early modern government: growing governmental authority often conflicted with charter-granted liberties and privileges. In this era of developing governmental institutions and imperial reach, such tensions would have particular relevance for the North American colonies.

Most Englishmen lived in small villages, such as John Winthrop's Groton, where the parish church dominated the landscape. During the early modern period, the central government increasingly assigned civil tasks to the parish and its leaders, creating a distinction between the parish as an ecclesiastical entity and the same community functioning as a "civil parish," dealing with social and economic challenges. Constables, key figures in carrying out the Crown's instructions and those of the Country Commission, came from the ranks of village worthies. Their effectiveness depended entirely upon village opinion. They served for only one year at a time and needed continually to maintain good relations with their neighbors. As Keith Wrightson has argued, constables came from the local communities they served and popular notions of order influenced the ways in which they carried the duties imposed by higher levels of local government.[12]

In many localities, the manor and its manorial court–presided over by the large local landowner–had previously served as the arbiter of local order. But as the Crown made more and more administrative duties the responsibility of the civil parish, it began to displace the manor as the primary secular authority at the lowest levels of society.[13] As in the case of boroughs, the organization of parishes could vary greatly. The governing body of the parish was the vestry, so named because it generally met in that portion of the parish church. In most places, the vestry was "open," meaning that it granted all male ratepayers in the parish the right to vote in parish affairs. In some parishes, particularly larger ones, a smaller number of well-to-do citizens—a "select vestry"—exercised power and co-opted new members when necessary, forming a self-perpetuating oligarchy. Whether open or select, the vestry chose lay church officers (the wardens and sextons) and those responsible for carrying out the new tasks imposed by Parliamentary legislation, such as overseers of the poor and surveyors of highways.[14] The constables, parish vestries, and anyone named to grand juries enforced the nation's laws and also served as the antennae of the king's government in rural areas. The channels of communication that connected the village constable, the justices of the peace, and the assize judges, worked two ways, transmitting royal will to the localities and enabling news and concerns to find their way to the capital.

This complex local political order should not be mistaken for an egalitarian or democratic society. John Winthrop began his 1630 lay sermon on "Christian Charity" with words that few Englishmen would dispute: "God almighty in his most holy and wise providence hath so disposed of the Condition of mankind, as in all times some must be rich some poor, some high and eminent in power and dignity, others mean and in subjection."[15] At each level of government, those of higher status expected the deference of the lower orders. The county judges tended to defer to those on the assize circuit; constables deferred to the county justices on the bench; the local vestry listened attentively to parish leaders. Yet, at each level, those higher up not only expected but needed the deference of those below them—little could be accomplished without it. This hierarchy allowed for an informal and subtle negotiation of interests and the establishment of institutions that served the needs of the English "middle sort," the local landowners, professionals, town merchants, and the lesser gentry.[16]

Successful government in England rested on a harmonious blending of dissimilar and unequal elements, each performing a distinctive role and acknowledging the role of others in the social and political hierarchy. Early modern English visions of society rested on acceptance of the idea, as Winthrop had written, that God created people as social unequals, but each with a necessary calling or vocation to fulfill. Whatever the humble status of a particular role, God designed it as vital to the health of the body politic. Thus, the well-known 1596 manifesto of parish notables in Swallowfield, Wiltshire, that demonstrated a general commitment to neighborliness, deference, order, and the idea that inferiors should not "malapertly compare [themselves] with their betters and set them at nought."[17]

In seeking to understand English local government, we should not presume social conflict; nearly all elements of society sought harmony and mutually beneficial relationships. English society looked back more to a medieval ideal than forward to a modern state. The relationship between the central government and the counties proved most successful when local magistrates adapted their legal powers to local conditions, often with the explicit approval of the central government. In local institutions, such as the Country Commission, and in other forums, such as the assizes or Parliament, national and local interests mingled. The assizes reinforced the connection of the Commission with royal authority and its sessions became a regional public forum where judges publicized the concerns of the Crown. But at the same time, the mingling of the judges of the central courts with the local justices not only enhanced the authority of the county judges, but gave local voices to reach the monarch and the Privy Council.

Parliament operated in a similarly balanced nature, with MPs seeking to satisfy the desires of the Crown while finding legislative solutions to local concerns.

Allowing local leaders to participate in their own governance could produce unexpected benefits for the Crown. In some areas of government activity, local officeholders proved assiduous and creative. For example, the Elizabethan poor law grew out of, and codified, a number of local initiatives. Boroughs burdened with growing numbers of poor and a troublesome level of immigration took on new administrative duties. The boroughs of London, Norwich, and Salisbury, among others, made important innovations that influenced national legislative policy and helped produce stability.[18] "The organization of incorporated boroughs varied greatly, from the complexity of London's government to that of small towns." Indeed, Englishmen proved less inclined to accept authority that did not involve local interests. The operation of government finances is a prime example. The record of local officials in raising money generally disappointed the Crown. England's financial system during the seventeenth century rested in part upon county, borough, and village officers setting and collecting rates. Local leaders, with an interest in preserving their own wealth, more often than not disappointed the central government with their revenue collections. As a result, the Crown increasingly turned to the employment of appointees to harvest revenues. Crown agents called purveyors received licenses to raise supplies for the royal household, arriving in the localities with warrants empowering them to take goods at the king's price—often considerably below market price. In one effort to rebuild the decaying value of royal revenues, "hunters after concealed lands" received licenses to search out questionable titles to lands that might have been alienated from the Crown. Royal agents "persuaded" monopolists and patentees to pay rents to the Crown or to forgo the repayment of debts in return for rights to collect fines or royalties on the production and sale of particular goods. Local interests often resented the assertion of authority by Crown appointees. County and village officeholders exercised political power as an extension of their broader "natural" authority, but Crown agents derived their authority from mere licenses. A magistrate was born and bred to rule by virtue of social preeminence, but the power of a licensee might only reflect specialized knowledge of legal title, mastery of the operations of markets in particular goods, or of the production and sale of commodities. Lacking any other legitimacy, and clearly acting for personal profit, their authority was closely scrutinized and often challenged.[19]

Englishmen such as John Winthrop believed that an alliance of local magistrates with godly ministers was essential to a well-ordered commonwealth. Even though Winthrop and his fellow colonial leaders had no interest in reconstituting the English Church in the new world, we must remember that the Church's institutional forms and religious order shaped New England's development. In particular, we must pay attention to the practice of religion in Winthrop's Stour Valley in the late sixteenth century, where negotiations between the Crown and the locality, laymen, and clergy promoted both reformed religion and a godly society.

In Elizabethan England, the established religious order allowed considerable local autonomy, creating the potential for local parishes to shape their own versions of faith and practice. The policies of the national church rested to a large degree on secular agencies of government—including the commission of the peace, constables, and parish vestries—and individuals responsible for implementing directives of the Queen or her bishops would not do so if it resulted in a loss of local harmony. Additionally, the right of presentment to benefices (advowsons) since the time of Henry VIII resided largely in lay hands. A benefice is an ecclesiastical office, in this case the possession of a rectory by a clergyman who ministers to the parish in question.[20] The laymen who held these rights were not totally free to choose their ministers. Candidates presented to benefices had to be ordained and, in most cases, licensed by the bishop. Nonetheless, the transfer of advowsons from clerical to lay hands after the Reformation clearly reduced the control exercised by the ecclesiastical hierarchy over local parishes. It represented, to some extent, an alienation of the control over who preached and, therefore, what was preached.

A second source of lay influence in such parishes involved control of resources. The transfer of benefices from monastic to lay control also meant that ecclesiastical revenue went through lay hands before reaching the minister. By installing the minister and determining how much of these funds he received, a lay patron possessed the power to help shape local religious practice. In the right hands, this could enhance the quality of local religion. On the other hand, misallocation of the funds by the lay leader keeping much of the parish tithes for himself would hinder the hiring of a highly qualified minister and contribute to what some perceived as the inadequacy of local religion.

To upgrade the quality of the clergy and local preaching, religious reformers undertook a variety of initiatives. Early in Elizabeth's reign, some bishops instituted prophesying, gatherings where a number of learned divines met to expound scripture to their fellows and to the laity. In some places, laymen who sought to make preaching more accessible to the godly contributed funds to establish lectures by "combination," which provided a forum where beneficed divines lectured in rotation. Clergymen who participated in such combination lectures often attended the sermons of their colleagues and then met over a meal to discuss issues facing both ministers and the church in general. Other lay patrons, and some town governments, endowed lectureships for a particular preacher in order to supplement the preaching normally available in their community. While this practice often augmented a poor benefice by providing a clergyman with extra income, in other cases such lectureships provided a preaching platform to a minister whom the local bishop would not license for a benefice. All these "extracurricular" efforts sought to upgrade the knowledge and effectiveness of parish clergy. In some areas, particularly Suffolk and Essex, the ecclesiastical hierarchy encouraged the establishment of such forums as a means of educating the laity in the essentials of reformed Christian faith and practice. The new measures also changed the power relationships between ecclesiastical authorities and the laity since in many cases laymen foot the bill for extraordinary preaching and, thus, exerted influence over the complexion of local religion.[21]

If the national leaders of the church—the monarch and the Archbishop of Canterbury—did not control preaching in many English parishes, neither did they control the enforcement of ecclesiastical law as much as they desired. The Church courts entertained two kinds of business: "office" and "instance." Instance business was analogous to civil business in the secular courts—cases initiated between individuals. Clearly, these cases depended on local willingness to present offenders. The dependence of church courts upon the willingness of ordinary Englishmen to bring complaints about their neighbors was no small matter. Churchwardens, the lay officers of the religious parish, held responsibility for bringing office business to the church courts. Living in the parish and valuing its harmony, churchwardens identified more with parishioners than with the church hierarchy, additionally shifting power to the localities. Churchwardens also became key figures in the system of visitation by which bishops oversaw standards of religious practice within their diocese. The bishop directed articles of enquiry (visitation articles) to them, who in turn usually crafted their responses to protect parish practices against the initiatives of an unpopular bishop. Officially the conduit of religious policy, churchwardens emerged from the ranks of the village worthies and applied their own or local standards of order.[22]

Religious divisions existed in England, affecting authorities in the Privy Council down to the parish vestry. The impact also could be seen in the propagation of the faith, colored by local lay interests. Practices considered a local norm in one part of the country might be accounted rank nonconformity elsewhere. Protestants who favored further reforms advanced their cause when they found allies in village, borough, and county government, or in diocesan palaces and regional church deaneries. Perhaps in no other region of England did local magistrates and ministers succeed so well in exploiting religious divisions to craft a distinct religious culture than the Stour Valley of south Suffolk and northern Essex, the region in which John Winthrop grew up and acquired his political education.

The absence of a single, powerful aristocrat who could have dominated the county, and the fact of religious division in Suffolk, made for some instability in the county's gentry politics at the time of Elizabeth's accession to the throne in 1558. Nevertheless, a county-wide sense of Protestant gentry solidarity emerged by the 1570s, leading to the exclusion of Catholics from the commission and ensconcing power in the hands of a Protestant elite.[23] Rich lay patrons such as Sir Robert Jermyn and Sir John Higham promoted godly preaching in alliance with the godly preachers already active in the county. The magistracy, with support of the ministry, used their positions as justices to promote moral and social reform: "In busying themselves so earnestly with a range of social offences, the Suffolk justices were in the van of what by Jacobean times was a groundswell of morally indignant and even Draconian magistracy."[24] The region to the south of Winthrop's Suffolk in Essex also included godly families such as the Riches and the Barringtons who promoted a reformed ministry and used their governing positions to advance their cause. Like the Suffolk magistrates, they too made great strides during Elizabeth's reign in changing the character of the region.

The "Godly Kingdon of the Stour Valley" stretched north and south from the Stour River that separated Essex from Suffolk and the diocese of Norwich from that of London.[25] The kingdom took shape by the late 1570s as the efforts of the lay magistrates, complemented by evangelical bishops in the two dioceses (men such as Parkhurst and Scrambler in Norwich and Grindal in London), promoted religious reform. In selecting archdeacons to govern the various regions along the valley, these bishops appointed clergymen (such as John Still in Sudbury and George Withers in Colchester) who supported reform. Both church and lay patrons turned to the graduates of the puritan colleges of Cambridge for the preaching clergy they appointed to livings and lectureships. This cultural region stretched sixteen miles on each side of the river from its source just east of Cambridge to its mouth on England's eastern coast. Within these boundaries, I have identified reformers in 103 of 213 Essex parishes, and in 95 of 183 Suffolk parishes between the late 1570s and the accession of Charles I.[26] Through official and unofficial means, religious leaders cooperated with godly magistrates to establish reformed religion in the region.

Local leaders in the Stour Valley created varieties of informal religious associations to shape the pattern of reform, unifying the region's clergy on a common agenda, and helping to select ministers for their parishes. Prophesyings first filled this function. Then, when Queen Elizabeth, troubled by the thought of what ideas were being advanced, suppressed those exercises, the clergy in the Stour Valley organized clerical conferences. The most famous of these was at Dedham, but it was closely linked to other conferences in the godly kingdom, such as the one presided over by John Knewstub in Cockfield, Suffolk, and the one attended by Ezekiel Culverwell and Richard Rogers in Braintree, Essex. During the 1580s, members of such conferences met to debate doctrine, discuss the moral and spiritual qualities of neighboring clergy, and resolve tensions with their congregations. Archbishops Whitgift (1583-1604) and Bancroft (1604-1610) feared this development (which Bancroft identified as a classis movement) as an attempt to create a presbyterian church within the church. Whitgift effectively suppressed the conferences by the early 1590s, but the spirit of clerical association rose, phoenix-like, in the form of combination lectureships.

The religious voluntarism which the reformers used to shape the area's religion was not inherently subversive, but the movement's clergy often refused to conform to the prescribed practices of the national church. Members of the conference movement also generally repudiated the three conservative articles of faith and practice that Archbishop Whitgift imposed in 1583. Clergymen of Essex and Suffolk who rejected the Archbishop's ecclesiastical policy received suspensions, but with the protection of noble patrons such as Lord Rich, Sir Francis Barrington, the godly still managed to extend their influence at the end of the sixteenth century. Later, under King James, the bishops again attempted to root godly clergy out of their livings and pulpits, but this campaign also failed due to "administrative laxity" and the persistence of local support. During the 1610s, the godly preachers in the Stour Valley enjoyed "almost complete peace."[27]

Jonathan Kalu identified seventy-two religious lecturers in Essex in the period 1603 to 1629. Of those whose religious sentiments could be identified, fifty-nine espoused puritanism and only three voiced orthodox or other sentiments.[28] Thus, the "tone" of the preaching in the region remained "hot"–of a character increasingly labeled puritan by detractors. Preached in most parishes, reinforced by the imprimatur of clerical associations, supported by reformist archdeacons and frequently by evangelical bishops, and endorsed by godly magistrates, the culture of reform became pervasive in the region. This godly preaching encouraged and ran parallel to a "culture of discipline" in local government, which became increasingly popular in the Stour Valley and its environs.[29]

Partnerships of godly magistrates and godly ministers reached down to the lowest levels of secular administration in the region. Together they worked to root out immoral behavior and institute programs of social and economic reform grounded in the gospels. In Elizabethan Ipswich, for instance, the constable patrolled the fields around the town and the inns and tippling houses on Sundays "in search of idle persons and players of unlawful games, imprisoning the stubborn and disobedient."[30] In the boroughs of Colchester and Sudbury, one can also find evidence of alliances between magistrates and reform ministers.[31] In Ipswich and Colchester, creation of town lectureships where clergy stirred their auditories to support reform earned these villages reputations as centers of godly reform.

In Terling, a Stour Valley village not too far from Winthrop's Groton, the substantial villagers dominated the offices of parish government and led a campaign against immorality—pre-marital sex, drinking, and gaming in particular. This had real effects on behavior within the village, most dramatically manifest in a declining illegitimacy rate. In 1585, not too far away from Terling, two ministers in Dedham, both of whom were members of the Dedham conference, agreed with the "ancient inhabitants" on a set of principles for the "better ordering" of the town. A monthly meeting was proposed and the ministers and vestrymen agreed to "visit the poor, and chiefly the suspected places, that understanding the miserable state of those that want, and the naughty disposition of disordered persons, they may provide for them accordingly."[32] A generation later, also in the region, measures against the settlement of poor cottagers were part of the constitution of the vestry of Finchingfield drawn up in 1626 and similar provisions were made by the vestries in Great Easton in 1603 and Braintree in 1619.[33] In Braintree and Finchingfield, godly incumbent clergymen regularly attended vestry meetings. In the Suffolk community of Boxford, next to Winthrop's Groton, on March 28, 1608, an agreement was "concluded by the chief of the inhabitants of the parish" in which they regulated trade on the Sabbath, required inhabitants taking in any laborers or servants without posting bond to guarantee they would not become public charges, and set other policies for the good ordering of their community.[34] One historian has suggested that the "culture of discipline" discerned in these Stour Valley villages was pretty consciously patterned on Calvin's Geneva, the "model of an ideally governed community."[35]

Winthrop, who would be the first governor and key architect of the Massachusetts Bay colony, closely observed and then joined the partnership of godly magistrates and ministers in the Stour Valley. Born in the valley in 1588, he grew up accustomed to reform practices. His uncle William Winthrop, a London merchant, used his wealth to support the placement of godly clergy in the Stour Valley as well as in London. John's father, Adam Winthrop, a barrister and small landowner, became a friend and ally of leading clerical figures in the region such as John Still, John Knewstub, and Henry Sandes, all of whom visited the Winthrop manor house in Groton. Adam observed the members of the Dedham conference gathering when they met at Boxford. As a friend of magistrates such as Sir Robert Jermyn and John Gurdon, Adam closely followed their work in erecting their godly kingdom. John Winthrop grew up in this atmosphere, listened to his father and his father's friends as they conversed around the Groton dinner table, and aspired to follow in their footsteps. When he purchased Groton Manor from his uncle John in 1613, he achieved a status that led in 1615 to his appointment to the commission of the peace. His rise to county leadership was furthered by service on the Suffolk Sewer Commission, which was responsible for supervising repairs of roads and waterways. He sought to use his growing influence to foster the reform cause.

As he achieved greater influence in Suffolk, Winthrop became more involved in national affairs, experiences that made him suspicious of the central government and that gradually led him to consider emigration. In 1625, King Charles appointed him to what became known as the Forced Loan Commission for Suffolk, a body authorized to raise funds for the king through loans. Like Sir Francis Barrington and other puritan magistrates, Winthrop saw the loan as an unjust imposition and refused to serve. Unlike Barrington, he escaped imprisonment for his opposition. He aspired to influence the nation's course by service in Parliament. Unsuccessful in his own bid for a parliamentary seat in 1626, he promoted the candidacy of others and assisted in the drafting of Parliamentary bills. One of those whom he supported was Sir Robert Naunton. In 1627, Sir Robert, Master of the Court of Wards and Liveries, appointed Winthrop an attorney of that national body. The court determined who managed the estates of minors who had inherited lands in which the king had an interest. Winthrop's business before that court generated further ties with national leaders and provided him with a first hand view of the workings of the central government.[36]

The efforts of the Jermyns and Knewstubs during the 1570s had created a dominant puritan culture in the godly kingdom of the Stour Valley. Winthrop witnessed good men using the forms of local civil and ecclesiastical order to advance both the secular and spiritual components of the commonwealth. But all of our attention on the creative possibilities available to local leadership obscures the fact that the ability of such men to craft a distinctive regional community ultimately depended on the tolerance of the Crown. It appointed commission members and determined the advancement of gentry and clerical leaders alike. In the late sixteenth and early seventeenth centuries, the Crown allowed the East Anglian magistracy considerable latitude in religious matters, permitting the godly to pursue their agenda without jeopardizing their own preferment. But by the 1610s, the king and archbishops came to see deviance from prescribed church procedures more seriously and to regard forms of local religious association as threats to the national agenda.

Magistrates quickly learned that a steep personal price might be paid for their commitment to the reform cause. Addressing members of the bench in 1579, John Knewstub dedicated his *Answeare unto Certaine Assertions* to "those gentlemen in Suffolk whom the true worshipping God hath made right worshipfull."[37] By the time John Winthrop joined the commission in 1615, circumstances had changed considerably. When he reflected on his attendance at one of the Suffolk Quarter Sessions that year, Winthrop expressed the sense of powerlessness that many godly magistrates experienced: "When I was at Sessions I kept a continual watch (as near I could), but yet when I saw and heard the great account and estimation that the wisdom, glory, wealth, pleasure and such like worldly felicity was in with all, me thought I heard all men telling me I was a fool, to set so light my honor, credit, wealth, jollity etc: which I saw so many wise men so much affect and joy in, to tie my comfort to a conversation in heaven, which was no where to be seen, no way regarded, which would bring my self and all my gifts into contempt."[38]

Changes at the local level foreshawdowed the declining influence of the godly over their own realm, eventually compelling Winthrop to consider immigration to New England. He attended the assizes session in 1618 to hear Samuel Ward's sermon which opened the proceedings. Ward claimed that he saw before him "a worthy bench yet mingled with some drosse and not so refined as I have seen it." He denounced, among many other things, the proliferation of "Judges that judge for reward . . . as also such mercenary Lawyers, as sell both their tongues and their silence, their clients causes and their own consciences: who keep life in the law so long as there is money in the purse," as well as of bailiffs who "vex poore Countrey-men with unjust summons to the assizes and Sessions, with the rest of that Rabble. These muck-wormes of the world, which like the Gentles breede of putrefecation, & Beetles fed in the dung, relishing nothing else but earthly things, thinke there is no other godlinesse but gaine, no happinesse but to scrape and gather, to have and to hold."[39]

Such anxieties, which both Ward and Winthrop harbored, possessed real foundation. The coming of more conservative bishops—Harsnet, Wren, and Laud—and the death of leading godly figures like Jermyn (in 1614) and Higham (in 1626) rendered the godly cause less secure. Clergy in the diocese of Norwich felt a pressure for closer conformity under Bishop Harsnet. His stringent visitation articles of 1620, for example, were designed to root out not only nonconformity but the institutions that supported it, and apparently caused the demise of various lectureships, including that at Boxford.[40] Harsnet's successor in Norwich, Bishop Wren, continued to press for closer conformity. The new bishops of London, including William Laud, applied even greater pressure in Essex, which was part of their diocese. If not "harried out of the land," at a minimum, puritan clergymen found themselves prohibited from lecturing and challenged anew in their parish ministries, especially following the appointment of William Laud as bishop of London in 1628.[41] In 1633, Nathaniel Ward, who had arranged for the publication of his brother Samuel's assize sermon, lost his pulpit at Stondon-Massey, Essex. Indeed, the list of clergymen who came to the Bay Colony in the 1630s amounted to a "who's who" of East Anglian evangelical Protestants.

The pressure for religious conformity being applied by Wren, Laud, and their fellow bishops was matched by what many in the Stour Valley and elsewhere considered the equally intrusive policies of Charles I. Charles sought to impose uniform standards of secular administration—some of them his own new initiatives—that challenged traditions of local government, and insisted on their consistent enforcement. The campaign for militia reform, for example, made clear that Charles would no longer be satisfied with formalities, but wanted "realities and effects."[42] This assertion of central authority caused frictions in a number of localities as did, famously, the king's unprecedented raising of ship money from inland communities to finance the rebuilding of English naval power. Not all of Charles's policies were controversial—the once-notorious "Book of Orders" is now known to have built on several generations of administrative practice and was remarkable for systemizing existing practice rather than promoting innovation.[43] Nevertheless, numerous conflicts did arise over matters of detail or the particularities of local circumstances. The fact that Charles closed off his subjects' normal means of protesting political and ecclesiastical innovations by refusing to call a parliament for over a decade heightened the concerns of many. By 1642 in the Stour Valley, fears for the future of the Protestant church would combine with a growing popular commitment to parliamentary rule to form powerful and widespread resistance to the Caroline regime. But long before that date, John Winthrop and many of his neighbors would give up on the chance of further reform at home and leave to establish a new, and they hoped, better England in North America.[44]

Winthrop's growing sense of discontent resulted from the failure of men as much as from the failure of institutions. The governance of the Stour Valley had been godly when headed by godly magistrates.

He did not dwell on the short-comings of local government; indeed, the distinction we make between local and other kinds of government would not have made much sense to him. The puritan sense of providentialism led him to look for signs of God's favor or disfavor, and he found the signs not just in his own neighborhood but also abroad in the struggles of the Protestant cause on the continent. In 1621, he called upon God to "looke mercifully upon this sinfull lande, and turne us to him by some repentance, otherwise we may feare it hath seen the best dayes." For a time he hoped for a parliamentary reformation. He recommended Sir Robert Naunton as a candidate the godly should support for Parliament because Naunton "is knowne to be sounde for religion, firme to the Com[mon] W[ealth] . . . and the meetest man to further the affaires of our Countrye, for our Clothiers businesse etc:."[45] Of course, Winthrop hoped to sit in Parliament and advance those causes himself, and he was disappointed when Sir Robert Crane's efforts to engineer his selection for the borough of Sudbury failed in 1625.[46] As the influence of the godly diminished on the county commission, as godly clergy were forced from their livings, and as new royal policies impinged on local rights Winthrop came to feel that "The night was closing in" on the godly kingdom of the Stour Valley, if not on England itself.[47] The promise of a second chance in Massachusetts would prove irresistable to Winthrop and many other disappointed reformers.

The political and social order that the Massachusetts settlers established possessed no direct legal analogy with forms of government in England. The colony's charter mostly resembled that of other trading companies and in some ways reflected the chartered powers of English boroughs. Generally, no English parallel existed for conditions in the New World. The colonists could, however, replicate those familiar forms of local government that they had used to protect their interests back home. In England, local leaders regularly adapted their powers to local conditions; similarly, the colonists could exploit their legal powers to establish a familiar political and social order. Godly governors in the old world had faced obstacles both nationally and locally, but colonists in Massachusetts Bay could improvise the forms and functions of government upon their arrival largely without interference from royal authorities.

The story of this experiment began when, on March 18, 1629, King Charles I bestowed a charter on the governor and company of the Massachusetts Bay in New England. In the summer of 1629, company leaders, having already initiated settlement in their grant, pondered moving their operations to the colony. On August 26, a group of company members met at Cambridge and agreed to settle in Massachusetts if the charter and company government moved. Three days later, a General Court of the Company voted to authorize such a removal. This agreement proved critical to the nature of social and institutional development. The godly kingdom of the Stour Valley had declined because of the new control asserted by Charles I and Archbishop Laud and Bay colonists interpreted their charter as a bulwark for their local institutions against any similar interference.

Some of the more prominent members of the Massachusetts Bay Company who remained in England gave up their ability to exercise a role in the governance of the colony. Thus, power came into the hands of men of relatively humble status, although the enterprise never attracted many noble backers. None of the original stockholders rose to the level of status of those who became investors in the soon-to-be-created Providence Island Company. The Massachusetts leadership included gentlemen of substance such as Sir Henry Rosewell, Sir John Young, Thomas Southcoat, John Humphrey, John Endecott, and Simon Whetcombe, while the Providence Island grandees included the Earl of Warwick, Lord Saye and Sele, Lord Brooke, Sir Thomas Barrington, Sir Gilbert Gerard, and John Pym.[48] The Massachusetts enterprise was striking for the relative ordinariness of its membership, and striking as well for the fact that the majority of the investors seem to have been more interested in promoting godliness than in amassing personal profits.[49]

In England, political stature was closely related to social status. The absence of England's aristocracy in the enterprise made the Bay Colony government's task of legitimizing itself to its own colonists all the more difficult. The men who assumed early control of the Bay Colony had limited experience with governing in England. Sir Richard Bellingham, one-time steward of the earl of Lincoln, had served (without distinction) in the Parliament of 1628, but he had little other governmental experience.[50] Sir Richard Saltonstall, knighted in 1618, had served as a member of the commission of the peace in the West Riding of Yorkshire and had been lord mayor of Ledsham, Yorkshire. He, however, returned to England shortly after his arrival in Massachusetts. A number of individuals had at least some formal training in the law, including Emmanuel Downing, Roger Ludlow, and Herbert Pelham, while Thomas Dudley had clerked for a judge.[51] Many of these men may have had some other experience with government or knowledge of the law garnered from service in the institutions of the hundred and the parish or from law handbooks. Clearly, John Winthrop stood head and shoulders above all his fellow colonists in governing experience. A relatively minor figure in Suffolk gentry circles, Winthrop stood out among the early magistrates of Massachusetts by his experience with governing at the county level. Perhaps more than anything else, his county experience led to his selection as governor and made him the key figure in shaping the political life of the Bay Colony.

John Winthrop believed that it was the task of those embarked on the puritan experiment in New England to create "a due form of government, both civil and ecclesiastical." Yet his famous speech on the *Arbella* spelled out none of the details of either church or civil polity.[52] Instead, he exhorted his fellow colonists to advance "Christian charity" in a strong restatement of the social gospel that countless puritan clergy had preached in the Stour Valley. In shaping the institutions of the Bay Colony, Winthrop and his fellow magistrates sought to replicate those patterns of governance that had allowed for the creation of their familiar godly kingdom. And in so raising their "city on a hill" they must, Winthrop said, labor so that "whatsoever we did or ought to have done when we lived in England, the same must we do and more also where we go."[53] Success in New England would depend entirely upon the leadership's ability to use the powers conferred by the charter to push local government in the direction of an alliance between magistrate and minister as had been the case back in England. Gradually, the complexity of the colony's affairs led to new initiatives and experiments in government. But for the first half decade, Winthrop and his fellow magistrates governed the Bay Colony in accord with the ideals that they had worked out in the Stour Valley.

Winthrop and the other magistrates sought to establish their legitimacy as rulers in two senses. First, they needed to assert the legality of the colony and their own authority, both of which rested on the company charter. Like their counterparts in chartered authorities in old England, the Massachusetts leadership interpreted their charter as a guarantee of the colony's legal status and of individual liberty. They openly and stoutly rejected any interpretation of their charter that challenged the colony's legitimacy or that curtailed their liberties. Second, Winthrop and the colony's other leaders sought to impress upon their fellow settlers the legitimacy of their authority. In his "Model of Christian Charity," Winthrop reminded the colonists that they had entered into a covenant with each other and with the Lord to advance godly ends.[54] Failure of government or the governed to abide by the covenant would bring divine wrath down upon all.

At its first meeting, held in Charleston on August 23, 1630, the Court of Assistants[55] designated its members and other specified individuals as justices of the peace, "in all things to have the power that Justices of the peace hath in England for reformacion of abuses and punishing of offenders, but not inflict any corporal punishment without the presence and consent of some one of the Assistants." They modeled the Court of Assistants after the English Commission of the Peace, in essence designating those justices who became Assistants as holding the authority that in England had been reserved to elite "quorum" members of the Commission. The Court also set out procedures, again modeled after English precedent, for calling people before the Court in civil actions and fixed prices for certain commodities and trades.[56] Average colonists easily recognized the parallels with familar English forms. The recently arrived John Wiswall wrote back home in 1638 that the "men called Assistants [were], in power, much like your justices."[57]

The New England colony in its early years combined the functions of England's central and county governments, adapting or changing those aspects of English governance to fit colonial circumstances. Thus, while modeling itself on the Commission of the Peace, the Court of Assistants assumed the responsibility for dealing with cases that in England the justices would have decided in conjunction with the assize judges. Because puritans opposed the traditional ecclesiastical courts, the Court of Assistants assumed responsibility for administration of estates and similar matters that back in England came before church courts.[58] In order to provide speedy responses to cases, the Court of Assistants met on a monthly basis, taking into its own hands the primary work load for hearing cases that in England would have been handled by the emerging petty sessions composed of local magistrates. Only in 1636, when the geographical size and population of the colony had grown substantially, did the Court create administrative divisions for the colony, each with its own court. At that point, the Court of Assistants abandoned its monthly meetings in favor of quarterly sessions. Similar to the practice in England, magistrates held the new inferior courts in or near the towns of the division and included any other magistrate who wished to attend. A minimum of three justices, one of whom had to be a colony magistrate (the equivalent of being "of the quorum" in England), was necessary for the inferior courts to render a decision.[59]

Anyone familiar with the surviving records of English justices of the peace will easily recognize the great extent to which the Court of Assistants assumed the role of the Commission of the Peace. In its first years, the records of the Court included various judicial acts, such as empanelling juries, conducting trials, and sentencing offenders to whippings, fines, appearances in stocks and bilboes, or even physical disfigurement. Each individual magistrate possessed the power to issue warrants, summonses, and attachments. The Court also bound individuals to appear before it and took sureties to insure that its orders were carried out. Legal historian George Haskins has shown that "Influential as English local customs appear to have been on Massachusetts civil procedure, that influence is also apparent in the colony's substantive law. For example, the orders and adjudications of the courts leave little doubt that the colonists were influenced by the concept of nuisance as it was understood in the English local courts at the time."[60] Written pleadings, promissory notes, articles of apprenticeship, wills, conveyances, and other such instruments were drawn up in accord with English legal forms, many probably drawn from standard formulary books such as William West's *Symboleography, Which May Bee Termed the Art, or Description of Instruments and Presidents* (London, 1598), which Winthrop owned.[61] Administratively, the

Court of Assistants took on responsibility for a vast area of public policy. It established prices for labor and goods; appointed militia officers and constables; set dates for musters; required town watchhouses to be built and watches to be kept; appointed days of fast and thanksgiving; regulated the sale of ale and liquor; administered estates and appointed estate commissioners; licensed ferry operators; required and regulated town maintenance of stocks, roads and bridges, and scales and weights; and set standards for the care of the poor. It also passed orders to regulate what magistrates conceived of as moral behavior, such as prohibitions on the use of tobacco and the wearing of costly apparel.

During the colony's early years, the Court of Assistants controlled town affairs, shaping local governance in ways reminiscent of English practice. Writing of the colony's first days, William Pynchon in 1647 reminded Winthrop of how the forms of governance had been modeled after their experience in England. "I remember at our first cominge as soon as ever the people were divided into severall plantations, you did presently nominate a constable for each plantation as the most common officers of the kings peace, and gave them their oath in true substance as the constables take it in England."[62] The 1636 Town Act constituted town governments to "resemble the limited structure of English parochial or manorial administration."[63] The law recognized that "particular townes have many things, which concerne only themselves, and the ordering of their owne affairs" and "it is therefore ordered that the Freemen of every towne, or the major parte of them, shall onely have power to dispose of their owne lands ... and make such orders as may concerne the well ordering of their owne townes, not repugnant to the lawes and orders here established by the General Court" and "to chuse their owne particular officers, as constables, surveyors for highways, and the like."[64]

Even before the Town Act of 1636, the residents of individual towns played a role in shaping their communities after the pattern of the English civil parish. Thus, in 1632 the Reverend George Philips gathered the citizens of Watertown together in the congregational meetinghouse to discuss the legitimacy of a tax rate levied by the General Court.[65] Just as adult male ratepayers were members of the parish vestry in England, adult males in the colony became town freemen, and town meetings held the same extensive authority as that exercised by the vestry back home. Administration of affairs not handled at town meetings was entrusted to boards of selectmen, a body not all that dissimilar from the select vestries of the English parish. Many towns drafted and subscribed to written covenants that are reminiscent of the articles drafted by Swallowfield and other English parish communities. Those subscribed to at Dedham, for instance, included:

> One. We whose names are here unto subscribed do, in the fear and reverence of our Almighty God, mutually and severally promise amongst ourselves and each other to profess and practice one truth according to that most perfect rule, the foundation whereof is everlasting love.... Two. That we shall by all means labor to keep off form us all such as are contrary minded, and receive only such unto us as may be probably of one heart with us.... [and] Three. That if at any time differences shall arise between parties of our said town, that then such party or parties shall presently resolve all differences unto some one, two, or three others of our said society to be fully accorded and determined without any further delay, if it possibly may be.[66]

The actual work of town selectmen and the town meeting as a whole can be traced in the *Second Report of the Record Commissioners of the City of Boston Containing the Boston Records, 1634-1660, and the Book of Possessions*. One can find there decisions for allocations of land, town orders for fencing in property, regulation of livestock, stipulations for arbitration of disputes, and the other nuts and bolts of running a town.[67] As David Grayson Allen and others have shown, even in making such everyday decisions, the colonists generally acted "in English ways," adapting to their new circumstances the parish and manorial policies of their places of origin.[68]

What one does *not* find in the Bay Colony also reflects the English puritan experience. Those elements of local government most closely tied to the Crown and most deeply resented never made the voyage across the ocean. One does not find in colonial New England a lord lieutenant, sheriff, purveyor, hunters after concealed lands, or licensees of the Crown. The militia was an important institution in the colony, whose effectiveness safeguard colonists against attack from hostile natives or foreign enemies. With no lord lieutenant, the militia came under the control of a commission, with the Assistants acting as muster commissioners much as the Suffolk Commission of the Peace had functioned as a muster commission. The Bay Assistants appointed town militia commanders, set requirements for training days, and mandated watches to be kept. Later, after the structure of the towns became legally established, the colony further modified the system in a voluntaristic direction by allowing the local militia companies to nominate the officers that would be appointed by the magistrates.

As they organized the affairs of their colony along the lines of county and local practice, colonial leaders also defined their relationship to the Crown. Unlike the members of the English commissions, these men were not appointees of the king. In this respect, their situation most closely resembled that of borough leaders, men chosen by their community in accord with the chartered rights of their corporation. The Massachusetts General Court and English boroughs, both derived from royal charters, owed their legal existences to the Crown, and jealously guarded their legal authority from encroachment.

Although they recognized their unity with all English people and the godly in the Church, the colonists seem to have come early to the view that their charter gave them virtual autonomy from the Crown and the central government in ordering local affairs.[69] In this they were little different from borough corporations at home, which had been largely free of concerted Crown interference in the generations prior to 1640.[70] Edmund S. Morgan described the situation nicely when he wrote that "Winthrop was content to acknowledge the subordination of Massachusetts to England, provided the mother country made no serious attempt to recover the powers which the King had so freely given."[71]

This is not to say that the magistrates conducted their business without fear of royal intervention. The oath that colony officers took included a statement swearing allegiance to the king, until 1643 when that portion was dropped. To help preserve their autonomy, colonial leaders relied on friends in England such as Emmanuel Downing to help them craft politic answers to the complaints of their critics. The magistrates only slapped John Endecott on the wrist for cutting the red cross out of the royal ensign during the mustering of the Salem militia in 1634, because they approved of his actions but feared the incident might provoke royal anger.[72] Additionally, many agreed with Roger Williams that the king had no right to grant to the settlers the land of Massachusetts, but they made every effort to stop him from publicly questioning the Crown's right, again fearing unwanted royal intervention.

The puritan character of the settlement attracted more than enough attention, and by the mid 1630s the charter and the very existence of the Bible commonwealth seemed in peril. In 1634, news of the Privy Council's creation of a Commission for Regulating Plantations, headed by the hated William Laud, prompted erection of new fortifications in Boston harbor, renewed attention to militia drills, and led to the appointment of a military council (muster commission) that included Winthrop and Endecott. When Charles I instructed Attorney General Sir John Banks to recall the Bay Colony's charter, colonial clergy urged the magistrates to defend Massachusetts by force if need be. When the Court of King's Bench ordered the colonists to surrender the charter, they ignored the demand. It is hard to say what might have happened if ill fortune and other events had not intervened. Sir Ferdinando Gorges, the king's appointee to assume control of the region, lost one of his ships upon launching and had insufficient resources on his own to proceed. The king, to whom Gorges looked for assistance, became preoccupied with the outbreak of the Bishops War in Scotland. Not until the time of a later King Charles in the 1680s would Massachusetts and other corporate bodies in England and the New World again fear loss of their charters.[73]

The New Englanders also found themselves defending their autonomy against potential parliamentary charter infringements during the 1640s. Massachusetts supported Parliament in the English Civil Wars, and in 1645 the General Court outlawed support for the royalist cause. The colonists welcomed a parliamentary order, which Winthrop recorded in September 1641, "that we should enjoy all our liberties, etc., according to our patent, whereby our patent, which had been condemned and called in upon an erroneous judgement in a quo warranto, was now implicitly revived and confirmed."[74] But Winthrop, among others, opposed any effort to make Massachusetts explicitly subject to parliamentary authority, arguing that "if we should put ourselves under the protection of the parliament, we must then be subject to such laws as they should make, or at least such as they might impose upon us."[75]

Whether from king or Parliament, the Bay Colony consistently resisted any attempt to decrease its autonomy. From its earliest days, the colony rejected the right of any settler to appeal decisions of the

General Court to authorities in England. Colonial officials repeatedly found themselves called upon to elaborate their understanding of the colony's relationship to imperial rule, and as time went on they did so with greater and greater precision. In a very detailed presentation, the magistrates in 1646 accepted the theoretical subordination of the colony to the mother country, but asserted that in practice Massachusetts enjoyed the same independence as the medieval English kings who ruled Normandy and Gascony. This astonishingly independent attitude casts new light on future relations between England and its colonial dependency.[76]

Winthrop exercised a critical role in shaping the evolving political system, although some historians have overestimated it. In Massachusetts, Winthrop enjoyed considerable respect and derived a certain amount of authority by virtue of serving as governor. But he was not a member of England's aristocracy who could claim authority based on lineage. Indeed, the Court of Assistants disfranchised and fined Thomas Dexter in 1633 for "saying this captious government will bring all to nought adding that the best of them *was but an Atturney*" (emphasis added). Thomas Dudley and others charged Winthrop with arbitrary rule. There is no evidence, however, that the governor exercised any power beyond that of the other magistrates, although Winthrop reserved the right to act more decisively if that served the best interests of the colony.[77] At most, the governor acted as a "custos rotulorum"—the chairman of the magisterial court who called meetings, set agendas, and guided deliberations.

By dressing their authority in the familiar garb of English local government, the magistrates won the support of the colonists and remained relatively free from royal interference during the first years of settlement. Nevertheless, the best efforts of Winthrop and his fellow magistrates could not insulate the godly kingdom of Massachusetts from the inevitable tensions of a rapidly growing society. Over the course of the Bay Colony's first decade, Massachusetts evolved from a compact settlement to the equivalent of a large county with many towns, to a burgeoning colony of many counties. The political localism that animated the entire settlement in 1630, a mere five years later became narrowed to a contentious defense of town rights, or of a county, against the policies of colony magistrates. Timothy Breen has argued that "Winthrop's experiences in England had been largely on the county level, and when he attempted to strengthen the hand of the Bay magistrates, to keep the colony's villages from spinning off in a dozen different directions, he found himself unwittingly portrayed as an enemy of the local communities."[78] These tensions influenced the further evolution of the colony's institutions.

More fundamental tensions developed from ambiguities inherent in the government's authority. Colonists at first accepted the rule of Winthrop and other magistrates because it resembled English local government. But growth of the colony quickly exposed the limitations of the English model. The Assistants, for instance, could justify setting rates for meeting the financial burden of defense or specific crises by the precedent of the Commission's ability to do so. But when it became necessary for the colony to create a general fund, no such precedent existed. A close reading of the political history of the 1630s reveals the magistrates, and especially Winthrop, grappling with the theoretical and practical limitations of the local government model. When challenged to justify certain acts that the magistrates could not claim to be based on the authority of the commission of the peace, no ready answer came to hand. On occasion, Winthrop claimed the vague justification of the precedent of common law usage. At other times, he made the dubious assertion of divine sanction, maintaining that God authorized the magistrates to serve the colony. Winthrop and the magistrates commonly invoked the charter, or patent, as they usually referred to it, to justify their actions. But the document represented more an emblem of legal status than a blueprint for government and within a few years so many changes had been made to the charter that it bore little resemblance to the original patent. As Morgan has put it, the "word 'freeman' as used in Massachusetts after 1630 meant something more and something less than was intended in the charter."[79]

While the charter could be used to deflect Royal or parliamentary interference and to reject appeals by dissidents to officials back home, the day-to-day legitimacy of the government depended on the colonists' approval of its actions. In what amounted to a nascent, informal democratic process, the shape of the charter emerged from ongoing negotiations between the magistrates and the populace. Such negotiation over acceptable boundaries of government action itself had been part of the colonists' English heritage. The process became more problematic with time, however, as new immigrants changed the political complexion of Massachusetts. Those who came to the Bay Colony in the mid 1630s possessed more distrust of authority than those who had journeyed to America at the start of the decade. Winthrop and the first colonists had perceived a danger of growing absolutism, but those who came later had felt the harsh hand of arbitrary government, making them more suspicious of authority, and particularly of discretionary authority, Winthrop's favorite theory of leadership.[80]

The Court of Assistants that met in September 1630 consisted of individuals who had been chosen by the company General Court in England. They could have ruled the colony themselves, co-opting new members to their body as necessary, but they chose to extend freemanship to others who had journeyed with them to the New World. To guarantee the godly nature of the commonwealth, the General Court limited new admissions to freeman status to church members. Thus, a new type of General Court emerged—one consisting of men who had invested not money but themselves in the errand into the wilderness. That General Court possessed the power to choose the assistants and the governor. Initially, this General Court met twice a year, reminiscent of the meetings of the assizes and, indeed, these sessions resembled the assizes in their solemnity and in the large audiences that witnessed the deliberations.[81] The company, however, apparently did not intend the General Court to serve as their equivalent. The assignment of power between the General Court—consisting of all the freemen—and the Assistants remained unclear and disputed.

Over time and through challenges to magisterial monopoly of power, the freemen and the political leadership developed a consensus on the meaning of the charter. As had been the case in England, "national" and local interests came to blows in Massachusetts over taxation for troop training and military preparedness. In 1632, for instance, the freemen of Watertown challenged the right of the Court of Assistants to levy a tax without their consent for colony fortifications. The dispute led to the right of the freemen of the various towns to appoint deputies to represent local interests at meetings of the General Court, where taxation issues would be decided.[82] Increasingly, the meetings of the General Court came to resemble Parliament and the assize sessions, serving as forums for the resolution of disputes between the central government and the localities.[83]

The debate over the necessity of a colonial code of laws best illustrates the dynamics of institutional development in Massachusetts.[84] Discussion of a new codes of laws continued an older English debate over the wide latitude exercised by common law courts in determining offenses and imposing sentences. Puritans and others had advocated review and codification of the penal statutes in the mother country, but with little success. Their efforts reached a peak during the Interregnum, when Englishmen began drawing upon the colonial experience in that debate.[85] Most colonists who backed the drive for codification expressed concerns that magisterial discretion in interpreting English laws and customs could lead to abuses of power. Clearly, some magistrates did earn a reputation for arbitrary rule. But other advocates of a code, including John Cotton, sought adoption of a new code based on Mosaic principles.[86]

Winthrop opposed the use of Mosaic law, remained highly suspicious of any legal codification, and for a time managed, along with other magistrates, to deflect the movement. He asserted that codification of colony "orders" as "laws" would "transgress the limits of our charter, which provide, we shall make no laws repugnant to the laws of England, and that we were assured we must do" by those who wished a code. Winthrop further explained that "to raise up laws by practice and custom had been no transgression; as in our church discipline, and in matters of marriage; to make a law that marriages should not be solemnized by ministers is repugnant to the laws of England; but to bring it to a custom by practice for the magistrates to perform it, is no law repugnant, etc."[87] Winthrop and several other magistrates had a more fundamental reason for opposing codification in the 1630s. As Winthrop once remarked, the colony lacked "of sufficient experience of the nature and disposition of the people, considered with the condition of the country and other circumstances, which made them conceive, that such laws would be fittest for us, which should rise *pro re nata*, upon occasions, etc., and so the laws of England and other states grew, and therefore the fundamental laws of England are called customs, consuetudines."[88] This view, often associated with the "common law mind," held "that the common law had developed through the gradual adaptation of natural principles of justice to peculiar English circumstances."[89] But by 1648, Winthrop could no longer defeat advocates of codification, and after many failed efforts and without fear of royal interference, the colonists adopted a body of "Laws and Liberties."[90]

Massachusetts colonists drew upon a larger political culture as they sought to interpret their formal legal powers in the light of their experiences with local government in old and New England. They clearly enjoyed unusual freedom to experiment in their new surroundings, but their actions owed much to the experience with local government in the Old World. The key to understanding this process lies not in seeking precise institutional analogies—for there are few—but in seeing how magistrates in the New World and the Old sought to exploit available legal instruments in pursuit of what they defined as the best interests of those under their authority. In Massachusetts, the settlers improvised, and in doing so created something new. The elements of their authority, however, were recognizably English. As Richard Ross wrote, "Puritanism . . . put its imprint on Massachusetts justice by intensifying selected strands of the English inheritance."[91]

In transferring their charter and seat of government to America, the settlers of Massachusetts also transferred familiar English forms of governance. They proved remarkably creative in adapting these forms to the New World situation. Given the relatively small population and the scarcity of trained judges, colonists could not transfer the multiplicity of national courts and legal procedures. Neither did they retain the strong English bond of the covenanted congregation and the civil parish—the township in New England. Magistrates came to be selected by freemen rather than by the Crown, and the distinction between assizes and Quarter Sessions became blurred. But the basic pattern of local justices maintaining order and meeting quarterly to deal with the broader concerns of the county (or colony), proved a familiar one calculated to create stability and order thousands of miles from home.

As in old England, colonial settlers used familiar institutions to reconcile local tensions over the appropriate use of legal and political power, and between particular local interests and a (developing) central government. The relative freedom from central oversight and control did not remove all obstacles to the establishment of godly rule, but it did permit them to improvise on elements of English institutional structure and political culture. In doing so, they did not act as "Americans," but as Englishmen giving expression both to a particular view of the old English past and of new English future.

This essay began as a collaborative effort with Michael J. Braddick. I wish to acknowledge Mike's contributions and advice, though responsibility for the final product is mine. The two of us offered versions of the essay at the Cambridge University Seminar on Tudor and Stuart England and also at the Massachusetts Historical Society's Early American History Seminar. I would like to thank those present on each occasion for their suggestions and comments.

1. Timothy H. Breen and Stephen Foster, "The Puritans' Greatest Achievement: A Study of Social Cohesion in Seventeenth-Century Massachusetts," *Journal of American History* 60(1973):5-22. Breen and Foster attribute that cohesion and peacefulness to factors such as the social unity and economic prosperity of the settlers, a widely accepted ideology, and the compact nature of the settlement. While not denying the importance of such factors, I argue in this essay that the successful establishment of familiar types of governing institutions played a major role in the colony's success.

2. For a good guide to local officeholding, see Anthony Fletcher, *Reform in the Provinces: The Government of Stuart England* (New Haven and London, 1986). For Suffolk, see Diarmaid MacCulloch, *Suffolk and the Tudors: Politics and Religion in an English County 1500-1600* (Oxford, 1986), appendix I; for Norfolk, see A. H. Smith, *County and Court: Government and Politics in Norfolk, 1558-1603* (Oxford, 1974), appendix I.

3. See T. G. Barnes, *Somerset 1625-1640: A County's Government During the 'Personal Rule'* (Chicago, 1961), 46.

4. J. S. Cockburn, *A History of English Assizes 1558-1714* (Cambridge, 1972). The Assizes are discussed extensively in Cynthia Herrup, The *Common*

Peace: Participation and the Criminal Law in Seventeenth-Century England (Cambridge, 1987). A detailed presentation and discussion of assizes and Sessions of the Peace in one county is Louis A. Knafla, *Kent at Law 1602, The County Jurisdiction: Assizes and Sessions of the Peace* (London, 1994).

5. Cockburn, *A History of English Assizes*, 2.
6. See Steve Hindle, *The State and Social Change in Early Modern England, c. 1550-1640* (Cambridge, 2000). Another viewpoint can be found in Michael J. Braddick, *State Formation in Early Modern England, c.1550-1700* (Cambridge, 2000).
7. Herrup, *The Common Peace*, 54-55.
8. For a discussion of this evolution, see Frederic A. Youngs, Jr., "Towards petty sessions: Tudor JPS and divisions of counties," in Delloyd J. Guth and John W. McKenna, eds., *Tudor Rule and Revolution: Essays for G. R. Elton from his American Friends* (Cambridge, 1982), 201-216.
9. Lancashire had no general Quarter Sessions and another local institutional innovation arose in its place. Magistrates met to discuss county business at the sheriff's table during assize week. B. W. Quintrell, ed., *Proceedings of the Lancashire Justices of the Peace at the Sheriff's Table During Assizes Week, 1578-1694*, Chester, Record Society of Lancashire and Cheshire, 121 (1981).
10. There is material on these offices in: J. R. Kent, *The English Village Constable 1580-1642: A Social and Administrative Study* (Oxford, 1986); John S. Morrill, *The Cheshire Grand Jury, 1625-1659: A Social and Administrative Study*, Leicester University Department of English Local History, Occasional Papers, 3rd Series, No. 1 (Leicester, Eng., 1976); and S. K. Roberts, "Initiative and Control: The Devon Quarter Sessions Grand Jury, 1649-70," *Bulletin of the Institute of Historical Research* 57 (1984):165-177.
11. Michael J. Braddick, *Parliamentary Taxation in Seventeenth-Century England: Local Administration and Response* (Woodbridge, Eng., 1994), 66-71.
12. Keith Wrightson, "Two Concepts of Order: Justices, Constables and Jurymen in Seventeenth Century England," in J. Brewer and J. Syles, eds., *An Ungovernable People The English and Their Law in the Seventeenth and Eighteenth Centuries* (London, 1980), 21-46. See also, Kent, *Village Constable*.
13. For the importance of manorial and other local courts down to 1600 and beyond, see Marjorie K. McIntosh, *Controlling Misbehavior in England, 1370-1600* (Cambridge, 1998).

14. As in the case of the commission of the peace, the most detailed explication of the operations of parish government is Sidney and Beatrice Webb, *English Local Government*. Vol. 1: *The Parish and the County* (London, 1906).
15. John Winthrop, "Modell of Christian Charity," *Winthrop Papers* (Boston, 1929-), 2:282.
16. Hindle, *The State and Social Change*, 29.
17. Quoted in Braddick, *State Formation*, 73.
18. Paul Slack, *Poverty and Policy in Tudor and Stuart England* (London, 1988), esp. 138-161; Slack, *From Reformation to Improvement: Public Welfare in Early Modern England* (Oxford, 1998), esp. 29-52.
19. For fuller discussion and reference, see Michael J. Braddick, *The Nerves of State: Taxation and the Financing of the English State, 1558-1714* (Manchester, 1996); Braddick, *State Formation*, 40-43.
20. An advowson is the right of nomination to a benefice. Laymen who purchased monastic lands following the dissolution of the monasteries might obtain the advowson for a benefice that had belonged to that monastery.
21. For a fuller discussion and further references, see Patrick Collinson, *The Religion of Protestants: The Church in English Society 1559-1625* (Oxford, 1982); Braddick, *State Formation*, 291-333.
22. John S. Craig, "Co-operation and Initiatives: Elizabethan Churchwardens and the Parish Accounts of Mildenhall," *Social History* 18(1993):357-380; Eric Carlson, "The Origins, Function and Status of the Office of Churchwarden, with Particular Reference to the Diocese of Ely," in Margaret Spufford, ed., *The World of Rural Dissenters, 1520-1725* (Cambridge, 1995), 164-207.
23. MacCulloch, *Suffolk and the Tudors*, 219.
24. Collinson, *Religion of Protestants*, 153-164, quotation at 159. Collinson's account also draws upon the MacCulloch's work.
25. For cultural regions, see A. Hassell Smith, "Puritanism and 'Neighbourhood': A Case Study in Late 16th and Early 17th Century Norfolk," in Edward Royle, ed., *Regional Studies in the History of Religion in Britain Since the Later Middle Ages* (York, 1984), a neglected but important work examining a religious cultural pays between the Stiffley and Galven rivers in north Norfolk, and suggesting ways of identifying cultural regions larger than the town and smaller than the county. Charles Phythian Adams also has argued for moving beyond political and ecclesiastical definitions of

place, most notably in *Societies, Cultures and Kinship, 1580-1850: Cultural Provinces and English Local History* (Leicester, Eng., 1997). I do not agree with all aspects of his analysis of the Stour region.

26. Unless otherwise indicated, material in this section is drawn from Francis J. Bremer, "Searching the Stour Valley for Puritans and Puritanism," paper delivered at the Institute of Historical Research Seminar in London on "The Religious History of Britain from the 15th to the 18th Centuries," Feb. 13, 2001.

27. William Hunt, *The Puritan Moment: The Coming of Revolution in an English County* (Cambridge, Mass, 1983), quotation, 109.

28. Hunt, *The Puritan Moment*, 111-112.

29. Hunt, *The Puritan Moment*, ch. 3; Wrightson and Levine, *Terling*.

30. Collinson, *Religion of Protestants*, ch. 4, quotation, 171.

31. Slack, *Poverty*, 150-151.

32. Hunt, *Puritan Moment*, 82.

33. Hunt, *Puritan Moment*, 71-72. Records of the Braintree and Finchingfield town meetings are to be found in F. G. Emmison, ed., *Early Essex Town Meetings: Braintree, 1619-1636: Finchingfield, 1626-1634* (Chichester, Eng., 1970).

34. Boxford Churchwardens Accounts, Suffolk Record Office/Bury.

35. Hunt, *Puritan Moment*, esp. 83-84.

36. Francis J. Bremer, "The Heritage of John Winthrop: Religion along the Stour Valley, 1548-1630," *New England Quarterly* 70(1997):515-547, quotation, 540. He seems to have been out of the commission in the mid 1620s. In advocating the election of Robert Naunton MP for Sudbury, in January 1626, he called on Sir Robert Crane to undertake the necessary lobbying at the quarter sessions: *Winthrop Papers*, 1:324-325. This may simply have been due to the fact of Crane's superior status, but the Crown Office Docquet Books note his restoration to the commission in June of that year. Public Record Office, C231/4 p. 203v, quoted from "John Winthrop as Justice of the Peace," http://marauder.millersville.edu/~winthrop/jp.html. For the possible significances of interrupted service as a JP see Smith, *County and Court*, ch. 4; and MacCulloch, *Suffolk and the Tudors*, 113-114.

37. John Knewstub, *An Answeare unto Certayne Assertions (1579)*, "Epistle"; Samuel Ward, *Jethro's Justice of the Peace* (n.p., 1618), 59-60.

38. John Winthrop, *Experiencia*, quoted from *Winthrop Papers*, 1:195-196. The text is also available on the web: http//www.millersv.edu/~winthrop/jwesp.html.
39. Ward, *Jethros Justice*, 51-52.
40. Bremer, "Heritage of John Winthrop," 540-543.
41. Two recent studies that examine the plight of puritan clergy in East Anglia at this time are Tom Webster, *Godly Clergy in Early Stuart England: The Caroline Puritan Movement c. 1620-1642* (Cambridge, 1997) and Francis J. Bremer, *Congregational Communion: Clerical Friendship in the Anglo American Puritan Community, 1610-1692* (Boston, 1994).
42. Kevin Sharpe, *The Personal Rule of Charles I* (New Haven and London, 1992), 32.
43. Sharpe, *Personal Rule*, esp. 403-506. There were some legal concerns expressed about powers of search for stores of grain during the harvest years 1630-1632, however. See Paul Slack, "Dearth and Social Policy in Early Modern England," *Social History of Medicine* 5(1992):1-17; R. B. Outhwaite, "Dearth and Government Intervention in English Grain Markets, 1590-1700," *Economic History Review* 34(1981):389-406.
44. John Walter, *Understanding Popular Violence in the English Revolution: The Colchester Plunderers* (Cambridge, 1999). There had been prominent opponents of the forced loan of 1626 in the region and John Winthrop refused to serve on the Suffolk Commission. His friend Sir Nathaniel Barnardiston was arrested for such a refusal. Richard Cust, *The Forced Loan and English Politics 1626-1628* (Oxford, 1987), 144-145. Cust has an extensive discussion of the resistance in East Anglia, including a map showing the large concentration of defaulters along the Stour Valley in northern Essex. In Essex, Sir Francis Barrington and Sir William Masham were committed to the Fleet for their opposition to the loan. Both the county commission and the king's Privy Council met often to decide how to respond to the widespread refusal to pay. Thomas Birch, comp., *The Court and Times of Charles the First* (London, 1849) 1:161-162, 207. John Winthrop communicated with Barrington through his son, John Winthrop, Jr., *Winthrop Papers*, 1:336-337. A few years later, in Witham, Essex, several others died in a melee that began when some youth tied red crosses to the tails of dogs to protest the billeting of Irish Catholic troops in their community, thus making a statement against the king's military policy and popery. G. E. Aylmer, "St Patrick's Day 1628 in

Witham, Essex," *Past & Present* 61(1973):139-148. See also: Timothy Breen, "The Covenanted Militia of Massachusetts Bay: English Background and New World Development," *Past & Present* 57(1972):74-96 and Francis J. Bremer, "Endecott and the Red Cross: Puritan Iconoclasm in the New World," *Journal of American Studies* 24(1990):5-22.

45. *Winthrop Papers*, 1:268, 325-326. For his providentialism, see esp. 238 and for his flirtation with service in the 1624 Parliament, 317-318. He kept notes about a variety of grievances to be presented to that Parliament, and also drafts of bills designed to combat drunkenness drawn up in the 1628 Parliament, 295-311, 371-374. For his fears about England's future, see 2:91-92. For the interconnections of religious and political grievances, and of local and national concerns, along the Stour Valley, see Walter, *Understanding Popular Violence*. For the hopes for parliamentary reformation in the 1640s, see Samuel Hartlib, *The Parliament's Reformation* (London, 1646). For the activities of the Hartlib circle, see C. Webster, *The Great Instauration: Science, Medicine and Reform 1626-1660* (London, 1975).

46. Sir Robert Crane, who had previously represented Sudbury in Parliament, used his influence to have Sir Nathaniel Barrington and John Winthrop chosen to represent the borough. But the freemen of the town chose Barrington and Thomas Smith, an alderman and former mayor. Winthrop's friend Brampton Gurdon wrote that "Sir Ro: Crane took it very unkindly." Brampton Gurdon to John Winthrop, Feb. 19, 1626, *Winthrop Papers*, 1:317-318. I would like to thank the staff of the History of Parliament Trust for permission to review their as-yet-unpublished information on Crane, Smith, and Sudbury.

47. Bremer, "Heritage of John Winthrop," 547.

48. For the Massachusetts Bay Company and the back ground of its membership, see Frances Rose-Troup, *The Massachusetts Bay Company and Its Predecessors* (New York, 1930); for the Providence Island Company, see Karen Kupperman, *Providence Island, 1630-1641: The Other Puritan Colony* (Cambridge, 1993).

49. The pursuit of profit and of reformation were not mutually exclusive goals, and the distinction between a godly north and commercial south in the American colonies is undoubtedly overdrawn. Kupperman, *Providence Island*. For profit and godliness in the American colonies, see also Webster, *Great Instauration*.

50. Except where noted, the information on early Massachusetts leaders comes from Robert Wall, *The Membership of the Massachusetts Bay General*

Court, 1630-1686 (New York, 1990), *Dictionary of National Biography*, and *American National Biography*.

51. George Haskins asserted in *Law and Authority in Early Massachusetts* (New York, 1960) that John Humphrey had been a member of Lincoln's Inn, but Wall's research does not support this. Haskins also followed Samuel Eliot Morison's lead in *Builders of the Bay Colony* (Boston, 1930) in claiming that William Pynchon was a justice of the peace, but Joseph Smith's examination of the Essex commissions for the peace for this period refutes that claim. Smith, *Colonial Justice in Western Massachusetts (1639-1702)* (Cambridge, Mass., 1961), 7. Smith also discounts the claim that Pynchon presided over manorial courts; his only public office seemed to be that of churchwarden.

52. *Winthrop Papers*, 2:293.

53. *Winthrop Papers*, 2:293.

54. John Witte, Jr., focuses on the covenant basis of early Massachusetts institutions in "How to Govern a City on a Hill: The Early Puritan Contribution to American Constitutionalism," *Emory Law Journal* 39(Winter 1990):41-64.

55. Structurally, the Assistants were the equivalent of a board of directors. The General Court should be seen as a meeting of all stockholders. The Assistants eventually evolved into an upper house of the general court that also served as the governor's council. That having been said, in 1630 the only stockholders (freemen) in the colony were Assistants, and so until freemanship was expanded, the membership of both groups was identical.

56. References to the activities of the Massachusetts Court of Assistants in this and succeeding paragraphs is based on John Noble, ed., *Records of the Court of Assistants of the Colony of the Massachusetts Bay 1630-1692* (Boston, 1904), 2.

57. John Wiswall to George Rigby, 1638, copy in Justin Winsor Papers, Massachusetts Historical Society, Box 10, "Notes for *Memorial History*," item 215.

58. This might also be seen as an effort by the colonists to achieve the reform of justice that many had demanded in England, where church courts were very unpopular and where justices of the peace had increasingly asserted their right to judge moral offenses.

59. Much of this ground has been previously covered by George Lee Haskins in *Law and Authority* (see n.51 for first cite). Our conclusions differ,

largely as a result of the scholarship on English law and society that has appeared in the four decades since Haskins wrote.

60. Haskins, *Law and Authority*, 169.
61. A copy of this work, with John Winthrop's signature, survives in the Winthrop Collection in the New York Society Library.
62. William Pynchon to John Winthrop, Mar. 9, 1646/7, *Winthrop Papers*, 5:134-135.
63. David Konig, *Law and Society in Puritan Massachusetts* (Chapel Hill, 1979), 21. Konig, whose study begins in 1636 and focuses on the decades that followed, regards the earliest government of the Bay Colony as modeled on that of English boroughs. It is also clear, however, that the model of the county commission, and the experience of the settlers in county government, was influential in molding the governance of the colony. The search for precise institutional analogies between old and New England is, in my view, a fruitless one. The important point is the way in which the settlers employed those powers for particular political and religious purposes.
64. *Massachusetts Records*, 1:172.
65. Roger Thompson, *Divided We Stand: Watertown, Massachusetts, 1630-1680* (Amherst, Mass., 2001), 40-41.
66. As quoted in Kenneth Lockridge, *A New England Town: The First Hundred Years* (New York, 1970), 4-6. Lockridge's study remains one of the most useful analyses of the workings of the seventeenth-century New England town community.
67. *Second Report of the Record Commissioners of the City of Boston Containing the Boston Records, 1634-1660, and the Book of Possessions* (Boston, 1902), which is a curiously neglected source.
68. David Grayson Allen, *In English Ways: The Movement of Societies and the Transferal of English Local Law and Custom to Massachusetts Bay in the Seventeenth Century* (Chapel Hill, 1981). Allen concludes that the inhabitants of the five Massachusetts towns he studied had "essentially reproduced what they wanted—the ordering of life as they knew it before their emigration" (205). Allen's focus is on land systems, agricultural methods, and to a lesser degree, town government.
69. Edmund S. Morgan, *The Puritan Dilemma: The Story of John Winthrop*, 2nd edition (New York, 1999), 175-176. The text of this edition is virtually identical to the original, published over forty years ago.

70. For a good, recent discussion of urban politics in that period, see C. F. Patterson, *Urban Patronage in Early Modern England: Corporate Boroughs, the Landed Elite, and the Crown, 1580-1640* (Stanford, 1999).
71. Morgan, *Puritan Dilemma*, 175.
72. A full discussion of the episode can be found in Bremer, "'Endecott and the Red Cross.'"
73. Francis J. Bremer, *The Puritan Experiment: New England Society from Bradford to Edwards*, rev. edition (Hanover, N. H., 1995), 70-72. For the assault on chartered authorities in England, see John Miller, "The Crown and the Borough Charters in the reign of Charles II," *English Historical Review* 100(1985):53-84.
74. Richard S. Dunn, James Savage, and Laetitia Yeandle, eds., *The Journal of John Winthrop 1630-1649* (Cambridge, Mass., 1996), 365; hereafter cited as Winthrop, *Journal*.
75. Winthrop, *Journal*, 346. In point of fact, as the 1640s advanced, Parliament did take actions to further the interests of the colonists—such as orders taken in 1642 and 1644 to free New England trade from customs duties—which the colonists welcomed, thus undercutting their claim to autonomy.
76. The full statement, as reported by Winthrop (who probably prepared it), is in his *Journal*: "by our Charter we had absolute power of Government: for thereby we have power to make laws, to erect all sorts of magistracy, to correct, punish, pardon, govern & Rule the people absolutely: which word implies 2 things: 1: a perfection of parts, so as we are thereby furnished with all parts of Government: 2: it implies a self sufficiency quoad subjectum materiam, & ergo, should not need the help of any superior power, either general Governor or &c to Complete our Government. Yet we did owe allegiance & subjection, 1. because our Common wealth was founded upon the power of that State, & so had been always on, 2. in regard of our tenure of our lands of the manner of East Greenwich, 3. we depended upon them for protection, &c 4. for Advice & Counsel when in great occasions we should crave it, 5. in the continuance of naturalization & free legeance of our selves & our posterity: yet me might be still independent in respect of Government, as Normandy, Gascony, &c, were, though they had dependence upon the Crown of France, & the Kings of England did homage, &c, yet in point of Government they were not dependent upon France." Winthrop, *Journal*, 648-649.

77. In August 1632, Thomas Dudley confronted Winthrop in front of a group of Bay Colony leaders and "demanded he of him the gronde & limittes of his Authoritye whither by the Patent or otherwise. The Governor answered that he was willing to stonde to that which he propounded & would challenge no greater Authoritye then he might by the Patent. the deputye replied that then he had no more Authoritye then everye Assistant (except power to call Courts & precedencye for honor & order.) the Governor answered he had more, for the Patent makinge him a Governor gave him whatsoever power belonged to a Governor by Common Lawe or the statutes, & desired him to shewe wherin he had exceeded &c: in speakinge this somewhat apprehensively the deputye beganne to be in a passion, & tould the Governor that if he were so ronde he would be rounde too, the Governor bvadd him vbe rounde if he would, so the deputye rose in a great furye & passion, & the Governor grewe verye hott allso, so as they bothe fell into bitternesse but by mediation of the mediators they were soon pacified. then the deputye proceeded to particulars," charging Winthrop with various excesses (Winthrop, *Journal*, 74-77). But Winthrop's answers all were based on the fact that either he had acted as a private person or he had been authorized by the body of Assistants to act as he had. This issue is complicated by the fact that Winthrop reported on Apr. 3: Winthrop, *Journal* (64): "At this Court an Act was made expressing the Governors power &c: & the office of Secretary & Treasurer, &c." No evidence of that order has been found. In the most famous challenge to Winthrop's authority (when he was put on trial before the General Court as a result of a petition from residents) when he delivered his "Little Speech on Liberty," the sources clearly reveal that he was singled out to defend actions he took as a member of a petite court composed of four magistrates.

78. Timothy Breen, "Persistent Localism: English Social Change and the Shaping of New England Institutions," in Breen, *Puritans and Adventurers: Change and Persistence in Early America* (New York, 1980), 3-4.

79. Morgan, *Puritan Dilemma*, 98.

80. This is discussed in Francis Bremer, *John Winthrop: America's Forgotten Founding Father* (New York, 2003).

81. Lechford, *Plain Dealing*, 162. Lechford's account has a brief discussion of the colony's civil government procedures, further reinforcing the adoption of English patterns.

82. The evolution of the colony's government in the years after 1636 has been traced by Robert E. Wall, *Massachusetts Bay: The Crucial Decade* (New Haven, 1972). The evolution of the relationship between the colony government and the towns is examined in Daniel K. Richter, "Town and Commonwealth in Massachusetts Bay 1630-1684" (MA thesis, Columbia University, 1977).

83. The political importance of the social interaction between the leaders of England's local communities during meetings of Parliament is discussed in Pauline Croft, "Capital Life: Members of Parliament Outside the House," in Thomas Cogswell, Richard Cust, and Peter Lake, eds., *Politics, Religion and Popularity in Early Stuart Britain: Essays in Honor of Conrad Russell* (Cambridge, 2002), 65-83.

84. For another discussion of Winthrop's views on the law and codification, see Rosezella Canty-Letsome, "John Winthrop's Concept of Law in 17th Century New England, One Notion of Puritan Thinking," *Duquesne Law Review* 16(1977-1978):331-357.

85. For the English debates over codification, see D. Veall, *The Popular Movement for Law Reform, 1640-1660* (London, 1970); Barbara Shapiro, "Law Reform in Seventeenth Century England," *American Journal of Legal History* 19(1975):280-312; and Barbara Black, "Aspects of Puritan Jurisprudence: Comment on the Puritan Revolution and English Law," *Valparaiso University Law Review* 18(1964):651-664. The Atlantic nature of this debate and the influence of New England on English thinking is touched upon in G. B. Warden, "Law Reform in England and New England, 1620 to 1660," *William and Mary Quarterly*, 3rd ser., 35(1978):668-690.

86. Cotton was the principle architect of one such code, "Moses His Judicials," which was not adopted in the colony but later became the basis for the New Haven Colony's laws. Puritans, like other Protestants, were divided over how much force the Mosaic code should have; see P. D. L. Avis, "Moses and the Magistrate: A Study in the Rise of Protestant Legalism," *Journal of Ecclesiastical History* 26(1975):149-172. For discussion of the arguments that led to codification in Massachusetts, see Mark D. Cahn, "Punishment, Discretion, and the Codification of Prescribed Penalties in Colonial Massachusetts," *American Journal of Legal History* 33(1989):107-136. There are numerous treatment of the transmission of English law to Massachusetts; see especially Richard Ross, "The Midwives and Morticians of Puritan Jurisprudence," paper delivered at the Millersville Uni-

versity Conference on the Worlds of John Winthrop, September 1999, which provides an excellent discussion of the historiography of early Massachusetts law.

87. Winthrop, *Journal*, 314-315.
88. Winthrop, *Journal*, 314.
89. For a very clear and concise account, see M. Smuts, *Culture and Power in England 1585-1685* (London, 1999), 17-27, quotation, 18. By implication, the law was not the creation of an act of will and, therefore, no individual or body could be said to be above the law or have existed prior to it. The law had evolved into a body of customs so complex as to be comprehensible only through the professional lawyers "artificial reason." That reason worked by balancing and adjusting conflicting claims, both among individuals and between the king's prerogative and the subjects' liberties.
90. While in England, John Winthrop shared the concern of many of his fellow attorneys about "barratry," the practice of many self-trained lawyers and solicitors in stirring up unnecessary lawsuits. In a statement of "Common Grievances Groaning for Reformation," Winthrop, who had a role in drafting the proposed bill for the last Parliament of James I, complained of an oppressive number of suits due to "the multitude of Attorneys in the courts," many of whom "will take out process against their neighbors upon very slight occasions." *Winthrop Papers*, 2:309. The early practice of Massachusetts reflected an effort to limit such practice, much to the dismay of Thomas Lechford. See Thomas G. Barnes, "Thomas Lechford and the Earliest Lawyering in Massachusetts, 1638-1641," and George L. Haskins, "Lay Judges: Magistrates and Justices in Early Massachusetts," both in Daniel Coquillette, ed., *Law in Colonial Massachusetts 1600-1800* (Boston, 1984).
91. Ross, "Midwives and Morticians," 5.

The Ancient Constitution in the Old World and the New

James S. Hart and Richard J. Ross

BELIEF IN THE GREAT antiquity and stability of England's constitution reached its highpoint in the early Stuart period, which also saw the beginnings of sustained New World colonization. Despite the conjunction of these events in time, historians have devoted little attention to ancient constitutionalist thought in the seventeenth-century American colonies.[1] This essay makes a start in that direction. It begins by discussing the timing and causes of the emergence of ancient constitutionalism in Stuart England, and the uses to which the concept was put. With this background established, it then explores the rather different career of ancient constitutionalism in seventeenth-century Massachusetts.

John Winthrop, an attorney in the Court of Wards, left a country suffused with ancient constitutionalist thought in order to help found a colony where the concept played little role. Within fifty years of his death, appeals to constitutional antiquity became common in Massachusetts politics. The reasons for the initial unimportance of ancient constitutionalism and for its revival shed light on the political and legal culture both of the world that Winthrop left and of the world that he and his successors built.

I.
The Ancient Constitution in Early Stuart England

Since the publication in 1957 of J. G. A. Pocock's seminal study of the common law mind, it has been taken as more or less axiomatic that political discourse in the early seventeenth century was shaped largely with reference to (and reverence for) England's so-called Ancient Constitution.[2] What Professor Pocock's study actually described was a set of perceptions, a "mentalité," what he called a "deep seated unconscious habit of mind," which was common to England's intellectual elite—and most especially to its common lawyers—and which conditioned their response to contemporary political conflict. The critical feature of that mentalité, indeed, its defining characteristic, was a faith in the rule of law. More particularly, it was a belief that England had always been governed with reference to its own "ancient constitution," to a set of principles—the common law—which had existed unchanged from the beginning of time. Professor Pocock's common lawyers—at least as exemplified by Sir Edward Coke—were deeply conservative and self-satisfied. They demonstrated little real sense of history and typically imagined that English law had remained impervious to substantive change over time, from either internal political forces or external influence. The fundamentals of common law had emerged fully formed before the memory of man, that is, "time out of mind," and remained substantially the same into the seventeenth century. Indeed, that was the common law's primary attribute—its consistency and the resulting continuity it provided. Common law represented "immemorial custom," a specifically English response to particular English needs. Common lawyers, in Pocock's view, were as a consequence antipathetic, or at the very least indifferent, toward other forms of law and other legal traditions, demonstrating little interest in, and even less absorption of continental jurisprudence. They remained (famously) "insular" in their outlook. The common law had proved itself so successful in solving English problems, over such long a period of time, that it had come to represent, for these men at least, an authoritative and infallible frame of reference for resolving the political controversies of the age. Hence, their mentalité gradually developed into something approaching a genuine political ideology.

Like all groundbreaking work, Professor Pocock's original thesis has been subjected to intense scrutiny, criticism, and modification, not least by the author himself.[3] The chief changes which have resulted have been to our understanding of the professional ethos of common lawyers. Pocock's initial concentration on Sir Edward Coke as a paradigm has been eschewed (sometimes rather too forcefully) in favor of a broader survey of contemporary common lawyers, not just men like Selden, Davies, or Dodderidge, but Sir Henry Finch, William Noy, or even Sir Francis Bacon, reflecting what was, in fact, a wider range of opinion and belief. Recent work has suggested that English common lawyers, as a group, were more worldly, more sophisticated, and more intellectually curious than Pocock's model might have suggested. It now seems certain, for instance, that most leading common lawyers had a working knowledge of (or at least a passing familiarity with) both Roman civil law and canon law, and, perhaps more to the point, were often fully conversant with the current trends of humanist legal scholarship on the Continent.[4] They understood and appreciated its influence on the development of English law and moreover were concerned with its continuing impact in English court proceedings. It also seems clear that few if any common lawyers (other than

Coke) seriously held to the Fortescuean position that the common law had remained static and immutable through the passage of time. Most understood that it had instead evolved gradually in response to changing circumstances and events—not least to the Norman Conquest. Recent scholarship has in fact suggested that a number of common lawyers were forced to come directly to terms with issue of the conquest, albeit largely to refute any suggestion that it represented a disruption—and therefore discontinuity—in the law and to avoid the more serious imputation that laws had been (or could be) created solely by the authority of the conqueror. Most seventeenth-century lawyers were by nature very conservative and resistant to arguments about radical change, especially in the law, for fear of creating uncertainty. But they understood that changes in the law had taken place in the past and would continue to do so in the future.[5]

For all of that, Pocock's original description of ancient constitutionalism remains entirely viable. Seventeenth-century common lawyers did articulate, in writing and speech alike, a relatively consistent and uniform vision of an ancient constitution which they believed had guided the conduct of English political affairs since the time of the Saxons. For most, the constitution was synonymous with the common law, which was itself a product of both custom and reason. At its core were certain fundamental, rational principles—what Christopher St. German called "dyverse generall Customes"—which were congruent with natural law and which had always proved "to be good and necessarye for the common welth of all the realme." These "immemorial" principles had shaped and controlled the development of particular local customs, had provided, in distilled form, legal maxims to guide the application of law by the courts in specific cases (Coke's famous "artificial reason"), and had, generally speaking, guided the interpretation of positive law as it applied to the formation of parliamentary statute.[6]

As such, the common law was seen to have provided all the answers. It was perfectly self contained.[7] It had evolved over time in direct response to English needs, and therefore accurately reflected English values and ideals. It was, said Sir John Davies, "so framed and fitted to the nature and disposition of this people, as we properly say it is connatural to the Nation, so as it cannot possibly be ruled by any other law."[8] It was also inherently rational and just, and so provided a moral center against which all behavior—but most especially political behavior—could be measured.[9] Good government in England was government conducted in strict conformity with dictates of the common law. That was the essence of the ancient constitution. Anything else was foreign and suspect or, at the very least, inappropriate to the history and character of the English polity.

Ironically, for all of the weight and authority accorded it, the concept of an ancient constitution was a relatively modern invention. That is to say, the concept itself does not appear to have had much currency before the beginning of the seventeenth century. Christopher Brooks has recently argued that sixteenth-century lawyers were largely unfamiliar with the kind of legal thinking that defined Pocock's "common law mind."[10] He suggests instead that Tudor legal professionals were far more influenced by European and classical traditions than by the imperatives of English historical experience; the two central works of English jurisprudence from this period, Fortescue's *De Laudibus Legum Angliae* and St. German's *Doctor and Student*, drew most heavily from Aristotle in the first case and from the French conciliarist Jean Gerson in the second.[11] Common lawyers, he argues, demonstrated little of the sort of reverence for historical antecedents later demonstrated by their Stuart counterparts and validated custom only insofar as it could be seen to concur with right reason. There was no discernible doctrine that past practice, in and of itself, should determine present and future law.[12]

Moreover, the commonplace attachment to the "rule of law" took on a greater variety of meanings in the sixteenth century. It was less often taken as a guarantor of the subjects' rights and liberties than as an expression of the subjects' obligations and responsibilities. That is, the law was more frequently seen, particularly in the later sixteenth century, as an attribute of government, as its primary means of maintaining order and stability, and as a guarantor of the subject's obedience to authority.[13] No doubt the uncertain and turbulent conditions of the late sixteenth century and the real (and recurring) threats to English security fostered a greater fear of disorder and consequently a greater willingness to allow the government greater latitude with regard to individual rights in the interests of protecting the commonwealth as a whole. But the contrast with the prevailing perceptions of the seventeenth century seems striking.

The purpose of what follows will be to suggest the ways in which ancient constitutionalism evolved as a peculiarly Stuart construct and to elucidate the specific conditions or circumstances that gave rise to key perceptions and attitudes. It would seem prudent here to draw a distinction between two phenomena; the evolving historicism of the common law mind, which gave rise to the notion of an ancient constitution, and the development of the political ideology that followed from it. The first must, in some measure, be traced to general conditions at work in the sixteenth century. Certainly English antiquarianism—itself a by-product of Renaissance humanism—which flourished under Elizabeth, played an important role here by offering a new and realistic view of England's past which simultaneously embraced notions of continuity and change. It accepted the true facts of historical development, while emphasizing the fundamental continuity of English law and legal institutions. These more sophisticated presentations and the traditions they initiated strengthened, rather than weakened, the case for the existence of an ancient constitution.[14]

English ecclesiology also exercised influence in the process.[15] The Reformation created a compelling need to defend the Church of England against the claims of schism, and therefore a need for a history of the English church that emphasized its antiquity as an example of primitive, pre-Roman, Christianity. The most notable example of this was Bishop Jewel's celebrated *Apology*, commissioned (unofficially) by the Crown and published in 1562, which argued that England's Reformation represented, above all else, a return to first principles.

> We have searched out of the Holy Bible, which we are sure cannot deceive, one sure form of religion, and have returned again unto the primitive church of the ancient fathers and apostles, that is to say to the first ground and beginnings of things, as unto the very foundations and headsprings of Christ's church.[16]

Jewel's argument presupposed the existence of an English church that predated the era of papal supremacy, a church which had taken its faith from the Scriptures and the teachings of the church fathers and its lead from the directives of the first four church Councils. In this, of course, Jewell was simply reflecting the assertions made explicitly in the Act of Supremacy.[17] England's new independence merely reflected the obligation of the Christian magistrate to reject papal leadership in the face of wholesale corruption and error. Quoting the prophet Isaiah ("A King ought to be a patron and nurse of the church"), Jewel insisted that "by histories and examples of the best times, good princes ever took the administration of ecclesiastical matters to pertain to their duty." In England's case, that decision had also been made in accordance with its own constitutional traditions. "The matter had been treated in open parliament, with long consultation, and before a notable synod and convocation."[18]

Archbishop Matthew Parker, (who served as editor of *The Apology*) followed similar lines of argument in his own efforts to celebrate the antiquity of the English church. His *Lives of the Archbishops of Canterbury* stressed the continuity of the Church's leadership from St. Augustine to his own archepiscopate—a line that stretched across the Reformation—and he insisted (citing the claims of English historians) that the origins of the "Christian Catholic Church of England" needed to be traced, not to the kings (and popes) of the sixth century, but to those of the second.[19] Richard Hooker, on the other hand, was less concerned about establishing the existence of a pre-Roman English church than with stressing its continuity with the broader Christian tradition, with the visible church of Christ (popish or otherwise), and in suggesting the ways in which the English church had struck an appropriate balance between the extremes of Christian faith.[20] In his famous *Of the Laws of Ecclesiastical Polity*, he implied that England's success in this endeavor owed much to its ability to undertake reform and establish ecclesiastical discipline and government in accord with its own indigenous political traditions. England's monarchy had proved a model because it had always been "tied unto the soundest perfectest and most indifferent rule; which rule is the law." He made clear that by the rule of law, he meant "not only the law of nature and of *God*, but the very national or municipal law consonant thereunto."

> Happier that people, whose law is their *King* in the greatest things than those whose *King* is himself their law. Where the *King* doth guide the state and the law the *King*, that commonwealth is like an harp or melodious instrument, the strings whereof are tuned and handled all by one hand, following as laws the rules and canons of Musical science.[21]

Consequently, his defense of the Royal supremacy stressed the role of Parliament (and hence public participation) in the making of law, spiritual and secular alike.

> Which laws being made amongst us are not by any of us so taken or interpreted as if they did receive their force from power which the *Prince* doth communicate unto the Parliament or to any other *Court* under him, but from the power which the whole body of this *Realm*, being naturally possessed with hath by free and deliberate assent derived unto him that ruleth over them.... So that our laws made concerning religion do take originally their essence from the power of the whole *Realm* and *Church of England* than which nothing can be more consonant unto the law of nature and the will of our Lord Jesus Christ.[22]

There was, as Hooker demonstrates, a kind of inevitable symbiosis between ecclesiastical and legal antiquarianism. Glen Burgess has recently suggested that ecclesiastical antiquarianism was important for precisely that reason: it simultaneously emphasized the singularity of England's solutions to the problems of religious settlement, and in so doing legitimized the notion of diversity of national customs and legal traditions. Furthermore, it celebrated England's reliance on the rule of law as the operating premise of its government.[23] Both characteristics would become central to the evolution of ancient constitutionalism.

Antiquarianism (of either kind) was itself a product of a highly charged and dynamic intellectual climate in the late sixteenth century, and that dynamism was clearly evident—with a variety of consequences—in the legal profession. Indeed, by the close of the sixteenth century the legal profession itself had been transformed. Not only had it grown dramatically in size (and political influence), it had become much more sophisticated and self-conscious as a professional class.[24] In no small measure, this resulted from advances in legal education. Lawyers were, in general, far better educated that they had been in the past—nearly 42 percent of those attending the Inns of Court were being admitted from universities by the last decade of the century.[25] But they were also (arguably) better trained. The print revolution had had an immediate impact by making available a wide variety of English legal sources (unauthorized and promiscuous though they may have been) in the form of yearbooks, law reports, abstracts of statutes, and treatises on special subjects. Immediate issues of pedagogy aside, growing access to those sources could only have inculcated in the neophyte lawyer a strong sense of the past and a respect for the singular heritage of the common law. Ultimately this translated into practice as well. As the century progressed, a perceptible shift took place toward greater reliance on case law and precedent—as opposed to general arguments from principle—in written pleadings. That is not to say that the courts had embraced a doctrine of *stare decisis*—judges did not trust the decisions of the past sufficiently (or at least lawyers' citations of them) to be bound by them in the present or future. Nevertheless, references to existing case law were pervasive and often influential and must gradually have worked to reinforce the notions of a customary body of law that would become the ancient constitution.

In immediate practical terms, of course, such ideas would have been advanced even more directly by the twice-yearly proceedings at the assizes. Common law judges consulted one another, shared ideas, and informed one another of their decisions before traveling circuit. "By this means," claimed Sir Matthew Hale, "their judgments, and their administrations of common justice, carry a consonancy, congruity and uniformity, one to another." As a consequence, "the laws and the administrations thereof are preserved from that confusion and disparity that would unavoidably ensue if the administration was by several incommunicating hands, or by provincial establishments."[26] Moreover, the active participation of the provincial community in those proceedings worked to the same end, at least insofar as local magistrates who served on the bench and local gentry who served on grand and petty juries were forced to familiarize themselves (if no more than that) with elements of the law and the traditions of legal procedure. The repeated exercise of those responsibilities, (whether in a coercive or a remedial capacity) inevitably conferred on the participants a shared proprietary interest in the common law and the ancient rights it protected.

Tudor common lawyers, and certainly Elizabethan lawyers, appreciated the importance of that legacy and understood their role as its guardians. But this was a professional view more than it was a political one. There was little apparent inclination to apply the lessons of legal history to matters of contemporary politics. In truth, Tudor monarchs gave them few occasions to do so. In general terms, they governed (or appeared to govern) according to expectation: that is, according to the rule of law. The deliberate reliance on Parliament, both as a court and a legislative assembly, was critical, of course, but so too was the frequent practice of consulting publicly with common law judges on delicate matters of policy and procedure. One thinks here of discussions over such matters as the status of royal proclamations, the authority of High Commission or the legality of the Statute of Uses. More to the point, Tudor monarchs, and especially Elizabeth, studiously avoided the kinds of confrontations that might lead to the development of adversarial politics—and competing ideologies. Part of her success resulted from simple good fortune, but part also came from sound political management. Faced with an increasingly well-educated and well-informed political elite, and determined to present to the wider world a picture of political unity at home, Elizabeth more often than not pursued compromise and conciliation (or, where necessary, obfuscation) on contentious issues. She evaded direct discussion of constitutional issues in order to avoid definition and clarification. As a consequence, the fundamental beliefs of the common lawyers were never (or very rarely) tested or seriously challenged in the arena of practical politics.

That would not, of course, be true of the Stuarts. Events—and personalities—conspired to raise legal and constitutional issues on a consistent basis, in Parliament and in the courts alike, and consequently worked to clarify beliefs in precisely the opposite way. The ideology of ancient constitutionalism emerged from this process, and it did so largely in adversarial fashion, as a defensive response to perceived threats to the supremacy of the common law. Much of the responsibility for this lies at the feet of James I. The new king combined great intelligence and cultivation with an unfortunate compulsion to instruct. Where Elizabeth avoided clarification, James doggedly pursued it. James also possessed deeply held political convictions, made evident in his two famous political treatises, *The Trew Law of Free Monarchies* and *Basilikon Doron*. Both made clear his commitment to the principles of Divine Right monarchy.[27] In so far as they can fairly be said to reflect his true opinion, they appeared to represent a direct and serious challenge to established English traditions.

This was especially true of the king's statements about the nature of the law and his relationship to it. James's notorious claim that the king was "above the Law, as both the author and the giver of strength thereunto," could perhaps have been tolerated as a general theoretical expression of his status as God's anointed, but the more practical assertions that he could mitigate the law of his own authority when he "sees the lawe doubtsome or rigorous," or suspend "general lawes made publikely in Parliament . . . upon causes knowen only to him," suggested something rather more frightening. James's assurance that a good king would always govern according to the law was likewise undermined by his subsequent claim that he was bound to do so "but of his good will, and for good example-giving to his subjects."[28]

These pronouncements must have made for sobering reading, but unease about James really developed over his relations with the legal profession and with Parliament. Given his background in Scotland and his status as monarch of three separate kingdoms, it is perhaps not surprising that James arrived in England with a less than reverential view of English common law. In speeches before Parliament, he happily conceded its native genius, but it always remained for him limited in its applicability. It was local law and offered only one kind of solution to the broader challenges of government.[29] That was made clear during the discussions on Union, a proposal which, in and of itself, terrified MPs and common lawyers alike because of its profound constitutional implications. As Conrad Russell has suggested, the immediate effect of combining two very different legal systems would have been to diminish the status of each in a greater Britain. More to the point, disputes over competing legal principles—seemingly unavoidable given the contrary nature of Scottish and English law—could only be effectively resolved through royal arbitration, and that in turn would inevitably reinforce James's claims to a sovereign "imperial" legal authority.[30] That was, after all, the underlying conclusion of Calvin's case, settled in 1608. Union threatened the hegemony of the common law and common lawyers responded by appealing to the inviolability of custom and the ancient constitution. The "imperial" reach, of course, extended to Ireland as well, and while James was amenable to governing colonial Ireland according to the principles and mechanisms of the common law, much of the legal and constitutional reform undertaken during his reign—directed primarily at the property rights and religious practices of native and old English populations—was accomplished through judicial fiat rather than through parliamentary statute. Justices in the Irish Privy Council repeatedly issued extra-judicial resolutions on key issues such as Irish land tenure and descent, religious conformity, and the political autonomy of municipal corporations, often with the complicity of the English bench in Exchequer Chamber. According to Sir John Davies, James's attorney general in Ireland, the right to impose this new judge-made law derived, in the wake of England's victory in the Nine Years War, not from common law, but from the civil law doctrine of conquest. Conquest conferred public law title to Ireland and justified the wholesale abrogation of all indigenous law and custom.[31]

In fact, James I had never really understood the attraction of unwritten law or the romance of custom. The comparative analysis of the Scottish and English legal systems, conducted as a preliminary to Union, only highlighted for him the seemingly disorganized and ill-defined nature of the latter and led him to spearhead a movement for comprehensive English law reform. His advocacy of reform was based in part on a genuine conviction that the law was uncertain and imprecise and therefore potentially unjust—a concern not without some merit. But he was also (or perhaps even more) concerned that England's unwritten common law allowed judges too much discretion. As he claimed in a speech to Parliament in 1607 "Where there is varietie and uncertaintie although a just judge may do rightly, yet an ill judge may take advantage and doe wrong. . . . Wherefore leave not the law to the pleasure of the Judge."[32]

On both counts, James was issuing a direct challenge to the common-law establishment. Common lawyers and judges prided themselves on mastering the essence of unwritten law. They celebrated their ability to understand and apply what was a very specialized form of knowledge—the ancient rules and procedures, the singular values and principles, "the native fund of moral preferences"[33]— which made up the common law. This was their stock in trade, their unique expertise. To suggest that it could be reduced to a simple code and that it could—and should—be made available for public consumption—"so the people should not depend upon the bare opinion of Judges and uncertain reports,"—was to demean the seriousness and importance of their profession.[34] It could only provoke a defensive reaction, one that would emphasize instead the inherent mystery of their discipline and the consequent need for greater, rather than lesser, judicial discretion; one which calls for the special character of an ancient constitution.

The same dynamic was evident in the courtroom as well, most notably perhaps in Sir Edward Coke's famous confrontation with James I in the case of Prohibitions (1608). James I's attempt to remove Fuller's case from Coke's court of Common Pleas, for his own determination, was predicated on two assumptions: first, that the authority delegated to the judges to determine cases in their own courts was transitory and could be suspended at the monarch's discretion; second, that this particular monarch possessed sufficient wisdom and understanding to effect a reasonable resolution in this (and implicitly in other) cases. Both assumptions seriously undermined the special status accorded the practitioners of the common law, both on and off the bench, and Coke's response went some way toward establishing the parameters of constitutional debate. In one of his most celebrated disquisitions, Coke denied the king the right to determine cases on his own authority: "no King after the Conquest assumed to himself to give any judgement in any cause whatsoever which concerned the administration of justice within this realm." Coke then explained that he was disqualified because he lacked the requisite training, the "long study and experience" which gave the common lawyer his special insight and understanding of English customary law—the famous "artificial reason," which characterized the judges' singular expertise.[35]

This was more than simple territorialism. Certainly Coke was attempting to defend the honor and historic privileges of his profession. But he was also attempting more broadly to assert the supremacy of the common law—of the ancient constitution—against a variety of other jurisprudential traditions (canon law in the church courts, equity in Chancery, and concilliar fiat in the prerogative jurisdictions of Star Chamber and High Commission) which lacked the historical pedigree of common law, but which seemed increasingly to be gaining coequal status in royal circles. In his view, the actions of those courts needed constantly to be monitored to ensure their congruence with the values and customs of England's bative legal culture and he argued that that job fell rightly to the common law bench.

James, of course, was not convinced, on either count. He continued to interfere directly in judicial proceedings in special cases—one thinks here of Peacham's case and the pivotal case of the Commendams—and he refused ever to accord the common law courts sovereign authority over other legal disciplines, a position emphatically restated in Coke's great conflict with Lord Chancellor Ellesmere in 1616. To do so was to concede Coke's point that the common law courts (and their judges) acted as the "golden mete-wand and measure to try the causes of the subjects" and "protect his Majesty in safety and peace."[36] It meant, very simply, that the king was under the law and neither James nor Charles I would ever accept that judgment. Indeed, that became the central problem: the early Stuart monarchs were keen to distinguish between the common law and the ancient constitution. They might revere the former, and wholly support its conventional proceedings, but they never equated its component parts with an ancient constitution capable of circumscribing their authority or course of action. Under the circumstances, disagreement was inevitable.

Much of the debate subsequently coalesced in the Parliament of 1610. Paul Christianson has recently argued that events in this Parliament helped crystallize the evolving issues.[37] He has suggested that James I gave particular shape to the debate by articulating his own interpretation of an ancient constitution. James's interpretation, however, was fluid and uncertain, frequently refashioned in response to changing political events. He proved quite capable of acknowledging his obligation to observe the fundamental laws of the kingdom, and on the occasion of his now famous address to Parliament on March 21, he solemnly pledged to frame his government accordingly. He recognized the supremacy of common law in matters concerning private property ("in any questions, either between the King and any of them, or amongst themselves in the points of *meum & Tuum*"), and he readily acknowledged the wisdom of governing through Parliament. He promised, for instance, that his ambitious plans to reform the law would only be undertaken "with the advise of Parliament: For the King with his parliament here are absolute (as I understand) in the making or forming of any sort of Lawes."[38]

What he would not do, however, was concede that those same laws could ultimately constrain his supreme authority. Only two months after this address, he returned to Parliament on May 21–this time in a fit of considerable pique over the Commons' continuing debate of his royal prerogative–and offered a rather different vision. His government would observe the rules of constitutional propriety, but they would do so entirely at his discretion. "Many things I *may* do without Parliament, which I *will* do in Parliament, for good Kings are helped by Parliament, *not*, for power, but for convenience, that the work may seem more glorious." The difference was telling. Parliament had been transformed from a necessity into an expendable "convenience," its participation emphatically a matter of grace rather than of right. Strictly speaking, of course, that was always true, insofar as it remained entirely within the king's prerogative to call and dissolve any assembly at will. But the sense of partnership in making law that James had emphasized in March went missing from the address in May. More ominously, perhaps, his attempt to circumscribe their debate on his prerogative came with a blunt warning: "You cannot so clip the wings of greatness. If a king be resolute to be a tyrannt, all you can do will not hinder him."[39] If, as Professor Christianson has suggested, James was at pains in 1610 to accommodate his earlier ideas to the traditions of ancient constitutionalism, the transition was perhaps proving more difficult that he may have anticipated. MPs could have been forgiven for being skeptical and confused.

As it was, they responded to this speech (and to James's earlier suggestions about the reform of the common law) directly, offering a much more affirmative view. The most coherent and thoughtful challenger was undoubtedly Thomas Hedley, who articulated what is now a classic précis of seventeenth-century constitutionalism.[40] He described the common law as "the life and soul of the politic body." Its essence was reason, tested over time, which was itself "the trier of truth, author of all human wisdom, learning and knowledge, and from which all human laws receive their chief strength, honor and estimation." Its evolution was determined by what was deemed to be "reasonable usage, throughout the whole realm, approved time out of mind in the King's courts of record . . . to be good and profitable for the commonwealth." The ancient constitution—the common law—had always maintained a perfect balance between the sovereignty of the king and the liberty of the subject. "To Sovereignty the law alloweth many prerogative rights of a large spread and many free exemptions, and to subjects such ingenuity and freedom as maintains him in spirit and courage and yet contains him in all duteous subjection."[41]

Turning to the particular case at hand, the issue of impositions, Hedley argued that in this kingdom of England, the laws of the kingdom are the inheritance not only of the King, but also of the subjects, of which the King ought not to disseise them or disinherit them. Therefore it followeth consequently and necessarily, that the king cannot alter the property of the lands or goods of any of his free subjects without their consent, for that is to disseise or disinherit them of the fruit and benefit of the law, which is all one as to disinherit them of the law itself. And this appeareth yet more plainly in the great Charter of the liberties of England, that the law is not only to protect us against the absolute power and prerogative of the King in life and member, but also in lands and goods. Therefore, he that cannot alter the law, cannot alter property.[42]

There were two underlying and unequivocal messages in this speech. The first was the central one that the king was subject to the law. Hedley echoed Coke in claiming that the happiness of the kingdom "resteth as well in the moderate and lawful freedom and liberty of the subjects as in the sovereignty of the king, but in the right combination and mixture of both (which by the common law is excellently performed)."[43] The second was that the constitution required public consent to change the law or to take the subjects' property, and consent required Parliament. In real, practical terms Parliament's participation was neither dispensable, nor a matter of grace, but a matter of right and in some cases a constitutional requirement.

The centrality of Parliament was the key feature of another singular interpretation offered in 1610, this time in print, by John Selden. Professor Christianson has suggested that Selden's *Jani Anglorum*, published later in the year, was written largely as a response to the claims made respectively by King James and Thomas Hedley in the aforementioned parliamentary debates. Selden's purpose was to offer a more coherent view of England's history (based on primary source material and careful humanist scholarship), which would demonstrate not only the evolution of England's ancient constitution, but more particularly its guiding principal of shared sovereignty. Selden's exposition of ancient British history emphasized the absence of a central (monarchical) authority and the gradual evolution of laws from commonly accepted practices, that is, from custom. His discussion of the Saxon period emphasized in turn the continual role of consultation between Saxon kings and their councils of wise men, from which he logically traced the evolution of parliaments. In Selden's history, the law had never been simply a product of the king's will, as James I had implied, but instead had always been the result of a cooperative enterprise undertaken between the king and his people.[44]

What had emerged from these dialogues were three "competing voices," three alternative interpretations of the ancient constitution, which Professor Christianson has described as: "constitutional monarchy created by Kings" (James I's), constitutional monarchy governed by the common law (Hedley's), and "mixed monarchy" (Selden's). He has argued that these interpretations not only provided alternative models for understanding the past, they gave definitive shape to political discourse in the present. There seems little question of that. The language of the ancient constitution plainly provided the fundamental tools (if certainly not the only tools) for discussion of the legal controversies of the age. What it did not provide, however, was resolution. The subtle differences between these interpretations point to their collective weakness: each of them conferred sovereign responsibility for interpreting the law on a different component institution. Taken to their logical conclusions, James I's view of the constitution would have placed final authority firmly in the king's hands, Hedley's in the common law bench, and Selden's in the High Court of Parliament. If these differences had remained speculative and theoretical, disagreement could have been tolerated, but increasingly, they played out in the arena of practical politics.

During the early decades of the seventeenth century, the Crown repeatedly found itself unable to meet the costs of government from ordinary resources. When Parliament denied extraordinary funds, the Crown resorted to extra legal (or at least legally questionable) measures—from impositions to benevolences, to forced loans, to military exactions and Ship Money—throwing into high relief critical matters of private property (and collaterally) personal liberty. When such issues were at stake, definitive arbitration was required. It proved unattainable. On the face of it, all "ancient constitutionalists" agreed that these matters should be tried at common law. But the integrity of that process was becoming increasingly uncertain. The king's relationship to the judges was complex and ill-defined and neither of the early Stuarts could resist interference, either directly or through indirect intimidation and pressure. James laid the groundwork with the dismissal of Coke in 1616—not for personal misconduct, as in the past, but for the content of his judicial opinions. Charles followed his lead, dismissing Chief Justice Crewe in 1626 for his opposition to the Forced Loan, Baron Walter in 1630 for his resistance to the criminal proceedings against Sir John Eliot and other MPs, and Chief Justice Heath in 1634 for his criticism of the Ship Money writs. Charles I, whatever his other claims to prerogative powers outside the law, could legitimately claim constitutional authority to direct and dismiss judges—they were, after all, servants of the Crown and their writs said they served at the pleasure of the king. But his actions hopelessly compromised the pretense of independent judgment and cruelly exposed the judges' vulnerability to public view.

Parliament, of course, played its part as well, exercising the entirely legitimate authority that Selden (among others) ascribed to the High

Court, by continually second guessing judicial decisions beginning with Bate's case and proceeding notably (and doggedly) through, among others, the Five Knights' case, the extrajudicial declarations on Ship Money, and ultimately Hampden's case. However legitimate their authority to do so—and their appellate jurisdiction was actually confirmed by statute—however noble their intention, however certain their defense of their legal rights and interests, the long-term effect undermined confidence in the bench and, therefore, in the security of the law. The process perhaps reached its apotheosis in 1640 with impeachment of six common law judges and Lord Keeper Finch. This proved a fatal development because the ancient constitution, however defined, was only as secure as public faith in the rule of law.

As Glen Burgess has recently argued, the centrality of common law discourse in domestic politics could not long survive these conditions.[45] When it became clear, as it had certainly by 1642, that Charles I and his supporters had abandoned the "agreed essentials" of constitutional government, members of Parliament were themselves forced to embrace new ideas to justify their resistance and to legitimize parliamentary administration in the Civil War. Ironically, they followed the lead provided by Charles himself: by adopting claims of necessity and effectively pleading "reasons of state." When Parliament attempted to defend itself in May 1642 against claims that it had acted without the "warrant of precedents" in declining the king access to the magazines at Hull, members responded by declaring that "And as some precedents ought not to be rules for us to follow, so none can be limits to bound our proceedings, which may and must vary according to different conditions of times." Members of Parliament acknowledged that all parties were now playing by a new and unchartered set of rules.[46]

The exchanges of the 1640s mark a dividing line in the career of the ancient constitution. In relative terms, it receded in importance as contemporaries employed a more varied repertoire of political arguments. Within these more pluralistic debates, it did remain significant, not least because controversialists expanded its range of uses. After 1642, advocates of a "mixed constitution" labored to prove the antiquity of the House of Commons in order to justify its "coordinate" lawmaking authority with the Lords and the Crown. Interregnum radicals used ancient constitutionalist arguments to justify deposing and executing Charles I, eliminating the Crown and the House of Lords, and governing England as a republic through the House of Commons alone. Champions of boroughs and corporations targeted by post-Restoration Stuart *quo warranto* proceedings pled antiquity in order to secure their privileges through prescription. By the early eighteenth century, opposition writers held up an idealized Saxon constitution of liberty to measure and condemn the corruptions and arbitrary overreachings of the government of their day–for instance, the influence peddling of Walpole's Whigs.[47]

But as contemporaries were putting the ancient constitution to more diverse uses, its centrality in political argument declined. The new and rapidly changing political circumstances of the Civil War encouraged arguments based on necessity, natural right, social contact, convenience, interest, and civic virtue. Disputes over the location of sovereignty undermined efforts to find ancient customs binding on Crown and Parliament alike. To be sure, there were moments when ancient constitutionalist arguments sounded with particular vigor: the Exclusion Crisis, the Whig rebuttal to Robert Brady's historiography, the legitimation of the Glorious Revolution, and Lord Bolingbroke's attacks on Walpole in the 1720s. But these instances punctuated a longer-term deterioration in the relative importance of ancient constitutionalism. Locke famously ignored it. Other writers portrayed selected elements of an ancient polity giving way to improvements in a process of progressive development. In the early eighteenth century, for example, supporters of Walpole styled the Whig regime a "modern constitution" that protected liberty better than predecessors tainted with feudal and absolutist elements. Still other writers treated ancient constitutionalism not as the framework establishing the objectives and methodology of political debate, but as a subordinate part of a rival framework. One might study the past through antiquarian techniques not to yield the binding obligations of Crown, Parliament, and subjects, but to discover an original contract, or to find in constitutional history the workings of reason or lessons about "convenience."[48] The "decay of genetic theories of politics and of fundamental law," R. J. Smith has observed, "meant that the historical debate on the English Constitution tended to decline from one of right to one of illustration."[49] Examined in long perspective, from 1640-1740, the influence of ancient constitutionalism traced a downward arc.

But not in Massachusetts. The historiography on ancient constitutionalism in England established a career for the concept that ill-suits developments in the seventeenth-century Bay Colony. Massachusetts not merely fails to match this pattern, but reverses it. Ancient constitutionalism there traced an upward arc. Largely ignored in the 1630s and 1640s, it took on a newfound importance in the 1680s and 1690s. Facing the loss of the first charter, confronting the Andros regime, and trying to secure and favorably interpret the second charter, colonial leaders spoke proudly of Massachusetts's own ancient constitution. Later, they began to think of their colony as part of an English ancient constitution, a young branch of a tree that drew stability and strength from its Saxon roots. By the early eighteenth century, Massachusetts colonists invoked two versions of the ancient constitution—indigenous and English—and used them selectively against encroachments by the empire and by prerogative. Understanding the timing and causes of this pattern requires, as a first step, explaining the curious uninterest in ancient constitutionalism among the first generation of Massachusetts settlers.

II.
The Career of the Ancient Constitution in Seventeenth-Century Massachusetts

The founders of Massachusetts planned the colony in the late 1620s and settled it in the 1630s, years when ancient constitutionalist ideas were at their height in England. Many of the Bay Colony's initial magistrates, ministers, and town notables suffered from royal and Episcopal campaigns against Puritans. They were a group disproportionately interested in political arguments used to restrain overreaching by the Crown against the Parliament and the towns, and by bishops against nonconformist ministers and lay religious leaders. Ancient constitutionalism proved one of the most potent of these arguments.[50]

Yet ancient constitutionalism played little role in the ongoing struggles of the colony's first generation over the proper nature and boundaries of central authority. Assistants, deputies, ministers, and town notables debated to what extent magisterial power was delegated from the deputies and populace (and hence bounded in extent and operation) and to what extent inherent in the office of magistrate (and hence, broad reaching and highly discretionary). Political elites disagreed over the proper demarcation of the powers of the colonial authorities and the towns. In these disputes, partisans drew on Scriptural injunctions and analogies, the charter, considerations of policy (or "convenience"), and local practice.[51] They ignored, rather than affirmatively rejected, the relevance of ancient constitutionalism.

Across the ocean in England, scholars, lawyers, courtiers, parliamentarians, and religious controversialists disputed the content, dating, and implications of the ancient constitution. Still others denied its existence. The civilians John Cowell and Thomas Ridley, the Catholic controversialist Robert Parsons, the historian John Hayward, and a group of high-royalist clerical writers believed that the Norman Conquest reconstituted the common law or, more radically, originated it.[52] Following Continental legal humanists, Crown servants Francis Bacon and Thomas Egerton undermined the supposed antiquity of English law by depicting it as developing over time in response to changing economic, social, and political conditions.[53] Both the efforts to define and refute the ancient constitution testified to its centrality in early Stuart political and legal thought. In first-generation Massachusetts, by contrast, political conflict inspired neither the use, amendment, nor denial of ancient constitutionalism. There was little engagement with this form of argument.

Why did the relative importance of ancient constitutionalist argument follow such different trajectories in England and Massachusetts? Before addressing this issue, we need to consider the objection that the question itself is ill-posed and misleading. A critic might ask how Massachusetts colonists could have used the rhetoric of the ancient constitution in the first two generations of settlement (from 1630 to about 1680)? How could they speak of their constitution as immemorial when they themselves, not distant ancestors, built their polity? Their inability to cast their constitution as ancient is exactly what one would expect. It needs no explanation.

This objection has some force, yet is also misconceived. To begin with, it proves too much. If the colonists took seriously the tests of antiquity current in seventeenth-century English legal thought, then they were no more entitled to speak of their constitution as ancient in the 1680s and 1690s (when they did) than in the 1640s, 1650s, and 1660s (when they did not).[54] English thinkers advanced several opinions about when the modifier "ancient" could be legitimately applied to the institutions, liberties, and customs that made up a constitution.[55] The most rigorous version required the principles and essence (but not all the details) of a constitution to be literally "immemorial." A constitution that existed "time out of mind" must have been in operation before the earliest available historical records, so that no act or decree could be said to have created it. For most who took this view, the English constitution was immemorial and flourished among the Saxons before the Norman Conquest, though Edward Coke claimed to glimpse it even further back in time.[56] A somewhat less demanding version styled a constitutional provision "ancient" if it met the common law's test of whether a custom derived from time out of mind. Common lawyers used the date of Richard I's coronation, September 3, 1189, as the dividing line between the time of memory and the time before memory. If a custom or institution existed before 1189, and if it had been used without interruption since that date, it earned the right to protection by the law. Prescription ratified and legitimated such ancient customs and institutions.[57] Shortening the period necessary to validate a custom through prescription yielded the third, and least rigorous, test of antiquity. What "measure of time shall make a custom?" asked Charles Calthrope in his 1574 Reading, (that is, Inns of Court lecture) on the law of copyhold. Some say seventy-six years validates a custom; others say one hundred years; but "the true measure" is

> that no man then in life, has not heard any thing, nor know any proof to the contrary. . . . [I]f lands have been demised by copy[hold] but 40 years, and there is none alive that can remember the same to be otherwise demised, this is a good copyhold, for the number of years makes not the matter, but the memory of man. . . . But if any chance to be alive, that remember the contrary, then such prescription must give place to such proof.[58]

John Cowell's *Interpreter* (1607) reported that some common lawyers accepted a custom "if two or more [witnesses] can depose, that they heard their fathers say, that it was a custom all their time, and that their fathers heard their fathers also say, that it was likewise a custom in their time."[59]

Under the first and second of these three tests, the liberties, institutions of governance, and constitution of Massachusetts were not ancient. And they could never become so. The passage of time could never change the damning facts that the colony came into existence after 1189 and that historical records amply documented its creation by royal charter. Massachusetts could only style its constitution as ancient under the third of the three tests, and then only under the loosest and most forgiving measures of prescription. The English lawyer John Palmer, who served as a judge under Andros's Dominion of New England, flatly denied that the colony had been in operation long enough to claim liberties through prescription.[60] The settlers could write off Palmer as ill disposed, but they could not so easily escape the force of his critique. How could the political leaders of the 1680s claim that their grandfathers lived under the constitution of Massachusetts when their fathers had built the colony? The colonists of the 1650s would have confronted even greater skepticism if they spoke of antiquity in a polity still so new.

In the first and second generations of Massachusetts, then, it was intellectually possible, but not fully persuasive, to point to a prescriptive ancient constitution. But the forensic difficulty of carrying off the position does not, by itself, explain the relative insignificance of ancient constitutionalism in those years. Massachusetts colonists used political arguments that were far more self-serving, awkward, even brazen, during their internal dissensions and in conflicts with imperial officials before 1680. They twisted their charter to style themselves a commonwealth rather than a trading company; they excluded propertied men from a colonial franchise based on church membership; they essentially freed themselves from the oversight of the Church of England; they exiled or executed religious dissenters; they undermined the Privy Council's right to hear judicial appeals and review legislation; and they temporized on whether the Navigation Acts and the common law bound them. By these standards, speaking of a Massachusetts prescriptive constitution was hardly forward.

There is a second problem in arguing that the inconsequential role of ancient constitutionalism in early Massachusetts is expected and not in need of an explanation. Whatever difficulties the newness of the polity created for proponents of an indigenous ancient constitution, why did colonists fail to invoke the ancient constitution of England? The settlers copied, or more typically adapted, many elements of English legal culture.[61] Why not this one? There must be something more at work to explain the first and second generations of settlers' lack of interest in ancient constitutionalism—more than simply the colony's "infancy," as Winthrop liked to call it.

That "something more" becomes clearer through a comparison to England. Political and intellectual conditions that fostered ancient constitutionalist thought in the mother country were absent or muted in Massachusetts. To begin with, the colonists' congregationalist religious order required different forms of legitimation than the Church of England. Both the gathered churches of Massachusetts and the national Church of England rejected claims that they represented new-modeled innovations (as the Catholics charged). Rather, they asserted consistency with the primitive Christianity of the era before the corrupt Roman Popes. The two religious orders connected this starting point to their present situation in different ways. The Church of England needed to fashion a historical legacy that justified national autonomy, royal supremacy, episcopal discipline, and the institutional, doctrinal, and liturgical compromises made by Henrician and

Elizabethan legislation. Advocates such as John Whitgift and Richard Hooker commonly argued that Christian commonwealths might arrange their ecclesiastical and civil administration in a variety of legitimate ways. The Church of England, which differed in organization and ceremonies from the Catholic church and other Protestant churches, followed a course rooted deep in its national history. Apologists engaged in both religious and legal antiquarian scholarship to find continuities between the ecclesiastical arrangements of the contemporary Church of England and its "primitive" forebear (not yet corrupted by the medieval Papacy). Ecclesiastical antiquarianism drew upon legal antiquarianism to construct an ecclesiastical-legal ancient constitution.[62]

The congregationalist churches of Massachusetts, while not separating from the Church of England, departed from it in many points of church organization and discipline. Their apologists commonly situated them in a European fellowship of advanced Reformed congregations who had modeled themselves most thoroughly on Scripture and the primitive church.[63] In Holland and Geneva were their peers. Since they did not replicate—indeed, since they criticized—the compromise with pre-Reformation episcopal church structure, discipline, and ceremonies arranged by Henrician and Elizabethan legislation, they did not need to defend that compromise as an authentically English pattern rooted in national ecclesiastical and legal history. The gathered churches of Massachusetts did not legitimate themselves through ecclesiastical antiquarianism pursued down through English history. For the first two generations of the colony, the Massachusetts Puritans' "primitivism" similarly restrained (though did not preclude) efforts to defend their church polity by invoking their own indigenous church history. The colonists lacked the drive to construct and defend a linked ecclesiastical and legal ancient constitution.

The Puritans' yearning to return to the purity of "primitive" days had not only a religious but a legal dimension. Legal primitivism was similarly uncongenial to ancient constitutionalism. In the legal sphere, the Puritans' primitivist impulses took the form of Biblicism in law—a desire to adopt rules based on those judicial laws of Moses infused with the moral law (and thus binding beyond the Jewish commonwealth).[64] To be sure, Massachusetts settlers subscribed to this Biblicist ideal to varying extents. And outside the capital statutes of the criminal law, their legal system honored Biblicism more in rhetoric than in practice. However qualified in application, Biblicism did mute ancient constitutionalism's role and appeal. Ancient constitutionalism used antiquarian scholarly techniques to document a continuous legal tradition running through a polity's history. Its key concepts of immemoriality and prescription assumed that the passage of time testified to a custom's rationality, ability to secure consent, or benefit to a community. Legal primitivism, by contrast, skipped over the practices and history of colonial and English law in order to focus attention on a Scriptural legal order of enduring worth and validity. Like ecclesiastical primitivism, legal primitivism tried to revivify an authoritative moment in the past. The relevant past was Scriptural, not English or colonial. Legal primitivism diverted attention away from the national focus and prescriptive logic of ancient constitutionalism, in both its English and indigenous varieties.

Not just the origins and legitimation, but the *content*, of the ancient constitution undermined its appeal to those committed to godly law. Both Englishmen and New Englanders lived by rules drawn from various bodies of law: common law, ecclesiastical law, local customs, the law merchant, the law of Admiralty and Star Chamber, and so forth.[65] The ancient constitution connected the present to the past not through these multiple, interlinked forms of law. It focused on (and overemphasized) one strand—the common law.[66] Puritans, though, had come to regard the common law with ambivalence. While they recognized its value in restraining royal prerogative and episcopal pressure, they decried its ungodly elements. It imposed capital punishment where God did not (as for theft) and cast aside God's Scriptural command to punish certain offenses with death (e.g. adultery). The common law differed from the judicial laws of Scripture on a host of particulars as varied as the use of primogeniture in inheritance and the acceptance of one instead of two witnesses in the proof of wrongdoing.[67] As heirs of a half-century campaign against ungodly blemishes on the common law, the Massachusetts Puritans treated it with a wariness they did not extend to other types of law in their colony, such as the charter or the local ordinances of England that they carried over.[68] Critics of the colony's government such as Samuel Gorton and Robert Child held up the common law as a restraint on the magistrates' power and as a symbol of English imperial authority. The association of the common law with the danger of metropolitan intervention in local affairs added another reason to look with suspicion on this law of uncertain godliness. To invoke the ancient constitution of England was to accept, even celebrate, the common law at its heart, which was no easy thing for Puritans to do in early Massachusetts.

If the ideological foundations of the Puritan colony worked against acceptance of ancient constitutionalism, the resistance that they created did not prove insurmountable. By the middle 1680s, spurred by the abrogation of the first charter, colonists invoked the ancient constitution of Massachusetts against Sir Edmund Andros's Dominion of New England. The Mathers, Increase and Cotton, proved the most vigorous exponents. During Increase's agency to London on behalf of Massachusetts, he condemned Andros's government for depriving the colony of its "ancient" polity and liberties through such means as governing and taxing without an assembly, calling land titles into question, and restricting town meetings. Increase appealed to King James II, King William III, and their officials to restore the colony's traditional polity. In a series of addresses and pamphlets, the Mathers cast Increase's mission and the second charter as the best possible defense of Massachusetts's ancient constitution given the political exigencies in England.[69]

The abrogation of the first Massachusetts charter came as part of a wider Stuart effort, in the middle 1680s, to expand the scope of royal prerogative by remodeling colonial charters and English municipal corporations. The Crown's defeat of London in a *quo warranto* proceeding in King's Bench in 1683 not only cost the city her charter, but induced dozens of other English towns and boroughs to surrender their franchises. James II continued Charles II's drive against municipal corporations until, fearing the arrival of William of Orange, he reversed course. In October 1688, James published a proclamation that restored the ancient constitution and liberties of London and numerous other cities. Though James had not spoken of colonial charters, Increase Mather tried to take advantage of this turn of policy. He tried to tie the fortunes of Massachusetts to those of the English municipal corporations by portraying all of them as polities stripped of their ancient constitutions and liberties and deserving restoration. The victory of King William only increased the power of this argument.[70] After the overthrow of Andros, the colonists followed Increase's lead. In May 1689, the Council for Safety and the convention of town representatives appealed to William to reinvest them with their "ancient" rights and privileges as part of his "universal restoration of charters and English liberties."[71]

The Mathers and their colonial supporters hinted at, rather than rigorously developed, the implications of the rhetoric of antiquity. The passage of time, the Mathers implied, had clothed Massachusetts's constitution in honor. Through prescription, a presumption had arisen in favor of the colony's inherited privileges and methods of governance. Deprivation of these by the Crown's servants was assumed to be wrongful. The Mathers' condemnation of Andros's illegalities and plea for the preservation of the colony's ancient constitution fell short of asserting that, as a matter of law, the English government could not alter the polity (a position that some of their countrymen would approach in later decades).

The notion that Massachusetts lived by an ancient constitution, which the Mathers popularized, spread widely throughout the colony. In 1691, Boston merchant Joshua Scottow published a tract lamenting declension from New England's "primitive constitution."[72] When William Phips returned to the colony in 1692 as governor under the second charter, he announced that "God had sent him there to serve his country and that he would not abridge them of their ancient laws and customs, but that all the laws, liberties and privileges that were practicable should be as before and should be maintained and upheld by him."[73] In 1696, the representatives in Massachusetts's General Court tried, unsuccessfully, to send an agent to England to restore the colony's "ancient privileges."[74] Wait Winthrop, three years later, accused colonists who had once worked with Andros of ruining the "ancient liberty of this country."[75]

After learning to celebrate, preserve, and shelter behind their own, indigenous ancient constitution—one not immemorial, but based on prescription—Massachusetts colonists later sought the protection of England's far older, immemorial constitution. This took some time. To contest Andros, colonists claimed to be upholding the rights of Englishmen as defined by the practices of the mother country. This political vocabulary, which drew strength from Whig justifications of the Glorious Revolution, initially had little historical dimension beyond loose invocations of Magna Carta.[76] It took until the early decades of the eighteenth century for New Englanders to ground the rights of Englishmen in an unbroken tradition dating back to a Saxon constitution of liberty. But once they became comfortable with this device, colonial Whigs made appeals to the immemorial and ancient English constitution an important part of their political repertoire.[77]

Since ancient constitutionalism had commonly been a bulwark against prerogative, it is not surprising, at first glance, that it made its appearance in reaction to Andros's Dominion of New England. Yet while the conflict with the English empire in the late 1680s provided the context for the rise of ancient constitutionalist argument in Massachusetts, it does not supply a full explanation. After all, Massachusetts worked to protect its charter, guard its political semi-autonomy, and minimize imperial oversight at many earlier points. One thinks, for instance, of the 1636-1638 *quo warranto* process, the arrival of the 1664 royal commissioners, and the persistent threats of new *quo warranto* proceedings in the 1670s fueled by Edward Randolph's censures against the colony. The rise of ancient constitutionalist thought required more than a collision with prerogative and the empire. A number of political and intellectual developments in the second and third generation of the colony facilitated its emergence, not least by complicating or contesting the ideological commitments of the early colony that had retarded its acceptance. In addition, ancient constitutionalism gained support by providing benefits within the colony's own domestic politics aside from its services against prerogative.

A precondition for believing in Massachusetts's own ancient constitution was a willingness to regard the colony as having a constitution. This took time to develop in a meaningful, robust way. To be sure, the first settlers understood that the colony had a set of laws and practices that "constituted" power and, in that most basic sense, was a constitution. But beginning around the Restoration, and accelerating in the 1670s, colonists replaced this vague, inchoate understanding of a constitution with a sharper appreciation that they lived under a patterned, coherent, and, importantly, a *distinctive* legal-political system. With the Restoration came pointed inquiries into Massachusetts's sectarianism and deviations from English law and trade policy. The Crown's generally adverse conclusions about the colony's civil and ecclesiastical institutions induced, in reaction, attempts to define favorably and justify Massachusetts's polity. This process encouraged both sides to describe the colony's laws and methods of governance as an integrated whole—that is, as a distinct constitution that might be defended, improved, or replaced. In a barrage of correspondence to King Charles II and other English notables, Edward Randolph poured scorn on the vices of the Massachusetts constitution and called for thoroughgoing revision.[78] The colony's agents in London complained, with justice, that Randolph planned the "total subversion of that constitution."[79] Enemies of the first charter government accused it of living by a "tyrannical and arbitrary constitution."[80] Massachusetts ministers' rallied to the defense of their polity in sermons. John Oxenbridge and Thomas Shepard called on settlers to guard the liberties established in the "early days of settlement" and passed down intact through the generations, the "first and best constitution and complexion of this colony."[81] Massachusetts's appreciation that it had a valuable and distinctive constitution came not only through struggle through England, but through comparison with other North American settlements. It was the singular beneficiary, wrote Oxenbridge, of "beautiful and precious liberties beyond other colonies."[82]

The growing salience of the Massachusetts constitution as a political concept laid the foundation for the colony's indigenous ancient constitutionalism, but there were still potential difficulties. In 1672, the elders of the gathered churches declared to the General Court that the colony's "civil constitution" rested on the charter, "by which we are incorporated into a body politic." This "makes us a people."[83]

Unfortunately, the charter that gave rise to the constitution and organized the people in a political society came from the decidedly ungodly Charles I. Perhaps the constitution and polity were tainted at the source? This potential obstacle faded over the seventeenth century as the Puritans became more insistent about describing their charter as a divine gift. After all, it enabled and protected the city on a hill.[84] By the turn of the eighteenth century, the minister Joseph Belcher could recount how God had founded "both an ecclesiastical and civil constitution here, together and at once, and thereby made us not only a people, but His people." God inspired his colonists to "endeavor a coalition of both those fundamental interest, viz., that of heaven and that of earth, which is to say, that of religion, and that of civil government, that the latter might be sanctified by the former."[85]

Belcher's formulation, typical of Massachusetts Puritans after the founding generation, made clear that the Stuart origins of the first charter did not compromise its godliness. But the position expressed by Belcher did more. It also suggested a way to mitigate a potential obstacle to indigenous ancient constitutionalism stemming from the political ideology of the founding generation. Puritans committed to primitivism—to the improvement of state and church by the commands in Scripture and the examples of the Jewish commonwealth and the early church—bore an ambivalent relationship to legal and political authority generated through custom (such as an ancient constitution). To live by Scripture and to copy primitive institutions and practices was to return to godliness. But customs generated by the repeated actions of men and women might or might not be in accordance with God's purposes. The Puritans declared in the 1648 Massachusetts law code that no "custom or prescription shall ever prevail amongst us in any moral case" if that custom or prescription "can be proved to be morally sinful by the word of God."[86] Built out of and legitimated by custom, an ancient constitution might contain ungodly corruptions, as did England's. The drift of Massachusetts intellectual life in the seventeenth century helped allay this concern in respect to the colony's own ancient constitution. It became common to depict as godly the first charter, the constitution that rested upon it, and the people that it organized politically. In so doing, colonists became prepared to see Massachusetts's ancient constitution—the confluence of its laws, institutions, practices, and liberties—as godly. Muting the potential tension between godly and traditional-customary legitimations of authority facilitated the emergence of indigenous ancient constitutionalism.

Helping along this process was the growing tendency, after 1660, to cite the charter and Massachusetts precedents that had grown up under the charter in political argument and in litigation. By the 1680s, in the words of T. H. Breen, "many colonists treated the charter with the kind of reverence that had previously been reserved for Scripture."[87] The first generation of magistrates and ministers gave stronger support than their successors to the Biblicist ideal of governing the colony through those judicial laws of Moses infused by the moral law (and hence perpetually binding).[88] Biblicism in law undermined ancient constitutionalism by skipping over developments in Massachusetts and England in order to find the current application of timeless legal authority—God's commands to the Jews and His oversight of their commonwealth. By the second and third generation, colonists wrestling with concrete political and legal disputes looked less to Deuteronomy and the examples of the kings of the Jewish commonwealth and more to the charter and to precedents set by Massachusetts's General Court, magistrates, and judicial tribunals. As the colony grew accustomed to looking for legal authority within its own history, it became better acclimated to the national focus and prescriptive logic of ancient constitutionalism. Although the magistrates and General Court of the second and third generation never abandoned

Biblicism, its lessening place in day-to-day politics and litigation undermined its potential resistance to ancient constitutionalism.

While the weakening of uncongenial ideological commitments from the first generation facilitated the emergence of ancient constitutionalism in late-seventeenth-century Massachusetts, colonists would not have taken up this form of argument unless it helped them accomplish political ends. Ancient constitutionalism served primarily as a weapon to defend inherited (or idealized) governmental institutions and practices against the intrusions of prerogative. But it also provided services in the colony's domestic politics, which added to its attractiveness.

Ancient constitutionalism proved especially valuable within Massachusetts politics insofar as it allowed colonists to protect and employ their traditional governmental practices and liberties after the invalidation of the first charter. While the charter lived, colonists had spoken of it as the foundation and guardian of their political and religious order. But as they were to learn, it was dangerous to identify the New England Way too closely with the charter. For once the charter fell, what was to become of the customs, liberties, and modes of governance that grew up under it? The 1683 *quo warranto* proceedings against the charter of London, a case that the colonists closely followed, shed some light on the question.[89] The litigation called into question the relationship between a polity's charter and the broader realm of practices and privileges encompassed by its constitution. Henry Pollexfen, defending the City before King's Bench, painted a dire picture of what would befall London should the Crown succeed in stripping the charter. The City, being dissolved as a political entity, could no longer collect its debts and its lands would revert to the donors. Loss of the charter would nullify its customary rights, including its political and economic structures and liberties, which were grounded in prescription. These rights were annexed to the charter and would be extinguished along with it. When the Crown issued a new charter for London, the customs and liberties of the City would not transfer to it and survive; they would die with the old charter. The Crown's advocates, trying to rebut this grievous prediction, claimed that many of the City's customary rights could continue after the elimination of the charter. At several points in the Middle Ages, they argued, the Crown had seized London's charter and placed a guardian ("*custos*") over the City to manage its government. Those seizures did not invalidate the City's prescriptive rights, and neither would the 1683 proceedings. The Crown would regrant London's customs and privileges along with a new charter. Indeed, some lawyers, including analysts sympathetic to London, thought that the City would retain the same legal rights and customs after the crown issued a new charter, except for the changes spelled out explicitly in the document.[90]

The London proceedings underscored the value of speaking about an ancient, prescriptive constitution broader than the charter and not reducible to it. Charters came from the Crown, and the king could abrogate subsequent charters no less easily than the first one. But the colony's constitution came, through prescription, from themselves. The constitution could live on beyond the death of the first charter and, if necessary, beyond the suspension or amendment of subsequent charters.

This implication of ancient constitutionalism—that it offered a way to preserve customs and privileges after the fall of the charter—provided two immediate advantages in the colony's domestic politics. First, institutions under the second charter could measure the extent of their authority and legitimate their power by reference to the political practices of the first charter period. In 1692, the General Court wrote into law some of the colony's "ancient" ways of governing. For example, Massachusetts, by statute, continued the "practice and custom" of towns choosing selectmen "for the ordering and managing

[of] . . . prudential affairs."⁹¹ Once again, the example of London served as a precedent. A 1690 parliamentary statute that restored the charter rights of London gauged the powers of officials according to the City's "ancient usage and custom."⁹² Second, the ancient constitution served in the second charter period as a protest ideal. Colonists often portrayed their ancient liberties as under siege, or slipping away and in need of revival. This argument presupposed that first charter practices were "supposed to" endure after the destruction of the charter that nurtured them.⁹³

Ancient constitutionalism came to occupy an important place in eighteenth-century Massachusetts political culture, as John Phillip Reid and Trevor Colbourn have shown.⁹⁴ The colonists' discovery (invention?) of their own indigenous ancient constitution in the late seventeenth century preceded and prepared the way for their later deployment of England's Saxon constitution of liberty in political argument. While these developments were an important chapter in Massachusetts's history, one might be tempted to dismiss them as having little importance beyond that one colony. After all, by English standards, Massachusetts's indigenous ancient constitutionalism never achieved the intellectual depth of the metropolis's version. No colonial equivalent of Coke, Selden, or even James I, put his mind to the elaboration, explanation, and defense of Massachusetts's ancient constitution. Competing versions of it did not emerge. It generated no program of research and documentation. Considered purely as an intellectual phenomenon, the colony's defense of its prescriptive rights seems derivative and underdeveloped.

Yet ancient constitutionalism in Massachusetts is of broader significance—not for its content, but rather for the timing and causes of its emergence, for its "career." The colony's ancient constitutionalism was out of synch with English political developments. Massachusetts showed little or no interest in ancient constitutionalism during the first half of the seventeenth century, the time of its greatest influence in the mother country, and only took it up as it declined in relative importance in metropolitan politics. A variety of ideological and political conditions particular to the colony at first retarded and then encouraged the use of ancient constitutionalism. Taken as a chapter in Massachusetts history, this story becomes a reception history of a political argument in a local context. Taken in broader perspective, this story suggests the value of studying the contrasting careers of ancient constitutionalism in the different colonies of the English transatlantic periphery. Scholars of English political history have explored the place of ancient constitutionalism in France, Scotland, Sicily, the Netherlands, and in other foreign lands better to understand its role at home.[95] Expanding this comparative project within as well as outside of the English speaking world could advance efforts to more precisely understand the special characteristics of ancient constitutionalism in England. And it could help illuminate the shared commitments—and the points of difference—within Anglophone transatlantic legal culture.

Notes

1. One notable exception is John Phillip Reid, "The Jurisprudence of Liberty: The Ancient Constitution in the Legal Historiography of the Seventeenth and Eighteenth Centuries," in *The Roots of Liberty: Magna Carta, Ancient Constitution, and the Anglo-American Tradition of the Rule of Law*, ed. Ellis Sandoz (Columbia, Mo., 1993), 147-231. On the importance of the ancient Saxon constitution in the historical thought of eighteenth-century Americans, see, e.g., Trevor Colbourn, *The Lamp of Experience: Whig History and the Intellectual Origins of the American Revolution* (Chapel Hill, 1965); J. C. D. Clark, *The Language of Liberty, 1660-1832: Political Discourse and Social Dynamics in the Anglo-American World* (Cambridge, 1994), 16-20, 276.

2. J. G. A. Pocock, *The Ancient Constitution and the Feudal Law* (1957), reissued with a retrospect (Cambridge, 1987).

3. The best survey of the criticisms and of the author's response is contained in Pocock's own retrospect in the second revised edition of *The Ancient Constitution*. The most important and comprehensive subsequent review of the central issues is contained in Glenn Burgess, *The Politics of the Ancient Constitution* (University Park, Penn., 1992).

4. Burgess, *The Politics of the Ancient Constitution*, 80. See also, Christopher Brooks and Kevin Sharpe, "Debate: History, English Law and the Renaissance," *Past & Present* 72(1976):133-142.

5. See especially, Burgess, *Ancient Constitution*, 20-37.

6. This summary is drawn largely from Christopher St. German, *St. German's Doctor and Student*, ed. T. F. T. Plucknett and J. L. Barton, Selden Society 91 (London, 1974), 45-47. Glen Burgess has argued that St. German's views were more influential among early modern lawyers than those of Fortescue. For a full and illuminating discussion of this matter, see Burgess, *Ancient Constitution*, 19-78.

7. Burgess, *Ancient Constitution*, 86.

8. Sir John Davies, *A Report of Cases*, pre., 6, cited in Burgess, *Ancient Constitution*, 52.

9. For a recent and interesting reconsideration of these perceptions, see Alan Cromartie, "The Constitutionalist Revolution: The Transformation of Political Culture in Early Stuart England," *Past & Present* 163(1999): 76-120.

10. Christopher W. Brooks, "The Place of Magna Carta and the Ancient Constitution in Sixteenth Century Legal Thought," in Ellis Sandoz, ed., *The Roots of Liberty, Magna Carta, Ancient Constitution, and the Anglo-American Tradition of the Rule of Law* (London, 1993), 57-88.

11. Brooks, "The Place of Magna Carta," 61-62.

12. Brooks, "The Place of Magna Carta," 75. Compare Janelle Greenberg, *The Radical Face of the Ancient Constitution: St. Edward's "Laws" in Early Modern Political Thought* (Cambridge, 2001), which argues for the importance of medieval and early Tudor ancient constitutionalism.

13. Brooks, "The Place of Magna Carta," 68-70.

14. For a more extensive discussion of this process, see Burgess, *Ancient Constitution*, 100-102.

15. Burgess, *Ancient Constitution*, 103-105. See also J. G. A. Pocock, "England," in Orest Ranum, ed., *National Consciousness, History and Political Culture in Early Modern England* (Baltimore, 1975), 106-110; and Pocock, "The History of British Political Thought: The Creation of a Center," *Journal of British Studies* 24(1985):290-292.

16. *The Apology* was republished in 1609, in a one-volume collection of Jewel's works, and a copy ordered to be placed in every parish church in England. John Jewel, *An Apology of the Church of England*, Ed., J. E. Booty (New York, 1963), xlii, 135.

17. I Elizabeth 1, cap 1, xx.

18. Jewel, *Apology*, 115. Jewel was attempting to defend the Church of England against the charge that it had reformed its church unilaterally, without proper consultation.

19. Peter White, "The *Via Media* in the early Stuart Church," in Kenneth Fincham, ed., *The Early Stuart Church, 1603-1642* (London, 1993), 211-230.

20. For a clear and thoughtful discussion of Hooker's ideas, see Peter Lake, *Anglicans and Puritans Presbyterianism and English Conformist Thought from Whitgift to Hooker* (London, 1988), esp. 145-231.

21. Richard Hooker, *Of the Laws of Ecclesiastical Polity*, Ed. Arthur Stephen McGrade (Cambridge, 1989), 146-147.

22. Hooker, *Ecclesiastical Polity*, 194-195.

23. Burgess, *Ancient Constitution*, 103-105.

24. For a useful look at the early modern legal profession, see C. W. Brooks, *Pettyfoggers and Vipers of the Commonwealth: The "Lower Branch" of the Legal Profession in Early Modern England* (Cambridge, 1986).

25. Louis A. Knafla, "The Matriculation Revolution and Education at the Inns of Court in Renaissance England," in A. J. Slavin, ed., *Tudor Men and Institutions* (Baton Rouge, La., 1972), 242.

26. Matthew Hale, *The History of the Common Law of England*, ed. Charles M. Gray (Chicago, 1971), 161.

27. Scholars remind us that the two treatises need to be read very carefully, with a clear view to their Scottish context, because James I had both a specific purpose and a specific audience in mind when he wrote them. The caution is appropriate, but it is equally important to remember that James went to some trouble to have both works published in England prior to his accession, and that whatever their original context, they were

the work of a thirty-three year old monarch of no little intelligence, education, and experience. Jenny Wormald, "James VI and I, *Basilikon Doron* and *The Trew Law of Free Monarchies*: The Scottish Context and the English Translation," in Linda Levy Peck, ed., *The Mental World of the Jacobean Court* (Cambridge, 1991), 36-54.

28. *The Political Works of James I*, ed. C. H. McIlwain (Cambridge, 1918), 63.

29. This point is developed more fully in Paul Christianson, "Royal and Parliamentary Voices on the Ancient Constitution c. 1604-21," in Peck, *The Mental World of the Jacobean Court*, 75.

30. Conrad Russell, "English Parliaments 1593-1606: One Epoch or Two?" in D. M. Dean and N. L. Jones, eds., *The Parliaments of Elizabethan England* (Oxford, 1990), 207-208.

31. For a detailed and illuminating discussion of this process, see Hans Pawlisch, *Sir John Davies and the Conquest of Ireland: A Study in Legal Imperialism* (Cambridge, 1985).

32. It is perhaps worth noting how radically this position differed from James's support of the use of judge-made law to achieve England's imperial needs and aims in Ireland.

33. Charles M. Gray, "Parliament, Liberty, and the Law," in J. H. Hexter, ed., *Parliament and Liberty from the Reign of Elizabeth to the Civil War* (Stanford, 1992), 160.

34. The quote is from a subsequent royal address to Parliament on the subject in 1610. McIlwain, *The Political Works of James I*, 311-312.

35. Coke, *Reports*, vi, 280-282 (pt. xii, 63-5), cited in J. P. Kenyon, ed., *The Stuart Constitution*, 2nd ed. (Cambridge, 1986), 80-81. This version, of course, reflects Coke's own account of the events.

36. Coke, *Reports*, vi, 280-282 (pt. xii, 63-65) in Kenyon, *The Stuart Constitution*, 80-81.

37. For the most recent and comprehensive presentation of his thesis, see Paul Christianson, *Discourse on History, Law, and Governance in the Public Career of John Selden* (Toronto, 1996); but see also "Royal and Parliamentary Voices on the Ancient Constitution, c. 1604-1621," in Peck, *The Mental World of the Jacobean Court*, 71-95; and "Ancient Constitutions in the Age of Sir Edward Coke and John Selden," in Sandoz, *The Roots of Liberty*, 89-146.

38. McIlwain, *The Political Works of James I*, 309-311.

39. E. R. Foster, *Proceedings in Parliament, 1610* (New Haven, 1966), 103-107.

40. Foster, *Proceedings in Parliament 1610*, 170-197. Professor Christianson makes the telling point that Hedley's speech predates the more celebrated discussions of the ancient constitution by both Sir Edward Coke and Sir John Davies. Christianson, "The Ancient Constitution, c. 1604-1621," 80.

41. Foster, *Proceedings in Parliament 1610*, 191.

42. Foster, *Proceedings in Parliament 1610*, 189.

43. Foster, *Proceedings in Parliament 1610*, 191.

44. This represents only a crude summary of the much more detailed exegesis offered by Christianson, *Discourse on History*, 14-32.

45. Burgess, *Ancient Constitution*, 212-231.

46. "Remonstrance of both Houses in answer to the King's Declaration concerning Hull, May 26, 1642," in Kenyon, *The Stuart Constitution*, 221.

47. Corinne C. Weston, "England: Ancient Constitution and Common Law," in *The Cambridge History of Political Thought, 1450-1700*, ed. J. H. Burns with the assistance of Mark Goldie (Cambridge, 1991), 399-405; Janelle Greenberg, *Radical Face*, 182-242; Pocock, *Ancient Constitution*, 361, 366-370; Reid, "Jurisprudence of Liberty."

48. Burgess, *Ancient Constitution*, 99-100, 231; Pocock, *Ancient Constitution*, 227, 230-232, 239, 361, 367-370; Greenberg, *Radical Face*, 270-296; J. W. Burrow, *A Liberal Descent: Victorian Historians and the English Past* (Cambridge, 1981), 21; Corinne Comstock Weston and Janelle Renfrow Greenberg, *Subjects and Sovereigns: The Grand Controversy over Legal Sovereignty in Stuart England* (Cambridge, 1981), 182-183; Martyn P. Thompson, "A Note on 'Reason' and 'History' in Late Seventeenth Century Thought," *Political Theory* 4(1976):491-504; James Coniff, "Reason and History in Early Whig Thought: The Case of Algernon Sidney," *Journal of the History of Ideas* 43(1982):397-416. In response to Lord Bolingbroke's deployment of the ancient constitution to attack Robert Walpole, the Robinarch's defenders in the 1720s and 1730 argued that the Whig regime embodied a "modern constitution" purged of absolutist excesses and made secure by the Glorious Revolution. Isaac Kramnick, *Bolingbroke and His Circle: The Politics of Nostalgia in the Age of Walpole* (Cambridge, Mass., 1968), 127-136.

49. R. J. Smith, *The Gothic Bequest: Medieval Institutions in British Thought, 1688-1863* (Cambridge, 1987), 41.

50. The core notion of ancient constitutionalism was legitimation through prescription: the antiquity of a custom or practice protected it from alteration against the will of the beneficiary. Understood in this broad sense,

ancient constitutionalism was an argument widely used in early modern England—in religion as well as politics, in struggles over economic rights as well as over governance, and in the boroughs and villages as well as the royal court and parliament. See David Underdown, *A Freeborn People: Politics and the Nation in Seventeenth-Century England* (Oxford, 1996), 48, 55-56.

51. See T. H. Breen, *The Character of the Good Ruler: A Study in Puritan Political Ideas in New England, 1630-1730* (New Haven, 1970); George L. Haskins, *Law and Authority in Early Massachusetts* (Lanham, Md., 1985); Robert Emmet Wall, Jr., *Massachusetts Bay: The Crucial Decade, 1640-1650* (New Haven, 1972).

52. John Hayward, *The Lives of the Three Norman Kings* (London, 1613), 96; Robert Parsons, *An Answer to the Fifth Part of Reports Lately Set Forth by Sir E. Cook* (St. Omer, 1606), 12-13, (English laws were "brought in principally by . . . a Conqueror, and such a one as intended to bridle the English by that means, and to bring them under by those laws, and the insolent dominion of the Normans"); Johann P. Sommerville, "History and Theory: The Norman Conquest in Early Stuart Political Thought," *Political Studies* 34(1986):255-256; William Klein, "The Ancient Constitution Revisited," in *Political Discourse in Early Modern Britain*, ed. Nicholas Phillipson and Quentin Skinner (Cambridge, 1993), 39-40. The "Bastard of Normandy came into England" and "gave the law, and took none, changed the laws, inverted the order of government," concluded Scotland's James VI five years before ascending the English throne as James I. James VI, *The True Law of Free Monarchies* (1598; London, 1603), in McIlwain, *The Political Works of James I*, 63.

53. "[A]ll human laws," wrote Egerton, "are but *leges temporis*." See "The Speech of the Lord Chancellor of England, in the Exchequer Chamber, Touching the Post-Nati" [1608], in Louis A. Knafla, *Law and Politics in Jacobean England: The Tracts of Lord Chancellor Ellesmere* (Cambridge, 1977), 223 and 49-50. Egerton went on to say: "And the wisdom of the judges found them to be unmeet for the time they lived in, though very good and necessary for the time wherein they were made." For Bacon's depiction, see, for example, Francis Bacon "Aphorisms" [MS c.1603-1622], in Mark S. Neustadt, "The Making of the Instauration: Science, Politics and Law in the Career of Francis Bacon" (Ph.D. diss., Johns Hopkins University, 1987), 272-282.

54. Settlers faced a particular challenge when they styled their own indigenous constitution as ancient. If they claimed the protection of England's

ancient constitution, they faced no more (or less) difficulty in proving the antiquity of particular customs and institutions than residents of the metropolis.

55. For a fuller exposition of the different interpretations of "antiquity" current in Stuart political thought, see the insightful recent monograph by Janelle Greenberg, *The Radical Face of the Ancient Constitution*, 20-26.
56. Pocock, *The Ancient Constitution and the Feudal Law* (1987), 37; W. H. Greenleaf, *Order, Empiricism and Politics: Two Traditions of English Political Thought, 1500-1700* (London, 1964), 193; Weston, "England," 384.
57. Corinne Comstock Weston, "Diverse Viewpoints on the Ancient Constitution," in Sandoz, *The Roots of Liberty*, 234-235; Mathew Hale, *History of the Common Law of England*, ed. Charles M. Grey (Chicago, 1971), 3-4.
58. Charles Calthrope, *The Relation Between the Lord of a Manor and the Copyholder his Tenant* (London, 1917), 15-16. Calthrope delivered his Reading in 1574; it was first published in 1635.
59. John Cowell, *Interpreter* (1607), V4.
60. John Palmer, *An Impartial Account of the State of New England; Or, the Late Government There Vindicated* (London, 1690), reprinted in William Henry Whitmore, ed., *The Andros Tracts* (New York, 1968), 1:47.
61. Haskins, *Law and Authority*; G. B. Warden, "Law Reform in England and New England, 1620 to 1660," *William and Mary Quarterly* 3d ser., 35(1978):668-690.
62. F. J. Levy, *Tudor Historical Thought* (San Marino, Calif., 1967), 79-123; Colin Kidd, *British Identities Before Nationalism: Ethnicity and Nationhood in the Atlantic World, 1600-1800* (Cambridge, 1999), 107-118; John Guy, "Thomas Cromwell and the Intellectual Origins of the Henrician Revolution," in *Reassessing the Henrician Age: Humanism, Politics, and Reform, 1500-1550*, ed. Alistair Fox and John Guy (Oxford, 1986), 151-178: Burgess, *Ancient Constitution*, 102-105.
63. Among many examples, one might cite John Cotton, *The Way of the Congregational Churches Cleared* (London, 1648), 93-99; and *A Platform of Church Discipline* (1648), in Williston Walker, ed., *The Creeds and Platforms of Congregationalism* (1893; Boston, 1960), 203-204. See generally Theodore Dwight Bozeman, *To Live Ancient Lives: The Primitivist Dimension in Puritanism* (Chapel Hill, 1988).
64. Bozeman, *To Live Ancient Lives*, 153-192.

65. Mark DeWolfe Howe, "The Sources and Nature of Law in Colonial Massachusetts," in *Law and Authority in Colonial America*, ed. George A. Billias (New York, 1965), 1-16; Haskins, *Law and Authority*.
66. Following contemporary usage, we include ancient statutes in the term "common law."
67. For a revealing assessment of the common law's fidelity to the demands of Scripture, see Henry Finch, "A Conference and Reformation of the Common Law by the Law of God" (MS, pre 1586), Bodleian Library, Rawlinson MS C43. Wilfrid Prest has astutely analyzed this document in "The Art of Law and the Law of God: Sir Henry Finch (1558-1625)," *Puritans and Revolutionaries: Essays in Seventeenth-Century History Presented to Christopher Hill*, ed. Donald Pennington and Keith Thomas (Oxford, 1978), 94-117.
68. The Puritans in Massachusetts did not extend to local law or the charter their ideologically driven ambivalence about the common law. The remembered practices of the English boroughs and villages of the original settlers supplied the bulk of workaday rules in early Massachusetts. See, e.g., Haskins, *Law and Authority*; David Grayson Allen, *In English Ways: The Movement of Societies and the Transferal of English Local Law and Custom to Massachusetts Bay in the Seventeenth Century* (Chapel Hill, 1981). Puritans insisted that this law, like all law, conform to God's requirements. But they did not look too closely since they lacked a pre-existing animus against the commercial practices of Dorchester or the land transfer rules of East Anglia. The charter, meanwhile, was the act of a Stuart king whose bishops were harrying Puritans in England. But over time, the colonists came to regard the charter as a divinely sanctioned instrument that protected their godly mission. By contrast, the Puritans' inherited misgivings about the common law remained. The common law underwent no cleansing, no rehabilitation.
69. Letter from Increase Mather to Thomas Hinckley, Sept. 12, 1689, in Robert Earle Moody and Richard Clive Simmons, eds., *The Glorious Revolution in Massachusetts: Selected Documents, 1689-1692, Publications of the Colonial Society of Massachusetts* 64 (Boston, 1988):443; Increase Mather, *A Narrative of the Miseries of New England by Reason of the Arbitrary Government Erected There* (London, 1688), 4-5; Increase Mather, *The Present State of New English Affairs* (Boston, 1689), in William Henry Whitmore, ed., *The Andros Tracts*, Prince Society, *Publications* 5-7 (New York, 1968), 2:17; Increase Mather, *Reasons for the Confirmation of the Charters of the Corporations*

in New England (London, 1689-1690), in *Andros Tracts*, 2:225; Increase Mather, *A Brief Account Concerning Several of the Agents of New England* (London, 1691), in *Andros Tracts*, 2:285; Cotton Mather, *The Serviceable Man* (Boston, 1690), 63; Cotton Mather, "Political Fables," in *Andros Tracts*, 2:325; A. B. [Cotton Mather], *An Account of the Late Revolutions in New England* (Boston, 1689), in *Andros Tracts*, 2:191; (identification of Cotton Mather as the author by Richard Johnson, *Adjustment to Empire: The New England Colonies, 1675-1715* [Leicester, Eng., 1981], 89n.45).

70. Philip S. Haffenden, "The Crown and the Colonial Charters, 1675-1688: Part I," *William and Mary Quarterly* 3d ser., 15(1958):297-311; Philip S. Haffenden, "The Crown and the Colonial Charters, 1675-1688: Part II," *William and Mary Quarterly* 15(1958):452-466; Jennifer Levin, *The Charter Controversy in the City of London, 1660-1688, and Its Consequences* (London, 1969), 93, 98-99; Johnson, *Adjustment*, 29, 52.

71. "At a Convention of the Representatives of the Several Towns and Villages of the Massachusetts Colony in New England" [May 24, 1689; Printed at Boston], in *Publications of the Colonial Society* 64:393; Council of Safety quoted in Viola F. Barnes, *The Dominion of New England* (New Haven, 1923), 254.

72. Joshua Scottow, *Old Men's Tears for their Own Declensions, Mixed with Fears of their and Posterities further Falling Off from New England's Primitive Constitution* (Boston, 1691).

73. Phips's remarks cited in Breen, *Character of the Good Ruler*, 190.

74. The Council vetoed the representative's initiative. Richard S. Dunn, *Puritans and Yankees: The Winthrop Dynasty of New England, 1630-1717* (1962; New York, 1971), 270.

75. Winthrop quoted in Johnson, *Adjustment*, 292.

76. After the abrogation of the first charter, the expiring General Court complained that the new government had the power to tax and legislate without an assembly, by which "the subjects are abridged of their liberty as Englishmen." General Court's Reply to His Majesty's Commissioners (May 1686), in Nathaniel Shurtleff, ed., *Records of the Governor and Company of the Massachusetts Bay* (Boston, 1854), 5:516. The "rights of Englishmen" was the rallying cry of protesters against Andros's taxes led by John Wise and of the Mathers in their lobbying and pamphleteering campaign. Wise and some of the pamphlet literature assailing Andros cited Magna Carta. Barnes, *Dominion*, 82-90; Breen, *Character of the Good Ruler*, 134-179.

77. Clinton Rossiter, *Seedtime of the Republic: The Origins of the American Tradition of Political Liberty* (New York, 1953), 217 (discussing John Wise in 1715); Breen, *Character of the Good Ruler*, 264 (discussing Franklin brothers' *New-England Courant* in the early 1720s); Colbourn, *The Lamp of Experience*; Reid, "Jurisprudence of Liberty"; Clark, *Language of Liberty*, 16-20, 276.

78. Letter from Randolph to King Charles II, Nov. 17, 1676, in *Edward Randolph, Including His Letters and Official Papers . . . 1676-1703*, ed. Robert N. Toppan and Alfred T. Goodrick (New York, 1967), 2:261; Letter from Randolph to Earl of Clarendon, June 14, 1682, in *Randolph Papers*, 3:157; Letter from Randolph to Archbishop of Canterbury, July 7, 1686, in *Randolph Papers*, 4:88. King Charles II, complaining that his directions had not been put into effect, spoke of the colony's "constitution." Letter from Charles II to Massachusetts, Sept. 20, 1680, in Thomas Hutchinson, *A Collection of Original Papers Relative to the History of the Colony of Massachusetts Bay* (1769; New York, 1967), 2:262-263.

79. Massachusetts Agents' Protest against Randolph's Appointment as Collector (1677?), in *Randolph Papers*, 6:76.

80. John Palmer, *An Impartial Account of the State of New England* (London, 1690), in *Andros Tracts*, 1:42.

81. John Oxenbridge, *New England Freemen Warned and Warmed* (Boston, 1673), 28-29; Thomas Shepard, *Eye Salve, Or Watchword from Our Lord Jesus Christ unto His Church . . . To Take Heed of Apostasy* (Cambridge, Mass., 1673), 22.

82. Oxenbridge, *New England Freemen Warned*, 28-29. Appreciation of Massachusetts's distinctive constitution grew hand in hand with what historians have termed the "invention of New England" in the realm of religious thought. Robert Middlekauff, *The Mathers: Three Generations of Puritan Intellectuals, 1596-1728* (New York, 1971), 96-112.

83. Elders' Advice to the General Court (1672), in Hutchinson, *Collection of Original Papers*, 2:167. The elders' image tacitly evoked the Aristotelian distinction, known to all educated New Englanders, between formal causes and material causes. The persons who lived in Massachusetts were the material that made up the colony. But this material, by itself, lacked organization. The constitution grounded in the charter served as the formal cause that organized and animated the material and turned it into a political society.

84. See "Arguments Against Relinquishing the [Massachusetts] Charter" (Nov. 1683?), in *Collections of the Massachusetts Historical Society*, 3rd ser.,

1:74-81; David S. Lovejoy, *The Glorious Revolution in America*, 2nd ed. (Middletown, Conn., 1987), 122, 142.

85. Joseph Belcher, *The Singular Happiness of Such Heads or Rulers As Are Able to Chose Out Their People's Way and Will Also Endeavor to their People's Comfort* (Boston, 1701), 3-4.

86. "Prescription," in *Laws and Liberties* (1648), in John D. Cushing, ed., *The Laws and Liberties of Massachusetts, 1641-1691* (Wilmington, Del., 1976), 1:51. To be sure, Massachusetts Puritans were not hostile to custom per se. They wished to insure that law built up through custom agreed with God's purposes.

87. Breen, *Character of the Good Ruler*, 132-133.

88. To be sure, the Biblicist ideal in law was always stronger in protestation than in practice, even in the first generation. On Biblicism's greater importance as a way of legitimating law than as a source of workaday rules, see Haskins, *Law and Authority*; Barbara A. Black, "Aspects of Puritan Jurisprudence: Comment on the Puritan Revolution and English Law," *Valparaiso University Law Review* 18(1984):651-664.

89. Massachusetts colonists cited the proceedings against London, as a warning, in "Arguments Against Relinquishing the [Massachusetts] Charter" (Nov. 1683?), *Collections of the Massachusetts Historical Society*, 3rd ser., 1:75-76, 79.

90. Argument of Pollexfen for the City, in *The Pleadings, Arguments, and Other Proceedings in the Court of King's Bench upon the Quo Warranto Touching the Charter of the City of London*, 2nd ed. (London, 1696), 112-113; Levin, *Charter Controversy*, 31, 38, 51-55, 105.

91. "An Act for Regulating of Townships," in Abner Goodell and Ellis Ames, eds., *Acts and Resolves of the Province of the Massachusetts Bay* (Boston, 1869), 1:65.

92. "An Act for Reversing the Judgment in a Quo Warranto against the City of London," 2 William and Mary c. 8 (1690).

93. The invocation of Massachusetts' ancient liberties by the General Court in 1696 and Wait Winthrop in 1699 (discussed earlier in this essay) employed the ancient constitution as a protest ideal.

94. Reid, "The Jurisprudence of Liberty"; Colbourn, *The Lamp of Experience*.

95. See Burgess, *Politics of the Ancient Constitution*, 15-17; Pocock, *The Ancient Constitution and the Feudal Law*, 16-17; J. P. Sommerville, "The Ancient Constitutionalism Reassessed: The Common Law, the Court and the Languages of Politics in Early Modern Europe," in *The Stuart Court and Europe: Essays in Politics and Political Culture*, ed. R. Malcolm Smuts (Cambridge, 1996), 39-64.

Performing Patriarchy: Gendered Roles and Hierarchies in Early Modern England and Seventeenth-Century New England

Richard Godbeer

WHEN IT COMES TO MATTERS of gender, contemporary western culture provides us with bipolar models that assert fundamental differences between men and women. From an early age, we all face intense pressure to conform with prepackaged gender identities. "Even in this jaded here and now," writes one observer of popular culture, "when nearly every border of human identity and behavior has been transgressed, gender still holds as fundamental, given, fixing most of us in one place or the other."[1] Recent theorists trained in a broad array of academic disciplines have challenged these bipolar models, rejecting as artificial the clear-cut distinctions on which they depend and calling for a more nuanced understanding of gender. Yet their reasoning has had relatively little impact upon the cultural mainstream. Indeed, the very newsworthiness of those who challenge gendered boundaries rests in large part upon our culture's generally rigid sense of male and female identity.

Despite some relaxation in the gendering of social roles and of dress, most people still expect women and men to embody fundamental difference. John Gray's bestseller, *Men Are From Mars, Women Are From Venus*, epitomizes such expectations. Gray argues that the route to a successful relationship between a man and a woman lies not in seeking common ground but in recognizing, accepting, and respecting members of the opposite sex as "inherently different" in their physiological and emotional makeup. Men and women "think, feel, perceive, react, respond, love, need, and appreciate differently." Indeed, Gray declares, "they almost seem to come from different planets."[2]

Supporters and critics of bipolar models such as Gray's often characterize these conceptions of gender as "traditional." Yet just how lengthy a pedigree do they have? Notions of gender in the seventeenth-century world of John Winthrop were in some respects much more fluid and capacious than paradigms of absolute and fixed difference between the sexes that rose to ascendancy during the eighteenth century and still prevail today. This might seem an odd claim, given that seventeenth-century society conceived of formal authority in male terms and that power rested for the most part with men. Women who threatened (or seemed to threaten) those conventions could find themselves under attack as scolds or witches.

John Winthrop's world certainly had a clear sense of masculinity and femininity as distinct constellations of qualities, the former associated with authority and the latter with subordination. Yet roles and attributes labeled as masculine or feminine were not attached inflexibly to male or female bodies. Women could assume male-identified roles in particular contexts and be treated in those contexts as male figures. Likewise, men could adopt feminine roles in certain circumstances and did so without qualm or public reproach. That flexibility in gender assignments was based in part upon biological assumptions that saw the differences between men and women as a good deal less absolute than later paradigms would insist.[3] As Laurel Thatcher Ulrich has written, a woman's life "was defined in a series of discrete duties," not in terms of a single identity that was "self-consistent and all-embracing," so that "unitary definitions of status" can be "misleading in any description of the lives of colonial women." As we will see, this was equally true of men. Women and men thought of themselves as embodying a variety of roles rather than a "unitary" identity.[4]

Women in early modern England and New England adopted what their society thought of as male roles on a regular basis, for the most part without arousing controversy. They not only acted on behalf of their husbands as male surrogates when occasion demanded, but also ran businesses in their own right as independent artisans. Many even joined guilds. Others became household heads, functioning in effect as female incarnations of patriarchal authority. This elasticity in gender roles also applied to men. Social, political, and spiritual order rested just as firmly on male as on female submission to authority figures. Men made sense of situations in which they deferred to male-identified authority by assuming in those contexts a female persona. John Cotton, in whose Boston congregation John Winthrop was a prominent member, declared that the relationship between "magistrates and subjects in the commonwealth" was equivalent to that between "husband and wife in the family," so that male subjects should defer to magistrates as wives deferred to their husbands. Pastors encouraged all believers, male and female, to envisage Christ as a prospective husband. "Men allowed themselves," writes Phyllis Mack, "a high degree of feminine expressiveness when, as worshipers, they assumed the role of loving spouse and supplicant." Dominance and subjection in seventeenth-century society found expression through the language of gender, but operated more in terms of situation than with regard to the sex of those involved. "Gender restrictions were," as Ulrich writes, "structural rather than psychological."[5]

The assumption that men and women could and should assume both male and female attributes made sense of a social order that regularly placed men in subordinate positions, often relative to women in positions of authority. Not only did widows become household heads, but women of high social status routinely exercised authority over low-status men. Rank outweighed gender. Situations such as these created what Mary Beth Norton refers to as "ambiguities in women's status" and, one might add, in that of men.[6] Poorer women were much less likely to command the obedience of male subordinates, but as we will see, even they could find themselves in positions of authority over men. It makes good sense to characterize hierarchical structures in the seventeenth century as patriarchal since contemporaries habitually described them in male terms: the gendered nature of authority was non-negotiable. Yet masculine and feminine attributes could become attached to either men or women; they were not limited to any one sex.

This essay draws on recent historical and literary studies to illuminate both the opportunities and dangers that flexible notions of gender afforded in Winthrop's lifetime on both sides of the Atlantic. Puritans in old and New England accentuated both the positive and negative potentialities in female agency. In this regard, New England differed from its culture of origin in degree, but not in kind. Early modern conceptions of gender were far from being unconditionally fluid. Context was crucial and the gender flexibility available to Winthrop's contemporaries sometimes came into conflict with the almost universal assumption that women rightfully occupied a subordinate position in society. For the most part, that tension remained implicit: characterizing women who exercised authority in male terms did, after all, reaffirm patriarchy as a cultural absolute. "Flexibility in familial and marital relations was possible," Susan Amussen writes, "because the underlying assumptions were rarely challenged."[7] Yet women in positions of authority had to pay close attention to the ambiguities in their situation since they could all-too-easily become the focus of suspicion and hostility if their behavior seemed to threaten patriarchal assumptions. A woman who sought to assume masculine prerogatives in a context seen by others as inappropriate or who challenged the need to conceptualize power in male terms became extremely vulnerable. She who appropriated male-identified authority, not as an ad hoc role but in her own right as a woman, turned implicit tension into outright contradiction and so became an abomination.

Order and hierarchy were ruling principles of the culture into which Winthrop was born and gender had a crucial role to play in that stratified world. The authority of man over woman in a patriarchal household was the fundamental hierarchical relationship, providing a model for all others. In practical terms, the family provided a basic unit of social identification and the principal site for economic production; but equally important was the informing role that familial and explicitly gendered language played in seventeenth-century conceptions of social, political, and religious order. Patriarchal terminology served to articulate all hierarchical relations: ministers invited believers to envisage God as a father and Christ as a husband; the redeemed should love, revere, and obey their savior as a wife loved, revered, and obeyed her spouse. When contemporaries thought about political authority, they did so in familial terms, equating the prerogatives of the ruler with those of a household head.[8] Orderly families laid the foundation for an orderly society. Puritan divine

William Gouge characterized the family as "a little commonwealth . . . a school wherein the first principles and grounds of government and subjection are learned." Issues of authority (whether in the context of family, politics, or society) were inextricably intertwined with gender. As Mary Beth Norton has pointed out, "the inherited language of power was infused with gender images." Theirs was, in David Underdown's words, a "gendered habit of mind."[9]

Winthrop and his contemporaries believed that disruptions of hierarchy would lead inevitably to chaos. Early modern writers used nightmarish images of the anarchy resulting from social insubordination to reaffirm the virtues of order and deference. Disorderly men certainly caused concern on both sides of the Atlantic, but disorderly women proved especially worrisome. Representations of unruly women figured prominently in cautionary depictions of social and moral chaos, reinforcing commitment to gender hierarchy and male governance. "Where the wife maketh head against the husband," declared one author in 1620, "all things go backward, and the whole house runneth to ruin."[10] Early modern depictions of women included both positive and negative stereotypes, pitting images of virtuous maids, wives, and widows against a disorderly and dangerous triad of whore, scold, and witch. Underlying these pejorative archetypes lay the notion that honorable womanhood was incompatible with any overt challenge to patriarchal assumptions.

Yet within an overarching paradigm of gender hierarchy, there was considerable leeway for assertive women. Olwen Hufton has observed that chapbooks, which targeted a popular market, often celebrated women who were "assertive, though within bounds," while more literary works frequently included female characters who assumed male-identified roles "with honour." Such scenarios generally proved "transitory" and sought "to cope with exigent circumstances," but they did acknowledge the possibility that women might assume roles and attributes labeled as masculine without becoming problematic.[11] As household mistresses and as affluent denizens of urban and rural communities, women regularly exercised an authority over male dependents that might strike modern eyes as incompatible with an ethos of female subjection. Women and men routinely adopted roles associated with the opposite sex. As Phyllis Mack reminds us, a subordinate male was "functionally feminine in relation to his female superior," who in turn was "functionally masculine in relation to her apprentices or dependents." In 1631, 16 percent of households in Southwark, a suburb of London, were headed by women.[12] By no means all women came to embody patriarchal authority as household heads, but even in more conventional situations hierarchies of age and social status regularly placed women in positions of authority over men.[13]

Informal female networks of knowledge and surveillance operated alongside and often in conjunction with more formal, male-dominated institutions to sustain communities and regulate behavior. Ulrich and Norton have shown in vivid detail the respect accorded to women in New England as producers of domestic goods, as skilled managers of household production, and as moral stewards. On both sides of the Atlantic, women played a pivotal role in regulating personal reputations. "Sexual honour was overwhelmingly a female concern," writes Laura Gowing. Although women could become the targets of oral networks that destroyed reputations, they also used such networks to exert an informal yet formidable power in and beyond their local neighborhoods. That power could extend into the realm of formal surveillance when issues of defamation came before the courts. Legal officials also drew upon female knowledge in cases of sexual transgression. Midwives were expected, for example, to question unmarried mothers during childbirth about the paternity of their children and might be called upon to repeat that information before a court. If a couple produced a child within nine months of their marriage, midwives could well be questioned as to whether the infant was premature or, most likely, had resulted from premarital sex. Female voices carried considerable, sometimes decisive, weight in such cases.[14]

The practical responsibilities that women fulfilled as household mistresses and their everyday contributions to the family economy required initiative and self-confidence as well as deference to the ultimate authority of male household heads. Those women who sold produce from their dairies or gardens at market would not be able to bargain successfully if they were "too demure." As Susan Amussen points out, women had to be both "assertive" and "obedient" as the occasion demanded.[15] If a husband fell ill or had to leave on a trip and so could not fulfill his duties as household head, society expected his wife to take his place. Ulrich has described the experiences of New England women who assumed male roles during the absence or indisposition of their husbands: they were treated by neighbors and business associates as though they were their husbands; they became functionally masculine. Women "could move rather easily from the role of housewife to the role of deputy husband." Consider a letter penned by Moses Gilman, who owned a lumber business in Exeter, New Hampshire. Gilman wrote to his wife Elizabeth from Boston in the 1670s, asking her to arrange for a shipment of "twelve thousand feet of merchantable boards," to be "rafted by Thursday next or sooner if possible." He evidently trusted that his wife could "order the matter" and also that all those involved would treat her as his credible surrogate. That assumption applied in poorer as well as more affluent households. Fishermen's wives routinely carried out business in the absence of their husbands, settled accounts, and even signed promisory notes.[16]

English women were actively engaged in a wide range of trades that in later periods would become almost exclusively male. They worked as artisans in three contexts. First, wives and daughters could acquire such skills informally through working alongside fathers and husbands who had been formally trained in a particular craft. In the second instance, widows often took over the family business and were able to function as independent artisans without having been apprenticed; it was assumed that such women already had the requisite skills. And third, other women became apprenticed in their own right and then operated as independent bootmakers, printers, pewterers, and armorers, to name but a few of the crafts in which they engaged. In 1574, Chester had five female blacksmiths; in early seventeenth-century Southampton, almost half of the town's apprentices were women. Women working as artisans were active as guild members and had apprentices of their own, both male and female. Most of the girls who were bound as apprentices came from modest or impoverished backgrounds; many of them were orphans. Training as an artisan could provide these young women with a means of support independent of men and conferred on them a measure of status and authority. That poorer women could and did become artisans and employers in their own right reminds us that the female assumption of male-identified roles and prerogatives was not limited to the upper ranks of society.[17]

Religion played an important role in fostering a sense of female confidence and agency on both sides of the Atlantic. Protestant emphasis upon "a priesthood of all believers" diminished the significance of male priests as intermediaries, enabling men and women to establish a more direct relationship with God. As Christina Larner has observed, Protestantism was "strongly patriarchal" in its sensibility, envisaging the household head as a quasi-clerical figure to whom family members would turn for spiritual guidance. Yet reformed faith demanded that women, as well as men, "for the first time become fully responsible for their own souls." This resulted in the "emergence of women as independent adults" in the spiritual realm.[18] Marie Rowlands and Frances Dolan have argued that Catholic women living in Protestant England also experienced a change in their spiritual status. They looked not to husbands but to priests for spiritual guidance and yet in many cases had no immediate access to Catholic clerics. Even if a priest were living in a recusant home, he depended as much on the household mistress as on the master of the house for protection, creating a significant ambiguity in their relationship. English Catholic women were thus less spiritually dependent than their counterparts in countries where it was possible to worship in the open.[19] In New England, ministers taught that Puritan women should defer to their husbands in spiritual as in other matters, yet they also lauded wives and mothers for their spiritual nurturance of husbands and children. Women who became full members of their local congregations could not participate equally with men in church governance, yet they nonetheless exercised appreciable, albeit generally informal, influence over their congregations' affairs.[20]

Most women in England and New England spent much of their time in and around the household. But their economic, social, and religious roles ensured that "the circle of female life spun outward," beyond the home and "into the web of community." Consider the epitaph written by New Englander Ann Bradstreet for her mother, Dorothy Dudley, who died in 1643:

> A worthy matron of unspotted life,
> A loving mother and obedient wife,
> A friendly neighbor, pitiful to poor,
> Whom oft she fed, and clothed with her store;
> To servants wisely aweful, but yet kind,
> And as they did, so they reward did find:
> A true instructer of her family,

> The which she ordered with dexterity.
> The public meetings ever did frequent,
> And in her closet constant hours she spent;
> Religious in all her words and ways,
> Preparing still for death, till end of days:
> Of all her children, children lived to see,
> Then dying, left a blessed memory.

She who left behind "a blessed memory" was a respected wife, mother, mistress, neighbor, and member of the Christian community. Though clearly subordinate to her husband, she wielded considerable moral and practical authority within the household and also in the larger community. A goodwife related to others in manifold capacities, some of which involved her exercising a "wisely aweful" authority, others requiring that she defer "obedient[ly]."[21]

It has long been a truism that family life conditioned the experiences and sensibility of women during this period, but only recently have scholars suggested that the same was true of men. Lisa Wilson has shown that New England men also spent most of their time "engaged in domestic concerns," "working and living together in the same space" with their wives. Their "power and identity originated in the home and like rings in a pond when a pebble is dropped reached to the outer shores." A New England man, writes Wilson, "was fundamentally dependent on his family for his sense of self." Just as "a worthy matron" brought honor to her husband, so a woman who failed to embody the qualities demanded of a godly helpmeet involved her husband as well as herself in shame and disapproval. Ironically, even the sexual double standard that defined adultery in terms of a married woman's infidelity rendered husbands dependent upon their wives for their reputation. A cuckolded husband was clearly "an insufficient husband" and "an inadequate member of society." Marriage and family life "tied men and women together in a complex series of mutual dependencies." The household head "positioned himself within a system of obligation and duty" that bound everyone, regardless of sex or status. He sought to fulfill his obligations as a man by proving himself "serviceable" to his family, the community, and God.[22]

The responsibility to serve involved everyone, women and men, in the assumption of roles that contemporaries labeled as masculine and feminine. This involved a "fluidity of self-perception" that was most explicit in the spiritual realm.[23] Images of Christ as a bridegroom entailed that all believers see themselves as brides. Puritan men and women expressed a deep yearning for Christ as their espoused lover, anticipating union with him in vividly sensual terms. John Cotton invited his flock to envisage marriage with Christ as an experience both romantic and sexual:

> Have you a strong and hearty desire to meet him in the bed of loves, whenever you come to the congregation, and desire you to have the seeds of his grace shed abroad in your hearts, and bring forth the fruits of grace to him?

Cotton urged unmarried men who were "troubled with lust after women" to "turn the strength of [their] affection to another that is white and ruddy, the fairest of ten thousand." John Winthrop referred to Christ as "my love, my dove, my undefiled," and prayed that he might be "possesse[d]" by his savior in "the love of marriage." Ministers taught their congregants to use Christ's marriage with the redeemed as a model for the union between husband and wife on earth. "[T]he ground and pattern of our love," wrote Winthrop to his third wife, Margaret Tyndal, "is no other than that between Christ and his dear spouse." Thus, in ways that may be alien to us, Winthrop combined gender constructs in his mind: he became both husband and wife.[24]

Over the course of the seventeenth century, New England pastors became increasingly effusive in their evocation of Christ as an object of romantic, sensual, and even erotic infatuation. Faced with the maturation of men and women who had not chosen to live in a godly commonwealth and who had to be persuaded to embrace orthodoxy, ministers sought to seduce young adults into the community of faith by stressing the voluptuous pleasures that awaited them in the form of union with their savior. Though the language that pastors used as they courted on Christ's behalf was at times exceptionally lurid, they drew their inspiration from images of Christ as a bridegroom that most people on both sides of the Atlantic would have considered familiar and unexceptionable.

Male New Englanders' conception of themselves as brides of Christ would have been facilitated by their pastors' depiction of the soul. Ministers taught that the soul did not adopt the sex of the body it inhabited: they characterized the soul sometimes as female and sometimes as sexually indeterminate. This interpretation mattered because the son of God was to marry not men and women but the souls of men and women. Elizabeth Reis has argued that a gendered distinction between body and soul allowed Puritan men to think of their souls as feminine while retaining a masculine "sense of themselves." I would suggest that such a distinction functioned in conjunction with and as part of a broad gender fluidity.[25]

Just as men would become the brides of Christ, so godly women would adopt male attributes through spiritual redemption. Ministers assured their flocks that those who submitted to God's will would become "members of Christ," dedicated to his service and empowered by their regeneration. Contemporaries used the word "member" to denote a penis. Puritans often wrote of their "spiritual ejaculations," referring to spontaneous prayer but surely aware of the word's double meaning. Thus, while the awakened souls of both men and women surrendered themselves to be penetrated and fertilized by their savior, they also became phallic and ejaculatory extensions of Christ. The repeated use of phallic images to denote spiritual power reminds us how dominant patriarchal conceptions were within Puritan culture and of the limits to gender fluidity. Yet women could assume masculine attributes and become correspondingly potent. A virtuous woman as much as any man had "the image of Christ and God upon her" and, on the Day of Judgment, her soul would "be marvellously changed into the likeness of the Lord Jesus Christ himself."[26]

Conversion narratives as well as prescriptive literature indicate "the fundamental sameness" of the conversion experience for men and women. "In all the expositions of grace," Charles Cohen has noted, "no one distinguished between the Spirit's operations in one sex or the other." Ulrich rightly insists that there was "no such thing" as a distinctive "female piety in early New England." Although ministers argued that the hazards of childbirth made women particularly susceptible to "the comforts of Christ," they "stressed the experience of childbirth, rather than the nature of the childbearer," and so "upheld the spiritual oneness of the sexes."[27]

Puritan ideology envisaged neither a wholly masculine identity for men nor a wholly feminine identity for women. Margaret Masson reminds us that New Englanders "had not yet arrived at definitions of sex roles or personality structure that were as fixed or mutually exclusive as those found in the nineteenth century." Thus, ministers could use "the female role as a typology for the regenerate Christian" without creating "role conflict" for men. "Sexual differentiation," she writes, "was still fluid enough for this to be possible." The bridal image evoked not femininity as such but instead a feminine role that both men and women could and should assume.[28]

Men adopted a bride-like posture not only as Christians but also in other contexts. Winthrop equated a citizen's "subjection to authority" with a wife's "subjection to her husband's authority" and that of "the church under the authority of Christ, her king and husband." That last phrase was telling in its equation of spiritual, political, and bridal comportment.[29] The "mutual dependencies" that sustained and gave meaning to the lives of men and women entailed both sexes performing male and female roles. That women could become functionally male and men functionally female suggests a complex and nuanced relationship between gender and authority. Because gender was to some extent fluid, so too was power. That flexible relationship between biological sex and cultural gender informed all social, political, and spiritual interactions. Engendering authority as male and subordination as female clearly reaffirmed the subordination of women to men as an ideal. The use of spousal imagery to describe relations between savior and saved, for example, surely reinforced a gender-based hierarchy within the family. But male Puritans developed a range of social capacities by relating to Christ as brides as well as emulating him in the role of bridegroom.

Conceptions of the body reinforced the measure of flexibility in gender roles and hierarchies that we find in the seventeenth century. "The basis for all thinking about the body at this time," writes Anthony Fletcher, was the humoral model. Four fundamental fluids (blood, choler, melancholy, and phlegm) present in both men and women governed "a common corporeal economy" in which all bodily functions and all disease could be explained in terms of humoral balance (thus Petruchio's insistence that his wife's cure in *The Taming of the Shrew* include the avoidance of meat, which "engenders choler"). The humors were in constant flux, which led to a never-ending struggle against disequilibrium. Men and women could be differentiated from each other to some degree by their distinct combination of these four fluids; the physical and moral frailty of women resulted from their particular humoral make-up. Yet the "line of difference between male and female" was "uncertain and unstable" because the humors were "fluid and indeterminate." Thus, "no sharp distinction between the sexes was possible."[30]

Equally significant in its implications for gender identity was Galen's "one-sex" model of the body, still influential though by no means unchallenged in Winthrop's time. As Thomas Laqueur has shown, this model assumed a basic structural homology in which female reproductive organs were nothing other than male organs inverted (the uterus an internal version of the scrotum, the ovaries resembling male testicles, and the penis appearing in women as the cervix and vagina). According to Galen, a failure of heat had prevented the female organs from thrusting outward, though under certain circumstances women's genitals could turn inside out and so effect a sex change. Women, according to this model, were beings who had failed to develop fully into men; they were imperfect versions of the male ideal.[31] Many early modern writers challenged this anatomical paradigm, depicting the female organs as distinct and arguing that women's bodies were perfect in their own right. But elements of the Galenic model were often combined with newer ideas in what Anthony Fletcher calls "a curious transitional world of neither one sex nor two." Even anatomists who affirmed the distinctiveness of women's bodies also believed that women could transmute into men.[32]

Body parts and physical processes associated with one sex, such as the lactating breast or ejaculating penis, were endowed with gendered attributes (the breast representing maternal nourishment and the penis, as we have already seen, connoting virility). Yet within the early modern cultural imagination, these organs and functions could be jettisoned by the sex with which they were normally associated or adopted by the other sex, at least figuratively, along with the cultural meanings that they carried. As Kathryn Schwarz has pointed out, "the maternal breast" functioned in early modern discourse as "an inescapable site of difference" between men and women, both physically and also in that the breast served to represent a series of roles "to which [women's] body parts confine[d] them." Yet that metonymic linkage was confining only in so far as breasts were irrevocably attached to women, and such was not always the case. Depictions of Amazonian women as missing a breast suggested that the female sex could escape an anatomically based patriarchy; removal of "the maternal breast" embodied their empowerment.[33] Conversely, spiritual texts sometimes represented men as acquiring maternal qualities through the metaphorical grafting of breasts onto their bodies. Male figures could assume the cultural roles associated with lactation. New Englander John Oxenbridge likened the role of a magistrate to that of "a nursing father" who "bears the sucking child." Ministers often referred to themselves as breasts of God from whom congregants would receive "the sincere milk of the Word." And Samuel Willard spoke of the world as "a sucking infant depending on the breasts of divine providence."[34]

For much of the seventeenth century, distinctions between maleness and femaleness remained much less absolute and more negotiable than in subsequent periods. (Once belief in the humoral economy faded and as a rigid "two-sex" paradigm eclipsed the one-sex model, cultural perceptions ossified into a form more recognizable to us today.) The notion that women were defective men mirrored theological teaching and itself served to justify patriarchy.[35] But in denying any clear-cut boundaries between male and female bodies, the humoral and one-sex models mirrored the complexity of gender politics. The ambiguities inherent in early modern perceptions of sexual difference reinforced flexible notions of gender, which in turn enabled women to exercise male-identified authority without appearing to subvert patriarchy.

Representations of Elizabeth I as a ruler exemplify the ways in which gender flexibility could mitigate somewhat the limitations imposed by patriarchal structures and rhetoric. One of the gravest challenges facing this monarch was her anomalous status as a powerful woman on the throne, fulfilling a role and exercising authority customarily associated with men. Protestant polemicist John Knox had excoriated female rule as inherently unnatural in *The First Blast of the Trumpet against the Monstrous Regiment of Women*, written in exile during the reign of Mary but published in the year of Elizabeth's accession. In light of such attacks, the new queen prudently showed herself to be as little "monstrous" as possible. She did so by adopting a persona that incorporated male as well as female components. The queen was, of course, unique in the potential threat that she posed and also in the resources available to her as she worked to assuage disquiet. Still, her assumption of male attributes was neither anomalous nor "monstrous" in an early modern context. Elizabeth dramatized the juxtaposition of masculine and feminine roles that pervaded the everyday lives of less exalted women.

Elizabeth bolstered her credibility as a female monarch by becoming, as Christopher Haigh puts it, "a political hermaphrodite, not only a queen, but a king as well." Leah Marcus has shown that Elizabeth took the time-honored notion of the ruler's two bodies (one mortal and fallible, the other transcendent and annointed by God) and superimposed onto that notion a gendered distinction. She treated her "earthly being" as "the body of a frail woman" and inscribed her "body politic" as male, presenting herself as "the incarnation of a sacred principle of kingship."[36] In 1563, the queen addressed a parliamentary delegation as follows: "though I be a woman yet I have as good a courage answerable to my place as ever my father had." She played on this duality in speeches throughout her reign, avowing her womanhood and recognizing that qualities "appropriate to my sex" might seem to disqualify her for leadership, yet assuring her male audience that "the princely seat and kingly throne" on which she sat had "constituted" her as a "Prince and head" who could and would rule effectively "for [their] safety." As Leah Marcus points out, she thus conceded and then immediately disabled "male discomfort at being commanded by a woman."[37]

The queen's dual nature became immortalized in the speech that tradition says she gave in 1588 to the troops at Tilbury, gathered to repulse the Spanish Armada. "I have the body of a weak and feeble woman," she declared, "but I have the heart and stomach of a king, and of a king of England too." In this much publicized address (which may or may not have represented accurately what she actually said that day), Elizabeth engaged the issue of her credibility as a military leader. "Rather than any dishonour should grow by me," she declared, "I myself will take up arms, I myself will be your general, judge, and rewarder of every one of your virtues in the field."[38] Yet she was careful to keep that male military persona within the rhetorical realm. Elizabeth was mounted on horseback and carried a truncheon, but the claim that she wore armor seems to have been a later invention. On this occasion and throughout her reign, Elizabeth avoided visual representations of her male persona. There were pictures of the queen as an Amazon, but these were produced either abroad or after her death. Elizabeth understood the limits of acceptable self-masculinization and abided by them. Availing herself of the opportunities afforded by gender flexibility and yet avoiding extremes that would almost certainly arouse new concerns, she sought with great cunning and at least intermittent success to quell anxieties about female rule.[39]

Elizabeth and her advisers crafted with equal circumspection that part of her public image which focused on her womanhood. Jodi Mikalachki has shown that sixteenth-century accounts of ancient English history made use of gendered images in ways that posed a significant problem for the queen. As the investigation of national origins became a major public preoccupation in early modern England, researchers uncovered evidence of licentious barbarism among ancient Britons that was anything but cause for celebration. In particular, English historiographers lamented their ancestors' apparent disregard for principles of "feminine subordination and chastity." Potent, ruthless, cruel, and sexually voracious women haunted early modern versions of English history. Queen Boadicca exemplified this "grotesquely feminized savagery." Historians described her, for example, as having arranged for the breasts of female prisoners to be cut off and sewn to their mouths in a "gruesome parody of maternal nurture." There were clear lessons in this grim past for Winthrop's times: the deplorable behavior of ancient women became a "a cautionary tale about the dangers of unrestricted female agency and rule."[40] Vilification of the savage Boadicca reflected and encouraged contemporary anxieties about female monarchy. If Elizabeth wished to forge an acceptable identity for herself as a ruler, she would have to avoid any kind of association with sixteenth-century depictions of ancient female sovereignty. Elizabeth's avoidance of military combat and her ostentatious virginity ensured that Boadicca functioned not as her prototype but as "the negative complement to Elizabeth's chaste embodiment of national security."[41]

Elizabethan propagandists forged for the queen an alternative and more acceptable version of empowered womanhood by using the queen's famed chastity to quell fears associated with images of women as sexually voracious. Comparing her to the chaste goddess Diana, to the Fairy Queen, and to the Virgin Mary, eulogists sought to swathe her in an aura of potent and pious womanhood that was stripped of danger. Despite her actual childlessness, Elizabeth became identified with a nurturing maternity. Eulogists encouraged the queen's subjects to envisage her as "the mother and nurse of this whole commonwealth and country." "How lamentable a thing is it," declared an address marking her departure from Norwich in 1578, "to pull away sucking babes from the breasts and bosoms of their most loving mothers."[42]

The queen's combination of apparent virginity and metaphoric fecundity freed her from the cumbersome restrictions that marriage and actual maternity would have entailed without depriving her of access to the positive attributes associated with marriage and motherhood. Such imagery allowed the queen "to preserve her independence while simultaneously tapping into the emotional power behind the images of wife and mother through fictionalized versions of herself."[43] Phyllis Mack has observed that this also enabled Elizabeth to sidestep potential contradictions as she sought to combine male and female attributes. However damaging it might have been in terms of the royal succession to avoid marriage and motherhood, she had "cleverly avoided confronting her subjects with the sight of a real mother on the throne."[44] Yet at the same time, her very public courtships kept in view the possibility that she might at some point fulfil such roles, enabling her to suggest without actually succumbing to a more sexually explicit version of womanhood.[45]

The tone of veneration that Elizabeth's propagandists sought to cultivate has resounded through the centuries to influence both scholarly and popular impressions of her reign. It is, then, important to keep in mind that the purpose of this dazzling exercise in self-fashioning was defensive. Many historians have drawn attention to the cult of Elizabeth I as Virgin Queen and its role in the Protestantization of England. That iconography shifted onto the monarch a ceremonial and even quasi-religious veneration previously focused on the Virgin

Mary. A potent image of faith associated with Catholicism was thus transposed as the tool of a Protestant state. Veneration of the new Virgin Queen expressed both patriotic loyalty and allegiance to the Protestant Church.[46] Helen Hackett's close study of this iconographic venture suggests that it should be understood in terms of Elizabeth's need to bolster her precarious authority as a woman and to present her potentially disastrous unmarried status as favorably as possible. The uses to which propagandists put images of the queen as a chaste figure changed over the course of her reign in accordance with the exigencies of the moment. Praise of the young monarch as a virgin who would presumably marry and bear children evolved into veneration of the queen as "a static icon of perpetual virginity" once it became increasingly unlikely that she would become a mother. During the middle decades of her reign, panegyrists sought to avoid Marian references in favor of other virginal figures to create "an iconography purified of Catholic associations." During the last phase of Elizabeth's life, the imagery that swathed her became increasingly extravagent and explicitly Marian in an attempt to counter "expressions of disallusionment and criticism."[47]

The gendered strategies, rhetorical and visual, adopted by Elizabeth I and her boosters bore eloquent testimony to the challenges facing any woman who sought to exercise authority in early modern England. Yet Elizabeth's reign demonstrated that careful manipulation of gendered roles and attributes could open up possibilities for female agency and rule. Such an enterprise required subtle calibration and always remained precarious. The queen became, as Sir Robert Cecil put it, "more than a man, and (in troth) sometyme less than a woman." Rumors of her sexual voracity and allegations of witchcraft by her enemies during the 1580s and 1590s remind us that Elizabeth was not immune to the fears directed against women who seemed to transgress gender norms.[48] Yet the queen deployed her composite persona to quite spectacular effect, especially during the middle years of her reign. Praised as "a maiden queen, and yet of courage stout," who inherited "more of her father than mother," Elizabeth I managed to become "king and queen both."[49]

The challenge facing Elizabeth I as a female ruler was doubtless intensified by dramatic demographic and economic changes which convinced many people that their world was spinning out of control. Population growth, inflation, land shortage and the dislocation that accompanied enclosure, an increase in poverty, and widespread vagrancy created an impression of growing instability and disorder. "Tis all in pieces," wrote John Donne, "all coherence gone. . . ."[50] Recent historians have argued that this "crisis of order" in early modern England included "a period of strained gender relations" as patriarchy itself seemed to come under threat from insubordinate women. Given an atmosphere of intense anxiety, fueled by a perceived "breakdown of the social order," women who pushed gender boundaries became increasingly vulnerable to attack. Some scholars have gone so far as to claim that "gender struggle" was central to social tensions during this period and reflects "a gender system under pressure."[51]

Those scholars who see early modern England as abnormally preoccupied with issues of gender draw upon multifarious sources to substantiate their claims. Their analysis of literary evidence from the late sixteenth and early seventeenth centuries, including material intended for a popular audience, suggests "considerable anxiety about the gender order." Historians such as Anthony Fletcher and David Underdown quote at length from Elizabethan and Jacobean authors who "seem to have been uncommonly preoccupied by themes of female independence and revolt."[52] They point to a surge in prosecution of witches and of scolds as evidence of rising hostility toward independent-minded, unruly, unneighborly, or otherwise threatening women.[53] They see "intense regulation of behaviour in both families and villages" as expressing an unusual degree of concern about the maintenance of "proper gender order" in local communities.[54] They argue that extralegal shaming rituals used in the late sixteenth and seventeenth centuries to humiliate cuckolded husbands and punish wives who cheated on, beat, or verbally abused their spouses point in a similar direction.[55]

Not all early modern scholars are convinced by these claims. David Cressy, for example, acknowledges that "there were strains in early modern society," including "questions about gender roles and identity," but doubts "that they were more acute than at other times or "that gender mattered more than other social, economic, religious and political problems." Martin Ingram has questioned whether prosecutions of women as scolds really did surge during this period, though he concedes that punishments for that offense did become more severe.[56] Cressy and Ingram caution that cases in which women were accused of disorderly behavior may have been more about order than they were about gender.

Yet contemporaries would have seen issues of order and of gender as inextricably intertwined. Witchcraft accusations in this period, though prompted in part by fears that had nothing to do with issues of gender, did clearly focus on women: four fifths of accused witches on both sides of the Atlantic were female. As Susan Amussen has argued, English culture conceived of family, society, and polity as interconnected. Given this "organic conception of society," anxieties about order in one aspect of people's lives would automatically prompt anxiety about all forms of order, including patriarchy. Since the latter figured in early modern discourse as the prototypical hierarchic relationship, it is hardly surprising that general anxiety about order would be played out, at least in part, through gendered channels so that disruptive women became, as Christina Larner puts it, "a prime symbol of disorder" in early modern culture.[57]

No fundamental challenge to conventional gender hierarchies emerged in the late sixteenth and early seventeenth centuries. As Susan Amussen rightly stresses, women did not "claim equality with their husbands or declare the family an irrelevant institution."[58] Yet there were a number of ways in which gender relations came under reconsideration during this period. Such scrutiny may have produced an unusual degree of sensitivity when it came to women who appeared to threaten patriarchal order. Larner has proposed that the escalation of witch accusations during this period may have been linked to the new ambiguity in women's status created by belief in a priesthood of all believers. Witch-hunting, "to some degree a synonym for woman-hunting," may have functioned "as a rearguard action against the emergence of women as independent adults" in the spiritual realm. After all, the decision to become a witch involved the exercise of "free will and responsibility."[59] Protestantism's emphasis upon the need for a loving partnership between husband and wife, in which the latter shared responsibility for the moral as well as practical welfare of the family household, mitigated somewhat and certainly complicated Protestant reaffirmation of patriarchal order. "The popularity of advice manuals and conduct books in this period," writes Underdown, "suggests that people were having to work out a new relationship between spouses, one that could no longer be taken for granted."[60]

Further evidence of gender-related anxiety comes from vehement attacks on cross-dressing that took place both on and off the Elizabethan and Jacobean stage. Those who attacked transvestism held that clothing represented God-ordained gender distinctions; cross-dressers contravened divine will as expressed in Deuteronomy 22:5. They also argued that clothing could act as an actual purveyor of identity and worried that those who cross-dressed might undergo fundamental transformation as a result of adopting the trappings of the opposite sex. Transvestism thus threatened to confound both externally and internally the distinctions between men and women without which an orderly and virtuous society could not survive. These writings exposed an underlying ambiguity in early modern English attitudes toward gender. On the one hand, antitheatrical polemicists insisted upon gender distinctions and hierarchies, while on the other, they acknowledged the contingency and instability of those very gendered boundaries that they affirmed to be natural and ordained by God.

Antitheatrical writers denounced cross-dressing on the grounds that it led male actors to acquire attributes associated with femininity. Masculinity connoted, among other things, self-control and thus the right to exercise authority; femininity signified passion and thus the need for subordination. Manhood demanded the governance of passion; enslavement by it constituted effeminization. Men who dressed as women adopted the insignia of female subordination and would become enslaved to passion. They thus abandoned their rightful position of authority; their social and moral manhood would seep away. Meanwhile, the mannish woman forsook modesty and chastity in favor of shameless self-assertion, including unfettered verbal and sexual expression. Running through attacks on women who adopted male dress was the sense that such behavior enabled the indulgence of unbridled sexual passion in a terrifying combination of female lust with male prerogative.[61]

Opponents of transvestism contended, furthermore, that theatrical performances would lead men both on and off the stage into illicit lusts. Boys who assumed female roles would become "changed by art" in ways over which they did not have full control, not least in their becoming more susceptible to unauthorized passions. "A woman's garment being put on a man" was "a great provocation of men to lust and lechery." Cross-dressing would "touch and move" the male wearer with "the remembrance and imagination of a woman," which in turn would "stir up the desire." Though the feelings "stirr[ed] up" related to "desire" between a man and a woman, an effeminated boy might assume a woman's attraction toward men. A situation in which men playing male roles had to kiss boys playing female roles might incite sodomitical lusts.[62] Meanwhile, male spectators would be incited to intemperate passions that could undermine masculine self-control. The latter might take the form of excessive lust for their own wives or illicit love for other women; their attraction to "players' boys thus clad in women's apparel" might lead them "so far as to solicit them by words, by letters, even actually to abuse them."[63]

In claiming that transvestism had the power to regender, critics assumed a metamorphic connection between sign and signified over which the individuals concerned had no apparent control. Boy actors and those around them risked losing their 'natural' male qualities, transformed by their performances in ways neither premeditated nor self-conscious. Polemicists argued that God had ordained clear distinctions between men and women. Those who contravened them "cast off God and Nature." But even as such critics defended allegedly natural and rightfully fixed gender categories, they also drew attention to the transformative potential of gendered performance.[64] At their most lurid, attacks on transvestism envisaged women growing beards and men acquiring breasts. The prospect of actual anatomical transformation exposed even physical manhood and womanhood as utterly unstable.[65]

In Elizabethan and Jacobean plays female characters played by boys often assumed male guise to advance their goals. Boys performing the roles of women pretending to be men would have enhanced a sense of gender instability, or so some recent scholars have argued. Jean Howard writes that female characters who disguised themselves as men put the image of a "speaking, plotting, roving" woman into "cultural circulation." As a site of "fluidity and multiplicity," Howard insists, the stage became "a vehicle for ideological contestation" and a platform for "gender struggle," expressing the era's gender-related anxieties.[66]

Other scholars have warned against treating antitheatrical tracts as representative and argue that transvestism on the stage was much less troubling for most audience members than such writings would suggest. David Cressy points out that cross-dressing was generally neither damaging to the character concerned nor ultimately transgressive: such plot devices usually enabled the cross-dressing character to win a husband or to humiliate an unsympathetic figure in the play. Even Howard acknowledges that most of the female characters who disguised themselves as men ended up in conventional marriages and that cross-dressing as a dramatic device did not necessarily have subversive implications. In Shakespeare's *Twelfth Night*, for example, Viola retains "a feminine subjectivity" throughout her performance as a young man. The real threat to patriarchy comes from Olivia, who remains dressed as a woman but who assumes control of her house and is eventually humiliated for her refusal to play a conventional role in courtship and the arrangement of marriage.[67]

We should not assume that male transvestism on the stage, so disturbing to antitheatrical writers, distressed the general public. Despite the negative connotations attached to effeminacy in some early modern writings, the assumption of female roles or feminine attributes was by no means always problematic in early modern culture.[68] Stephen Orgel reminds us that "everyone in this culture was in some respects a woman, feminized in relation to someone." Given that everyday life included a measure of gender flexibility, the idea of a man playing a feminine role would not have struck most theatergoers as inherently anomalous or troubling.[69]

Anxieties about theatrical transvestism are inseparable from broader concerns about issues of gender in early modern society. Yet that does not mean that most people were constantly preoccupied with either. "It is necessary to remember," writes Stephen Orgel, "that antitheatrical tracts are pathological. They share assumptions with the culture as a whole, but their conclusions are eccentric." Cross-dressing on the early modern English stage clearly had the potential to arouse concern, especially given concurrent anxieties relating to issues of order and stability, but these experiments were "safely contained within the theatre's walls." And such performances did not strike all observers as necessarily subversive. The mostly comic transvestite scenarios in early modern drama, condemned by antitheatrical writers as transgressive and subversive, would surely have struck the vast majority of spectators as an amusing play upon the ambiguities and multipotentialities of gender.[70]

However "pathological" antitheatrical writings may have been, they highlight potential conflicts between the culture's fluid conceptions of gender and the dictates of patriarchal order. That potential would have existed even in circumstances where there was no extraordinary anxiety regarding the threat of disorder. Just as Elizabeth I had to exercise her avowedly masculine role as monarch without appearing to forsake her womanhood, so women in general on both sides of the Atlantic had to employ great caution as they assumed male roles, lest their behavior appear transgressive. Context and tone played crucial roles in defining when and under what circumstances the blurring of gender boundaries was acceptable. A household mistress could, for example, quite legitimately assume male prerogatives as a "deputy husband" with the permission of her spouse, but social expectations compelled her to surrender them when her husband reasserted his authority. Thus, when William and Ann Hibbens, a wealthy Bostonian couple, decided in the late 1630s to have a carpenter make some alterations in their home, Hibbens could give his wife "leave to agree with the joiner and to order the business with him as she thought good." But when a quarrel developed over the cost and quality of the alterations, William Hibbens negotiated a compromise, expecting his wife to defer, and expressed his displeasure when she refused to do so: "[I] was very willing to stand to that agreement," he later testified, "and did persuade my wife, and could have wished with all my heart [that] she had been willing to have done the same; and I have had some exercise of spirit with her, that she hath not done so."[71]

When Mistress Hibbens resisted all attempts at informal arbitration, her church became involved and initiated disciplinary proceedings against her. Some of her alleged "transgressions" ("sowing of discord . . . several lies and untruths . . . uncharitable thoughts . . . slanders and evil reports") would not have struck church members as intrinsically gendered and would have provoked censure even if she had been a man. But other allegations, which related specifically to her behavior as a woman, became increasingly prominent as the proceedings wore on. The gender troubles surrounding Ann Hibbens went far deeper than her refusal to resign her role as deputy husband. Mistress Hibbens had voiced her "judgement that husbands must hearken to their wives and be guided by them in all things." She claimed that such was the teaching of her minister and indeed it is not difficult to believe that Cotton had dwelt in his sermons upon the respect due to women as wives and mothers. But her neighbors believed that Ann Hibbens had distorted that message so that it became a "corrupt opinion" that she used to "usurp authority." She had "exalted her own wit and will and way" over "her guide and head," behaving toward her husband "as if he was a nobody," flaunting her "want of subjection."[72]

Even when Ann Hibbens acted on her husband's behalf with his explicit sanction, the tone in which she carried out her duties placed her in danger. A woman who adopted a male role could not afford to behave entirely like a man, or, as John Cotton put it, to "exceed the bounds of womanly modesty."[73] Jane Kamensky has emphasized that Hibbens's aggressive and disputatious way of talking played a critical role in establishing her reputation as a transgressor. New England's "rules of right speaking" prescribed different speech codes for men and women. The content and tone of Hibbens's words bore little resemblance to "the judicious, infrequent, and sober conversation" expected of goodwives.[74]

Developing the ability and self-confidence to become a "deputy husband" and yet maintaining in all other respects a feminine sense of oneself cannot have been easy. Deputy husbands had to enter into a male space without succumbing to the "aggressive, contentious, [and] disorderly" dynamic that so often characterized that realm. As surrogate men, women had to behave as men and yet not like men. As Carol Karlsen has shown, women who became witch suspects often displayed "outspoken and abrasive" qualities that would have been much less subversive if displayed by men. Unless they acted with great care, women who assumed roles that conferred authority could become "[un]womanly" in their neighbors' eyes and so disturbing symbols of disorder.[75]

The congregation in Boston excommunicated Hibbens. Sixteen years later, soon after the death of her husband, she was indicted, convicted, and executed on charges of witchcraft. Hibbens's grim fate illustrates the limits of gender flexibility and, equally important, the ways in which that flexibility could itself create danger, especially for women. Ann Hibbens's ordeal began with her empowerment as a deputy husband: it was the way in which she enacted that role and her refusal to surrender it that placed her in mortal danger.

The social threat that Hibbens posed would have been inseparable in the minds of her neighbors from her spiritual frailties as a woman, which marked her as a potential witch. Here again we encounter a fundamental ambiguity in early modern gender ideology. Puritan theologians held that men and women were equal before God, both capable of piety though highly susceptible to sin. Yet there were limits to this spiritual egalitarianism. Ministers held that women were more vulnerable than men to diabolical temptation. After all, they taught, it was Eve who first gave way to Satan and then seduced Adam, when she should have served him in obedience to God. Cotton Mather argued in *Ornaments for the Daughters of Zion* that "the female sex" was "naturally the fearful sex" because all women as daughters of Eve inherited her traits and should live in "fearful" awareness of their implications. "A virtuous woman," Mather wrote, must fear both her own capacity for sin and the wrath of God, "whom she had by the sin and the fall of her first mother departed from."[76] Puritans did not believe that women were intrinsically more evil than men, but they did see them as more susceptible to sinful temptation. Elizabeth Reis has pointed out that "colonists shared with their English brethren the belief that women's bodies were physically weaker than men's" and therefore that "the devil could more frequently and successfully gain access to and possess women's souls." That four-fifths of accused witches in New England were women was due, at least in part, to the currency of these assumptions about female vulnerability.[77]

Puritan faith in seventeenth-century New England intensified the ambiguous attitudes toward female agency that permeated early modern Anglo-American society. Puritans' emphasis upon the centrality of the family in promoting moral order and personal devotion prompted them to laud the roles played by Daughters of Zion as wives, mothers, and household mistresses. Yet their intense fear of the Devil and their conviction that women were especially susceptible to his insinuations reinforced and deepened anxieties about the dangers posed by disorderly women. New Englanders sought to ensure a constructive and respected place for women as pious helpmeets in godly society. But as Carol Karlsen points out, lingering fear of "women-as-witches" led them to suspect and attack those who seemed to express "dissatisfaction, however indirectly, with the power relations of their society."[78]

Given the interrelated nature of all social roles and personal relationships in Winthrop's world, questioning a husband's authority carried an all-encompassing significance: such conduct presented an implicit challenge to all forms of social, political, and religious hierarchy. In a fledgling colony, still establishing its own version of social order, such challenges could not have been more unwelcome. Anne Hutchinson, another Bostonian, had been convicted of heresy and banished from Massachusetts in 1638, two years prior to Hibbens's excommunication. The colonial government accused her of behaving as "a husband rather than a wife and a preacher than a hearer and a magistrate than a subject." This formulation emphasized the crucial roles that gender played in the family, church, and state, exposing the broad implications of her having "stepped out of [her] place." Ann Hibbens's alleged challenge to "nature" and "the institution of God" doubtless reminded Bostonians of Hutchinson and the disorder that she represented.[79]

"See we not plainly," wrote seventeenth-century clergyman Richard Hooker, "that obedience of creatures unto the law of nature is the stay of the whole world." Gender was clearly a crucial component of that hierarchical order. It constituted, as Joan Scott has written, "a primary way of signifying relationships of power."[80] This essay does not intend to gainsay the patriarchal nature of early modern Anglo-American society. Recent scholars have alerted us to the many restrictions placed upon seventeenth-century women by social, political, legal, economic, and religious structures. Even as women routinely assumed male-identified roles that conferred on them considerable authority, the tension between such scenarios and generally accepted theories of female subordination remained controllable only if women performed masculine roles with careful attention to nuance and tone. Because contemporaries saw the subordination of women to men as the most fundamental of hierarchic relationships, because they often used gendered language to characterize other variants of hierarchy, and because they thought about their world in organic terms, destabilization of the gendered order betokened general chaos. Transgressive women thus became archetypes of social and moral disorder.

Yet the patriarchal world of seventeenth-century England and New England incorporated and accommodated fluid conceptions of gender; patriarchy and gender flexibility intertwined in a complex and multipotential choreography. It would be misleading to portray this period as one in which men and women deployed gender as a free-floating tool of self-expression. Nonetheless, the ways in which women and men made sense of themselves as gendered beings reveals a culture of intricate possibilities rather than of rigid categories. Gendered power was not reserved exclusively for any one sex. In recognizing the very real restrictions that women in particular faced on both sides of the Atlantic, we should not forget the remarkable, though sometimes perilous, opportunities that resulted from conceiving of gender as transferable attributes rather than as absolute and fixed identities. Because both men and women could become functionally masculine or feminine as circumstances dictated, women as well as men in the world of John Winthrop could and did perform patriarchy.

Endnotes:

The author wishes to thank Catherine Allgor, Lynn Botelho, Francis Bremer, Thomas Cogswell, Jennifer Hildebrand, Wendy Lucas, and Donald Yacovone for their astute comments and advice.

1. Carol Anshaw, "Gender Pretender," *The Advocate*, Mar. 16, 1999.
2. John Gray, *Men Are From Mars, Women Are From Venus* (New York, 1992), 5, 11.
3. Thomas Laqueur reconstructs premodern conceptions of the body in *Making Sex: Body and Gender from the Greeks to Freud* (Cambridge, Mass., 1990). That anatomical paradigm is discussed below.
4. Laurel Thatcher Ulrich, *Good Wives: Image and Reality in the Lives of Women in Northern New England, 1650-1750* (New York, 1982), 8.
5. John Cotton, *The Way of the Churches of Christ in New-England* (London, 1645), 4; Phyllis Mack, *Visionary Women: Ecstatic Prophecy in Seventeenth-Century England* (Berkeley, 1992), 49; Ulrich, *Good Wives*, 38.
6. Mary Beth Norton, *Founding Mothers and Fathers: Gendered Power and the Forming of American Society* (New York, 1996), 10.
7. Susan Dwyer Amussen, *An Ordered Society: Gender and Class in Early Modern England* (New York, 1988), 3, 133; see also Norton, *Founding Mothers and Fathers*, esp. 10. Tina Krontiris concludes that women writers in early modern England rarely "attack[ed] basic assumptions in the ideologies that oppress[ed] them," adopting instead "strategies of appropriation, accommodation, and modification." Tina Krontiris, *Oppositional Voices: Women as Writers and Translators of lierature in the English Renaissance* (New York, 1992), 142, 143.
8. E. M. W. Tillyard, *The Elizabethan World Picture* (London, 1943); Amussen, *An Ordered Society*; Gordon J. Schochet, *Patriarchalism in Political Thought: The Authoritarian Family and Political Speculation and Attitudes Especially in Seventeenth-Century New England* (New York, 1975); and James Daly, *Sir Robert Filmer and English Political Thought* (Toronto, 1979).
9. William Gouge, *Of Domestical Duties* (London, 1634), 17; Norton, *Founding Mothers and Fathers*, 6; David E. Underdown, *A Freeborn People: Politics and the Nation in Seventeenth-Century England* (Oxford, 1996), 62. See also Edmund S. Morgan, *The Puritan Family: Religion and Domestic Relations in*

Seventeenth-Century New England (1944; New York, 1966); John Demos, *A Little Commonwealth: Family Life in Plymouth Colony* (New York, 1970), and Carol Karlsen, *The Devil in the Shape of a Woman: Witchcraft in Colonial New England* (New York, 1987), 160-165.

10. Thomas Gataker, *Marriage Duties Briefly Couched Together* (London, 1620), 10.

11. Olwen Hufton, *The Prospect Before Her: A History of Women in Western Europe, 1500-1800* (New York, 1996), 52-53.

12. Mack, *Visionary Women*, 49; Jeremy Boulton, *Neighbourhood and Society: A London Suburb in the Seventeenth Century* (Cambridge, 1987), 126.

13. See Anthony Fletcher, *Gender, Sex, and Subordination in England, 1500-1800* (New Haven, 1995), 403; Amussen, *An Ordered Society*, 3; and Norton, *Founding Mothers and Fathers*, 10.

14. Ulrich, *Good Wives*, passim; Norton, *Founding Mothers and Fathers*, esp. 10, 21, 236; and Laura Gowing, *Domestic Dangers: Women, Words, and Sex in Early Modern London* (Oxford, 1996), esp. 109. See also Cornelia Hughes Dayton, *Women Before the Bar: Gender, Law, and Society in Connecticut, 1639-1789* (Chapel Hill, 1995), 21. Dayton's fine study shows that Puritan values created unusual opportunities for women's voices to be heard in court. Dayton argues that cultural, legal, and economic changes diminished those opportunities by the mid eighteenth century. Mary Beth Norton argues that patriarchal conceptions of polity gave way in the late seventeenth century to Lockean contractual theory that perceived political obligation in terms of a voluntary agreement between men. That shift from what Norton has termed "a unified theory of power" to "a dichotomous theory of power in which the sources of authority in the family differed from those in society and the polity" had profoundly negative implications for women because it removed familial analogies from political discussion and indeed firmly separated instead of conflating family and state. (Norton, *Founding Mothers and Fathers*, 11). A gradual transformation in the conceptualization of economic production had a parallel impact: as the focus of male economic activity shifted away from the home and an integrated working partnership between husband and wife toward individual employment and wage labor, so women's work was reconceived as separate from and less productive than male economic activity. Whereas Alice Clark located this transformation squarely in the seventeenth century, more recent historians such as Amussen see that chronology as premature, insisting that the family during that period was still "the fundamental eco-

nomic unit of society" as well as "the basis for political and social order." Susan Cahn argues that the transformation was underway during Winthrop's lifetime, but concedes this to have been "a lengthy process which, for many families, was incomplete in 1700." Alice Clark, *Working Life of Women in the Seventeenth Century* (London, 1919); Amussen, *An Ordered Society*, 1; and Susan Cahn, *Industry of Devotion: The Transformation of Women's Work in England, 1500-1660* (New York, 1987), 8. See also Michael McKeon, "Historicizing Patriarchy: The Emergence of Gender Difference in England, 1660-1760," *Eighteenth-Century Studies* 28(1995):295-322. Historians have, furthermore, examined sectarian challenges to gender norms during the Civil War and the subsequent reassertion of male authority, partly in response to those challenges. See Patricia Crawford, *Women and Religion in Seventeenth-Century England* (London, 1993); Mack, *Visionary Women*; Rachel Trubowitz, "Female Preachers and Male Wives: Gender and Authority in Civil War England," *Prose Studies* 14(1991):112-133; Elaine Hobby, *Virtue of Necessity: English Women's Writing, 1649-1688* (Ann Arbor, Mich., 1988); Christina Berg and Phillipa Berry, "Spiritual Whoredom: An Essay on Female Prophets in the Seventeenth Century," in Francis Baker et al., ed., *Literature and Power in the Seventeenth Century* (Colchester, Eng., 1981); and Keith Thomas, "Women and the Civil War Sects," *Past & Present* 13(1958):42-62.

15. Amussen, *An Ordered Society*, 119.
16. Ulrich, *Good Wives*, 39-41, 50.
17. K. D. M. Snell, *Annals of the Labouring Poor* (Cambridge, 1985), 270-319.
18. Christina Larner, *Enemies of God: The Witch-Hunt in Scotland* (Baltimore, 1981), 101, 102.
19. Marie B. Rowlands, "Recusant Women, 1560-1640," in Mary Prior, ed., *Women in English Society, 1500-1800* (London, 1985), 149-180, and Frances Dolan, "Gender Identities" (paper given at The Worlds of John Winthrop conference in September 1999), 4-5. Alexandra Walsham cautions us not to read all signs of "proselytism, autonomy, and enterprise" by recusant woman as "invariably" at the expense of "male religious initiative." She suggests that female recusant activity was "just as often a natural division of labour in the management of dissent." Alexandra Walsham, *Church Papists: Catholicism, Conformity, and Confessional Polemic in Early Modern England* (Rochester, N.Y., 1993), 78-81.
20. Ulrich, *Good Wives*, 215-235.

21. Ulrich, *Good Wives*, 8-9, 239-240; John Howard Ellis, ed., *The Works of Anne Bradstreet* (Gloucester, Mass., 1962), 220. We should beware of confusing agency or affirmation with modern notions of individuality. Margaret Ferguson argues persuasively that recent attempts to find "autonomy" and "selfhood" in early modern women's lives are sometimes problematic, not least because these notions would have made little sense to women or men of that period. Margaret W. Ferguson, "Moderation and Its Discontents: Recent Work on Renaissance Women," *Feminist Studies* 20(1994):349-366. As Susan Frye and Karen Robertson have pointed out, "the individual subject" acquired meaning "within a matrix of interactions." Men and women conceived of themselves in relation to others. Susan Frye and Karen Robertson, eds. *Maids and Mistresses, Cousins and Queens: Women's Alliances in Early Modern England* (New York, 1999), 4.

22. Lisa Wilson, *Ye Heart of a Man: The Domestic Life of Men in Colonial New England* (New Haven, 1999), 1-3, 92-93, 98, 186-187.

23. Mack, *Visionary Women*, 49-50.

24. John Cotton, *Christ the Fountain of Life* (London, 1651), 36-37, and *A Practical Commentary* (London, 1656), 131; Robert C. Winthrop, ed., *The Life and Letters of John Winthrop* (Boston, 1864-1867), 1:136, 397.

25. Richard Godbeer, *Sexual Revolution in Early America* (Baltimore, 2002), 79-82; Elizabeth Reis, *Damned Women: Sinners and Witches in Puritan New England* (Ithaca, N.Y., 1997), 93-120 (quotation 101); see also Margaret Masson, "The Typology of the Female as a Model for the Regenerate: Puritan Preaching, 1690-1730," *Signs* 2(1976):313-315.

26. Cotton Mather, *Ornaments for the Daughters of Zion* (Cambridge, 1692), 39, 42.

27. Charles Lloyd Cohen, *God's Caress: The Psychology of Puritan Religious Experience* (New York, 1986), 222-223; Laurel Thatcher Ulrich, "'Vertuous Women Found': New England Ministerial Literature, 1668-1735," in Jane Wilson James, ed., *Women in American Religion* (Philadelphia, 1980), 75, 78, 79. See also Masson, "Typology of the Female," 312-13, and Emory Elliott, "The Development of the Puritan Funeral Sermon and Elegy: 1660-1750," *Early American Literature* 15(1980):154-155.

28. Masson, "Typology of the Female," 305, 315. See also Amanda Porterfield, *Female Piety in Puritan New England: The Emergence of Religious Humanism* (New York, 1992), 6-7, 156.

29. John Winthrop, *The History of New England from 1630 to 1649*, ed. James Savage (Boston, 1825-1826), 2:281.
30. Fletcher, *Gender, Sex, and Subordination*, 33, 44, 79, 82, 108; *The Taming of the Shrew*, act IV, scene ii.
31. Laqueur, *Making Sex*, passim.
32. Fletcher, *Gender, Sex, and Subordination*, 41; see also Janet Adelman, "Making Defect Perfection: Shakespeare and the One-Sex Model," in Viviana Comensoli and Anne Russell, eds., *Enacting Gender on the English Renaissance Stage* (Urbana, Ill., 1999), 23-52, and Stephen Orgel, *Impersonations: The Performance of Gender in Shakespeare's England* (Cambridge, 1996), 21-23.
33. Kathryn Schwarz, "Missing the Breast," in David Hillman and Carla Mazzio, eds., *The Body in Parts: Fantasies of Corporeality in Early Modern Europe* (New York, 1997), 147, 148. As Mary Fissell has noted, it might be tempting when dealing with a period in which men and women were understood to be physical variants of each other, rather than utterly distinct, to shift "the burden of sexual difference" away from the body and onto society. Yet "bodily difference" and "cultural difference" informed each other; they were "mutually constitutive" rather than "different domains." Mary Fissell, "Gender and Generation: Representing Reproduction in Early Modern England," *Gender and History* 7(1995):448.
34. John Oxenbridge, *New England Freemen...* (Cambridge, Mass., 1673), 36-37; John Cotton, quoted in David Leverenz, *The Language of Puritan Feeling: An Exploration in Literature, Psychology, and Social History* (New Brunswick, N.J., 1980), 143; Samuel Willard, *A Complete Body of Divinity* (Boston, 1726), 131. For references to male breasts and bosoms in English plays, see Peter Stallybrass, "Transvestism and the 'Body Beneath': Speculating on the Boy Actor," in Susan Zimmerman, ed., *Erotic Politics: Desire on the Renaissance Stage* (New York, 1992), 70.
35. Milton's *Paradise Lost*, for example, had Adam address Eve as "this fair defect of nature."(10: 891-92). For Shakespearean references to women as distinct from men because lacking male body parts or qualities, see Adelman, "Making Defect Perfection," 23-24.
36. Christopher Haigh, *Elizabeth I* (London, 1988), 22; Leah S. Marcus, *Puzzling Shakespeare: Local Reading and Its Discontents* (Berkeley, 1988), 54; see also Marie Axton, *The Queen's Two Bodies: Drama and the Elizabethan Succession* (London, 1977), esp. 38.

37. T. E. Hartley, ed., *Proceedings in the Parliaments of Elizabeth I, 1558-1581* (Wilmington, Del., 1981), 94, 148; Marcus, *Puzzling Shakespeare*, 55-56. Elizabeth I's dual engendering of her political authority was also exemplified in her frequent assertions that she was married to her kingdom. The queen characterized herself sometimes as wife to her subjects but increasingly toward the end of her reign as their husband. She made cunning use of this dual nature when dealing with actual male suitors, winning over potential husbands "by giving rein to her flirtatious, feminine side" and then using male-identified language to quell their insistent demands. Marcus, *Puzzling Shakespeare*, 59-60.

38. Quoted in Paul Johnson, *Elizabeth I: A Biography* (New York, 1974), 320.

39. Susan Frye, "The Myth of Elizabeth I at Tilbury," *Sixteenth Century Journal* 23(1992):95-114; Marcus, *Puzzling Shakespeare*, 62; and Winfried Schleiner, "Divina Virago: Queen Elizabeth as an Amazon," *Studies in Philology* 75(1978):163-180. In 1675, the queen assumed the role of a chivalric knight in the royal entertainment at Kennilworth, but she did not adopt male costume; see Philippa Berry, *Of Chastity and Power: Elizabethan Literature and the Unmarried Queen* (New York, 1989), 95-100.

40. The images of female excess through which scholars depicted ancient barbarism were, Mikalachki notes, "analagous" to sixteenth-century "constructions of insubordinate womanhood." In particular, the cruelty, lust, and inversion of maternal nurture present in these accounts bore more than a passing resemblance to the qualities associated with witches. See Jodi Mikalachki, *The Legacy of Boadicea: Gender and Nation in Early Modern England* (New York, 1998), 11, 13, 14, 15, 116.

41. It was not until the late seventeenth century that English representations of Boadicca became mostly flattering and only rarely during Elizabeth's reign did panegyrists draw parallels between the two queens. Mikalachki, *Legacy of Boadicea*, 117, 126, 129.

42. Quotations from Helen Hackett, *Virgin Mother, Maiden Queen: Elizabeth I and the Cult of the Virgin Mary* (New York, 1995), 4. The association of Elizabeth I with mythic and religious figures provided an additional means to assuage fears regarding female rule. "One way to accommodate a powerful woman," writes Hackett, "without disrupting a predominant cultural framework which regards women as inferiors and subordinates, is to present her as a wonder and a miracle, an 'exceptional woman' whose marvelous gifts stand out in contrast to the general fallibility or even depravity of her sex." Hackett, *Virgin Mother, Maiden Queen*, 238-239; see

also Sara Mendelson and Patricia Crawford, *Women in Early Modern England* (New York, 1988), 65, and Haigh, *Elizabeth I*, 21.

43. Marcus, *Puzzling Shakespeare*, 53.
44. Mack, *Visionary Women*, 251.
45. See Carole Levin, *The Heart and Stomach of a King: Elizabeth I and the Politics of Sex and Power* (Philadelphia, 1994), 39-65.
46. See especially Elkin Calhoun Wilson, *England's Eliza* (1939; New York, 1966); Frances A. Yates, *Astraea: The Imperial Theme in the Sixteenth Century* (London, 1975); and Roy Strong, *The Cult of Elizabeth: Elizabethan Portraiture and Pageantry* (London, 1977). These works have exerted a powerful influence over more recent scholarship, for examples of which see Hackett, *Virgin Mother, Maiden Queen*, 7.
47. Hackett, *Virgin Mother, Maiden Queen*, esp. 10, 236-237, 239.
48. Sir Robert Cecil to Sir John Harington, 1603, in Thomas Park, ed., *Nugae Antiquae: Being a Miscellaneous Collection of Original Papers* (London, 1804), 1:345; Levin, *The Heart and Stomach of a King*, chap. 4; Marcus, *Puzzling Shakespeare*, 70-71, 81.
49. Quotations from Hackett, *Virgin Mother, Maiden Queen*, 165, and Marcus, *Puzzling Shakespeare*, 58.
50. Frank J. Warnke, ed., *John Donne: Poetry and Prose* (New York, 1967), 207. For discussion of the preoccupation with disorder in early modern England, see Keith Wrightson, *English Society, 1580-1680* (London, 1982), 121-182.
51. David E. Underdown, "The Taming of the Scold: The Enforcement of Patriarchal Authority in Early Modern England," in Anthony Fletcher and John Stevenson, eds., *Order and Disorder in Early Modern England* (Cambridge, 1985), 116, 136; Jean E. Howard, *The Stage and Social Struggle in Early Modern England* (London, 1994), 16, 94.
52. Fletcher, *Gender, Sex, and Subordination*, 28; Underdown, "The Taming of the Scold," 117. See also Katherine Usher Henderson and Barbara F. McManus, eds., *Half Humankind: Contexts and Texts of the Controversy About Women in England, 1540-1640* (Urbana, Ill., 1985) and Linda Woodbridge, *Women and the English Renaissance: Literature and the Nature of Women* (Urbana, Ill., 1984).
53. For the prosecution of women as scolds, see Underdown, "The Taming of the Scold," passim; for scholarship on witchcraft as woman-hunting,

see Elspeth Whitney, "The Witch 'She'/ The Historian 'He': Gender and the Historiography of the European Witch-Hunts," *Journal of Women's History* 7(1995):77-101.

54. Amussen, *An Ordered Society*, 181, 182.
55. See Underdown's discussion of this scholarship in "The Taming of the Scold," 121.
56. David Cressy, "Gender Trouble and Cross-Dressing in Early Modern England," *Journal of British Studies* 35(1996):464; Martin Ingram, "'Scolding Women Cucked or Washed': A Crisis in Gender Relations in Early Modern England?" in Jenny Kermode and Garthine Walker, eds., *Women, Crime, and the Courts in Early Modern England* (London, 1994), 48-80.
57. Amussen, *An Ordered Society*, 188; Larner, *Witchcraft and Religion*, 86, and in general her thoughtful engagement with claims that witch-hunting was not necessarily woman-hunting, 84-88.
58. Amussen, *An Ordered Society*, 182.
59. Larner, *Enemies of God*, 3, 101, 102.
60. Underdown, "The Taming of the Scold," 136. For further discussion of this issue, see R. Hamilton, *The Liberation of Women: A Study of Patriarchy and Capitalism* (London, 1978), 56-63; Elizabeth Dale, "The Marriage Metaphor in Seventeenth-Century Massachusetts," in Larry D. Eldridge, ed., *Women and Freedom in Early America* (New York, 1997), 229-243; Morgan, *The Puritan Family*, 29-64; and Demos, *A Little Commonwealth*, 82-99. Underdown suggests, furthermore, that the rapid expansion of a market economy may have involved a growing number of women in selling produce at the marketplace and in running households while their husbands were away from home, which could have created a sense of threat. (Underdown, "The Taming of the Scold," 135-136).
61. See Orgel, *Impersonations*, esp. 119, and Mark Breitenberg, *Anxious Masculinity in Early Modern England* (Cambridge, 1996), 150-174. For sumptuary laws and their significance, see Richard Godbeer, "Perversions of Anatomy, Anatomies of Perversion: The Periwig Controversy in Colonial Massachusetts," *Proceedings of the Massachusetts Historical Society* 109(1998):4-6.
62. William Prynne, *Histrio-Mastix: The Player's Scourge, or, Actor's Tragedy* (London, 1633), 169; John Rainolds, *Th'Overthrow of Stage-Playes* (London, 1599), 97; Orgel, *Impersonations*, 34, 160n9.

63. Prynne, *Histrio-Mastix*, 211-212; see also Orgel, *Impersonations*, 27-30, and Fletcher, *Gender, Sex, and Subordination*, chap. 5.

64. Prynne, *Histrio-Mastix*, 190; see Stallybrass, "Transvestism," 76; Laura Levine, *Men in Women's Clothing: Anti-Theatricality and Effeminization, 1579-1642* (Cambridge, 1994), 15; and Breitenberg, *Anxious Masculinity*, esp. 152-154.

65. Levine, *Men in Women's Clothing*, 5; Orgel, *Impersonations*, 25. Attacks on wig-wearing in early modern England and colonial New England were animated by similar concerns to those underlying criticism of cross-dressing. For English examples of this genre, see William Prynne, *The Unloveliness of Lovelocks* (London, 1628); Thomas Hall, *The Loathsomeness of Long Hair* (London, 1653); *The Hairy Comet* (London, 1676); John Mulliner, *A Testimony Against Periwigs and Periwig-Making* (Northampton, 1677); Richard Richardson, *A Declaration against Wigs and Periwigs* (London, 1682); and Vincent Alsop, "What distance ought we to keep in following the strange fashions of apparel which come up in the days wherein we live?" in Samuel Annesley, *A Continuation of Morning-Exercise Questions and Cases of Conscience* (London, 1683), 589-632. For attacks on wig-wearing in New England, see Godbeer, "Perversions of Anatomy, Anatomies of Perversion," passim.

66. Howard, *The Stage and Social Struggle*, 17.

67. Cressy, "Gender Trouble," 452-458; Howard, *The Stage and Social Struggle*, esp. 115-116.

68. Nor should we assume that masculinity had a unitary or universally accepted meaning; see Susan Dwyer Amussen, "'The Part of a Christian Man': The Cultural Politics of Manhood in Early Modern England," in Amussen and Mark A. Kishlansky, eds., *Political Culture and Cultural Politics in Early Modern England: Essays Presented to David Underdown* (Manchester, Eng., 1995), 213-233.

69. Orgel, *Impersonations*, 35.

70. Orgel, *Impersonations*, 106, 124.

71. "Proceedings of Excommunication against Mistress Ann Hibbens of Boston," in John Demos, ed., *Remarkable Providences: Readings in Early American History* (Boston, 1991), 271-272.

72. "Proceedings of Excommunication," 277, 279, 280.

73. Quoted in Jane Kamensky, *Governing the Tongue: The Politics of Speech in Early New England* (New York, 1997), 94.

74. Kamensky, *Governing the Tongue*, 4, 7-8, 94, 152. Malicious, gossipy, or trouble-making speech could play an important role in a woman's becoming a witch suspect. Those associated with "the timbre of witchspeak" were liable to be thought of in feminine terms, whether or not they were female. A man who threatened or scolded ("no substitutes for masculine, authoritative speech") had "a woman's tongue in his head" and so might also become suspect. "In this sense," Kamensky writes, "all witchspeak was feminine, regardless of the sex of the speaker." While this further underlines the degree to which Puritans believed men and women could adopt gendered attributes associated with the other sex, it also highlights the insidious values attached to specifically gendered qualities. Kamensky, *Governing the Tongue*, 159, and "Talk Like a Man: Speech, Power, and Masculinity in Early New England," in Laura McCall and Donald Yacovone, eds., *A Shared Experience: Men, Women, and the History of Gender* (New York, 1998), 35.

75. A striking number of accused witches in seventeenth-century New England were women who had inherited or stood to inherit property in the absence of male heirs, thus acquiring a form of power usually reserved for men. Karlsen, *The Devil in the Shape of a Woman*, 77-116, 118.

76. Mather, *Ornaments for the Daughters of Zion*, 19-20. Karlsen analyzes Samuel Willard's discussion of Eve's culpability in *The Devil in the Shape of a Woman*, esp. 176-177.

77. Reis, *Damned Women*, 108, 110. At least some women appear to have internalized these assumptions, see 38, 41, 42, 124.

78. Karlsen, *The Devil in the Shape of a Woman*, xiii-iv, 152. Meanwhile, unconventional attitudes toward gender within marginal groups such as the Quakers created exceptional opportunities for women that in turn gave rise to controversy and opprobrium directed against those who espoused such ideas.

79. "Report of the Trial of Mrs. Anne Hutchinson before the Church in Boston," David D. Hall, ed., *The Antinomian Controversy, 1636-1638* (Durham, N. C., 1990), 383; "Proceedings of Excommunication," 280; see also Kamensky, *Governing the Tongue*, esp. 71-73.

80. John Keble, ed., *The Works of that Learned and Judicious Divine, Mr. Richard Hooker* (Oxford, 1888), 1:208; Joan Wallach Scott, *Gender and the Politics of History* (New York, 1988), 42.

"Justification by Print Alone?": Protestantism, Literacy, and Communications in the Anglo-American World of John Winthrop

David D. Hall and Alexandra Walsham

IN AUGUST 1629, THE Suffolk antiquary Robert Reyce wrote to his friend and confidant John Winthrop entreating him not to emigrate to New England. "The church and common welthe heere at home, hathe more neede of your best abyllytie in these dangerous tymes, then any remote plantation . . . How harde wyll it bee for one broughte up amonge boockes and learned men to lyve in a barbarous place where is no learnynge and lesse cyvillyte."[1]

Reyce's earnest persuasions proved fruitless, but in equating "civilization" with the use of letters and alphabetic writing he was giving expression to a deeply rooted contemporary conviction, the commonplace that literacy and literature distinguished superior races from heathen savages. This sacralization of the western book as the archetype of wisdom shaped and informed the English, and more generally, the European encounter with the non-Christian, native peoples of the New World.[2] In a culture that revered the Bible as a living text and regarded nature as "Gods great booke in Folio,"[3] such logocentric assumptions are hardly surprising. They were part of a wider Renaissance privileging of literacy which also inaugurated a prolonged process of cultural polarization within European society itself, the beginnings of a divide between intellectual elites and their unlearned and "vulgar" social inferiors. As early as 1513, a Benedictine monk was claiming that "without lytterature and good informacyon" the "comyn people Ben lyke to Brute beestes." Nearly two centuries later, in 1691, Richard Baxter echoed him, alleging that mass illiteracy would lead to "a generation of barbarians in a happy Christian land."[4] The concept of "Literature" with a capital L was a product of the same historical moment. The humanists and their successors promoted the idea of an exalted sphere of writing characterized by aesthetic beauty and timeless transcendence, thus encouraging the construction of a canon of great works of "art" sharply demarcated from the inelegant output of untalented scribblers.[5]

This privileging of literacy, literature, and the printed book has persisted to the present day. The notion that the invention of printing represented a "revolutionary" moment and helped to precipitate a major mental and conceptual shift from "orality" to "literacy" (and indeed from the "medieval" to the "modern") still exercises considerable influence in scholarly circles.[6] Equally enduring is the "mythical charter" within western culture which recognizes a single kind of reading–the ability to decipher written texts–and portrays history as a march of progress up and away from the confusing uncertainties of the oral and the visual.[7] Religion enters this narrative in the guise of the Protestant Reformation, which is widely believed to have eroded illiteracy and extinguished both "popish" superstition and oral tradition. The emphasis which Protestantism placed upon "the Word" has been transmuted into the idea that it regarded printed texts as indispensable.

The reasons for the resilience of these paradigms and their wider ramifications cannot be taken up in this essay.[8] Our chief concern here is narrower, to re-examine one part of this larger story, the connections between Protestantism in early modern England and New England and the forces of writing, literacy, and print. We say "re-examine" because recent work on both sides of the Atlantic has called into question the dominance of print in communication and unsettled a number of conventional assumptions about the printing press as an agent of orthodoxy and standardization and as a critical factor in the making of public opinion and a "public sphere." This work has also served to emphasize that the relationship between religious communities and particular textual practices and communicative strategies is strongly affected by the circumstances in which such groups find themselves. Nor can we separate the distinctive modes of speech and writing these groups employed from the complexities of the marketplace: in both old and New England such communities depended on the commercial book-trade in a way that inevitably compromised the ideal relationship between writer and reader.[9] In our survey, three key themes will emerge: (1) the continuing juxtaposition of the printed book with oral, scribal, and visual modes of communication that retained a versatile utility throughout this period; (2) the mediations that occurred as texts were transmitted along the speech-writing continuum, and the manner in which these mediations alter our understanding of texts; and (3) the role of the various media in relation to political opposition, censorship, and public opinion.

This essay is but a prolegomena to a scholarship on "communication and religion" which, for the most part, has yet to be written: that is, historically specific descriptions of how particular groups or communities deployed the technologies of speech, writing, and printing in the maintaining of religion. We may, however, hazard a few general remarks. Within some versions of English Protestantism, Scripture was considered self-authenticating and accessible to everyone who possessed the "eye of faith." Anxious that their own words should have the same transparency, speakers and writers sought to imitate the "humble" or "plain" style that Jesus himself was presumed to have employed, insisting too that the "practical divinity" they wrote had a value far higher than any product of commerce or of "literary" culture since their own works were addressed to the "chief end" of life, to become one with God. From these assumptions followed certain narrative structures and conventions; from them flowed a construction of the ideal reader as someone for whom listening and reading were intimately linked with spiritual self-discipline. Though Quakers and Anglicans largely fall outside the scope of the present discussion, they supplemented these presuppositions in their own distinctive manner.[10]

The many similarities between communicative practices in early modern England and New England warrant an essay that bridges the Atlantic. At certain points, therefore, examples from both societies are integrated into a single narrative, with the emphasis falling upon the transfer from the old world to the new of technologies and the practices that arose around them. Yet, as we shall see, a transatlantic perspective also exposes some significant and illuminating differences. Because the emigrants of the 1630s included very few of the rural poor or landless tenants, more of them were literate than was true of the English people as a whole. The "dark corners of the land" deplored by puritan evangelists in England did not exist in early New England, though this would change in the second half of the century as settlers dispersed ever more widely into the interior and as coastal towns such as Marblehead developed a distinctive identity and culture.[11] Initially, the precarious economic situation of the colonists placed severe limits on the business of printing and the traffic in imported books. Not until the 1670s did a competitive book trade begin to emerge. Even then, its dimensions were modest, as was the scale of importation from the old world. A third circumstance was the long-lasting hegemony of a particular version of Protestantism in New England and of the meanings it assigned to speech, writing, literacy, and print.[12] Accordingly, communicative practices here were in some sense a simplified version of the range employed in Tudor and Stuart England. Ironically, the colonists would also anticipate, in events such as the Antinomian controversy of 1636-1638, the sectarian disturbances of the Civil War period and the strain these placed on orthodox expectations about speech and writing. Because the conflict between orthodoxy and dissent in New England could be played out through the medium of the English book trade, certain colonists were able to speak and write with a remarkable degree of freedom.[13]

Elizabethan and early Stuart commentators repeatedly complained about the chaotic proliferation of books being churned out by commercial printing houses in England. Scholars and wits deplored the stylistic deficiencies of the vast majority of published works and ministers and moralists thundered against the "godlesse & childish vanity, that hath now blotted so many papers." Laurence Chaderton lamented that "vaine glory, and desire of popular fame in the writers, and desire of filthy lucre in the printers, have stuffed our English studies with many superflous and unnecessary bookes. . . ." According to the Canterbury preacher Thomas Jackson, most were "good for nothing but an Ephesian bonfire."[14] The statistics compiled by modern bibliographers offer independent proof that output from

English presses was indeed on the increase: it rose nearly four-fold between 1555 and 1640.[15] Almanacs sold at a rate of 400,000 a year in the later seventeenth century; there may have been as many as three or four million ballads in circulation by 1660; and the production of bibles, catechisms, and prayer books was no less prodigious.[16] This last point warns us against taking clerical outrage about the profusion of "filthy" and "frivolous" books too much at face value. In the long run, the primary function of cheap print may have shifted from edification to entertainment, but "religious" works, as conventionally defined, were undoubtedly the bread and butter of most Elizabethan, Jacobean, and Caroline printers.[17]

Nevertheless the sheer range of literature is deserving of emphasis. A glance at entries in the *Stationers' Register* in the year of John Winthrop's birth, 1588, reveals a wide variety of genres and formats: grammars, law books, government propaganda, and ecclesiastical proformas; news pamphlets describing battle victories, gory crimes, and providential wonders; chivalric romances, histories, and accounts of foreign adventures; sermons, devotional tracts, and diatribes against the pope and his priestly minions; medical texts and manuals of handy advice for "huswyves"; Sir Philip Sidney's *Arcadia*; and dozens of jingoistic ditties celebrating the defeat of the Spanish Armada.[18] The presence of numerous translations from Italian and French reminds us that the English book trade was a part of an international enterprise. Just as continental favorites found their way across the Channel and were hastily "Englished," so did home-bred successes travel in the opposite direction, taking their chances at the famous book fair in Frankfurt.[19] And if exiles employed Dutch and German presses to sway public opinion in England, religious classics like the works of William Perkins would help to succor Calvinists in Hungary, Bohemia, Switzerland, and Spain.[20] This cross fertilization continued in the guise of the news-sheets or corantoes produced in the context of the Thirty Years' War. By the time Winthrop died in 1649, the English Revolution had led to an imaginative explosion of new printed forms and left traditional rhetorical categories in a state of confusion.[21]

The sharp upward curve in the graph of book production is testimony to the rapid expansion and growing maturity and sophistication of the publishing industry in early modern England. The granting of a monopoly to the Stationers' Company in 1557 ensured that, by comparison with other countries in Europe, a relatively small number of printers were at work at any one time. A handful labored in Oxford and Cambridge, but the vast majority in London.[22] It was not until the lifting of this restriction in 1695 that provincial presses could be established legally, though by 1640 a fair number of towns had booksellers of their own, including Shrewsbury, Canterbury, Exeter, and York, some of whom sponsored publications of special local interest.[23]

Despite this urban, indeed metropolitan bias, books do seem to have penetrated the outlying countryside. Margaret Spufford, Tessa Watt, and Michael Frearson have demonstrated that chapmen, peddlers, and carriers distributed printed wares in rural areas. These traveling salesmen dealt in ballads, chapbooks, and other portable texts mainly as a sideline, carrying them in their packs alongside pins, needles, handkerchiefs, and other small goods.[24] Print was also disseminated outwards from London by means of more informal, private networks: Joseph Mede, fellow of Christ's College, Cambridge, received weekly packages of printed and manuscript news from a semi-professional supplier in the city and sent them on to Sir Martin Stuteville at Dalham in Suffolk, while John Winthrop relied on the kindness of friends and relatives passing by the bookselling center of the capital, St. Paul's Churchyard.[25]

The development of effective distribution systems was one symptom of the increasingly entrepreneurial character of the contemporary book trade. Closely regulated by its elected officers, the Stationers' Company was highly protective of its privileges: the frequency with which these were infringed is suggestive of the competitive and proto-capitalist instincts of printers and publisher booksellers.[26] In pursuit of profit, these businessmen were no less ready to print bawdy ballads about courtship and marriage than collections of pious prayers and meditations, and although some, including Robert Waldegrave and Thomas Jenner, used their presses to promote a partisan cause, most appear to have adjusted their opinions according to the prevailing wind. John Charlewood, for example, issued rabidly anti-Catholic tracts but also published works by the Jesuit Robert Southwell.[27] Piracy of bestselling titles was widely practiced, one of the most celebrated cases being the violation of John Day's patent for printing *The ABC with Little Catechism* in 1582. Arthur Dent's *Sermon of Repentance*, reprinted thirty-seven times between 1582 and 1638, was another item which led more than one publisher to infringe the rights of his rivals in pursuit of a share of its profits.[28] Recycling and updating of old stories of "strange," "true," and "wonderful newes" was something of a speciality of John ("Reade and Tremble") Trundle, and the simultaneous publication of ballads and pamphlets on the same theme became a well-established method of securing a journalistic scoop.[29] By the early seventeenth century, syndicates of printers were common and there were signs of growing specialization within the market: no less than eleven partners financed the production of the fifth impression of Foxe's famous "Book of Martyrs" in 1596[30] and in 1624 a group of six booksellers established copyright over a stock of some 127 Elizabethan ballads. The same decade saw John Wright invent a new publishing staple, the religious chapbook or penny godly.[31] The success enjoyed by such works serves to underline the point that religious publishing was highly lucrative.

On the eve of John Winthrop's departure for Massachusetts, then, books had clearly become valuable commodities and publishing in England was evolving into an increasingly prosperous industry. At first glance, the situation in New England after Winthrop had arrived and commercial and religious life had become relatively stable presents us with some striking contrasts.

In September 1638, the widow of the Reverend Jose Glover watched as the crew of the ship on which her husband had died unloaded the printing press he was bringing with him to Massachusetts. Whether anyone who knew how to operate it arrived at the same time remains doubtful. Stephen Day, who would manage the press during the early years, was a locksmith who may have depended on the services of Gregory Dexter, an experienced printer living in Rhode Island, until Samuel Green and his son became involved in the mid 1640s. Nor do we know precisely why Glover was bringing over a press, although the darkening situation in England and the necessity, long since acted upon by "forward" puritans in England and the Netherlands, of resorting to clandestine or unlicensed printing,[32] offer some clues. The decision to locate the press in Harvard Yard was in keeping with English attitudes and practice: outside London, the two universities of Oxford and Cambridge were each authorized to undertake certain forms of printing, and from the start, the political and religious leaders of Massachusetts envisioned the press as an instrument of official policy and "orthodoxy."

However, as Hugh Amory has emphasized in his revisionist account of the Cambridge printing office,[33] its history for the first thirty years is chiefly one of inactivity. Many writers continued to rely on the London book trade: the controversies which beset the colonists—

Roger Williams's protests, the transatlantic exchanges about church order, the insurgency of Anne Hutchinson, and the Robert Child affair—were all played out in print by means of presses thousands of miles away. Little changed until the 1660s, when the New England Company, an English philanthropic organization founded in 1649, undertook to finance John Eliot's translation of the Bible into Algonquian, together with the texts that made up Eliot's "Indian library," which would eventually include a *Primer* and several Protestant devotional classics. All this work required a second printing press and a trained printer, Marmaduke Johnson, who joined the Greens in Cambridge in 1659.

In the preceding period, the Greens had relied on institutional patrons for most of their business: the civil government, for which their press issued broadsides containing laws or other orders and the 1648 *Laws and Liberties;* congregations, for which it published catechisms written by various emigrant ministers; and Harvard College, for which it produced Commencement *Theses* and *Questionaes.* Edition sizes of books that were the product of such patronage were small and distribution often confined to officeholders and/or a list of towns. With the exception of the annual almanac, very few items were undertaken at the expense either of the Greens and Johnson or of any merchant-bookseller. It is a sign of the slow pace of consumer demand that copies of a broadside edition of the Massachusetts *Capitall Laws* issued in 1642 continued to be available in the 1670s, when the selectmen of Watertown ordered copies to distribute among householders.[34] No less notable is the apparent near absence in the early years of the colony of a body of cheap print comparable with that which flowed from presses in England, that is, ephemeral ballads and pamphlets which catered to the appetite of the populace for moralizing news stories spiced with sensation. And not one Cambridge or

Boston printer issued any school books until the belated arrival in the 1680s of Benjamin Harris, temporarily a refugee from the heated politics of England at the time of the Popish Plot and Exclusion Crisis.

While few details survive of the trade in imported books, the quantities that the merchant John Usher was receiving from London in the 1680s—a total in one shipment of twenty copies—underscore its limited scope at the end of the seventeenth century.[35] The scale of private importation is even more difficult to gauge, though there is evidence that in the 1630s John Winthrop, Jr., was having crates of volumes shipped out to him in New England, along with the latest catalogues. Nevertheless, it is clear that the stock of books which the emigrants brought over from England on their original voyages (which were undoubtedly predominantly religious in character) did not begin to be replenished significantly until at least a generation later.[36]

That so little in the way of printing, bookbinding, and bookselling took place during the first twenty or thirty years of the settlement, and no competition at all existed within the trade until the mid 1660s, means that piracy was non-existent. On the other side of the coin, local printers ignored patents and monopolies within the English trade (and continued to do so for the entire colonial period), while the two Massachusetts printers who tentatively competed against each other in the 1660s, Samuel Green and Marmaduke Johnson, did not have to petition for privileges, there being no literary text that needed such protection.[37] The sole exception was the Massachusetts statutes: in 1672, the merchant-bookseller Usher obtained an exclusive right to print a new edition of the laws of the colony.

In the light of the above, it might be suggested not only that early Americans were familiar with a much narrower range of publications than their counterparts in England but that they came into contact with relatively few printed texts at all. Just how widely were books diffused in early Massachusetts society? A study of surviving probate inventories from Essex, Suffolk, and Middlesex counties dating mainly from after 1650 indicates that 50-60 percent of the deceased owned books worth enough to be noted among their household goods. The omission of almanacs, primers, printed broadsides, psalters, catechisms, and similar items from these lists makes it unclear whether such unbound pamphlet books were not owned, not conserved, or simply not deemed sufficiently valuable to be counted. This caveat aside, the Bible, predominantly in the format of quarto, is by far the most commonly specified title, appearing in two thirds of the Essex inventories mentioning books and 30 percent of those from Middlesex. When these figures are reversed to indicate absence, it is apparent that half or more of these households did not possess a copy of the Scriptures.[38] These statistics may help us to understand why a Massachusetts clergyman complained in an election sermon in 1673 that "in multitudes of Families there is (it may be) . . . no Bible, or onely a torn Bible to be found[.] I mean but a part of a Bible."[39] Such figures are also at odds with the commonplace that Protestantism, especially in its domestic setting, revolved around the perusal and recitation of edifying texts.[40] The paucity of devotional tracts and the large number of homes without a Bible strongly suggest that the vitality of religious practice among lay people in New England was unrelated, in the main, to printed books, notwithstanding the emphasis which godly magistrates and ministers on both sides of the Atlantic placed on reading God's Word, sometimes celebrating it in terms that implied it was nothing less than an agent of salvation.[41]

Such observations should give scholars of post-Reformation England serious pause for thought, since it has been conventional to emphasize the major spurt of growth in this regard which occurred between 1560 and 1640. Peter Clark's analysis of the records relating to Canterbury, Maidstone, and Faversham in Kent reveals that only 40 percent of men and 25 percent of women owned books by the early seventeenth century, while they feature in a mere 7.8 percent of inventories from rural Leicestershire between 1600 and 1624.[42] Likewise, cases like that of the laborer lodging in the Forest of Arden in 1614 who kept "Sertyane small bookes" in his rented room were probably rare, and it remains difficult to assess if the library assembled by London artisan Nehemiah Wallington is as unique as the personal archive in which they are described.[43] A conservative reading of this evidence sets a similar question mark beside the assumption that the explosion of printing in this period was largely a consequence of the advent of Protestantism. It also indirectly casts doubt upon the ingrained idea that the spread of Protestant piety was the chief engine behind the significant expansion of literacy in late sixteenth- and early seventeenth-century England. It is to a more detailed consideration of these issues that we must now turn.

Historians have long followed in the footsteps of early Protestant apologists in presupposing the existence of a causal nexus between the success of the Reformation and the invention of the mechanical press. Martin Luther spoke of the press as an instrument of liberation—God's "highest and extremest act of grace, whereby the business of the Gospel is driven forward"—and John Foxe blustered that "[e]ither the pope must abolish knowledge and printing, or printing must at length root him out."[44] The new medium of mass communication has been credited with transforming the abstract ideal of a "priesthood of all believers" into practical reality by eliminating the need for clerical mediation. A. G. Dickens once wrote, only half jokingly, of the "Doctrine of Justification by Print Alone."[45] By extension Roman Catholicism is still sometimes presented as an archenemy of technological change in the realm of communications. Many modern accounts continue to perpetuate the confessional stereotypes enshrined in contemporary woodcuts and engravings contrasting Protestant congregations assiduously following the preacher's text in a book on their knees with ignorant "popish" ones fingering their rosary beads.[46]

However, recent work is beginning to qualify both aspects of this topos. On the one hand, there is growing recognition that the post-Reformation English Catholic community utilized the instrument of print with great ingenuity. Forced to rely on books as a vital supplement to, if not substitute for, a small band of missionary priests, its clerical leaders skillfully exploited the press, disseminating spiritual guidance to the faithful in small formats which could easily be concealed and drawing on the rich literary resources of international Catholicism to resist its annihilation in England.[47] Such was the success of works like Robert Persons' *First Book of Christian Exercise* (1583), better known as *The Book of Resolution*, that puritan divines conscious of the scarcity of devotional works on their own side sometimes resorted to "purging" them of doctrinal error and republishing for the benefit of Protestant readers.[48] Even the royal chaplain, Daniel Featley, had to concede that "the Romanists for the most part exceed [us] in bulke," though he insisted that his colleagues surpassed them "in weight."[49] The centrality that books of this kind acquired in recusant households like that of Dorothy Lawson in Newcastle-upon-Tyne[50] suggests that we should seriously consider the possibility that post-Reformation English Catholicism provided at least as much of an incentive to read as Protestantism.

On the other hand, the bibliocentricity of Protestant culture has itself come under critical scrutiny. Repeated complaints about the "common sort" irreverently discussing scripture on the ale bench remind us that evangelical ideas spread initially through established networks of rumor and gossip and in centers of popular sociability.[51] In its first generation, as Patrick Collinson and other scholars have shown, English Protestantism made imaginative use of pictures, plays, songs, and carnivalesque ritual to convey its message that the pope was Antichrist and the mass a mummery.[52] And, above all, the Reformation in England, as in Europe in general, was a preaching revival.[53] Stephen Egerton spoke of the word of God "soundly, plainly, and zealously preached" as the "principall meanes and bellowes" by which the Holy Spirit kindled a fire in the hearts of believers. "Of all the Senses," he said, "none is more needfull, or use-full, then Hearing."[54] It was not necessary to be able to read to be consoled by the comforting discourse of a talented "spiritual physician" or roused by a fire-and-brimstone sermon predicting that plagues would soon fall on an iniquitous nation. Catechizing was likewise essentially an oral mode, a dialogue between ministers and the congregations under their care.[55] In New England too the clergy, civil leaders, and heads of households had other means than printed books at their disposal for transmitting religious instruction. One index of the overwhelming importance of speech in fashioning people's self-understanding as saints and sinners is that allusions to sermons far outnumber references to printed texts in the confessional relations made by candidates applying for membership in Thomas Shepard's church in Cambridge, Massachusetts.[56] The practice of memorizing and repeating sermons at home serves as another reminder of the power of the spoken word in a society in which children were taught reading itself through the verbal recitation of liturgical texts. In this manner the sick and housebound were enabled to enjoy the fruits of public preaching vicariously. In the 1670s, for example, the Ipswich matron Sarah Goodhue relied on hearing her husband's notes read aloud when she was left behind to nurse infants and recover from the rigors of childbirth. Far from sapping the vitality of oral culture—a mode of literacy that, in this period, was always in a relationship of exchange with print-based literacy—Protestantism may have served, at least in the short term, to reinforce it.[57]

"Justification by Print Alone?"

We also need to note that Protestants often expressed strong reservations about utilizing the new-fangled medium of print and about what James Rigney has called "the duplicity of duplication."[58] Many a preacher protested in the preface to his sermon that reading it as a text could never compare with hearing it in the flesh. Writing in 1626, Humphrey Sydenham was not the first or the last to fear that his would "loose some of the lustre in perusall, which it found in the delivery." This was not always a self-deprecating formula. Conceiving of themselves as divine messengers and prophets, puritan ministers tended to regard books as vastly inferior to the experience of being ravished by the living Logos. This self-understanding helps explain the reluctance of a significant number of clergymen to take the plunge into print, including some of the most energetic and celebrated preachers of the age, Archbishop Tobie Matthew of York among them.[59] Another retiring figure was Stephen Egerton, who refused to publish any of his thousands of lectures at Blackfriars in the course of his lifetime, and only belatedly and somewhat begrudgingly sanctioned the printing of one taken down by "characterie" or shorthand. When he published Richard Rogers's *Practice of Christianitie* in 1618, he did so—"not without much conflict and doubting"—to forestall unauthorized editions of copies that had been prepared for private use.[60]

In New England, as in England, much use was made of scribal publication, a technology which printing failed to displace. First-generation ministers frequently distributed manuscript copies of catechisms to their congregations. Religious verse, especially the elegy, was chiefly confined to this medium.[61] Letters offering pastoral advice were reproduced by hand, as were conversion narratives and key documents exemplifying the intimate link between religion and civil society, such as the Massachusetts "Body of Liberties" of 1641 and John Winthrop's "Model of Christian Charity."[62] Handwritten texts associated with the Antinomian Controversy, including John Wheelwright's inflammatory fast-day sermon of 1637 and the conferences between the elders and John Cotton in 1636 and 1637, appear to have circulated widely.[63] Returning to the Old World, the Scottish Covenanter Samuel Rutherford's "letters" of spiritual counsel were disseminated chirographically in the 1630s, when access to print was limited.[64]

Certainly, the clergy did come to recognize the value of the press in preserving for posterity the works of dead colleagues, who might thereby preach from the grave. The editors of the London lecturer Thomas Taylor's collected sermons, which did not appear in print until 1653 because the "iniquity" of former times "could not bear such burning and shining light," celebrated the book's ability to "make him once again speak to the good of the Church after so many years silence."[65] John Norton played upon the interchangeability of speech, writing, and printing, and the permanence of the last medium, in entitling his biography of John Cotton, *Abel being dead yet speaketh*. With Robert Bedingfield, student of Christ Church in Oxford, ministers began to insist that though it was better to preach, it was still good to print, reasoning that "the understanding is not informed, nor the will moved alwaies by the Eare, but sometimes by the Eye; otherwise the suttle Romanists would unclaspe the Bibles of the Laitie. . . ."[66] In England, there was nothing like being suspended from the ministry for refusing to subscribe or wear the surplice for persuading nonconformists like John Dod and Robert Cleaver that the moment had come to set their inhibitions firmly to one side. Some saw persecution as a providential encouragement to the public dissemination of their writings: God "suffered the violence of men to silence their tongues, that they might have a greater vacancy for this kinde of instruction."[67] And in the 1640s, mainstream Protestant ministers increasingly fell back upon the authority of print to counter the impact of the "pretended Revelations" of radical sectarians who valued private inspiration above the written word.[68]

Publishing presented other problems for Protestants which it would be unwise to overlook. Some expressed concern that the availability of sermon texts would erode the foundations of communal worship. John Barlow suspected people might be tempted to "sit at hom[e] with a printed paper, dreaming that will suffice to get faith for salvation, and so absent themselves from the more powerfull meanes in the publicke congregation."[69] Another danger was that men and women would spend their time reading the wrong sort of literature: English ministers and social commentators constantly lamented the moral corruption of the multitude by bawdy ballads, Italian romances, and other "bableries," declaring such publications to be the "Library of the Devil" and "the very poyson of youth."[70] In this sense literacy was a double-edged sword. Even Scripture itself could be a source of disorder if misinterpreted, as Martin Luther had discovered to his horror during the German Peasants' War.[71] The debate about unmediated Bible-reading cut across the confessional divide between Catholics and Protestants. Calvin himself would assert that God wanted "the bread to be cut for us, the pieces to be put in our mouths, and the chewing to be done for us,"[72] a sentiment which does much to explain the reliance of the second-generation Protestant clergy on catechizing and the famous marginalia in the Geneva Bible. These were safe ways of predigesting the Word.

The body of evidence assembled above does much to qualify and weaken the presumed link between literacy and Protestantism which pervades so much of the historical scholarship on old and New England. We need to recognize that religion may not have been the sole or even the primary reason why people might wish to become literate and why others were eager to promote the widespread diffusion of reading and writing.[73] Influenced by humanist works such as Thomas Elyot's *The Boke Named the Governour* (1531) and Roger Ascham's *The Scholemaster* (1570), gentlemen began to regard learning as an essential emblem of their rank. This, in turn, encouraged ambitious individuals at the other end of the social spectrum to see literacy as a vehicle for personal advancement and upward mobility. Literacy also lessened the chances of being cheated in the course of credit transactions and helped shopkeepers and tradesmen keep their businesses afloat in an age witnessing the growth of commerce and a market economy. Reading opened the door to a world of entertainment and armchair adventure and it could even be a means of medical self-help: A.T.'s *Rich store-house or treasury for the diseased* (1596) presented itself as of "great benefit and comfort" to "the poorest sort of people that are not of ability to go to the Physicians."[74] Educational writers, meanwhile, argued that schooling was a key to breeding good citizens and a safeguard against the perils presented by political insubordination. As these attitudes and practices suggest, piety was by no means the only factor which prompted town corporations to found and maintain pedagogic institutions.

The double-edged qualities of literacy—an instrument of discipline, yet also of empowerment—re-emerged in the uses of schooling in New England. Always wary of reading, speaking, and listening as potentially capable of subverting theological orthodoxy and inciting sedition, the authorities in New England sought to ensure that these practices served the ends of order. Hence the close association between learning how to read and memorizing (and reciting aloud) a catechism; no fewer that thirteen of the first-generation ministers prepared catechisms for their congregations, while others relied on versions printed in England.[75] The Massachusetts General Court voted in May 1642 to hold parents accountable for their children's "ability to read & understand the principles of religion & the capitall lawes of this country." A subsequent "school law" of 1647 required each town of fifty households or more to "appoint [some] one ... to teach all such children as shall resort to him to write & reade," but did not mandate that children participate in this instruction. Justifying the law, the General Court invoked the Protestant principle that everyone should have access to "the true sence & meaning of the originall" of Scripture, a second benefit being that literacy would prevent "learning" from being "buried in the grave of our fathers in the church & commonwealth."[76] In thus validating education, the Court was also signaling its awareness of the sectarian turmoil in England during the 1640s, when the authority of an institutional, learned clergy was called into question. Several years later, in 1652, the General Court vetoed a motion by Second Church, Boston, to elect an orthodox though unlearned man to the office of minister, noting as it did so "the unsutablenes of these times complyinge with such unsound tenents as now abound, for the subversion of an able ministery."[77] At Harvard College, dedicated to the social task of educating an "able clergy," the assumption reigned that a full understanding of the Bible, and especially the means of deciphering any of its "mysteries," required training in the "arts" of logic and rhetoric that were beyond the reach of most laity.[78] Lest we exaggerate either the aspects of regulation or those of liberation, it must be noted that laxness within towns and families, together with gender-related assumptions about the importance of reading and writing, belied statutory prescriptions that ought to have ensured the near universal ability to read.[79]

At the same time, it is important to emphasize that the boundary between literacy and illiteracy was permeable and blurred. Many printed artifacts were themselves hybrid media, interweaving typography with traditional forms of oral and visual communication and functioning more as mnemonic aids than as receptacles and reservoirs of new information. Broadside ballads mediated messages to those unable to read through melody and music; woodcut pictures continued to give life to the Gregorian dictum that images were the books of the illiterate; and in the same way that catechizing stimulated oral exchange, so printed sermons fed back into the domain of speech via the practice of repeating them in what the suspicious English authorities were liable to regard as household conventicles.[80] A second key insight is the need to replace a narrow and singular definition of literacy with the notion of "an elaborate hierarchy of literacy skills," "a diversity of literacies" depending on class, age, occupation, geography, and gender.[81] Probably the most significant division was between writers and readers. Since reading was taught before writing (and before many children were snatched away from school to contribute to the income of the household), statistics for literacy based on counting signatures are likely to represent a "spectacular underestimate" of how many could read.[82] This is true of New England no less than England. In both contexts, the presence of professional scriveners, schoolmasters, and ministers meant that an inability to write was not necessarily a terrible handicap. Further complicating the picture are the many individuals who recognized the vernacular alphabet but lacked the capacity to fathom texts written in Latin; fluent readers of print who struggled to decipher secretary and other scribal hands; and people who could manage the heavy Gothic black letter but not the Roman font revived by the humanists. Finally, we may cite the remarkable familiarity of uneducated Lollards, Baptists, and other sectarian groups with vast portions of the Bible. The ability of such individuals to recite long passages with astonishing accuracy challenges us to rethink the meaning of illiteracy itself and further qualifies the cliché that early modern Protestantism was a religion of the book.[83]

Much of the evidence presented in the preceding sections points towards a larger unsettling that has occurred in our understanding of texts, whether printed or scribally produced. To ask "what is a text?" has become a question that invites, indeed demands, attention to the circumstances of reproduction, transmission, and reception, circumstances that in turn allow us to situate any given text within its social and historical contexts. In adopting this perspective, we find ourselves not only removing the author from a position of unique authority and autonomy, but extracting texts themselves from any space—"Literature" is the leading example—postulated as lying outside history. In other words, the effect of recognizing texts as products of collective negotiation and exchange rather than emanations of individual creativity is to break down the distinction between writers and readers and to assault the concept of an immortal literary canon, not least with regard to the icon that is William Shakespeare.[84] It is also a means of uncovering the fluidity of communicative practices in the past.

Texts in early modern England and early New England underwent many forms of mediation. In a climate in which books were increasingly regarded as articles of commerce, it should not surprise us that published authors had negligible rights. The licensing records of the Stationers' Company rarely registered their names; printers sometimes stripped them from the title pages of books which did not sell and substituted that of someone else; and the legal concepts of plagiarism and intellectual property were scarcely embryonic.[85] This state of affairs assists in explaining why many preachers, like poets, playwrights, and musicians, preferred to circulate their works in manuscript. Chirographical transmission afforded a writer greater control over the process of reproduction and enabled the author to select an exclusive circle of readers rather than suffer the indignity of promiscuous consumption.[86] In England the forces of the marketplace were gradually dissolving traditional client-patron relations. The commercialization of printing was helping both to "canonize" literary figures like Philip Sidney, Ben Jonson, George Herbert, and John Donne[87] and to bring about the birth of the semi-professional writer. However, the majority of those who made a living by "scribbling" in London were balladmongers, pamphlet "stitchers," and hack translators, hirelings of printers who mercilessly exploited their meager talents and to a large extent dictated the nature of their output.[88]

Indeed, just as the process of material transmission by scriveners and copyists introduced changes into an original, so did printers and bookseller-publishers play an important part in molding the form and content of texts.[89] The personnel of printing offices were commonly responsible for punctuating copy texts and correcting proofs; on many occasions they made even more forceful editorial interventions in transforming a manuscript into a saleable book. Here we need to pay attention to the "packaging" strategies employed by these businessmen, including the eye-catching woodcuts they inserted in English news pamphlets and ballads to hook potential buyers, and to their role in preparing the preliminary apparatus of title page, epistle "to the reader," and dedication.

This prefatory matter or "pre-text,"[90] which might also be produced by a well-meaning patron or friend, instructed readers how they should understand and use the texts that followed—in the case of devotional tracts, as an aid to meditation, penitence, and, ultimately, inward reception of the Holy Spirit. However they may have been influenced by these "pretexts," people clearly brought their own beliefs and experiences to a text and re-made it yet again. Roger Chartier, Bill Sherman, and others have taught us that reading is not a passive, mechanical process, but an act of "poaching" in which readers are not submissive inferiors but "equal partners" with authors and printers "in the creation of meaning."[91] As Barbara A. Johnson has shown in her study of the reception of John Bunyan's *Pilgrim's Progress*, readers appropriated books in keeping with their own expectations, though the materialities of a text and all that counts as "pre-text" enter into this process as well. The ways in which the laity "read" the quasi-official definition of Congregational church order in New England, the "Cambridge Platform" of 1648, is another example of this process.⁹² Readers were even more literally involved in the making of John Foxe's *Actes and Monuments*, supplying fresh accounts of the sufferings of the martyrs and the hideous providential punishments that had befallen their persecutors to be incorporated in subsequent editions.⁹³

Sermons are exceptionally revealing about the fluidities of transmission for two telling reasons: only a tiny fraction of all sermons that were preached survive in manuscript or printed texts, and in making the transition from speech to script or print a sermon underwent substantial changes. Echoing countless Elizabethan and early Stuart clergymen, the New England minister Increase Mather frankly acknowledged in the preface to *The Wicked Mans Portion* (1675) that the lecture as heard by his original audience and the version he now presented to the reading public were considerably different.⁹⁴ This difference was due in large part to the puritan practice of delivering sermons from memory or from skeletal notes, it being assumed that a full text compromised the likeness between the preacher and a divinely inspired prophet in the Israelite mould. In attempting to reconstruct many months later the rousing discourses they had declared from the pulpit, busy ministers such as Thomas Gataker inevitably introduced significant alterations.⁹⁵ If such discrepancies were characteristic of sermons seen through the press by their progenitors, they must have been even more prevalent in those derived from manuscript notes taken down in shorthand by admiring auditors or edited posthumously by grieving colleagues. Francis Marbury's *Notes on the Doctrine of Repentance* (1602), for instance, was published "without anie reforming of mine own," while the oeuvre of "silver-tongued" Henry Smith presents particularly intractable problems to modern bibliographers.⁹⁶ Detailed examination of the printed sermon-series of Thomas Hooker reveals how extensively his London bookseller-publishers revised their copies, some of which were products of the art of "brachigraphy," and Kenneth Parker and Eric Carlson's careful study has shown that much material of uncertain provenance was incorporated into printed editions of the celebrated "sayings" of the Cambridgeshire minister Richard Greenham, a collection of axioms which had hithero circulated scribally and orally.[97]

The shaping and reshaping of religious texts also had much to do with how authors, editors, and booksellers responded to the constraints of genre, audience, and regulation. As Ian Green has pointed out, for instance, hundreds of catechisms published in early modern England forgo extended discussion of knotty theological topics such as the doctrine of election. The Calvinist clergy who prepared them evidently felt that it was wise to steer clear of controversy and concentrate instead on fostering clear understanding of the basic tenets of Christianity and on inculcating personal morality.[98] Only in the rarefied atmosphere of the university or in the context of a "plaine syllogistical" dispute, as occurred among the New England ministers at the synod of 1637, was it appropriate to air and debate predestinarian dogma, though here too the pressure of ecclesiastical politics in the Stuart period often left its mark in subtle equivocations and readjustments.[99] For evidence of a different type of mediation, we may turn to J. C. Davis's stimulating analysis of the short-lived Ranter frenzy of 1650-1651, which suggests that enterprising booksellers may have invented an enemy to satisfy the thirst of readers with an avid interest in lurid tales of deviants.[100]

Cheap print in general strongly reinforces many of the points made in this section. Penny "godlies," narratives of executions, "last dying speeches" of notorious criminals, and reports of strange prodigies are preeminent examples of texts that were the outcome of dialogue, compromise, and struggle between authors, publishers and readers. Often anonymous as well as theologically ambivalent, these ballads and chapbooks seem to have been produced by a combination of "pot poets" and evangelical pastors, both of whom were at the mercy of the financial ambitions of the publishers who specialized in such ephemera. Popular moralists such as Philip Stubbes straddled the boundary between Grub Street and godly society ambidextrously. The slavish imitation of homiletic discourse practiced by professional writers often makes it difficult to distinguish between ordained ministers and laymen who mimicked them.[101] The "marketplace theologians" of early-seventeenth-century England are equally elusive figures, at least some of whom may have been versatile hacks employed by profit-seeking stationers rather than beneficed preachers.[102] Similarly, "Robert and Richard Burton" were nothing more than pseudonyms under which the bookseller Nathaniel Crouch compiled inexpensive histories and sensational anthologies of wonders.[103] Research by Patrick Collinson, Tessa Watt, and Peter Lake adds a further dimension. In the early years of Elizabeth's reign a number of preachers actively appropriated the ballad as an evangelizing tool, writing Reformed lyrics to the devil's own tunes. Half a century later, ministers like Henry Goodcole were ingeniously converting the murder pamphlet into a vehicle for teaching distinctively Calvinist lessons about the machinations of Satan and the human propensity to sin, while Eamon Duffy has identified some late-seventeenth-century "penny godlies" as the work of nonconformist ministers such as Richard Baxter, Henry Stubbs, and Thomas Wadsworth intent on using print as an arm of their mission to the poor.[104] Across the Atlantic, comparable attempts were made to reshape the almanac into a providential primer, with only limited success in the longer run. Harvard graduates like Samuel Danforth purified local imprints of red-letter days, references to Christmas, and the detailed prognostications which were a hallmark of the ancient science of judicial astrology.[105]

To describe this body of material as a form of "religious literature" is to stretch conventional categories, for it contradicts the Weberian assumption that the Protestant Reformation, in alliance with the press, suppressed beliefs which would now be labeled "superstitious" and "irrational." It is also to call into question the highly intellectualized picture of Protestantism in early modern England and New England painted by historians who have focused on a narrow range of texts with little heed to how they were mediated. And it is to draw attention to the complex interactions between piety and profit, business initiative and clerical zeal that were characteristic of the print cultures of both these societies.

The last remaining task of this essay is double-stranded: to explore the ways in which speech, writing, and print were implicated in the expression of public opinion and political opposition in the two worlds of John Winthrop, and to consider the role of religion in these processes.

Censorship has a place in this story, for it affected the reproduction and transmission of texts. In an era in which modern concepts of freedom of expression are anachronistic, the right of the established Church and government to regulate the press and utilize it as an instrument of hegemony was almost uncontested. In England, the essential organs of the system were the Privy Council, Court of Star Chamber, High Commission, and the Corporation of London, while the linchpins of its daily operations were the episcopal chaplains who acted as licensers. The massive erosion of religious consensus caused by the Reformation presented particular challenges. In the reigns of Henry VIII, Mary, and Elizabeth I, a series of statutes and proclamations prohibiting publication of "lewd," "seditious," and "heretical" works by Jesuits, seminary priests, familists, and separatists streamed forth, betraying intense anxiety about books as begetters of "schism" and corrupters of the "simpler sort."[106] The Star Chamber decree of 1586 significantly tightened up the procedures for licensing, and the 1590s saw a sharp assault on acerbic satires in the wake of the Marprelate Controversy and its acrimonious spin-off, the Nashe-Harvey flyting. The controversies surrounding the rise of Arminianism in the reign of James prompted the suppression of several provocative works, including Richard Montagu's *Appello Caesarem* in 1625. Both overt and oblique criticism of the Spanish Match and Protestant England's lukewarm stance in the Thirty Years' War caught the eye of the censor in the course of that decade. The years of Personal Rule saw the proscription of a number of dissident puritan tracts and the corporeal punishment of those who had authored them: William Prynne's *Histrio-mastix* (1633) notoriously made martyrs of this outspoken barrister's ears.[107]

Whereas an older generation of historians tended to depict censorship in the Laudian period as a tyrannical device and to integrate it into a whiggish narrative of Stuart absolutism, more recent work by Sheila Lambert and others has strongly questioned the ability of the government to stifle the articulation of radical views. The intermittent and spasmodic character of regulation in the 1620s and 1630s has become a keynote of revisionist accounts, and the claims made in Milton's passionate apology for free speech, *Aeropagitica* (1644), have been cut down to size.[108] On balance, censorship in this period seems to have been neither a crippling straitjacket nor a flimsy scarecrow. The summoning of the Long Parliament and the descent into Civil War witnessed the collapse of Caroline control of the press (however effective), though ironically the later 1640s and 1650s were marked by fresh calls for regulation by those who had formerly been its victims. In his famous *Gangraena* (1646), for instance, the presbyterian lecturer Thomas Edwards insisted that censorship was the only cure for the cancer of radical sectarianism.[109]

At least initially, operations in early New England were on such a small scale and the relations among press, church, state, and Harvard College so close that there was little need for elaborate regulatory mechanisms. Contrary to the situation in pre-1640 England, no attempt was made to regulate the contents of the almanacs that the Cambridge printer began to issue in the 1640s, doubtless because the authors were suitably orthodox graduates of and tutors at Harvard College.[110] Not until the 1660s did the Massachusetts government finally introduce a formal system of licensing, shortly after the English Parliament passed the Licensing Act of 1662. It did so in response both to the stirrings of competition between the printers Marmaduke Johnson and Samuel Green and to the sharper factionalism within orthodox circles that became dramatically evident in the aftermath of the Synod of 1662, when for the first time a book appeared in which three ministers, John Davenport, Charles Chauncy, and Increase Mather attacked the position taken by the majority of their colleagues on the question of baptism as a privilege available to parents who were not "full" members of the Church and, even more significantly, appealed over their heads to the laity.[111] Hitherto the only printed texts that had been subject to any form of suppression were John Eliot's embarrassingly "republican" description of *The Christian Commonwealth*, published in London in 1659, William Pynchoon's *The Meritorious Price of Our Redemption* (London, 1650), and heterodox books brought across the Atlantic by stray Baptists and Quaker itinerants during the period of the Civil War and Commonwealth–books whose doctrinal and political range attest to the near absence and inefficiency of external restrictions in revolutionary England.[112]

Throughout the period script and print could be powerful weapons in the hands of the persecuted, exiled, and dispossessed. Members of marginalized religious groups made adept use of the press as a proselytizing agent. The connection between Lollardy and illicit texts was well cemented by the late fifteenth century and conventicles drew strength from the circulation of vernacular translations of the scriptures and other spiritual tracts.[113] Under Mary I, Protestant refugees on the Continent mounted an impressive propaganda campaign to reclaim their country from the clutches of popery; separatists who found a safe haven in the Low Countries smuggled polemic against the established Church back across the Channel; and the imported writings of the mysterious "H. N." helped sustain the secretive nicodemite sect of the Family of Love.[114] Illegal publishing likewise played a vital role in the development of early Quakerism into a coherent national movement, helping its leaders to maintain internal discipline among the "Friends" as well as to engage in an external dialogue with the Interregnum regime on the vexed question of a religious settlement.[115] No less notable is the way in which the post-Reformation Catholic community made a virtue out of the necessity of its dependence on print, utilizing books as "domme preachers" and surrogate priests.[116] No clandestine printing occurred in New England because it was not in the interests of the Cambridge or Boston printers to defy the civil government, but some critics did turn to scribal publication.[117]

So, in both contexts, censorship is perhaps better described as a loosely woven mesh than a heavy iron grille. Yet this does not mean that it can be dismissed as insignificant. The fact that contemporaries perceived regulation of the press to be more than a paper tiger is a point of some importance: among other things it encouraged forms of dissimulation, evasion, and self-imposed silence. Alison Shell observes that a perfunctory denunciation of popery in the preface sometimes permitted Catholic devotional tracts to slip by the censor undetected,[118] while Anthony Milton has illuminated some of the more subtle and insidious ways in which opinion was manipulated and conditioned in the 1620s and 1630s, showing how licensers "massaged" texts to make them "speak with a Laudian accent" and benignly removed starkly presbyterian or anti-ceremonialist sentiments from Calvinist works to render them innocuous in a changing theological climate.[119] Wishing to conceal and simultaneously to reveal their opinions, many writers resorted to indirection, employing allusion and other textual strategies to disguise subversive statements, strategies which Annabel Patterson has argued were critical in the making of "imaginative literature."[120] In the case of the politicized election sermons of mid-seventeenth-century New England or the much-debated radicalism of John Milton, devices of this kind can make these texts almost impenetrable to modern readers.[121] Never quite certain of what was acceptable to the ecclesiastical mainstream, authors engaged in still another species of self-censorship when the boundaries of orthodoxy shifted. After the Restoration, for instance, Richard Baxter rejected or reinterpreted some of what he had written earlier about a holy commonwealth. Baxter's own autobiography received rough handling from his editors, who removed passages which did not accord with their politics, while George Fox's journal was stripped of some of the ecstatic apocalypticism he had expressed in the 1650s when it was printed posthumously forty years later.[122]

The presence of a system of censorship also helps to explain the prevalence of scribal publication. In Elizabethan and Jacobean England, prudence moved many a writer who objected to state or church policy to circulate his criticism in manuscript. This was the medium Philip Sidney selected for a letter protesting against the proposed Anjou marriage, a move which seems wise in the light of John Stubbs' savage punishment for publishing *The Discoverie of the Gaping Gulf* in 1579.[123] Anonymous handwritten libels are another indication of the pervasiveness of this practice, together with the many scribal copies of defiant Catholic texts like *Leicesters Commonwealth* (1585) and Edmund Campion's famous "Brag," which did the rounds of the recusant underground and survive in British archives.[124] Indeed, Harold Love has suggested that in the seventeenth century script as a medium was inherently oppositional—"a vehicle for ideological debate within the governing class"— and insisted that its significance was greatest during decades marked by the airing of dissent.[125] For the troubled 1620s and 1630s, an abundance of evidence supports this assertion. Provincial gentlemen like William Davenport kept in touch with developments in the capital by means of the widespread circulation of newsletters and "separates" containing transcripts of speeches and proceedings in parliament, state trials, diplomatic negotiations and military dispatches;[126] at a lower social level, scurrilous libels and mocking rhymes dispersed in public places gave expression to popular hatred of political scapegoats such as the Duke of Buckingham.[127] Moreover, much of the anti-Laudian polemic that flooded from the presses in the early 1640s had been scribally published during the Personal Rule. As the London schoolmaster John Vicars had confided to a colleague in 1636, "MS[S] are nowe the best help Gods people have to vindicate the Truth, printing being now a dayes prohibited to them, especially if their writings have any least tang or tincture of opposition to Arminianisme yea or even to Poperie itself."[128] Arthur Marotti has also called attention to the volume of obscene verse and political satire that circulated in manuscript, citing, among many other examples, Royalist writings denouncing the Cromwellian regime in the 1650s.[129] This is not to say that scribal publication was an entirely fail-safe way of expressing dissident views: fear of official interception of private letters seems to have induced Robert Reyce to adopt various pseudonyms when writing to John Winthrop in Massachusetts with news of the imposition of ship money and the attack on the puritan sabbath enshrined in the revived Book of Sports of 1633.[130]

The New England side of the story has never been adequately studied, but a close reading of Winthrop's journal-history indicates that his political opponents within the civil government made effective use of scribal transmission to mobilize dissent. By the early 1640s, a coalition of gentry from Middlesex and Essex counties was challenging Winthrop and his allies on a variety of issues. These included a long-running dispute over the ownership of a pig and the proposal, backed by Winthrop, for a "Standing Council" that would exercise substantial authority between sessions of the General Court. Thus at a General Court meeting in the spring of 1642 the legislators debated what to do about an unsigned handwritten text criticizing the Standing Council as "a sinful innovation." This manuscript had already circulated, having been transmitted to William Hathorne and passed on to a freeman before coming into the hands of Thomas Dudley, who, together with one of the Salem ministers, had written a reply. The majority resisted Winthrop's call for inquiry to be made after the author, apparently knowing his identity all too well, and after prolonged debate it was agreed that the guilty party would not be subject to censor. Later that year when the stray sow, or Robert Keayne affair, was arousing "much contention" in the General Court and "great expectation in the country," the governor and his supporters "publish[ed] a declaration of the true state of the cause" in an attempt to sway public opinion. Probably distributed in multiple copies, this too elicited a scribal counter-text airing the views of the plaintiffs. Much to Winthrop's dissatisfaction, it persuaded "many of the elders that justice had yet to be done."[131] As these and other episodes reveal, script could be a supple and flexible device for disseminating ideas at odds with those of the political establishment.

So too could the slippery and ephemeral medium of speech. In recent years, the ears of historians of early modern England and New England have become more attuned to the part which rumor, gossip, conversation, and orally disseminated news played in the formation of what it is fashionable to call "the public sphere." Alastair Bellany,

Pauline Croft, and Adam Fox have shown that libels, rhymes, and lampoons were a means by which Englishmen and women of humble origin not only reproved their social superiors but expressed their views on local and national political issues. Yielding insight into popular attitudes towards popery and puritanism, the court, constitution, and monarchy, they both reflected and engendered the discontent that culminated in the outbreak of fighting between King and Parliament in 1642.[132] Richard Cust has similarly argued that the oral (and scribal) dissemination of news helped create a perception of politics as an adversarial rather than a consensual process and to undermine the legitimacy of the Stuart regime.[133] The work of Dagmar Freist extends this insight for our understanding of the turbulent early 1640s, when the participation of the ordinary people in political discourse assumed new depth and direction.[134] Jane Kamensky has adopted a similar perspective in exploring the threat which the spoken word often presented to uniformity, hierarchy, and patriarchy in New England.[135] Here, as in England, contemporaries struggled with the contradictions that inhered in the understanding of speech itself, a medium they regarded as a vehicle of divine revelation and order but also as one prone to instability and subversion. Indeed, in the early years of Massachusetts's history, the authorities moved quickly to punish transgressions of the tongue, and did so far more frequently than they punished offenses of the pen and press. These processes were gendered in the sense that speech in general and gossip in particular were widely regarded as women's weapons, even if in practice men were just as frequently accused of misspeaking.[136] And they acquired confessional and denominational overtones because religious minorities were quick to realize that oral modes had the advantage of leaving behind no incriminating evidence.

This survey of the links between communicative practices and the forging of public opinion may serve as a commentary upon Jürgen

Habermas's influential model of the emergence of a "public sphere" in the eighteenth century, a space aside from that claimed by Europe's absolute monarchies in which civil society could conduct "rational public discussion."[137] Habermas's thesis has stimulated much critical interest in historical circles, not least his claim that the birth of "public opinion" as a critical factor in politics was essentially a consequence of the Enlightenment.[138] In a recent book, David Zaret has contested this chronology and argued that the origins of the "public sphere" and of "democratic culture" lie in the mid seventeenth-century English Revolution. He sees them as byproducts of the profound practical transformations that the technology of print wrought in the realm of political communication.[139] But his suggestion that print alone provided the right conditions in which open ideological debate could occur surely runs the risk of according the press exaggerated importance as a revolutionary force and reviving an historical trope that it has been one of the chief aims of this essay to question and unsettle. His argument privileges print over oral and scribal modes such as preaching and letter-writing, which, as we have seen, played a crucial role in undermining orthodoxy and fostering criticism and opposition.[140] It also implicitly perpetuates the assumption that illiteracy effectively barred people from exercising a "political" voice.

Both in England and New England, then, print, script, and speech coexisted in a complex symbiosis. In two societies where literacy was a highly fluid and pluralistic phenomenon, there was a lively interface between the typographical medium and the thriving cultures of the written and spoken word which predated, and throughout this period, were neither displaced nor dominated by it. This may be particularly true of early Massachusetts, where the book trade was relatively primitive and underdeveloped for at least a generation. Texts of all kinds were the outcome of a series of interactions and transactions, interactions between different media and transactions between authors, publishers, and readers and between commercial incentives, the constraints of censorship, and religious and political ideals and priorities. These insights strike at the heart of the other influential paradigm that we have placed under the microscope, the assumption that Protestantism and the Reformation had a peculiar affinity with literacy, writing, and print. Scrutiny of seventeenth-century religious culture on both sides of the Atlantic suggests that this is a commonplace in need of serious refinement. It demonstrates that the relationship between them was far more interesting, equivocal, and intricate.

The scholarship we have been summarizing also has important wider implications for our understanding of "religion" and, perhaps especially, "religious belief." In seeking to describe sixteenth- and seventeenth-century piety, historians of early modern England and New England have commonly relied upon sermons and treatises written by ordained clergy trained at Oxford, Cambridge, or Harvard. Anyone attempting to delineate the history of doctrine must rely on texts of this kind, as must any systematic account of the "practical divinity" that was the substance of parish preaching. Historians who are interested in popular religion may draw on such texts, but are more inclined to rely on the formats and genres of "cheap print," together with the "texts" of visual or material culture. None of this evidence is unproblematic. For no printed text can authorial control be taken for granted; few, if any, are free from the interventions of the book trade or from some form of censorship, and in the special case of cheap print, some if not most of it seems to have been written by professional writers who recycled stock characters and tropes. Too often, text-based generalizations about "religion" have rested (as Anne Hutchinson said of a works-based assurance of salvation) on "sandy foundations," that is, upon an insufficient awareness of the mechanisms of cultural production as sketched in this essay. As Ian Green's study of religious bestsellers has recently demonstrated, these interventions greatly complicate our assumptions about the shape, meaning, and monolithic character of theology, popular belief, and, indeed, of Protestantism.[141] And in those rare cases where the sources permit us to penetrate an individual mentality more deeply, intellectual coherence gives way to an extraordinary patchwork that cannot be found in any single text or set of texts.[142] We need, in conclusion, to become more closely attuned to the fluidity, heterogeneity, and plurality of the religion of Protestants in both England and New England.

Notes

*Readers should note that this essay was completed and sent to press in 2001. Apart from an indication of some work published in the years since in the footnotes, it has not been possible to take full account of historiographical developments in the interim.

1. *The Winthrop Papers* (Boston, 1929-), 2:105-106; hereafter cited as *Winthrop Papers*.
2. See Anthony Pagden, *The Fall of Natural Man: The American Indian and the Origins of Comparative Ethnology* (Cambridge, 1982), esp. 127-131, 162-164, 179-190; Stephen Greenblatt, *Marvelous Possessions: The Wonder of the New World* (Oxford, 1991), esp. 7-12; Walter D. Mignolo, *The Darker Side of the Renaissance: Literacy, Territoriality and Colonization* (Ann Arbor, Mich., 1995), 69-122.
3. L. Brinkmair, *The Warnings of Germany* (London, 1638), sig. *2v.
4. Henry Bradshaw, *The Life of Saint Werburge of Chester*, ed. Carl Horstmann, Early English Text Society, Old Series 88 (London, 1887), 131; Richard Baxter, *The Poor Husbandman's Advocate* (1691), quoted in David Cressy, *Literacy and the Social Order: Reading and Writing in Tudor and Stuart England* (Cambridge, 1980), 4.
5. See the comments of Jonathan Barry, "Literacy and Literature in Popular Culture: Reading and Writing in Historical Perspective," in *Popular Culture in England, c. 1500-1850*, ed. Tim Harris (Basingstoke, Eng., 1995), 90-91;

and Raymond Williams, *Keywords: A Vocabulary of Culture and Society* (London, 1976, 1983), 183-188.

6. See Alexandra Walsham and Julia Crick, "Introduction: Script, Print and History," in Julia Crick and Alexandra Walsham, eds., *The Uses of Script and Print 1300-1700* (Cambridge, 2004), 1-26.

7. Ruth Finegan, "Literacy as Mythical Charter," in *Literacy: Interdisciplinary Conversations*, ed. Deborah Keller-Cohen (Cresskill, N.J., 1994), 38.

8. But see Sandra L. Gustafson, *Eloquence is Power: Oratory and Performance in Early America* (Chapel Hill, 2000), 1-39, and Alexandra Walsham, "Reformed Folklore? Cautionary Tales and Oral Tradition in Early Modern England," in *The Spoken Word: Oral Culture in the British Isles 1500-1850*, ed. Adam Fox and Daniel Woolf (Manchester, Eng., 2001), 173-195.

9. See, generally, Ian Green, *Print and Protestantism in Early Modern England* (Oxford, 2000), and, with particular reference to the sermon, James Rigney, "'To Lye Upon a Stationer's Stall, Like a Piece of Course Flesh in a Shambles': The Sermon, Print and the English Civil War," in *The English Sermon Revised: Religion, Literature and History 1600-1750*, ed. Lori Anne Ferrell and Peter McCullough (Manchester, Eng., 2000), 188-207.

10. See Barbara A. Johnson, *Reading Piers Plowman and The Pilgrim's Progress: Reception and the Protestant Reader* (Carbondale, Ill., 1992); John R. Knott, *The Sword of the Spirit: Puritan Responses to the Bible* (Chicago, 1980); David D. Hall, *Worlds of Wonder, Days of Judgment: Popular Religious Belief in Early New England* (New York, 1989), 21-70.

11. See, e.g., Daniel Vickers, *Farmers and Fisherman: Two Centuries of Work in Essex County, Massachusetts, 1630-1850* (Chapel Hill, 1994).

12. Americanists do not hesitate to use the name "Puritanism" for this version of English Protestantism, even as students of English Protestantism have been questioning the merits of the term. For a fuller account of communicative practices in early New England than can be provided here, see Hugh Amory and David D. Hall, eds., *A History of the Book in America*. vol. 1, *The Colonial Book in the Atlantic World* (New York, 2000) [hereafter *CBAW*], 83-151. For England, see John Barnard and D. F. McKenzie with Maureen Bell, eds., *The Cambridge History of the Book in Britain* Vol. 4, *1557-1695* (Cambridge, 2002) [hereafter *CHBB 4*].

13. Grantland Rice, *The Transformation of Authorship in America* (Chicago, 1997); Philip Round, *"By Nature and By Custom Cursed": Transatlantic Civil Discourse and New England Cultural Production* (Hanover, N.H., 1998).

14. Quotations from *A Briefe and Necessarie Catachisme of Instruction, in Maister Derings Workes* (London, 1590), sig. A1v (now thought to be the work of John More); Laurence Chaderton, *An Excellent and Godly Sermon, Most Needefull for this Time* (London, 1580), sig. A3r; Thomas Jackson, *Londons New-Yeeres Gift* (London, 1609), sigs. A2r-v.

15. Maureen Bell and John Barnard, "Provisional Count of STC Titles 1475-1640," *Publishing History* 31(1992):48-64.

16. On almanacs, see Bernard Capp, *Astrology and the Popular Press: English Almanacs 1500-1800* (London, 1979), 23; on ballads, Tessa Watt, *Cheap Print and Popular Piety 1550-1640* (Cambridge, 1991), 11-127; on catechisms, Ian Green, *The Christian's ABC: Catechisms and Catechizing in England, c. 1530-1740* (Oxford, 1996), 45-92; on bibles, Green, *Print and Protestantism*, 42-100; on longer "theological" books, Kari Konkola, "'People of the Book': The Production of Theological Texts in Early Modern England," *Papers of the Bibliographical Society of America*, 94(2000/1):5-34, and on other kinds of devotional literature, Green, *Print and Protestantism*, 168-444.

17. See Keith Thomas, "From Edification to Entertainment: Oral Tradition and the Printed Word in Early Modern England," *Times Literary Supplement* (Aug. 23, 1991), 5-6.

18. Edward Arber, ed., *A Transcript of the Registers of the Company of Stationers of London 1554-1640 A.D.* (London, 1875-1894), 2:482-512. Sidney's *The Countess of Pembroke's Arcadia* was entered on Aug. 23, 1588, but not published until 1590. For a survey of the variety of books, see H. S. Bennett, *English Books and Readers, 1558-1603* (Cambridge, 1965), 112-258, and *English Books and Readers, 1603-1640* (Cambridge, 1970), 87-198.

19. For just one example of a translated English pamphlet, see *Discours veritable et tres-piteux, de l'inondation et debordement de mer, survenu en six diverses provinces d'Angleterre* (Paris, 1607). See A. W. Pollard and G. R. Redgrave, *A Short-Title Catalogue of Books Printed in England, Scotland, and Ireland and of English Books Printed Abroad 1475-1640*, 2nd ed., rev. and enl. by W. A. Jackson, F. S. Ferguson and Katharine F. Pantzer (London, 1976-1991) [hereafter *STC*], a translation of STC 22915.

20. See Ian Breward, ed., *The Work of William Perkins*, The Courtenay Library of Reformation Classics (Abingdon, Eng., 1970), 613-632.

21. See Nigel Smith, *Literature and Revolution in England, 1640-1660* (New Haven, 1994), esp. 19, 257-263.

22. Bennett, *English Books and Readers 1558-1603*, 20-30.

23. For provincial booksellers, see Alexander Rodger, "Roger Ward's Shrewsbury Stock: An Inventory of 1585," *The Library*, 5th ser. 13(1958):247-268; Robert Davies, *A Memoir of the York Press . . . in the Sixteenth, Seventeenth and Eighteenth Centuries* (London, 1868); Ian Maxted, ed., "A Common Culture? The Inventory of Michael Harte, Bookseller of Exeter, 1615," in Todd Gray, ed., *Devon Documents: In Honour of Mrs Margery Rowe* (Tiverton, Eng., 1996), 119-126; John Barnard and Maureen Bell, "The English Provinces," in *CHBB* 4, 665-686.

24. See Margaret Spufford, *Small Books and Pleasant Histories: Popular Fiction and its Readership in Seventeenth Century England* (Cambridge, 1981), 111-128; Spufford, *The Great Reclothing of Rural England: Petty Chapmen and their Wares in the Seventeenth Century* (London, 1984); Watt, *Cheap Print*, 11-38; Michael Frearson, "The Distribution and Readership of London Corantos in the 1620s," in Robin Myers and Michael Harris, eds., *Serials and their Readers 1620-1914* (Winchester, Eng., 1993), 1-25.

25. British Library, Harleian MSS 389-90; *Winthrop Papers*, 1:290; 3:96.

26. As documented in Arber, *Stationers' Register*.

27. For the output of these printers, see *STC*, vol. 3. On Charlewood, Watt, *Cheap Print*, 51.

28. Bennett, *English Books and Readers 1558-1603*, 71-73; Bennett, *English Books and Readers 1603-40*, 59-66. Roger Ward, Nathaniel Butter, and Edward Wright were all fined for illegally printing copies of Arthur Dent's *A Sermon of Repentaunce* (1583), *STC* 6649.5-6670.

29. See Gerald D. Johnson, "John Trundle and the Book-Trade 1603-1626," *Studies in Bibliography* 39(1986):177-199. For an example of simultaneous publication of a ballad and pamphlet, Arber, *Stationers' Register*, 2: 570.

30. Bennett, *English Books and Readers 1603-1640*, 272-273.

31. Watt, *Cheap Print*, 74-127, 257-320.

32. As pursued, for instance, by William Brewster in the Netherlands, where he published, among others, William Ames. Keith L. Sprunger, *Trumpets from the Tower: English Puritan Printing in the Netherlands, 1600-1640* (New York, 1994).

33. Hugh Amory, "Printing and Bookselling in New England, 1638-1713," in *CBAW*, 83-116.

34. Amory, "Printing and Bookselling," 112-113.

35. Worthington C. Ford, *The Boston Book Market, 1670-1700* (Boston, 1917); Hugh Amory, "Under the Exchange: The Unprofitable Business of

Michael Perry, a Seventeenth-Century Boston Bookseller," *Proceedings of the American Antiquarian Society* 83(1993):31-60. Both this essay and that cited in n.36 have been reprinted in Hugh Amory, *Bibliography and the Booktrades: Essays on the Print Culture of Early New England*, ed. David D. Hall (Philadelphia, 2004).

36. *Winthrop Papers*, 3:118; Hugh Amory, "'A Bible and Other Books': Enumerating the Copies in Seventeenth-Century Essex County," in *Order and Connexion*, ed. R. C. Alston (Cambridge, 1997), 17-37.

37. Amory remarks, however, that Samuel Green "treated his license to print English as a privilege from which the printer of Indian books, Johnson, should rightly have been excluded." *CBAW*, 84.

38. Amory, "'A Bible and Other Books,'" in *CBAW*, 117-151; Hall, *Worlds of Wonder*, 251-255.

39. Thomas Shepard, *Eye-Salve* (Cambridge, Mass., 1673), 42.

40. See, for example, Christopher Durston and Jacqeline Eales, eds., *The Culture of English Puritanism, 1560-1700* (Basingstoke, Eng., 1996), 16.

41. In the 1670s, for example, Richard Baxter warned parents that if they neglected to teach their children to read they would thereby "deprive them of a singular help to their instruction and salvation." *A Christian Directory* (London, 1673), 548.

42. Peter Clark, "The Ownership of Books in England, 1560-1640: The Example of Some Kentish Townsfolk," in Lawrence Stone, ed., *Schooling and Society: Studies in the History of Education* (Baltimore, 1976), 99 and passim. The Leicestershire figures are cited in Laura Caroline Stevenson, *Praise and Paradox: Merchants and Craftsmen in Elizabethan Popular Literature* (Cambridge, 1984), 68-69.

43. The case of the laborer is cited in Margaret Spufford, "The Importance of Religion in the Sixteenth and Seventeenth Centuries," in Spufford, ed., *The World of Rural Dissenters 1520-1725* (Cambridge, 1995), 47. For Wallington, see Paul S. Seaver, *Wallington's World: A Puritan Artisan in Seventeenth Century London* (London, 1985), 5.

44. Luther is cited in M. H. Black, "The Printed Bible," in S. L. Greenslade, ed., *The Cambridge History of the Bible* (Cambridge, 1963), 3:432; John Foxe, *Acts and Monuments*, ed. S. R. Cattley (London, 1853-59), 3:720.

45. A. G. Dickens, *The German Nation of Martin Luther* (London, 1974), 103. See also the discussions of this theme in Jean-François Gilmont, ed., *The*

Reformation and the Book, trans. Karin Maag (Aldershot, Eng., 1998), esp. 1-9, 469-493.

46. For example, on the title-page of Foxe's *Acts and Monuments* (1563 and subsequent editions).

47. See Alexandra Walsham, "'Domme Preachers'? Post-Reformation English Catholicism and the Culture of Print," *Past & Present*, 168(2000): 72-123.

48. Persons' book was "purged" by Edmund Bunny. See R. McNulty, "A Protestant Version of Robert Persons' First Book of the Christian Exercise," *Huntington Library Quarterly* 23(1959-1960):221-300; Brad S. Gregory, "The 'True and Zealouse Service of God': Robert Parsons, Edmund Bunny and the *First Booke of the Christian Exercise*," *Journal of Ecclesiastical History* 45(1994):238-268; and Victor Houliston, "Why Robert Persons would not be Pacified: Edmund Bunny's Theft of The Book of Resolution," in Thomas McCoog, ed., *The Reckoned Expense: Edmund Campion and the Early English Jesuits* (Woodbridge, Eng., 1996), 159-177.

49. Daniel Featley, *Ancilla Pietatis* (London, 1626), sig. A6r.

50. See William Palmes, *The Life of Mrs Dorothy Lawson, of St Anthony's, near Newcastle-on-Tyne* (London, 1855).

51. See Patrick Collinson, *From Iconoclasm to Iconophobia: The Cultural Impact of the Second English Reformation*, The Stenton Lecture 1985 (Reading, Eng., 1986), 9.

52. Patrick Collinson, *The Birthpangs of Protestant England: Religious and Cultural Change in the Sixteenth and Seventeenth Centuries* (New York, 1988), 106-112; Watt, *Cheap Print*, 39-73; John King, *English Reformation Literature: The Tudor Origins of the Protestant Tradition* (Princeton, 1982) and Paul Whitfield White, *Theatre and Reformation: Protestantism, Patronage and Playing in Tudor England* (Cambridge, 1993).

53. See R. W. Scribner, "Oral Culture and the Diffusion of Reformation Ideas," repr. in his *Popular Culture and Popular Movements in Reformation Germany* (London, 1986), 49-69.

54. Stephen Egerton's dedicatory epistle to Richard Rogers, *The Practice of Christinaitie* (London, 1618), sigs. A3v-4r; and Egerton's *The Boring of the Eare* (London, 1623), sig. A8r.

55. Green, *The Christian's ABC*, esp. 93-229.

56. *Thomas Shepard's Confessions*, ed. George Selement and Bruce C. Woolley, *Publications of the Colonial Society of Massachusetts*, 58(1981). It is also telling that Shepard wrote *A Treatise on Ineffectual Hearing of the Word*, bound with *Subjection to Christ* (London, 1654), but little or nothing on how to read.

57. Sarah Goodhue, *A Valedictory and Monitory Writing* ([Cambridge?, 1681?], repr. in Thomas J. Waters, *Ipswich in the Massachusetts Bay Colony* (Ipswich, Mass., 1905), 1:519-524; Adam Fox, *Oral and Literate Culture in England, 1500-1700* (Oxford, 2000); Keith Thomas, "The Meaning of Literacy in Early Modern England," in Gerd Baumann, ed., *The Written Word: Literacy in Transition* (Oxford, 1986), 97-131.

58. Rigney, "The Sermon, Print and the Civil War," 196.

59. On this subject, see D. F. McKenzie, "Speech-Manuscript-Print," *The Library Chronicle of the University of Texas at Austin* 20(1990):87-109; Alexandra Walsham, *Providence in Early Modern England* (Oxford, 1999), 52-55. Humphrey Sydenham, *Natures Overthrow, and Deaths Triumph* (London, 1626), sig. a3v. On Tobie Matthew, who recorded 1992 sermons in his preaching diary, none of which were printed, see W. J. Sheils, "An Archbishop in the Pulpit: Tobie Matthew's Preaching Diary, 1606-1622," in Diana Wood, ed., *Life and Thought in the Northern Church, c. 1100-c.1700*, Studies in Church History, Subsidia 12 (Woodbridge, Eng., 1999), 381-405.

60. *An Ordinarie Lecture . . . Preached at the Blacke-Friers. And Taken as it was Uttered by Characterie* [by A. S.] (London, 1589). This was reprinted the same year "perused, corrected and amended by the author." He did, however, publish other material, including a catechism, much of it reluctantly. See *STC* 7527.5-7539. Rogers, *The Practice of Christianitie*, sig. a4r-v.

61. Harold Stein Jantz, *The First Century of New England Verse* (Worcester, Mass., 1944).

62. *Winthrop Papers*, 2:23, 25.

63. For the documents of the Antinomian Controversy, see David D. Hall, ed., *The Antinomian Controversy, 1636-1638: A Documentary History* 2nd ed. (Durham, N.C., 1990), ix, 44, 153, 174-175.

64. When eventually printed, the letters went through some eighty editions in English. John Coffey, *Politics, Religion and the British Revolutions: The Mind of Samuel Rutherford* (Cambridge, 1997), 26 and n.142.

65. Thomas Taylor, *The Works of that Faithful Servant of Jesus Christ, Dr. Thom. Taylor . . . Not Hitherto Published*, ed. Edmund Calamy et al (London, 1653), title page and sig. A3r.

66. Robert Bedingfield, *A Sermon Preached at Paules Crosse the 24. of October. 1624* (Oxford, 1625), sig. 2v.
67. John Dod and Robert Cleaver, *A Plaine and Familiar Exposition of the Ninth and Tenth Chapters of the Proverbs of Salomon* (London, 1612), sig. A3r. Quotation from the editors' epistle to the reader in Taylor, *Works*, sig. b1r.
68. See Rigney, "The Sermon, Print and the English Civil War," 196.
69. John Barlow, *Hierons Last Fare-well* (London, 1618), sig. A4r.
70. Richard Baxter, *A Treatise of Self-Denyall* (London, 1660), 126-128. Not until the close of the seventeenth century—the timing had much to do with the delayed arrival of a commercial book trade in the colonies—did anyone in New England decry the presence of "bad books," by which were meant certain ballads, romances, and tracts about fortune telling. See *The Diary of Cotton Mather*, ed. Worthington C. Ford (1911-1912; New York, 1957), 2:242.
71. See Gerald Strauss and Richard Gawthrop, "Protestantism and Literacy in Early Modern Germany," *Past & Present* 104(1984):31-55; and Strauss, "Lutheranism and Literacy: A Reassessment," in Kaspar von Greyerz, ed., *Religion and Society in Early Modern Europe* (London, 1984), 109-123.
72. Gilmont, ed., *The Reformation and the Book*, "Conclusion," quotation at 475. See also Alexandra Walsham, "Unclasping the Book? Post-Reformation English Catholicism and the Vernacular Bible," *Journal of British Studies* 42(2003):141-166.
73. See Cressy, *Literacy*, 1-18; Thomas, "Meaning of Literacy," 110-112; Thomas Lacqueur, "The Cultural Origins of Popular Literacy in England 1500-1850," *Oxford Review of Education* 2 (1976): 255-275; R. A. Houston, *Scottish Literacy and the Scottish Identity: Illiteracy and Society in Scotland and Northern England, 1600-1800* (Cambridge, 1985).
74. Thomas Elyot, *The Boke Named the Governour* (London, 1531); Roger Ascham, *The Scholemaster* (1570); A. T., *A Rich Store-house or Treasury for the Diseased* (London, 1596), title page. A good example of literacy as an aid to commercial success and upward mobility is Thomas Tyron, the son of an Oxfordshire tiler and plasterer who became a merchant after recognizing "the vast usefulness of Reading" at the age of thirteen. Tyron is discussed in Margaret Spufford, "First Steps in Literacy: The Reading and Writing Experiences of the Humblest Seventeenth-Century Autobiographers," *Social History* 4(1979):416.

75. Wilberforce Eames, "Early New England Catechisms," *Proceedings of the American Antiquarian Society* 12(1898):76-182.

76. *Records of the Governor and Company of the Massachusetts Bay in New England*, ed. Nathaniel B. Shurtleff (Boston, 1844-1854), 2:6-7, 203.

77. Shurtleff, *Records of Massachusetts Bay*, 3: 293, 294, 331.

78. Charles Chauncy, *Gods Mercy Shewed to His People in Giving Them a Faithful Ministry and Schooles of Learning* (Cambridge, Mass., 1665).

79. Geraldine J. Murphy, "Massachusetts Bay Colony: The Role of Government in Education" (Ph.D. diss., Radcliffe College, 1960).

80. On these themes, see Watt, *Cheap Print*, 11-253; Natasha Würzbach, *The Rise of the English Street Ballad, 1550-1650*, trans. Gayna Walls (Cambridge, 1990). On sermon repetition, see Patrick Collinson, "The English Conventicle," in W. J. Sheils and Diana Wood eds., *Voluntary Religion*, Studies in Church History 23 (Oxford, 1986), 240-244.

81. Quotations from Thomas, "Meaning of Literacy," 101; Barry Reay, *Popular Cultures in England 1550-1750* (London, 1998), 45 (and see 36-70 passim).

82. For England, see Spufford, "First Steps in Literacy," Thomas, "Meaning of Literacy," 101-103, commenting on Cressy's figures in *Literacy*, 176-177. For New England, Hall, *Worlds of Wonder*, 71-116; *CBAW*, 550 n.13.

83. See Thomas, "Meaning of Literacy," 104-105.

84. For an excellent summary of current bibliographical theory on the transmission of literary texts, see Douglas A. Brooks, "Prologue," in *From Playhouse to Printing House: Drama and Authorship in Early Modern England* (Cambridge, 2000).

85. Not until 1709 did a statute of Queen Anne formally locate literary property rights in authors rather than stationers.

86. See J. W. Saunders, "The Stigma of Print: A Note on the Social Bases of Tudor Poetry," *Essays in Criticism* 1(1951):139-164; Saunders, "From Manuscript to Print: A Note on the Circulation of Poetic MSS in the Sixteenth Century," *Proceedings of the Leeds Philosophical and Literary Society, Literary and Historical Section* 6(1951):507-528; Harold Love, *Scribal Publication in Seventeenth Century England* (Oxford, 1993); H. R. Woudhuysen, *Sir Philip Sidney and the Circulation of Manuscripts 1558-1640* (Oxford, 1996); McKenzie, "Speech-Manuscript-Print."

87. See Arthur F. Marotti, *Manuscript, Print, and the English Renaissance Lyric* (Ithaca, N.Y., 1995), 209-290 and passim; Joseph Loewenstein, "The

Script in the Marketplace," *Representations* 12(1985):101-114; Richard Helgerson, *Self-Crowned Laureates: Spenser, Jonson, Milton and the Literary System* (Berkeley, 1983).

88. See Lawrence Manley, *Literature and Culture in Early Modern England* (Cambridge, 1995), 297-371; Phoebe Sheavyn, *The Literary Profession in the Elizabethan Age*, 2nd edn, rev. by J. W. Saunders (Manchester, Eng., 1967); Edwin Haviland Miller, *The Professional Writer in Elizabethan England: A Study of Nondramatic Literature* (Cambridge, Mass., 1959).

89. For a powerful exposition of this theme, see Adrian Johns, *The Nature of the Book: Print and Knowledge in the Making* (Chicago, 1998).

90. Larzer Ziff, "Upon What Pretext: The Book and Literary History," *Proceedings of the American Antiquarian Society* 95(1985):297-315.

91. See, among Roger Chartier's many works on this topic, "Culture as Appropriation: Popular Cultural Uses in Early Modern France," in Steven L. Kaplan, ed., *Understanding Popular Culture: Europe from the Middle Ages to the Nineteenth Century* (Berlin, 1984), 229-253; "Texts, Printing, Readings," in Lynn Hunt, ed., *The New Cultural History* (Berkeley, 1989), 154-175; and Chartier, ed., *The Culture of Print: Power and the Uses of Print in Early Modern Europe*, trans. L. G. Cochrane (Cambridge, 1989). William H. Sherman, *John Dee: The Politics of Reading and Writing in the English Renaissance* (Amherst, Mass., 1995), quotation at 54. For an important discussion in the medieval context, see Suzanne Reynolds, *Medieval Reading: Grammar, Rhetoric and the Classical Text* (Cambridge, 1996).

92. Johnson, *Reading Piers Plowman and The Pilgrim's Progress*; Hall, *Worlds of Wonder*, 68-69.

93. On Foxe, see Walsham, *Providence*, 102-103; Thomas S. Freeman, "Fate, Faction and Fiction in Foxe's *Book of Martyrs*," *Historical Journal* 43(2000):601-623.

94. Increase Mather, *The Wicked Mans Portion* (Boston, 1675), preface; for another example see the essay by Winfred Herget cited in n.97. For just two examples of English preachers discussing the differences between the sermon as preached and the sermon as printed, see John Lawrence, *A Golden Trumpet to Rowse up a Drowsie Magistrate* (London, 1624), sig. a1r-v and Abraham Gibson, *The Lands Mourning, for Vaine Swearing: or the Downefall of Oathes* (London, 1613), sig. A4r.

95. See Thomas Gataker, *A Sparke Toward the Kindling of Sorrow for Sion* (London, 1621), sig. A4r.

96. Francis Marbury, *Notes on the Doctrine of Repentance* (1602), sig. A2r-v. On Smith, see *STC* 22656-22783.7.

97. Winifred Herget, "The Transcription and Transmission of the Hooker Corpus," in *Thomas Hooker: Writings in England and Holland, 1626-1633*, ed. George H. Williams et al. (Cambridge, Mass., 1975), 253-270. To compare the surviving scribal copies of documents thrown up by the Antinomian Controversy with each other and with contemporary printed versions based on other copies is to gain some sense of the level of mistakes that inevitably rose in the course of scribal transmission. See Hall, *The Antinomian Controversy*. Kenneth L. Parker and Eric J. Carlson, *Practical Divinity: The Works and Life of Reverend Richard Greenham* (Aldershot, Eng., 1998), 31-57.

98. Green, *The Christian's ABC*, 386 and 350-386, passim.

99. See Nicholas Tyacke, *Anti-Calvinists: The Rise of English Arminianism c. 1590-1640* (Oxford, 1987) and Peter White, *Predestination, Policy and Polemic: Conflict and Consensus in the English Church from the Reformation to the Civil War* (Cambridge, 1992), studies based largely on texts that circulated within university culture. Hall, *Antinomian Controversy*, 213.

100. J. C. Davis, *Fear, Myth and History: The Ranters and the Historians* (Cambridge, 1986), 107-110. For a parallel reading of the Synod of 1637's huffing and puffing about "Antinomian" errors, see Stephen Foster, "New England and the Challenge of Heresy, 1630-1660: The Puritan Crisis in Transatlantic Perspective," *William and Mary Quarterly*, 3rd series, 38(1981):624-660, and Michael P. Winship, *Making Heretics: Militant Protestantism and Free Grace in Massachusetts, 1636-1641* (Princeton, 2002).

101. See Walsham, *Providence*, 8-64, and "'A Glose of Godlines': Philip Stubbes, Elizabethan Grub Street and the Invention of Puritanism," in Susan Wabuda and Caroline Litzenberger, eds., *Belief and Practice in Reformation England* (Aldershot, Eng., 1998), 177-206.

102. See Hall, *Worlds of Wonder*, 52-53; Green, *Print and Protestantism*, 473-487; see also Watt, *Cheap Print*, 306-311.

103. See Robert Mayer, "Nathaniel Crouch, Bookseller and Historian: Popular Historiography and Cultural Power in Late Seventeenth-Century England," *Eighteenth Century Studies* 27 (1994):391-419.

104. Collinson, *Birthpangs*, 106-112; Watt, *Cheap Print*, 39-73; Peter Lake, "Deeds against Nature: Cheap Print, Protestantism and Murder in Early Seventeenth Century England," in Kevin Sharpe and Peter Lake, eds.,

Culture and Politics in Early Stuart England (Basingstoke, Eng., 1994), 257-283; Eamon Duffy, "The Godly and the Multitude in Stuart England," *The Seventeenth Century* 1(1986):47-49. See also Peter Lake with Michael Questier, *The Antichrist's Lewd Hat: Protestants, Papists & Players in Post-Reformation England* (New Haven, 2002).

105. See Hall, *Worlds of Wonder*, 58-61.

106. For examples, see 34 & 35 Henry VIII c. 1; 1 & 2 Philip and Mary c. 3; 1 Elizabeth c. 6; 23 Elizabeth c. 2; Paul L. Hughes and James F. Larkin, eds., *Tudor Royal Proclamations* (New Haven, 1964-1969), nos. 432, 443, 460, 561, 577, 580, 598, 652, 667, 672, 699, 709; James F. Larkin and Paul L. Hughes, eds., *Stuart Royal Proclamations*, Vol.1 *1603-1625* (Oxford, 1973), nos. 247, 256.

107. See, among other discussions, Bennett, *English Books and Readers 1558-1603*, 30-55; Bennett *English Books and Readers 1603-1640*, 40-58; Leona Rostenberg, *The Minority Press and the English Crown: A Study in Repression 1558-1625* (Niewkoop, Neth., 1979). On Montagu, see Sheila Lambert, "Richard Montagu, Arminianism and Censorship," *Past and Present* 124(1989):36-68.

108. For the notion of censorship as a crippling system, see Christopher Hill, "Censorship and English Literature," in his *Collected Essays* vol. 1 *Writing and Revolution in Seventeenth Century England* (Brighton, Eng., 1985), 32-71. For more recent revisionist accounts, Sheila Lambert, "State Control of the Press in Theory and Practice: The Role of the Stationers' Company before 1640," in Robin Myers and Michael Harris, eds., *Censorship and Control of Print in England and France 1600-1910* (Winchester, Eng., 1992), 1-32; Lambert, "The Printers and the Government, 1604-1637," in Robin Myers and Michael Harris, eds., *Aspects of Printing from 1600* (Oxford, 1987), 1-29; Lambert, "Richard Montagu, Arminianism and Censorship"; A. B. Worden, "Literature and Political Censorship in Early Modern England," in A. C. Duke and C. A. Tamse, eds., *Too Mighty to be Free: Censorship in Britain and the Netherlands* (Zutphen, Neth., 1987), 45-62; C. S. Clegg, *Press Censorship in Elizabethan England* (Cambridge, 1997) and *Press Censorship in Jacobean England* (Cambridge, 2001). For a useful summary of conflicting positions, see Nigel Wheale, *Writing and Society: Literacy, Print and Politics in Britain 1590-1660* (London, 1999), 69-84.

109. Thomas Edwards, *Gangraena: Or a Catalogue and Discovery of Many of the Errours, Heresies, Blasphemies and Pernicious Practices of the Sectaries of this Time*

(London, 1646), the subject of Ann Hughes's, *Gangraena and the Struggle for the English Revolution* (Oxford, 2004).

110. Capp, *Astrology*, 46-50, 273-274.

111. David D. Hall, "Readers and Writers in Early New England," in *CBAW*, 130.

112. Hall, "Readers and Writers in Early New England," in *CBAW*, 128-130.

113. See the relevant essays in Anne Hudson, *Lollards and their Books* (London, 1985); Hudson, *The Premature Reformation: Wycliffite Texts and Lollard History* (Oxford, 1988), esp. 166-168, 186-188, 460-461, 464, 467-468, 470-471; Margaret Aston, "Lollardy and Literacy," reprinted in her *Lollards and Reformers: Images and Literacy in Late Medieval England* (London, 1984), 193-217. For the theme of this paragraph, see generally Alexandra Walsham, "Preaching without Speaking: Script, Print and Religious Dissent," in Crick and Walsham, *The Uses of Script and Print 1300-1700*, 211-234; and Nigel Smith, "Nonconformist Voices and Books," in *CHBB* 4, 410-430.

114. For Marian Protestant initiatives, see David Loades, "Books and the English Reformation Prior to 1558," in Gilmont, *The Reformation and the Book*, 264-291; Andrew Pettegree, *Marian Protestantism: Six Studies* (Aldershot, Eng., 1996). For the separatists, Rostenberg, *Minority Press*, 190-198. For the Family of Love, Christopher W. Marsh, *The Family of Love in English Society, 1550-1630* (Cambridge, 1994), esp. 79-85; and for other pre-Civil War radicals' reliance on scribal publication, including translations of the *Theologia Germanica*, see David R. Como, *Blown by the Spirit: Puritanism and the Emergence of an Antinomian Underground in Pre-Civil-War England* (Stanford, 2004).

115. See Kate Peters, "Quaker Pamphleteering and the Development of the Quaker Movement, 1652-1656" (Ph.D. thesis, Cambridge University, 1996); Peters, "'The Quakers Quaking': Print and the Spread of a Movement," in Wabuda and Litzenberger, *Belief and Practice in Reformation England*, 250-267.

116. Walsham, "'Domme Preachers'?"

117. The first instance of a false imprint, at a moment when the governor had banned any publications on the subject, was Samuel Willard's critique of the judicial process in the Salem witch hunt of 1692, identified on the title page as the work of a printer-bookseller in New York, but the work of one of the Boston printers.

118. Alison Shell, "Catholic Texts and Anti-Catholic Prejudice in the Seventeenth-Century Book Trade," in Myers and Harris, *Censorship and Control of the Press*, 42.

119. Anthony Milton, "Licensing, Censorship and Religious Orthodoxy in Early Stuart England," *Historical Journal* 41(1998):625-651, quotation at 647.

120. Annabel Patterson, *Censorship and Interpretation: The Conditions of Reading and Writing in Early Modern England* (Madison, Wisc., 1984), building on the ideas of Leo Strauss, *Persecution and the Art of Writing* (Glencoe, Ill, 1952). See also Michael Wilding, *Dragon's Teeth: Literature in the English Revolution* (Oxford, 1987), 2, who comments that "to circumvent the consensus of non-political readings, new points of entry and departure can be taken . . . . The significant absence can illuminate the enigmatic. Rather than looking for overall political allegory . . . at a time of censorship, repression, and ready reprisal, it can sometimes be more profitable to assemble a network of allusions, to establish a field of potentially political reference."

121. See the reading of these sermons in Emory Elliott, *Power and the Pulpit in Puritan New England* (Princeton, 1975).

122. William Lamont, *Puritanism and Historical Controversy* (Montreal, 1996), 46, 73, 114; *The Journal of George Fox*, ed. John Nickalls (London, 1952), preface.

123. Woudhuysen, *Sir Philip Sidney*, 151 and in general 145-153.

124. Thomas H. Clancy, *Papist Pamphleteers: The Allen-Persons Party and the Political Thought of the Counter Reformation in England, 1572-1615* (Chicago, 1964), 237, 239; Nancy Pollard Brown, "Paperchase: The Dissemination of Catholic Texts in Elizabethan England," in Peter Beal and Jeremy Griffiths, eds., *English Manuscript Studies 1100-1700*, vol. 1 (Oxford, 1989), 121, 128.

125. Love, *Scribal Publication*, 184, 177-230 passim.

126. J. S. Morrill, "William Davenport and the 'Silent Majority' of Early Stuart England," *Journal of the Chester Archaeological Society*, 58(1975):115-129; F. J. Levy, "How Information Spread among the Gentry, 1550-1640," *Journal of British Studies* 21(1982):11-34; Richard Cust, "News and Politics in Early Seventeenth Century England," *Past & Present*, 112(1986):60-90.

127. Alastair Bellany, "'Raylinge Rymes and Vaunting Verse': Libellous Politics in Early Stuart England, 1603-1628," in Sharpe and Lake, *Culture and Politics*, 285-310, and "Libels in Action: Ritual, Subversion and the English Lit-

erary Underground, 1603-42," in Tim Harris, ed., *The Politics of the Excluded, c.1500-1850* (Basingstoke, Eng., 2001), 99-124; Pauline Croft, "Libels, Popular Literacy and Public Opinion in Early Modern England," *Historical Research* 68(1995):266-285; David Underdown, *A Freeborn People: Politics and the Nation in Seventeenth-Century England* (Oxford, 1996), 45-67.

128. Frederick S. Boas, ed., *The Diary of Thomas Crosfield M.A., B. D. Fellow of Queen's College, Oxford* (London, 1935), 89.

129. Marotti, *Manuscript, Print and the English Renaissance Lyric*, 75-133.

130. *Winthrop Papers*, 3:298, 356.

131. *The Journal of John Winthrop 1630-1649*, ed. Richard S. Dunn, James Savage, and Laetitia Yeandle (Cambridge, Mass, 1996), 390-391, 395-398.

132. See the references cited in n.127, and Martin Ingram, "Ridings, Rough Music and Mocking Rhymes in Early Modern England," in Barry Reay, ed., *Popular Culture in Seventeenth Century England* (London, 1985), 166-197; Adam Fox, "Ballads, Libels and Popular Ridicule in Jacobean England," *Past & Present* 145(1994):47-83; Patrick Collinson, "Ecclesiastical Vitriol: Religious Satire in the 1590s and the Invention of Puritanism," in John Guy, ed., *The Reign of Elizabeth I: Court and Culture in the Last Decade* (Cambridge, 1995), 150-170.

133. Cust, "News and Politics"; Adam Fox, "Rumour, News and Popular Political Opinion in Elizabethan and Early Stuart England," *Historical Journal* 40(1997):597-620. The single best New England source that demonstrates the circulating of news via speech is *The Diary of Samuel Sewall*, ed. M. Halsey Thomas (New York, 1973). See also Richard D. Brown, *Knowledge Is Power: The Diffusion of Information in Early America, 1700-1865* (New York, 1989).

134. Dagmar Freist, *Governed by Opinion: Politics, Religion and the Dynamics of Communication in Stuart London 1637-1645* (London, 1997).

135. Jane Kamensky, *Governing the Tongue: The Politics of Speech in Early New England* (New York, 1997). It should be noted, however, that court records do not support Kamensky's argument for three major crises, and that she has exaggerated the participation of women in crimes of speech.

136. For New England, see Mary Beth Norton, *Founding Mothers and Fathers: Gendered Power and the Forming of American Society* (New York, 1996), 243, 253. For England, see among others, Laura Gowing, *Domestic Dangers: Women, Words and Sex in Early Modern London* (Oxford, 1996), esp. 59-138; Steve Hindle, "The Shaming of Margaret Knowsley: Gossip, Gender and

the Experience of Authority in Early Modern England," *Continuity and Change* 9(1994):391-419; Bernard Capp, *When Gossips Meet: Women, Family, and Neighbourhood in Early Modern England* (Oxford, 2003).

137. Jürgen Habermas, *Structural Transformation of the Public Sphere* (1962; Cambridge, Mass., 1989).

138. See, for example, Craig Calhoun, ed., *Habermas and the Public Sphere* (Cambridge, Mass., 1992); Jonathan Barry, "A Historical Postscript," in Dario Castiglione and Lesley Sharpe, eds., *Shifting the Boundaries: Transformation of the Languages of Public and Private in the Eighteenth Century* (Exeter, Eng., 1995), 220-237.

139. David Zaret, *Origins of Democratic Culture: Printing, Petitions, and the Public Sphere in Early-Modern England* (Princeton, 2000). For an attempt to insert the marketplace into Habermas's model, see Alexandra Halasz, *The Marketplace of Print: Pamphlets and the Public Sphere in Early Modern England* (Cambridge, 1997).

140. On sermons and the public sphere, see Tony Claydon, "The Sermon, the 'Public Sphere' and the Political Culture of Late Seventeenth-Century England," in Ferrell and McCullough, *English Sermon Revised*, 208-234.

141. Green, *Print and Protestantism*.

142. See, for instance, the studies of Nehemiah Wallington, Richard Napier, Samuel Sewall, and John Taylor by Seaver, *Wallington's World*; Michael MacDonald, *Mystical Bedlam: Madness, Anxiety, and Healing in Seventeenth-Century England* (Cambridge, 1981); Hall, *Worlds of Wonder*, 213-238; and Bernard Capp, *The World of John Taylor the Water-Poet 1578-1653* (Oxford, 1994). The classic example is Carlo Ginzburg, *The Cheese and the Worms: The Cosmos of a Sixteenth-Century Miller*, trans. John and Anne Tedeschi (London, 1980).

Notes on Contributors

Lynn Botelho is associate professor of history at Indiana University of Pennsylvania and author of *Old Age and the English Poor Law, 1500-1700* (2004). She also co-authored *Women and Ageing in British Society Since 1500* (2001) and has written a number of articles on ageing in early modern England. She is currently working on a book about the ageing body and popular medicine.

Francis J. Bremer is chair of the history department at Millersville University of Pennsylvania and editor of the Winthrop Papers for the Massachusetts Historical Society. He is author of a number of books on Puritanism, most recently *John Winthrop: America's Forgotten Founding Father* (2003). He is preparing his next book, *Puritanism: An Early Attempt to Create the Kingdom of God in America*.

Richard Godbeer is professor of history at the University of Miami. He is author of *The Devil's Dominion* (1992), *Sexual Revolution in Early*

America (2002), *Escaping Salem: The Other Witch Hunt of 1692* (2004), and is currently writing a study of male friendship and romantic love in colonial and revolutionary America.

DAVID D. HALL, Bartlett Professor of New England Church History at the Harvard Divinity School, has written extensively on religion and society in seventeenth-century New England and England. Among his many books are: *The Faithful Shepard: A History of the New England Ministry in the Seventeenth Century* (1972) and *Worlds of Wonder, Days of Judgment: Popular Religious Belief in Early New England* (1989). Together with Hugh Amory, he edited and contributed to *The Colonial Book in the Atlantic World* (2000). Most recently, he published *Puritans in the New World: A Critical Anthology* (2004).

JAMES S. HART, JR., is professor of history at the University of Oklahoma and specializes in the legal and constitutional history of early modern Britain. His scholarship includes *Justice Upon Petition: The House of Lords and the Reformation of Justice, 1621-1675* and *The Rule of Law, 1603-1660: Crowns, Courts and Judges* (2003).

MARK A. PETERSON is associate professor of history at the University of Iowa and author of *The Price of Redemption: The Spiritual Economy of Puritan New England* (1997) as well as many articles about early New England history. He is currently at work on a book about Boston in the Atlantic World, 1630-1865.

RICHARD J. ROSS is professor of law and history at the University of Illinois (Urbana-Champaign) and specializes in the legal history of early America and early modern England. His most recent publication is: "Legal Communications and Imperial Governance in Colonial British and Spanish America," in *The Cambridge History of Law in America*, eds. Christopher Tomlins and Michael Grossberg (forthcoming, 2006).

MARK VALERI is E. T. Thompson Professor of Church History at Union Theological Seminary of Virginia. He has written about religious thought and social issues in eighteenth-century New England and is author of *Law and Providence in Joseph Bellamy's New England: The Origins of the New Divinity in Revolutionary New England* (1994). He has edited *Sermons and Discourses, 1730-1733* (1999) of Jonathan Edwards, and he currently is writing about religion and commercial exchange in Massachusetts from 1630 through 1770.

ALDEN T. VAUGHAN taught early American history and culture for many years at Columbia University, where he is now professor emeritus of history. Among his many publications are *New England Frontier: Puritans and Indians, 1620-1675* (1965; 3d ed., 1995); *The Puritan Tradition in America, 1620-1730* (1972); *American Genesis: Captain John Smith and the Founding of Virginia* (1975), and a collection of his essays, *Roots of American Racism* (1995). He is completing a book on indigenous Americans in the British Isles, 1500-1776.

VIRGINIA MASON VAUGHAN is professor of English at Clark University. She has published extensively on Shakespeare's plays, most notably *Shakespeare's Caliban: A Cultural History*, with Alden Vaughan (1991) and *Othello: A Contextual History* (1994). Her most recent book is *Performing Blackness on English Stages, 1500-1800* (2005).

ALEXANDRA WALSHAM is senior lecturer in history at the University of Exeter and has published widely on the religious and cultural history of early modern England. Among her works is *Providence in Early Modern England* (1999). Her most recent book is *Charitable Hatred: Tolerance and Intolerance in England 1500-1700* (2006). She is now working on *The Reformation of the Landscape: Religion, Memory, and Legend in Early Modern Britain*.

TOM WEBSTER, lecturer at the University of Edinburgh, specializes in religious history and the philosophy of history. He has written *Godly Clergy in Early Stuart England* (2003) and published an edition of the *Diary of Samuel Rogers, 1634-1638* (2004). He is co-editing the new *Encyclopedia on Puritanism* and researching possession and dispossession in Tudor and Stuart England.

INDEX

Abbot, George, 24, 28, 33, 41, 45
The ABC with Little Catechism (Day), 341
Abel being dead yet speaketh (Cotton), 350
Absolutism, 221, 260, 361
Act of supremacy, 243
Actors, 315–317
Adam, 53, 321
Admonition to Parliament (Field), 154
Adultery, 13, 267, 300
Advice manuals, 314, 339
Advowsons, 196–198
Aeropagitica (Milton), 361
Africans, 25–26, 60;
  court cases and, 73n.111;
  English attitudes toward, 40–45, 55–59;
  mentioned, 9. *See also*, slavery
Alchemy, 88, 96
Alcohol, 169, 170, 214
Alehouse keepers, 190
Algonquian Indians, 49, 343
Allgor, Catherine, 323
Almanacs, 339, 343, 345, 359, 363
Alms, 166
Alphabet, vernacular, 354
Amazons, 45
Ambrose, Isaac, 132
American Antiquarian Society, 93

American Indians, 16, 343;
  English and, 25, 26, 35, 45–55, 59, 60;
  mentioned, 9, 216.
  See also individual tribes
Ames, William, 3, 156, 157
Amory, Hugh, 342
Amurath, 38
Amussen, Susan, 294, 297, 313, 314
Anabaptist, 161
Ancient and Honorable Artillery Company, Boston, 95
Ancient constitution, 12–13;
  in England, 237–260;
  in Massachusetts, 260–278;
  primitive, 270;
  Saxon constitution and, 259, 263, 270, 277
Andrews, Charles M., 2
Andros, Sir Edmund, 269–270
Angleria, Peter Martyr, 41
Anglicans. *See* Church of England
Anglo-Irish, 29
Answeare unto Certaine Assertions (Knewstub), 205
Anti-ceremonialists, 364
Antichrist, 348. *See also* Catholicism
Antinomian Controversy, 90, 338, 349
Antinomians, 84, 147, 161

Antiquarianism, 245–246, 266
Anti-Semitism, 33–34. *See also* Jews
Apocalypticism, 364
Apology (Jewel), 243, 244
Apostates, 39
Appello Caesarem (Montagu), 361
Apprentices, 213, 298. *See also* Artisans, Women
Arbella (vessel), 50, 175, 211
Arbitration, 173, 176, 190, 216
Arcadia (Sidney), 339
Archbishops, 153, 201, 205, 244;
   of Canterbury, 154, 198;
   John Whitgift and, 201, 265;
   William Laud and, 200, 207, 209;
   of York, 134, 349.
Archdeacons, 200, 202
Aristotle, 241
Armada, Spanish, 6, 23, 31, 308, 339
Armado, Adriano de, Don, 32
Arminianism, 134, 362
Armitage, David, 1–2
Armorers, female, 298
Arson, 171
Articles of Enquiry, 198–199
Articles of Faith, 201
Artificial reason, 240, 251
Artisans, 81, 158, 160, 346;
   females as, 292, 298;
   shortage of, 168
Ascham, Roger, 351
Assimilation, 29–30, 54–55
Assistants, colonial, 220, 261
Assizes sessions, 12, 189, 194, 222, 246;
   John Winthrop and 205–206;
   judges and, 193, 212
Astrology, judicial, 360
Atheists, 129
Atlantic history, 1–5
Augustine, Saint, 244
Authority, 196, 291, 298;
   author and, 355;
   contempt of, 170;
   discretionary, 221;
   ecclesiastical, 198;
   gendering of, 93–94, 292, 293, 294–296, 304, 311;
   imperial, 249, 268;
   political, 94;
   practical, 300;
   royal, 194, 209, 253–254
Avarice, 147, 150

Bacon, Sir Francis, 152, 239, 262
Badger, Goodman, 166
Bailiffs, 189
Bailyn, Bernard, 165
Balkan Peninsula, 34
Ballads, 340, 343, 351, 356;
   popularity of, 339, 341, 353, 359
Bancroft, Archbishop, 201
Banks, Sir John, 218
Baptism, 34, 51, 354, 362
Barbados, 77
Barbary, 37, 54
Barlow, John, 351
Barratry, 172
Barrington, Sir Francis, 200, 201, 204, 210
Barry, John, 137
Bartholomew, William, 171
Basilikon Doron (James I), 248
Bate's Case, 258
Battle of Alcazar (Peele), 43
Baxter, Richard, 86, 335, 359, 364
Bay Psalm Book, 92
Bayly, Lewis, 75, 86
Baynes, Paul, 44
Beaver pelts, 169
Bedford, Bedfordshire, 118
Bedingfield, Robert, 350
Belcher, Joseph, 273
Bellany, Alastair, 367
Bellingham, Sir Richard, 210
Benefices. *See* Advowsons
Berkeley, William, 82
Bermuda, 55, 77, 82–84, 92
Best, George, 42–43
Beza, Theodore, 156
Bible, 157, 172, 335;
   access to, 353;
   Algonquian and, 343;
   economy and, 157, 166;
   Genevan, 132, 351;
   John Davenport and, 173–174;
   law and, 171–173, 266–267, 274;

Index

sales of, 339
Bibliographers, 339
Bilboes, 213
Bildeston, Suffolk, 151, 156
Bills of exchange, 169
Bishops War, 218
Bishops, 196, 197, 243, 261;
   as evangelicals, 200, 202;
   Matthew Wren and, 121, 122, 206, 207;
   powers of, 198–199;
   Puritans and, 80, 152, 154–156, 162, 206–207;
   Samuel Harsnet and, 134, 206
Black magic, 46
Blackfriars, 349
Blacksmiths, female, 298
Boadicca, Queen, 309
Body, conceptions of, 304–307;
   breasts and, 305, 306, 309, 316;
   penis and, 302, 305
"Body of Liberties" (Massachusetts), 349
Boemus, Joannes, 41
Bohemia, 339
Boke Named the Governour (Elyot), 351
Bolingbroke, Lord, 259
Bolton, Robert, 113, 117–120, 122–123, 125, 134
Bonds, 150, 176, 190, 203
Book of Common Prayer, 92
Book of Martyrs (Foxe), 132, 341, 357
"Book of Orders," 207
Book of Resolution. See First Book of Christian Exercise
Book of Sports, 80, 365
Bookbinding, 344
Books, 24, 34, 93;
   importance of, 334–335, 338–342;
   importation of, 338, 344;
   oral, visual, scribal communication and, 336;
   ownership of, 345–346;
   religion and, 348;
   selling of, 336, 338, 340, 341, 343, 344, 356, 358, 369
Bootmakers, female, 298
Borde, Andrew, 22, 26–27, 41
Boroughs, 192, 193, 195, 199, 216

Boston, Lincolnshire, 77, 129
Boston, Mass., 59, 147, 170, 217;
   economy in, 169;
   excommunications in, 163–165, 320;
   lawsuits and, 172;
   publication in, 99, 270, 344, 363;
   trade and, 147;
   mentioned, 77, 91, 292, 297, 319, 322
Bownd, Nicholas, 133
Boxford, Suffolk, 203, 206
Boyle, Robert, 88
Brachigraphy, 358
Braddick, Michael J., 225
Bradford, William, 49
Bradstreet, Anne, 87, 299
Brady, Robert, 259
Braintree, Essex, 201, 203
Brauer, Jerald, 129
Breen, Timothy, 12, 77, 220, 274, 323
Breslow, Marvin Arthur, 31
Bribery, 158
Briefe and Plaine Declaration (Fulke), 154
Brinsley, John, 60, 112, 122, 126
Broadsides, 343, 345, 353
Brooke, Lord, 83, 84, 210
Brooks, Christopher, 241
Brooks, Thomas, 135
Brownists, 129–130
Bucer, Martin, 159
Buckingham, Duke of, 3, 65
Budapest, 38
Bunyan, John, 118, 356
Burgess, Glen, 245, 258
Burroughes, Jeremiah, 116
Burton, Richard (pseudo), 359
Burton, Robert (pseudo), 359
Bury St. Edmunds, Suffolk, 156

Cain (Cham), 42–43
Calvin, John, 154, 159, 351;
   works published, 155–156;
   mentioned, 149, 172, 175, 203, 249
Calvinism, 98, 100, 158, 159, 161, 358
Cambridge, Cambridgeshire, 166, 200, 209, 340, 343, 358
Cambridge, Mass., 348, 363
Cambridge Platform, 166, 357

Cambridge University, 4, 90, 200, 342, 369
Camden, William, 23, 27
Campion, Edmund, 365
Canada, 173
Cannibalism, 40, 45
Canon law, 12, 239, 252
Canterbury, Kent, 124, 338, 340, 345
Canticles, 135
Capital punishment, 189, 267
Capitall Laws (Massachusetts), 343
Captivity, 37, 58
Carew, Thomas, 151
Caribbean, 57, 83
Carlson, Eric, 358
Carpenters, 164, 168, 319
Carter, Bezaleel, 152
Carter, Brenda, 17
Case law, 246
Catechisms, 92, 358;
  manuscript distribution of, 349;
  oral tradition and, 77, 348, 353;
  print culture and, 339, 345
Catholicism, 25, 80, 244, 265, 311;
  France and, 173;
  print culture and, 346–347, 363;
  reaction against, 199, 341, 348;
  Spain and, 29, 31;
  women and, 299;
  mentioned, 51. *See also* Papacy
Cathrope, Charles, 263
Cattle, 28
Cavaliers, 169
Cavenham, Suffolk, 152
Cecil, Sir Robert, 311
Censorship, 15, 336, 360–365, 369
Central courts, 194
Chaderton, Laurence, 338
Chancery, 252
Channel Isles, 37
Chapbooks, 295, 340, 359, 360
Chaplains, 341, 360
Chariter, Roger, 356
Charity, 158, 173
Charles I, 207, 209, 218, 258, 273;
  church courts and, 153;
  execution of, 259;
  forced loan and, 257;
  John Winthrop and, 6, 204;
  mentioned, 200, 252
Charles II, 98, 269, 272
Charles, Prince, 31
Charlestown, Mass., 90, 212
Charlewood, John, 341
Charters, 4, 13, 192, 216–217. *See also* Massachusetts Bay Colony
Chauncy, Charles, 362
Chesapeake, 25, 83
Chester, Chestershire, 298
Chiauses (emissaries), 37
Chickahominy Indians, 48
Child, Robert, 85, 88, 268, 343
Children, 296, 299, 303, 310, 348
Chorographies, 24
Christ, 292, 294, 301–304;
  mentioned, 33, 41, 46, 94, 244
Christ Church, Oxford, 350
Christ's College, Cambridge, 340
The Christian Commonwealth (Eliot), 362
Christianson, Paul, 252–253, 254, 255, 256
Christmas, 359
Church of England, 264–266;
  church courts and, 153, 198, 212, 252;
  churchwardens and, 153, 193, 198, 199;
  classis and, 156, 201;
  deaneries of, 199; discipline in, 91, 156–157, 162, 165, 167, 171, 173;
  Henry Newman and, 98;
  John Winthrop and, 196;
  lay influence in, 197;
  market place and, 162;
  parishes of, 134, 193;
  Richard Hooker and, 244;
  structure of, 198–199;
  Wethersfield congregation and, 129;
  usury and, 153
Church-Government and Church-Covenant Discussed (Mather), 161
Clark, J. C. D., 4
Clark, Peter, 345
Clarke, Samuel, 114
Classis, 156, 201
Cleaver, Robert, 350
Clothing, 24, 171, 214, 314–315

Index

Cockburn, J. S., 189
Cockfield, Suffolk, 201
Cogswell, Thomas, 323
Cohen, Charles, 303
Coke, Sir Edward,
    English constitution and, 263;
    J.G.A. Pocock and, 238–240;
    James I and, 251–252, 257;
    Thomas Hedley and, 255;
    mentioned, 277
Colbourn, Trevor, 277
Colchester, Essex, 200, 202
Collinson, Patrick, 111, 138, 347, 359
Colman, Benjamin, 98
Commission for Regulating Plantations, 217
Commission of the Peace, 6, 188–191;
    quorum and, 189, 212;
    in Suffolk, 196, 199, 204, 205, 210, 212, 213, 216, 220
Common law,
    England and, 189, 223, 238–242, 246, 248, 249, 250, 252–254, 257, 258, 261;
    lawyers and, 238, 239, 240, 247, 248, 249, 263;
    Massachusetts and, 167, 173, 176, 220, 265, 267–268;
    mentioned, 12, 13
Communion, 80, 94, 135–137, 158, 163
Conciliar fiat, 252
Conferences, 200–201
Conformity, religious, 207
Connecticut, 54–55, 85, 90
Consistories, 156
Constables, 189–193, 196, 202, 214
Constitution. *See* Ancient Constitution
Conventicles, 80, 83, 137, 156, 354
Conversion, 26, 39, 52–53, 59, 86, 87
Cooper, Rev. Thomas, 43
Copyhold, law of, 263
Copyists, 356
Copyright, 341
Corantoes, 340
Coroners, 189
Corporation of London, 360
Costello, Elvis, 126
Cottagers, 203
Cotton, John,
    Abel being dead yet speaketh and, 350;
    covenants and, 129;
    code of laws and, 223;
    discipline and, 162, 163, 168, 175;
    ideas of authority and, 292, 319–320;
    publications of, 161;
    sexual metaphors of, 301;
    mentioned, 3, 95, 157
Cotton, John, Jr., 92
Council for Safety, 269
Country Commission, 192, 194
County, functions of, 188, 193, 199, 210
Court of Assistants, 170, 171, 172, 212–214, 219, 221
Court of Common Pleas, 189, 251
Court of King's Bench, 189, 218, 269, 275
Court of Record, 254
Court of Star Chamber, 123, 252, 267, 360, 361
Court of Wards and Liveries, 204, 237
Courtiers, 261
Courts,
    archdeaconate, 153;
    borough, 192;
    Calvinist ethics and, 172;
    chancery, 189;
    church, 152, 198;
    diocesan, 153, 171;
    ecclesiastical, 11, 12, 134, 136, 153;
    secular, 11, 152, 172, 192, 198;
    in Westminster, 189.
    See also specific courts
Courtship, 310, 317, 341
Covenants, 173, 211–223;
    community and, 129;
    congregations and, 224;
    Scottish style, 350;
    theology of, 128–130, 156
Covetousness, 165, 166
Cowell, John, 262, 264
Crane, Sir Robert, 208
Crashaw, William, 46
Credit, 150, 170–171, 176, 352;
    pricing and, 158;
    mentioned, 11, 151
Cressy, David, 4, 313, 317

Crewe, Chief Justice, 257
Croft, Pauline, 367
Cromwell, Oliver, 16, 24, 30, 35, 365
Cross-dressing, 14, 314–318
Crouch, Nathaniel, 359
Cuckold, 300–301, 313
Cudworth, James, 162
Culverwell, Ezekiel, 201
Cust, Richard, 124, 367

D'Aulnay, Charles, 173
Dalham, Suffolk, 340
Dancing, 95–96
Dane, John, 162
Danforth, Samuel, 359
Daughters of Zion, 321
Davenport, John, 82, 167, 173–176, 362, 365
Davies, Sir John,
  Englishness of 24, 241;
  Ireland and, 29, 30;
  racial ideas of 42;
  mentioned, 239
Davis, J. C., 358
Day, John, 341
Day, Stephen, 342
Deacons, 91, 162
Decades of the Newe Worlde of West India (Angleria), 41
Debt,
  American Indians and, 51, 53;
  Crown and, 195–196;
  legal action and, 170, 173;
  Max Weber and, 176;
  Robert Keayne and, 165;
  seizure for, 171;
  mentioned, 166, 167
Deceit, 158, 163, 164
Decker, Thomas, 151
Dedham classis, 156
Dedham conference, 202, 203
Dedham, Essex, 118, 156, 200, 202, 215
Deference, 193–194, 295
Dekker, Thomas, 43
Denmark, 99
Dent, Arthur, 341
Description of England (Harrison), 23
Desmond, Earl of, 27

Deuteronomy, 274
Devil, 115, 123, 139, 321–322, 351;
  racism and, 46;
  Shakespeare and, 43;
  mentioned, 359
Devotional tracts, 92, 129, 339, 345, 356;
  Catholics and, 363–364
Dexter, Gregory, 342
Dexter, Thomas, 219
Diana, goddess, 309
Dickens, A. G., 346
Discoverie of the Gaping Gulf (Stubbs), 364
Discoverie of Witchcraft (Scot), 43
Doctor and Student (St. German), 241
Dod, John, 350
Dolan, Frances, 299
Dominion of New England, 260, 264, 271, 368
Donne, John, 312, 355
Dorchester, England, 129, 156, 159
Dorchester, Mass., 59, 169
Downing, Emmanuel, 57, 58, 210, 217
Drinking, 162–163, 167, 170, 202
Dublin, Ireland, 77
Dudley, Dorothy, 299
Dudley, Thomas, 210, 219, 366
Duffy, Eamon, 359
Durand, William, 83
Dutch, 164, 147
Dutch Reformed Church, 158

Eales, Jacqueline, 120
East Anglia, England, 6, 76, 187–188, 207
East Indians, 24
Ecclesiology, 243
Eckert, Jerry, 17
Economy,
  Puritans and, 147–186;
  Elizabeth I and, 312;
  engrossing and, 150, 153, 156;
  literacy and, 352;
  women and, 297
Eden, Richard, 41, 42
Edict of Nantes, 98
Education,
  American Indians and, 48;
  at Halle, 100;
  Massachusetts and, 92, 352–353;

Index

religion and, 92, 100, 137, 197–198;
women and, 100;
mentioned, 79, 89
Edward I, 33
Edwards, Thomas, 362
Egerton, Stephen, 348, 349
Egerton, Thomas, 262
Eliot, Sir John, 52–53, 86–87, 257, 343, 362
Elizabeth I, 247–248, 318, 360;
Commission of the Peace and, 188;
excommunication of, 31;
expels Africans, 44;
Puritans and, 200;
Roderigo Lopez and, 34;
Spain and, 31;
symbolism of, 23, 307–312;
mentioned, 14, 27, 28, 111, 197, 199, 242, 359
Elizabeth of Arragon, 32–33
Ellesmere, Lord Chancellor, 252
Elyot, Thomas, 351
Enclosure, 150, 312
Endecott, John, 209, 217, 218
English Civil War, 218, 361;
mentioned, 4, 13, 150, 340, 368
Engrossing, 150, 153, 156
Ephesian bonfire, 338
Essex, England, 187;
Archbishop Whitgift and, 201;
Puritans in, 198, 199, 200;
William Laud and, 206
Essex County, Mass., 170–171, 345, 366
Estate commissioners, 214
Ethiopia, 40
Ethnography, 25, 45, 76, 78
Eucharist, 135–136
Eulogists, 309–310
Eve, 321
Exchequer, 250
Exclusion crisis, 259, 344
Excommunication, 153, 155, 157;
Elizabeth I, and, 31;
Puritans and, 162, 163–165, 167, 320, 322
Executions, 264, 358
Exeter, England, 132, 340
Exeter, N. H., 297

Extortion, 164

Familists, 361
Family,
gender and, 87, 322;
piety and, 77, 116;
structure of, 294, 301
Family of Love, 363
Farming, 28, 160, 166, 170. *See also* Husbandry
Fast days, 80, 118, 134, 214
Fathers, 264, 298
Faversham, Kent, 345
Featley, Daniel, 347
Federal theology, 156. *See also* Covenants
Feoffees for Impropriation, 134
Ferdinando of Arragon, 32–33
Feudalism, 260
Field, Thomas, 154
Fills, Robert, 155
Finch, Sir Henry, 239
Finch, John, Lord Keeper, 258
Finchingfield, England, 203
First Blast of the Trumpet against the Monstrous Regiment of Women (Knox), 307
First Book of Christian Exercise (Person), 347
First Church, Boston, 163, 164, 173
Fishermen, 160, 297
Fiske, John, 165–166
Fiske, Phineas, 166
Five Knights Case, 258
Fletcher, Anthony, 30, 305, 312
Fluellen, Captain, 26
Forced Loan, 204, 257
Forest of Arden, England, 346
Fornication, 162, 163, 170
Fort Hill, Plymouth Colony, 50
Fortescue, Sir John, 241
Fox, Adam, 367
Fox, George, 364
Foxe, John, 6, 132, 341, 346, 357
Francke, August Hermann, 86, 99, 100
Franklin, William, 164
Fraud, 150, 170
Frearson, Michael, 340
Freemen, 214, 215, 221, 222
Freist, Dagmar, 367
Fulke, William, 154–155

Funerals, 95

Gainsh, Robert, 42
Galen of Pergamum, 305
Gaming, 171, 202
Gascony, France, 219
Gataker, Thomas, 357
Geere, Dennis, 162
Gender, 87, 290–333, 353
Geneva, 156, 177, 266;
    John Calvin and, 149, 203;
    Marian exiles and, 155
Geneva Bible, 132, 351
Genevan Consistory Court, 155
Gentry, 81, 194, 210, 247
Gerard, Sir Gilbert, 210
German Peasants' War, 351
Germany, 35
Gerson, Jean, 241
Gifford, Mr., 136
Gilman, Elizabeth, 297
Gilman, Moses, 297
Gipson, Lawrence Henry, 2
Glendower, Owen, 26
Glorious Revolution, 98, 259, 270
Glover, Rev. Jose, 342
Goodcole, Henry, 359
Goodhue, Sarah, 348
Goodwin, Thomas, 125, 135
Gorges, Sir Ferdinando, 218
Gorton, Samuel, 85, 268
Gossip, 15, 347, 367
Gouge, William, 133
Gowing, Laura, 296
Gowing, Robert, 166
Grace, 10, 89, 132
Grand juries, 193
Gray, John, 291
Great Easton, Essex, 203
Great Migration, 6, 80
Greeks, 35
Green, Ian, 358, 370
Green, Samuel, 342, 343, 344, 362
Greene, Robert, 23, 38
Greenham, Richard, 126, 358
Grent, John, 151
Grey, Lord, 28
Grindal, Bishop, 200

Groton, Suffolk, 192, 202, 203, 204
Grub Street, 359
Guilds, female members, 292
Guinea, 58
Gurdon, John, 203

Habermas, Jürgen, 368
Hackett, Helen, 311
Haigh, Christopher, 307
Hakluyt, Richard, 24, 39
Hale, Sir Matthew, 246
Halfway Covenant, 97
Hall, David D., 3, 13, 14–15
Halle, Saxony, 99, 100, 101
Halle Institute, 86
Hambrick-Stowe, Charles, 75, 92
Hampden's Case, 258
Hariot, Thomas, 47
Harley, Lady Brilliana, 132
Harley, Sir Robert, 114, 120, 124, 134
Harris, Benjamin, 344
Harris, Robert, 114
Harrison, William, 23, 150
Harsnet, Bishop Samuel, 134, 206
Hart, James, 12–13
Hartlib, Samuel, 88
Harvard, John, 95
Harvard College, 90, 353, 362, 369;
    printing and, 342, 343;
    mentioned, 88, 359
Harvey, William, 164
Haskins, George, 213
Hathorne, William, 366
Hayward, John, 261
Heads of Agreement, 98
Heath, Chief Justice, 25
Hebrew, 33, 35
Hedley, Thomas, 254–257
Hedonism, 39
Hemlyn, John, 152–153
Henrico, Virginia, 49
Henry V, 38
Henry IV (Shakespeare), 39
Henry VIII, 9, 197, 360
Henry, Prince, 31
Herbert, George, 355
Hereford, England, 24
Heresy, 8, 29, 90, 162, 163

Index

Herodotus, 40
Hibbens, Anne, 164, 319–322
Hibbens, William, 319
High Commission, 247, 252, 360
High Court, 257
Higham, Sir John, 199, 206
Hildebrand, Jennifer, 323
Hildersham, Arthur, 131
Historie of the Turkes (Knolles), 37
Histrio-mastix (Prynne), 361
Hobbamock, 49–50
Hoffman, Ronald, 17
Holland, 266
Holy Ghost, 115, 348, 356
Honor, 296
Hooker, Richard, 161, 244, 245, 265, 322
Hooker, Thomas, 85, 162, 358
Howard, Jean, 316–317
Hufton, Olwen, 295
Hughes, Lewis, 82
Huguenots, 98
Hull, England, 258
Humanists, 335, 354
Hume, David, 111
Humors, 304–305
Humphrey, John, 209
Hundreds, 191, 210
Hungary, 35, 339
Hunger, 147
Hunters after concealed lands, 216
Husbands, 322;
  as metaphor, 302;
  theater and, 317;
  wives and, 292, 295, 297, 301, 318–320
Husbandry, 150, 292, 298, 299, 314.
  See also Farming
Hutchinson, Anne, 84–85, 87, 322, 343, 369–370

Iberia, 33, 44
Idleness, 159, 163, 167
Illegitimacy, 202
Illiteracy, 335
Indenture, 55–56
Indian Library, 343
Indians. *See* American Indians
Infants, 348

Ingram, Martin, 313
Inheritance, 167, 268
Innkeepers, 161
Inns of Court, 246, 263
Intellectual property, 355
Interest rates, 158, 159, 167, 169.
  See also Usury
Interpreter (Cowell), 264
Interregnum, 17, 222, 259, 363
Ipswich, Suffolk, 202, 348
Ireland, 4, 249;
  English characterizations of, 8, 9, 24, 25, 27–30, 39, 40, 46, 51, 59, 60;
  John Winthrop and, 6;
  Privy Council of, 250;
  mentioned, 4, 37, 53, 54
Iron, 150, 169
Isaiah, 243
Ishmael, 38, 124
Isle of Wight County, Va., 82
Islam, 36–38

Jackson, Thomas, 338
James I, *Book of Sports* and, 80;
  Church courts and, 153;
  legal views of, 248–252;
  Puritans and, 6;
  Scotland and, 27;
  Spain and, 30;
  mentioned, 48, 121, 201, 277, 361
James II, 98, 268, 269
James River, Va., 82
Jamestown, Va., 47
Jani Anglorum (Selden), 255
Janizaries, 35
Japheth, 46
Jeffries, Joyce, 159
Jenner, Thomas, 341
Jeremiads, 176
Jermyn, Sir Robert, 199, 203, 204, 206
Jerusalem, 122
Jesuits, 361
Jesus Christ, 14, 60, 112, 245
Jewel, Bishop, 243
Jew of Malta, 34–35
Jews, 39, 274;
  English anti-Semitism and, 24, 25, 33–35, 37, 51

Johnson, Barbara A., 356
Johnson, Ben, 96, 355
Johnson, Edward, 147, 148, 161, 176
Johnson, John, 123
Johnson, Marmaduke, 343, 344, 362
Johnson, Richard, 3
Jordan, Ignatius, 132
Josselin, Ralph, 112
Judges, 161, 206, 224, 250–251, 257;
   assizes and, 189, 194;
   as spiritual advisors, 172;
   mentioned, 210, 364
Judicial astrology, 359
Juries, 189, 213, 247
Jurisprudence, 52–53, 173–174, 241, 252
Justices of the peace, 12, 188–191, 212, 213;
   mentioned, 193, 194, 199

Kalu, Jonathan, 201
Kamensky, Jane, 320, 367
Karlsen, Carol, 320, 322
Keayne, Robert, 154, 164, 168, 366
Keys of the Kingdom of Heaven (Cotton), 161
King Philip's War, 87
Knewstub, John, 201, 203, 204, 205
Knolles, Richard, 37, 38
Knox, John, 307

Laborers, 167, 168, 169, 203, 346
Lake, Peter, 125, 359
Lambert, Sheila, 361
Lancaster, Mass., 173
Laqueur, Thomas, 305
Larner, Christina, 298, 314
Lathes, 191
Latin texts, 354
Laud, Archbishop William, 206, 207, 209
De Laudibus Legum Angliae (Fortescue), 241
Laurence, Anne, 53
Law, 16–17, 188, 237–289;
   admiralty and, 267;
   codification of, 16, 223;
   colonial leaders and, 210;
   John Davenport on, 176;
   Irish and, 30;
   Mosaic law and, 167, 223;
   natural, 173;
   printing and, 339;
   Thomas Shepard on, 174
Laws and Statues of Geneva (Fills), 155
Lawson, Dorothy, 347
Lawsuits, 11, 172
Lawyers, 175–176, 206, 240–241, 245–247, 249;
   banned from New Haven Colony, 173;
   John Winthrop as, 175, 237;
   mentioned, 11, 13, 176, 261
Lechford, Thomas, 167
Lectures, 201–202, 349, 350, 357;
   endowed lectureships and, 197–198;
   mentioned, 137, 200, 206, 263
Ledsham, Yorkshire, 210
Legal humanists, 262
Legal primitivism, 266–267
Leicesters Commonwealth, 365
Leicestershire, England, 346
Leiden, 77
Lepanto, 35
Libels, publishing and, 364, 365;
   mentioned, 163, 167, 170, 367
Libertines, 161
Licensing Act, 362
Life of the Renowned John Eliot (Mather), 86
Lincoln, Earl of, 210
Linen, 150
Literacy, 14, 334–370
Lives of the Archbishops of Canterbury, 244
Livestock regulation, 216
Loans, 158, 159, 166, 204;
   brokers and, 151;
   usury and, 169, 170
Locke, John, 259
Locksmith, 342
Lollards, 354, 363
London, England,
   Africans in, 44;
   charter and, 276–277;
   ethnicity of, 25;
   Increase Mather and, 268;
   James I, and, 269, 275;
   Jews in, 33, 39;
   poverty in, 191;
   Puritans and, 154, 155, 159;
   publishing and, 340, 342, 344, 356, 358, 365;

Index

office holding in, 191;
Turks and, 37;
usury in, 150–151, 162;
mentioned, 88, 98, 99, 129, 158, 195, 200, 203, 206, 272, 346, 350
Lopez, Roderigo, 34
Louis XIV, 98
Love, Harold, 365
Low Countries, 23, 29, 31, 342, 363
Lucas, Wendy, 323
Ludlow, Roger, 210
Lumber, 297
Lust's Dominion (Dekker), 43
Luther, Martin, 346, 351
Lutherans, 100
Lying, 158, 162–164, 166, 171

Mack, Phyllis, 292, 296, 310
Magisterial court, 219
Magna Carta, 270
Mahomet, 38, 41
Maidstone, Kent, 345
Malabar coast, India, 100
Maldon, Essex, 136
Malnutrition, 56
Mammonism, 151
Mandeville, John, 40
Manhood,
    English identity and, 22, 296–297, 315–316;
    New England society and, 95–96, 291–292, 300
Manicongo, 40
Manteo, 47
Marblehead, Mass., 337
Marbury, Francis, 357
Marcus, Leah, 307, 308
Marian exiles, 155, 363
Marlowe, Christopher, 24, 34
Marottie, Arthur, 365
Marprelate Controversy, 361
Marriage, 297, 310, 317, 341;
    dynastic, 31;
    John Winthrop and, 223, 301
Marshall, Stephen, 133, 139
Marshall, Thomas, 164
Martha's Vineyard, 52
Maryland, 58, 83

Masons, 168
Massachusetts Bay Colony,
    alchemy and, 88;
    American Indians and, 51;
    economic forces and, 147–186;
    first charter of, 90, 208, 209, 218–221, 260, 264, 268, 269, 271–276;
    General Court of, 58–60, 81, 147, 167–171, 209, 214–216, 218–219, 221–222, 270, 272, 274, 276, 352, 353, 366;
    governance and, 187–236;
    John Winthrop and, 6, 9, 45;
    Puritanism and, 9–12, 80–81, 83;
    second charter of, 260, 268–270;
    slaves in, 57;
    stockholders of, 86, 209;
    voting qualifications in, 174
Massasoit, 49, 52
Masson, Margaret, 303
Matar, Nabil, 39
Mather, Cotton, 86, 93, 98–100, 269, 321
Mather, Increase, 86, 93, 268–269, 357, 362
Mather, Richard, 93, 161
Mathew, Tobie, 349
Maverick, Samuel, 59
Mayflower (vessel), 49
McNeill, William, 96
Mede, Joseph, 340
Memorizing, 235, 263, 348
Men Are from Mars, Women Are From Venus (Gray), 291
Mercator, Gerard, 24
Merchant of Venice (Shakespeare), 34
The Meritorious Price of Our Redemption (Pyncheon), 362
Middlesex, England, 170, 345
Middlesex County, Mass., 173, 366
Midwives, 296, 297
Mikalachki, Jodi, 309
Militia 95, 147, 214, 216–217;
    boroughs and, 192;
    reform and, 207
Miller, Perry, 3, 76
Milton, John, 364
Missionaries, 53, 60, 85, 87, 98–99
Mnemonic aids, 353

Model of Christian Charity (Winthrop), 9, 159, 175, 349
Mohammed, 37
Moneylenders. *See* Usury
Monopolies, 160, 195, 340, 344
Montagu, Richard, 361
Moors,
    English identity and, 24, 25, 32, 40, 41, 51, 55, 60. *See also* Muslims
Moral law, 266, 274
Morgan, Edmund S., 3, 217, 220
Morison, Samuel Eliot, 3
Mornay, Philip Duplessis, 156
Mortgages, 176
Morton, Thomas, 45, 80
Moryson, Fynes, 28, 29
Moses, 46
Mosse, Miles, 152
Mothers, 296, 300, 310, 311, 321. *See also* Wives, Women
Mountjoy, Lord, 28
Municipal corporations, 13, 269
Musicians, 355
Muslims, 37, 38, 51
Mysticism, 26, 29

Nansemond County, Va., 82
Napier, Richard, 159
Nashe-Harvey flyting, 361
Natick, Mass., 53
Native American. *See* American Indians
Natural law, 167, 173, 176
Natural right, 13, 259
Naunton, Sir Robert, 204, 208
Navigation Acts, 265
Neill, Michael, 30
Netherlands. *See* Low Countries
New England Company, 343
New England Mind (Miller), 76
New Haven Colony, 52, 90, 91, 172, 173
New Spain, 42
Newcastle-upon-Tyne, Northumberland, 347
Newman, Henry, 98, 99
Newtown, Mass., 90
Nine Years War, 250
Noah, 46
Norman Conquest, 240, 261, 263

Normandy, 219
Northamptonshire, England, 137, 156
Norton, John, 350
Norton, Mary Beth, 293, 295, 296
Norwich, diocese of, 121, 200, 206
Norwich, Norfolk, 156, 191, 195, 200, 206, 310
Notes on the Doctrine of Repentance (Marbury), 357
Nuttall, Geoffrey, 114

O'Neill, Shane, 27
Of the Laws of Ecclesiastical Polity (Hooker), 244
Old English, 29, 249–250
Omnium Gentium Mores (Boemus), 41
One-sex model, 305–306
Oral culture, 348, 353, 366–367
Orgel, Stephen, 318, 319
Ornaments for the Daughters of Zion (Mather), 321
Orphans, 99, 298
Ortelius, Abraham, 24, 35
Osgood, Herbert, 2
Ottoman Empire, 24, 34–39, 40, 51, 60
Overseers of the poor, 193
Oxenbridge, John, 92, 272, 306
Oxford, England, 340
Oxford University, 3, 7, 90, 342, 269

Palmer, John, 264
Pamphlets, 24, 93, 154;
    popularity of, 339, 343, 356
Papacy, 31, 243, 266–267;
    as antichrist, 348;
    printing and, 339;
    mentioned, 134, 244, 265, 344.
    See also Catholicism
Parker, Henry, 138
Parker, Kenneth, 358
Parker, Matthew, Archbishop, 244
Parkhurst, John, Bishop, 200
Parliament, 247–253, 362;
    Crown and, 195, 255, 257–259, 261;
    John Winthrop and, 204, 207, 208;
    Long Parliament of, 139, 361;
    printed record of, 365;
    Puritans and, 152, 210, 221;

Richard Hooker and, 244–245;
   mentioned, 6, 134, 194
Parson, Robert, 261
Patriarchy, 13, 290–323, 367
Patterson, Annabel, 364
Paul's Cross, 152
Payne, Robert, 171
Peacham's Case, 252
Peele, George, 43
Peirce, Capt. William, 57
Pelham, Herbert, 210
Penny godlies, 358, 359, 341
Pequot Indians, 51, 57, 58
Perkins, William, 113, 156, 157, 339
Persons, Robert, 347
Pestana, Carla G., 2
Peter, Hugh, 166
Peterson, Mark, 10
Petit, Larry, 17
Petruchio, 304
Pewterers, female, 298
Philip II, 27, 29, 31
Philips, George, 215
Phips, William, 270
Physicians, 22, 159
Plagiarism, 355
Plays, 316–317, 347–348, 355
Pliny, 40
Plymouth Colony, 80, 90, 92, 95;
   American Indians and, 49–50, 52
Pocahontas, 47, 48
Pocock, J. G. A., 238, 239, 240, 241
Pollexfen, Henry, 275
Poor law, 195
Poor, 150, 202–203, 359;
   education and, 100;
   New England and, 147;
   relief for, 137, 150, 166, 190, 191, 195, 214;
   mentioned, 312
Portuguese, 33, 41, 45, 147
Powhatan Indians, 47, 48, 50, 54
Practical divinity, 79, 87, 114, 132, 337, 369
Practice of Christianitie (Rogers), 349
Practise of Pietie (Bayly), 75, 86
Preaching,
   Puritans and, 199, 201–202;
   in England, 197–198, 206, 348;
   mentioned, 157, 163, 197
Premarital sex, 297
Presbyterians, 8, 98, 156, 201, 364
Preston, John, 114, 128, 131, 135, 136
Priests, 298, 299, 361
Primers, 345, 359
Primitive church, 266
Primogeniture, 268
Prince, Thomas, 98
Printers, 344, 355, 356;
   female, 298;
   increased production of 339;
   profitability of, 341–342
Printing, 24, 89, 334–386;
   cheap press and, 339, 343, 358, 369;
   distribution networks for, 340–341;
   importance of, 24, 246, 346;
   in New England, 91–100;
   Protestantism and, 335–370;
   Roman font and, 354;
   unlicensed, 342;
   mentioned, 14, 15, 16. *See also* Publishing
Prisoners, female, 309
Privy Council, 152–153, 194, 199, 217, 360;
   judicial appeals and, 265
Probate inventories, 344–345
Proformas, ecclesiastical, 339
Prohibitions, Case of (1608), 251
Promissory notes, 213, 297
Prophesying, 197, 200
Prophets, 349
Providence Island, 57, 77, 84, 209–210
Providentialism, 208, 339
Prynne, William, 361
Psalms, 95–96, 137
Psalters, 345
Publishing, 14, 79, 89, 369;
   Liturgical texts and, 348;
   illegal, 363;
   grammar books and, 339;
   religious books and, 339, 342;
   royalties and, 196. *See also* Printing
Purchas, Samuel, 24, 25, 43
Pym, John, 210
Pyncheon, William, 85, 214, 362

Quakers, 51, 263, 337, 362
Quarter Sessions, 89–191, 112, 224;
  administrative duties and, 190;
  judicial duties and, 190;
  in Suffolk, 205
Quinnipiac Indians, 52
Quo warranto, 218, 259, 269, 271

Randolph, Edward, 271, 272
Ranters, 358
Ratepayers, 193, 215
Read, Mr., 167
Reading, 77, 335–370
Reciting, 352, 354
Recusants, 129, 299
Reformation, 44, 197, 243, 346, 369;
  economy and, 157;
  printing press and, 346;
  mentioned, 3, 9
Regrating, 150
Reid, John Phillip, 277
Reis, Elizabeth, 302, 321
Renagadoes, 39
Renaissance humanism, 242
Rents, 151, 155, 195
Reproductive organs, 305
Reyce, Robert, 334, 365
Rhode Island, 51, 58, 342
Rich, Lord, 201
Rich store-house or treasury for the diseased (A.T.), 352
Richard I, 263
Ridley, Thomas, 261
Right of presentment, 196–197
Rigney, James, 349
Roanoke Island, Va., 47, 48
Rogers, John, 113, 134–135
Rogers, Richard, 129, 132, 201, 349
Rogers, Samuel, 121–122, 133, 135–137
Rolfe, John, 45, 48
Rolfe, Rebecca, 47
Roman Catholicism. *See* Catholicism
Roman civil law, 239
Romances, 339, 351
Romans, 26, 35
Rosewell, Sir Henry, 209
Ross, Richard, 12–13, 224

Rowlands, Marie, 299
Royal Chaplain, 347
Royal commissioners, 271
Royal prerogative, 253, 254, 257, 267, 269
Royal succession, 310
Royal supremacy, 245, 265
Rule of law, 242, 245, 247, 258
Rules of constitutional propriety, 253
Rumor, 67, 347
Russell, Conrad, 249
Rutherford, Samuel, 350

Sabbath, 80, 138, 203, 366;
  breaking of, 162, 163, 166, 167
Sacramenta, 84, 135, 136
Sacramental bread and wine, 94
Sahara Desert, 40
St. George, Robert, 95
St. German, Christopher, 240, 241
St. Matthias Cathedral, 38
St. Paul's Cathedral, 151
St. Paul's Churchyard, 340
Salem, Mass., 57, 166, 366
Salisbury, England, 195
Saltonstall, Sir Richard, 210
Sandes, Henry, 203
Sandys, George, 43
Satan. *See* Devil
Saugus, Mass., 169
Saxons, 240, 256
Saxony, 86
Saye and Sele, Lord, 3, 210
The Scholemaster (Ascham), 351
Schoolmasters, 354, 365
Schwarz, Kathryn, 306
Scot, Reginald, 43
Scotland, 26–27, 218, 249;
  mentioned, 4, 7, 8, 9, 25, 51, 96
Scott, Joan, 322
Scott, Thomas, 124
Scottow, Joshua, 270
Scrambler, Bishop, 200
Scribal publication, 349–350, 354, 364, 365, 366
Scriveners, 354, 356
Second Church, Boston, 353
Second Report of the Record Commissioners of the

Index

City of Boston, 215
Seldon, John, 239, 255–256, 257, 277
Selectmen, 215, 343
Selimus, 38
Sermon of Repentance (Dent), 341
Sermons, piety and 114, 115, 116;
    importance of, 80, 127, 134–135, 137, 158, 348–349;
    John Winthrop and, 193;
    laity and, 80, 197, 348;
    publication and, 206, 339, 345, 350, 357–358, 364;
    scarcity of, 89;
    mentioned, 77, 133, 156, 369
Servants, 51, 59, 169, 203;
    African, 44–45;
    military training and, 59;
    treatment of, 170. *See also* Slavery
Sewall, Samuel, 95
Sewer Commission, Suffolk, 204
Sextons, 193
Sexuality,
    adultery and, 300;
    differences in, 304–307;
    gender and, 305–306;
    illicit, 202, 296;
    Turkish, 39;
    mentioned, 24
Shakespeare, William, 24, 26, 43, 355;
    Henry IV and, 26, 39;
    Jews and, 32, 33, 34;
    Twelfth Night and, 317
Shamans, 53
Shapiro, James, 33
Shawmut Peninsula. *See* Boston
Shell, Alison, 363
Shepard, Thomas, 161–162, 174, 272, 348
Sheriffs, 12, 189, 216
Sherman, Bill, 356
Sherrard, Hope, 84
Ship money, 207, 257, 258, 366
Shoemaking, 147
Shopkeepers, 352
Shrewsbury, England, 340
Shylock, 34
Sibbes, Richard, 113–114, 116, 118, 123;
    piety and, 131, 133;
    sin and 115; mentioned, 3
Sidney, Sir Philip, 88, 339, 355, 364
Silver trade, 94
Sin, 161, 162–163, 321, 348
Skelton, Samuel, 129
Slander, 164, 166
Slavery, 25, 41, 167;
    Africans and, 43–45, 47, 60;
    Christian, 37;
    English colonies and, 56–59, 73n.111;
    Indians and 32. *See also* Indenture
Smith, Henry, 357
Smith, John, 45
Smith, R. J., 260
Social contract, 13, 259
Society for the Promotion of Christian Knowledge, 98
Sodomy, 39
Some, Robert, 133
Southampton, Hampshire, 298
Southcoat, Thomas, 209
Southwark, London, 296
Southwell, Robert, 341
Spain,
    American Indians and, 45, 46;
    England and, 30–33, 48, 57;
    Philip II of, 27, 29, 31;
    Spanish Armada and, 23, 339;
    Spanish Infanta and, 31;
    Spanish Match and, 134, 361;
    mentioned, 24, 25, 35, 51
Sparrowhawk, Nathaniel, 118
Speech, 336–337, 348, 354, 365–367;
    subversion and, 170, 352;
    mentioned, 249
Speed, John, 35;
    Africans and, 40;
    Jews and, 33;
    Scotland and, 27
    travel narrative of, 24;
    Turkey and, 37, 39;
    Welsh character and 26;
Spenser, Edmund, 28, 29, 32
Spinners, 151
Sprint, John, 117
Spufford, Margaret, 340
Squanto, 49
Stackhouse, Anthony, 137

Stage. *See* Theater
Standing Council, 366
Standish, Miles, 80
Stare decisis, doctrine of, 246
Starkey, George, 88–89, 96
State of the Church of England (Udall), 154
Stationers' Company, 340, 341, 355
Stationers' Register, 339
Statutes,
　printing and, 246, 344, 360–361;
　economic regulation and, 169–170;
　Statute of Uses and, 247;
　mentioned, 249
Still, John, 200, 203
Stocks, 189, 213, 214
Stondon-Massey, Essex, 206
Stone, Gov. William, 83
Stour River, England, 200
Stour Valley, England,
　piety in, 77, 101, 196, 199–208, 211;
　mentioned, 6, 12, 156
Strachey, William, 45
Stuart monarchs, 27, 248
Stubbes, Philip, 359
Stubbs, Henry, 359
Stubbs, John, 364
Stuteville, Sir Martin, 340
Subsidy collectors, 191
Sudbury, Suffolk, 191, 200, 202
Suffering, spiritual, 121–123
Suffolk, England, 188–189, 198–200;
　Commission of the Peace and, 190–191;
　Forced Loan Commission and, 204;
　Quarter Session at, 205;
　mentioned, 12, 101, 129, 187, 334
Suffolk County, Mass., 170, 345
Sumptuary violations, 170, 171
Superstition, 28, 29, 30, 32
Sureties, 190, 213
Surplice, 350
Survey of the Summe of Church-Discipline (Hooker), 161
Surveyors, 147, 193
Swallowfield, Wiltshire, 194, 215
Swearing, 170
Sweete, Temperance, 163
Switzerland, 339. *See also* Geneva

Sydenham, Humphrey, 349
Symboleography, Which May Bee Termed the Art. (West), 213
Synod, 243, 362

Tailors, 163, 164
Taming of the Shrew (Shakespeare), 304
Tanners, 164
Taverners, 161
Taxation, 215, 222, 268
Taylor, Thomas, 131, 134, 350
Ten Commandments, 159
Terling, Essex, 202
Thanksgiving days, 214
Theater, 14, 314–318
Thirty Years War, 121, 340, 361
Thompson, Roger, 2
Thorpe, George, 47
Tilbury, Essex, 308
Timber, 169
Tippling houses, 202. *See also* Taverners
Tithes, 197
Tobacco, 21, 171
de la Tour, Charles, 173
Town Act of 1636, 214–215
Town marshal, 171
Town meeting, 172, 215, 268
Town representatives, 269
Town watchhouses, 214
Trade,
　Boston and, 147–148;
　Indians and, 161, 169, 171;
　John Winthrop and, 160–161, 165, 170;
　Trading companies and, 208, 264;
　women and, 297–298;
　mentioned, 4, 11, 25, 35, 190, 212
Tradesmen, 11, 352
Training days, 216
Transvestism, 314–318
Treason, 82
The Trew Law of Free Monarchies (James I), 248
Trundle, John, 341
Tudor, Mary, 31, 307, 360, 363
Tudor monarchs, 247
Twelfth Night (Shakespeare), 317
Two-sex model, 306

Index

Tyndal, Margaret. *See* Winthrop, Margaret Tyndal
Tyrone, Earl of, 27

Udall, John, 154
Ulrich, Laurel Thatcher, 292, 293, 296, 297, 303
Underdown, David, 295, 312
Unemployed, 163
United Colonies, 90
Usher, John, 344
Usury, 150–159, 164–165, 167, 169, 171; mentioned, 11, 12
Utopia, 50

Vagrancy, 312
Venice, 35
Vestry, 193, 196, 199, 202–203, 215
Vicars, John, 365
Vienna, 38
Virgin Mary, 309
Virginia Company of London, 46, 50
Virginia,
  American Indians and, 48–50, 52, 53, 54;
  Africans and, 55–56, 58;
  Lower Norfolk county of, 82;
  New England and, 147;
  population of, 56;
  Puritans and, 60, 83
Visitation, 198–199, 206
Vitkus, Daniel J., 35
von Rohr, John, 128
Voting qualifications, 174

Wade, Mr., 171
Wadsworth, Thomas, 359
Wages, 155, 168
Waldegrave, Robert, 341
Wales, 8, 26, 59, 60
Wallington, Nehemiah, 11, 158–159, 346
Walpole, Sir Robert, 259
Walter, Baron, 257
Wampanoag Indians, 49, 50
Wantonness, 160
Wapentakes, 191
Ward, Nathaniel, 139, 206

Ward, Samuel, 115, 124–125, 129–130, 206
Warrants, 213
Warwick, Earl of, 83, 84, 210
Watch, 171, 214, 216
Watertown, Mass., 215, 222, 343
Watt, Tessa, 34, 359
Wayte, Richard, 163
Weavers, 151
Webb, George, 152
Webb, Stephen S., 3
Weber, Max, 176
Webster, Tom, 77
Wenham, Mass., 166
West, William, 213
West Africa, 58
West Indies, 24, 147
West Riding, Yorkshire, 210
Wethersfield Covenant, 129, 130
Wharves, 170
Wheelwright, John, 349–350
Whetcombe, Simon, 209
Whigs, 259–260
Whipping, 189, 213
Whitbourne, Richard, 46
White, John, 159, 160
White, Thomas, 154
Whitelock, Bulstrode, 122
Whitgift, John, Archbishop, 201, 265
Wonder-Working Providence (Johnson), 147
Whore, 295
Wicked Mans Portion (Mather), 357
Widows, 159, 293, 295, 298, 342;
  home for, 99. *See also* Women
Wilcox, Thomas, 154
Willard, Samuel, 3, 305
William III, 269
William of Orange, 269
Williams, Roger, 85, 217, 343;
  American Indians and, 45, 59;
  mentioned, 60
Wills, 213
Wilson, Lisa, 300
Wiltshire, England, 152
Windsor, England, 150
Wine, 163
Winship, Michael, 85
Winthrop, Adam, 203

Winthrop, John, 187–225, 291, 292, 366;
  American Indians and, 45, 48, 50, 53;
  birth of, 339;
  books and, 340;
  Christian Charity sermon and, 9, 159, 175, 349;
  death of, 340;
  early life, 23, 25;
  emigration of, 6, 160, 342;
  female roles and, 304, 323;
  as governor, 170–175;
  Jews and 35;
  as a lawyer, 175, 237;
  moral stewardship of, 160–161, 163, 165, 169–170, 174–175;
  Parliament and, 204, 207, 208
  piety and, 77, 101, 129, 133, 301–302, 304;
  Robert Keayne and, 165;
  slavery and, 58;
  suffrage and 81;
  Virginia and, 82;
  wife of, 301;
  mentioned, 11, 12, 26, 51, 157, 334, 365
Winthrop, John, Jr., 88, 344
Winthrop, Margaret Tyndal, 301
Winthrop, Wait, 270
Winthrop, William, 6, 203
Wiswall, John, 212
Witchcraft, 291, 312–314, 320–322;
  Africans and, 43;
  Catholicism and, 29;
  Elizabeth I and, 311;
  mentioned, 88, 295
Withers, George, 200
Wives, 292, 295, 297, 301, 318–320.
  See also Mothers, Women

Woburn, Mass., 147
Wolves, 147
Women, 291–300, 314, 318;
  as amazons, 306;
  as armorers, 298;
  as artisans, 292;
  assertiveness of, 293, 295–296, 309, 311–312, 323;
  business dealings of, 297;
  as defective men, 305–306;
  as devil, 321;
  disorderliness of, 295;
  education of, 100;
  male roles and, 292, 303, 304, 307, 323;
  marriage and, 294, 295, 297–300, 302, 304, 316, 321, 322;
  scolds and, 291, 295, 312–313;
  witchcraft and, 291, 313–314,
  See also Widows, Wives
Wonder-Working Providence (Johnson), 147
Wood, William, 45
Woodcuts, 353, 356
Woodworkers, 158
Wool, 150
Worksop, Nottinghamshire, 129
Wren, Matthew, Bishop, 121, 122, 206, 207
Wright, John, 341
Wrightson, Keith, 192

Yearbooks, 246
York, England, 340
Young, Sir John, 209

Zaret, David, 368

www.ingramcontent.com/pod-product-compliance
Lightning Source LLC
Chambersburg PA
CBHW031959220426
43664CB00005B/70